The Windows®
Interface Guidelines
for Software Design

PUBLISHED BY
Microsoft Press
A Division of Microsoft Corporation
One Microsoft Way
Redmond, Washington 98052-6399

Library of Congress Cataloging-in-Publication Data
The Windows interface guidelines for software design.
      p.   cm.
  Includes index.
  ISBN 1-55615-679-0
  1. Microsoft Windows (Computer file)   2. User interfaces (Computer
systems)   3. Computer software--Development. I. Microsoft
Corporation.
QA76. 76.W56W553   1995
005.265--dc20   95-330
                                            CIP

Printed and bound in the United States of America.

1 2 3 4 5 6 7 8 9   QEQE   0 9 8 7 6 5

Distributed to the book trade in Canada by Macmillan of Canada, a division of Canada Publishing
Corporation.

A CIP catalogue record for this book is available from the British Library.

Microsoft Press books are available through booksellers and distributors worldwide. For further
information about international editions, contact your local Microsoft Corporation office. Or
contact Microsoft Press International directly at fax (206) 936-7329.

Contents

PART I FUNDAMENTALS OF DESIGNING USER INTERACTION

Chapter 1 Design Principles and Methodology

Chapter 5 General Interaction Techniques

PART II   WINDOWS INTERFACE COMPONENTS

Chapter 6   Windows

Chapter 7   Menus, Controls, and Toolbars

Chapter 8   Secondary Windows

Contents

PART III DESIGN SPECIFICATIONS AND GUIDELINES

Chapter 9 Window Management

Chapter 10 Integrating with the System

Chapter 11 Working with OLE Embedded and OLE Linked Objects

Chapter 12 User Assistance

Chapter 13 Visual Design

PART IV APPENDIXES

Appendix A Mouse Interface Summary

Appendix B Keyboard Interface Summary

Appendix C Guidelines Summary

Appendix D Supporting Specific Versions of Microsoft Windows

Appendix E International Word Lists

Introduction

Welcome to *The Windows Interface Guidelines for Software Design*, an indispensable guide to designing software that runs with the Microsoft® Windows® operating system. The design of your software's interface, more than anything else, affects how a user experiences your product. This guide promotes good interface design and visual and functional consistency within and across Windows-based applications.

What's New

Continuing the direction set by Microsoft OLE, the enhancements in the Windows user interface provide a design evolution from the basic and graphical to the more object oriented — that is, from an application-centered interface to a more data-centered one. In response, developers and designers may need to rethink the interface of their software — the basic components and the respective operations and properties that apply to them. This is important because, from a user's perspective, applications have become less the primary focus and more the engines behind the objects in the interface. Users can now interact with data without having to think about applications, allowing them to better concentrate on their tasks.

When adapting your existing Windows-based software, make certain you consider the following important design aspects:

- Title bar text and icons
- Property sheets
- Transfer model (including drag and drop)

- Pop-up menus

- New controls

- Integration with the system

- Help interface

- OLE embedding and OLE linking

- Visual design of windows, controls, and icons

- Window management

- Presentation of minimized windows

These elements are covered in depth throughout this guide.

How to Use This Guide

This guide is intended for those who are designing and developing Windows-based software. It may also be appropriate for those interested in a better understanding of the Windows environment and the human-computer interface principles it supports. The content of the guide covers the following areas:

- Basic design principles and process — fundamental design philosophy, assumptions about human behavior, design methodology, and concepts embodied in the interface.

- Interface elements — descriptive information about the various components in the interface as well as when and how to use them.

- Design details — specific information about the details of effective design and style when using the elements of the interface.

- Additional information — summary and quick reference information, a bibliography, a comprehensive word list in numerous languages to assist in product localization, and a glossary.

This guide focuses on the design and elements of an application's user interface. Although an occasional technical reference is included, this guide does not generally cover detailed information about technical implementation or application programming interfaces (APIs), because there are many different types of development tools that you can use to develop software for Windows. The documentation included with the Microsoft® Win32® Software Development Kit (SDK) is one source of information about specific APIs.

How to Apply the Guidelines

This guide promotes visual and functional consistency within and across the Windows operating system. Although following these guidelines is encouraged, you are free to adopt the guidelines that best suit your software. However, by following these guidelines, you enable users to transfer their skills and experience from one task to the next and to learn new tasks easily. In addition, evolution toward data-centered design breaks down the lines between traditional application domains, making inconsistencies in the interface more obvious and distracting to users.

Conversely, adhering to the design guidelines does not guarantee usability. The guidelines are valuable tools, but they must be combined with other factors as part of an effective software design process, such as application of design principles, task analysis, prototyping, and usability evaluation.

You may extend these guidelines, provided that you do so in the spirit of the principles on which they are based, and maintain a reasonable level of consistency with the visual and behavioral aspects of the Windows interface. In general, avoid adding new elements or behaviors unless the interface does not otherwise support them. More importantly, avoid changing an existing behavior for common elements. A user builds up expectations about the workings of an interface. Inconsistencies not only confuse the user, they also add unnecessary complexity.

These guidelines supersede those issued for Windows version 3.1 and all previous releases and are specific to the development of applications designed for Microsoft® Windows®, Microsoft® Windows NT™ Workstation, and Microsoft® Windows NT Server. There is no direct relationship between these guidelines and those provided for other operating systems.

For more information about special considerations concerning developing applications for both Windows 95 and Windows NT operating system, see Appendix D, "Supporting Specific Versions of Windows."

Conventions Used in This Guide

The following conventions are used throughout this guide.

Convention	Indicates
	A reference to related topics in this guide or other books that provide more information about the topic.
	Additional or special information about the topic.
SMALL CAPITAL LETTERS	Names of keys on the keyboard — for example, SHIFT, CTRL, or ALT.
KEY+KEY	Key combinations for which the user must press and hold down one key and then press another — for example, CTRL+P or ALT+F4.
Italic text	New terms and variable expressions, such as parameters.
Bold text	Win32 API keywords and registry key entries.
Registry text	Examples of registry entries.
[ ]	Optional information.

Part I

Fundamentals of
Designing User
Interaction

Design Principles and Methodology

A well-designed user interface is built on principles and a development process that centers on users and their tasks. This chapter summarizes the basic principles of the interface design for Microsoft Windows. It also includes techniques and methodologies employed in an effective human-computer interface design process.

User-Centered Design Principles

The information in this section describes the design principles on which Windows and the guidelines in this book are based. You will find these principles valuable when designing software for Windows.

User in Control

An important principle of user interface design is that the user should always feel in control of the software, rather than feeling controlled by the software. This principle has a number of implications.

The first implication is the operational assumption that the user initiates actions, not the computer or software — the user plays an active, rather than reactive, role. You can use techniques to automate tasks, but implement them in a way that allows the user to chose or control the automation.

The second implication is that users, because of their widely varying skills and preferences, must be able to personalize aspects of the interface. The system software provides user access to many of these aspects. Your software should reflect user settings for different system properties, such as color, fonts, or other options.

The final implication is that your software should be as interactive and responsive as possible. Avoid modes whenever possible. A *mode* is a state that excludes general interaction or otherwise limits the user to specific interactions. When a mode is the only or the best design alternative — for example, for selecting a particular tool in a drawing program — make certain the mode is obvious, visible, the result of an explicit user choice, and easy to cancel.

For information about applying the design principle of user in control, see Chapter 4, "Input Basics," and Chapter 5, "General Interaction Techniques." These chapters cover the basic forms of interaction your software should support.

Directness

Design your software so that users can directly manipulate software representations of information. Whether dragging an object to relocate it or navigating to a location in a document, users should see how the actions they take affect the objects on the screen. Visibility of information and choices also reduce the user's mental workload. Users can recognize a command easier than they can recall its syntax.

Familiar metaphors provide a direct and intuitive interface to user tasks. By allowing users to transfer their knowledge and experience, metaphors make it easier to predict and learn the behaviors of software-based representations.

When using metaphors, you need not limit a computer-based implementation to its "real world" counterpart. For example, unlike its paper-based counterpart, a folder on the Windows desktop can be used to organize a variety of objects such as printers, calculators, and other folders. Similarly, a Windows folder can be more easily resorted. The purpose of using metaphor in the interface is to provide a cognitive bridge; the metaphor is not an end in itself.

Metaphors support user recognition rather than recollection. Users remember a meaning associated with a familiar object more easily than they remember the name of a particular command.

For information about applying the principle of directness and metaphor, see Chapter 5, "General Interaction Techniques," and Chapter 13, "Visual Design." These chapters cover, respectively, the use of directness in the interface (including drag and drop) and the use of metaphors when designing icons or other graphical elements.

Consistency

Consistency allows users to transfer existing knowledge to new tasks, learn new things more quickly, and focus more on tasks because they need not spend time trying to remember the differences in interaction. By providing a sense of stability, consistency makes the interface familiar and predictable.

Consistency is important through all aspects of the interface, including names of commands, visual presentation of information, and operational behavior. To design consistency into software, you must consider several aspects:

- Consistency within a product. Present common functions using a consistent set of commands and interfaces. For example, avoid implementing a Copy command that immediately carries out an operation in one situation but in another presents a dialog box that requires a user to type in a destination. As a corollary to this example, use the same command to carry out functions that seem similar to the user.

- Consistency within the operating environment. By maintaining a high level of consistency between the interaction and interface conventions provided by Windows, your software benefits from users' ability to apply interaction skills they have already learned.

- Consistency with metaphors. If a particular behavior is more characteristic of a different object than its metaphor implies, the user may have difficulty learning to associate that behavior with an object. For example, an incinerator communicates a different model than a wastebasket for the recoverability of objects placed in it.

Although applying the principle of consistency is the primary goal of this guide, the following chapters focus on the elements common to all Windows-based software: Chapter 6, "Windows," Chapter 7, "Menus, Controls, and Toolbars," and Chapter 8, "Secondary Windows." For information about closely integrating your software with the Windows environment, see Chapter 10, "Integrating with the System," and Chapter 11, "Working with OLE Embedded and OLE Linked Objects."

Forgiveness

Users like to explore an interface and often learn by trial and error. An effective interface allows for interactive discovery. It provides only appropriate sets of choices and warns users about potential situations where they may damage the system or data, or better, makes actions reversible or recoverable.

Even within the best designed interface, users can make mistakes. These mistakes can be both physical (accidentally pointing to the wrong command or data) and mental (making a wrong decision about which command or data to select). An effective design avoids situations that are likely to result in errors. It also accommodates potential user errors and makes it easy for the user to recover.

For information about applying the principle of forgiveness, see Chapter 12, "User Assistance," which provides information about supporting discoverability in the interface through the use of contextual, task-oriented, and reference forms of user assistance. For information about designing for the widest range of users, see Chapter 14, "Special Design Considerations."

Feedback

Always provide feedback for a user's actions. Visual, and sometimes audio, cues should be presented with every user interaction to confirm that the software is responding to the user's input and to communicate details that distinguish the nature of the action.

Effective feedback is timely, and is presented as close to the point of the user's interaction as possible. Even when the computer is processing a particular task, provide the user with information regarding the state of the process and how to cancel that process if that is an option. Nothing is more disconcerting than a "dead" screen that is unresponsive to input. A typical user will tolerate only a few seconds of an unresponsive interface.

It is equally important that the type of feedback you use be appropriate to the task. Pointer changes or a status bar message can communicate simple information; more complex feedback may require the display of a message box.

For information about applying the principle of visual and audio feedback, see Chapter 13, "Visual Design," and Chapter 14, "Special Design Considerations."

Aesthetics

The visual design is an important part of a software's interface. Visual attributes provide valuable impressions and communicate important cues to the interaction behavior of particular objects. At the same time, it is important to remember that every visual element that appears on the screen potentially competes for the user's attention. Provide a pleasant environment that clearly contributes to the user's understanding of the information presented. A graphics or visual designer may be invaluable with this aspect of the design.

For information and guidelines related to the aesthetics of your interface, see Chapter 13, "Visual Design." This chapter covers everything from individual element design to font use and window layout.

Simplicity

An interface should be simple (not simplistic), easy to learn, and easy to use. It must also provide access to all functionality provided by an application. Maximizing functionality and maintaining simplicity work against each other in the interface. An effective design balances these objectives.

One way to support simplicity is to reduce the presentation of information to the minimum required to communicate adequately. For example, avoid wordy descriptions for command names or messages. Irrelevant or verbose phrases clutter your design, making it difficult for users to easily extract essential information. Another way to design a simple but useful interface is to use natural mappings and semantics. The arrangement and presentation of elements affects their meaning and association.

You can also help users manage complexity by using progressive disclosure. *Progressive disclosure* involves careful organization of information so that it is shown only at the appropriate time. By "hiding" information presented to the user, you reduce the amount of information to process. For example, clicking a menu displays its choices; the use of dialog boxes can reduce the number of menu options.

Progressive disclosure does not imply using unconventional techniques for revealing information, such as requiring a modifier key as the only way to access basic functions or forcing the user down a longer sequence of hierarchical interaction. This can make an interface more complex and cumbersome.

For information about applying the principle of simplicity, see Chapter 7, "Menus, Controls, and Toolbars." This chapter discusses progressive disclosure in detail and describes how and when to use the standard (system-supplied) elements in your interface.

Design Methodology

Effective interface design is more than just following a set of rules. It requires a user-centered attitude and design methodology. It also involves early planning of the interface and continued work through the software development process.

A Balanced Design Team

An important consideration in the design of a product is the composition of the team that designs and builds it. Always try to balance disciplines and skills, including development, visual design, writing, human factors, and usability assessment. Rarely are these characteristics found in a single individual, so create a team of individuals who specialize in these areas and who can contribute uniquely to the final design.

Ensure that the design team can effectively work and communicate together. Locating them in close proximity or providing them with a common area to work out design details often fosters better communication and interaction.

The Design Cycle

An effective user-centered design process involves a number of important phases: designing, prototyping, testing, and iterating. The following sections describe these phases.

Design

The initial work on a software's design can be the most critical because, during this phase, you decide the general shape of your product. If the foundation work is flawed, it is difficult to correct afterwards.

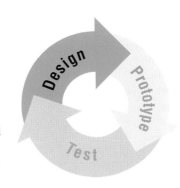

This part of the process involves not only defining the objectives and features for your product, but understanding who your users are and their tasks, intentions, and goals. This includes understanding factors such as their background — age, gender, expertise, experience level, physical limitations, and special needs; their work environment —

equipment, social and cultural influences, and physical surroundings; and their current task organization — the steps required, the dependencies, redundant activities, and the output objective. An order-entry system may have very different users and requirements than an information kiosk.

At this point, begin defining your conceptual framework to represent your product with the knowledge and experience of your target audience. Ideally, you want to create a design model that fits the user's conceptual view of the tasks to be performed. Consider the basic organization and different types of metaphors that can be employed. Observing users at their current tasks can provide ideas on effective metaphors to use.

Document your design. Committing your planned design to a written format not only provides a valuable reference point and form of communication, but often helps make the design more concrete and reveals issues and gaps.

Prototype

After you have defined a design model, prototype some of the basic aspects of the design. This can be done with "pencil and paper" models — where you create illustrations of your interface to which other elements can be attached; storyboards — comic book-like sequences of sketches that illustrate specific processes; animation — movie-like simulations; or operational software using a prototyping tool or normal development tools.

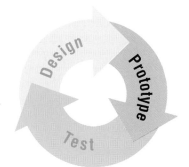

A prototype is a valuable asset in many ways. First, it provides an effective tool for communicating the design. Second, it can help you define task flow and better visualize the design. Finally, it provides a low-cost vehicle for getting user input on a design. This is particularly useful early in the design process.

The type of prototype you build depends on your goal. Functionality, task flow, interface, operation, and documentation are just some of the different aspects of a product that need to be assessed. For example, pen and paper models or storyboards may work when defining task organization or conceptual ideas. Operational prototypes are usually best for the mechanics of user interaction.

Consider whether to focus your prototype on breadth or depth. The broader the prototype, the more features you should try to include to gain an understanding about how users react to concepts and organization. When your objective is focused more on detailed usage of a particular feature or area of the design, use depth-oriented prototypes that include more detail for a given feature or task.

Test

User-centered design involves the user in the design process. Usability testing a design, or a particular aspect of a design, provides valuable information and is a key part of a product's success. Usability testing is different than quality assurance testing in that, rather than find programming defects, you assess how well the interface fits user needs and expectations. Of course, defects can sometimes affect how well the interface will fit.

There can be different reasons for testing. You can use testing to look for potential problems in a proposed design. You can also focus on comparative studies of two or more designs to determine which is better, given a specific task or set of tasks.

Usability testing provides you not only with task efficiency and success-or-failure data, it also can provide you with information about the user's perceptions, satisfaction, questions, and problems, which may be just as significant as the ability to complete a particular task.

When testing, it is important to use participants who fit the profile of your target audience. Using fellow workers from down the hall might be a quick way to find participants, but software developers rarely have the same experience as their customers. The section, "Usability Assessment in the Design Process," provides details about conducting a usability test.

Iterate

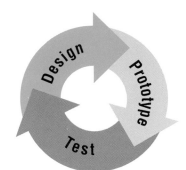

Because testing often uncovers design weaknesses, or at least provides additional information you will want to use, repeat the entire process, taking what you have learned and reworking your design or moving onto reprototyping and retesting. Continue this refining cycle through the development process until you are satisfied with the results.

During this iterative process, you can begin substituting the actual application for prototypes as the application code becomes available. However, avoid delaying your design cycle waiting for the application code to be complete enough; you can lose valuable time and input that you could have captured with a prototype. Moreover, by the time most applications are complete enough for testing, it is difficult to consider significant changes, because it becomes easier to ignore usability defects because of the time resources invested. In addition, changes at this point may affect the application's delivery schedule.

Usability Assessment in the Design Process

As described in the previous section, usability testing is a key part of the design process, but testing design prototypes is only one part of the picture. Usability assessment should begin in the early stages of product development, where you can use it to gather data about how users do their work. You then roll your findings back into the design process. As the design progresses, usability assessment continues to provide valuable input for analyzing initial design concepts and, in the later stages of product development, can be used to test specific product tasks. Apply usability assessment early and often.

Consider the user's entire experience as part of a product's usability. The usability assessment should include all of a product's components. A software interface is more than just what shows up on the screen or in the documentation.

Usability Testing Techniques

Usability testing involves a wide range of techniques and investment of resources, including trained specialists working in sound-proofed labs with one-way mirrors and sophisticated recording equipment. However, even the simplest investment of an office or conference room, tape recorder, stopwatch, and notepad can produce benefits. Similarly, all tests need not involve great numbers of subjects. More typically, quick, iterative tests with a small, well-targeted sample, 6-10 participants, can identify 80 to 90 percent of most design problems.

Like the design process itself, usability testing begins with defining the target audience and test goals. When designing a test, focus on tasks — not features. Even if your goal is testing specific features, remember that your customers will use them within the context of particular tasks. It is also a good idea to run a pilot test to work out the bugs of the tasks to be tested and make certain the task scenarios, prototype, and equipment work smoothly.

When conducting the usability test, provide an environment comparable to the target setting; usually a quiet location, free from distractions, is best. Make participants feel comfortable. Unless you have participated yourself, you may be surprised by the pressure many test participants feel. You can alleviate some pressure by explaining the testing process and equipment to the participants, and stating your objective in testing the software and not them; if they become confused or frustrated, it is not a reflection upon them.

Allow the user reasonable time to try and work through any difficult situations. Although it is generally best to not interrupt participants during a test, they may get stuck or end up in situations that require intervention. This need not necessarily disqualify the test data, as long as the test coordinator carefully guides or hints around a problem. Give general hints before moving to specific advice. For more difficult situations, you may need to stop the test and make adjustments. Keep in mind that less intervention usually yields better results. Always record the techniques and search patterns that users employ when attempting to work through a difficulty, and the number and type of hints you have to provide.

Ask subjects to think aloud as they work, so you can hear what assumptions and inferences they are making. As the participants work, record the time they take to perform a task as well as any problems they encounter. You may also want to follow up the session with a questionnaire that asks the participants to evaluate the product or tasks they performed.

Record the test results using a portable tape recorder, or better, a video camera. Since even the best observer can miss details, reviewing the data later will prove invaluable. Recorded data also allows more direct comparisons between multiple participants. It is usually risky to base conclusions on observing a single subject. Recorded data also allows all the design team to review and evaluate the results.

Whenever possible, involve *all* members of the design team in observing the test and reviewing the results. This ensures a common reference point and better design solutions as team members apply their own insights to what they observe. If direct observation is not possible, make the recorded results available to the entire team.

Other Assessment Techniques

There are many techniques you can use to gather usability information. In addition to those already mentioned, "focus groups" are helpful for generating initial ideas or trying out ideas. A focus group requires a moderator who directs the discussion about aspects of a task or design, but allows participants to freely express their opinions. You can also conduct demonstrations, or "walkthroughs," in which you take the user through a set of sample scenarios and ask about their impressions along the way. In a so-called "Wizard of Oz" technique, a testing specialist simulates the interaction of an interface. Although these latter techniques can be valuable, they often require a trained, experienced test coordinator.

Understanding Users

The design and usability techniques described in the previous sections have been used in the development of Windows and in many of the guidelines included in this book. That process has yielded the following general characteristics about users. Consider these characteristics in the design of your software:

- Beginning Windows users often have difficulty with the mouse. For example, dragging and double-clicking are skills that may take time for beginning mouse users to master. Dragging can be difficult because it requires continued pressure on the mouse button and involves properly targeting the correct destination. Double-clicking is not the same as two separate clicks, so many beginning users have difficulty handling the timing necessary to distinguish these two actions, or they overgeneralize the behavior to assume that everything needs double-clicking. Design your interface so that double-clicking and dragging are not the only ways to perform basic tasks; allow the user to conduct those tasks using single click operations.

- Beginning users often have difficulty with window management. They do not always realize that overlapping windows represent a three-dimensional space. As a result, when a window is hidden by another, a user may assume it no longer exists.

- Beginning users often have difficulty with file management. The organization of files and folders nested more than two levels is more difficult to understand because it is not as obvious in the real world.

- Intermediate users may understand file hierarchies, but have difficulty with other aspects of file management — such as moving and copying files. This may be because most of their experience working with files is often from within an application.

- Advanced, or "power," users want efficiency. The challenge in designing for advanced users is providing for efficiency without introducing complexity for less-experienced users. (Shortcut methods are often useful for supporting these users.) In addition, advanced users may be dependent upon particular interfaces, making it difficult for them to adapt to significant rearrangement or changes in an interface.

- To develop for the widest audience, consider international users and users with disabilities. Including these users as part of your planning and design cycle is the best way to ensure that you can accommodate them.

Design Tradeoffs

A number of additional factors may affect the design of a product. For example, marketing considerations may require you to deliver a product with a minimal design process, or comparative evaluations may force you to consider additional features. Remember that shortcuts and additional features can affect the product. There is no simple equation to determine when a design tradeoff is appropriate. So in evaluating the impact, consider the following:

- Every additional feature potentially affects performance, complexity, stability, maintenance, and the support costs of an application.

- It is harder to fix a design problem after the release of a product because users may adapt, or even become dependent on, a peculiarity in the design.

- Simplicity is not the same as being simplistic. Making something simple to use often requires a good deal of work and code.

- Features implemented by a small extension in the application code do not necessarily have a proportional effect in a user interface. For example, if the primary task is selecting a single object, extending it to support selection of multiple objects could make the frequent, simple task more difficult to carry out.

Basic Concepts

Microsoft Windows supports the evolution and design of software
from a basic graphical user interface to a data-centered interface that
is better focused on users and their tasks. This chapter outlines the
fundamental concepts of data-centered design. It covers some of the
basic definitions used throughout this guide and provides the fundamental model for how to define your interface to fit well within the
Windows environment.

Data-Centered Design

Data-centered design means that the design of the interface supports
a model where a user can browse for data and edit it directly instead
of having to first locate an appropriate editor or application. As a
user interacts with data, the corresponding commands and tools to
manipulate the data or the view of the data become available to the
user automatically. This frees a user to focus on the information and
tasks rather than on applications and how applications interact.

In this data-centered context, a *document* is a common unit of data
used in tasks and exchanged between users. The use of the term is
not limited to the output of a word-processing or spreadsheet application, but it emphasizes that the focus of design is on data, rather
than the underlying application.

Objects as Metaphor

A well-designed user interface provides an understandable, consistent framework in which users can work, without being confounded by the details of the underlying technology. To help accomplish this, the design model of the Windows user interface uses the metaphor of objects. This is a natural way we interpret and interact with the world around us. In the interface, *objects* not only describe files or icons, but any unit of information, including cells, paragraphs, characters, and circles, and the documents in which they reside.

Object Characteristics

Objects, whether real-world or computer representations, have certain characteristics that help us understand what they are and how they behave. The following concepts describe the aspects and characteristics of computer representations:

- Properties — Objects have certain characteristics or attributes, called *properties*, that define their appearance or state — for example, color, size, and modification date. Properties are not limited to the external or visible traits of an object. They may reflect the internal or operational state of an object, such as an option in a spelling check utility that automatically suggests alternative spellings.

- Operations — Things that can be done with or to an object are considered its *operations*. Moving or copying an object are examples of operations. You can expose operations in the interface through a variety of mechanisms, including commands and direct manipulation.

- Relationships — Objects always exist within the context of other objects. The context, or *relationships*, that an object may have often affects the way the object appears or behaves. Common kinds of relationships include collections, constraints, and composites.

Relationships

The simplest relationship is a *collection*, in which objects in a set share a common aspect. The results of a query or a multiple selection of objects are examples of a collection. The significance of a collection is that it enables operations to be applied to a set of objects.

A *constraint* is a stronger relationship between a set of objects in that changing an object in the set affects some other object in the set. The way a text box streams text, the way a drawing application layers its objects, and even the way a word-processing application organizes a document into pages are all examples of constraints.

When a relationship between objects becomes so significant that the aggregation can be identified as an object itself with its own set of properties and operations, the relationship is called a *composite*. A range of cells, a paragraph, and a grouped set of drawing objects are examples of composites.

Another common kind of relationship found in the interface is containment. A *container* is an object that is the place where other objects exist, such as text in a document or documents in a folder. A container often influences the behavior of its content. It may add or suppress certain properties or operations of an object placed in it. In addition, a container controls access to its content as well as what kind of object it will accept as its content. This may affect the results when transferring objects from one container to another.

All these aspects contribute to an object's *type*, a descriptive way of distinguishing or classifying objects. Objects of a common type have similar traits and behaviors.

Composition

As in the natural world, the metaphor of objects implies a constructed environment. Objects are compositions of other objects. You can define most tasks supported by applications as a specialized combination or set of relationships between objects. A text document is a composition of text, paragraphs, footnotes, or other items. A table is a combination of cells; a chart is a particular organization of graphics. When you define user interaction with objects to be as consistent as possible at any level, you can produce complex constructions while maintaining a small, basic set of conventions. These conventions can apply throughout the interface, increasing ease of use. In addition, using composition to model tasks encourages modular, component-oriented design. This allows objects to be adapted or recombined for other uses.

Persistence

In the natural world, objects persist in their existing state unless changed or destroyed. When you use a pen to write a note, you need not invoke a command to ensure that the ink is preserved on the paper. The act of writing implicitly preserves the information. This is the long term direction for objects in the interface as well. Although it is still appropriate to design software that requires explicit user actions to preserve data, consider whether data can be preserved automatically. In addition, view state information, such as cursor position, scroll position, and window size and location, should be preserved so it can be restored when an object's view is reopened.

Putting Theory into Practice

Using objects in an interface design does not guarantee usability. But applying object-based concepts does offer greater potential for a well-designed interface. As with any good user interface design, a good user-centered design process ensures the success and quality of the interface.

The first step to object-based design should begin as any good design with a thorough understanding of what users' objectives and tasks are. When doing the task analysis, identify the basic components or objects used in those tasks and the behavior and the characteristics that differentiate each kind of object, including the relationships of the objects to each other and to the user. Also identify the actions that are performed, the objects to which they apply, and the state information or attributes that each object in the task must preserve, display, and allow to be edited.

Once the analysis is complete, you can start identifying the user interfaces for the objects. Define how the objects you identified are to be presented, either as icons or data elements in a form. Use icons primarily for representing composite or container objects that need to be opened into their own windows. Attribute or state information should typically be presented as properties of the associated object, most often using property sheets. Map behaviors and operations to specific kinds of interaction, such as menu commands, direct manipulation, or both. Make these accessible when the object is selected by the user. The information in this guide will help you define how to apply the interfaces provided by the system.

Redesigning an existing Windows 3.1-based application to a more data-centered interface need not require an immediate, complete overhaul. You can begin the evolution by adding contextual interfaces such as pop-up menus, property sheets, and OLE drag and drop and by following the recommendations for designing your window title bars and icons.

The Windows Environment

This chapter provides a brief overview of some of the basic elements included in the Microsoft Windows operating system that allow the user to control the environment (sometimes collectively referred to as the *shell*). These elements provide not only the backdrop for a user's environment, but can be landmarks for the user's interaction with your application as well.

The Desktop

The *desktop* represents a user's primary work area; it fills the screen and forms the visual background for all operations (as shown in Figure 3.1). However, the desktop is more than just a background. It can also be used as a convenient location to place objects that are stored in the file system. In addition, for a computer connected to a network, the desktop also serves as a private work area through which a user can still browse and access objects remotely located on the network.

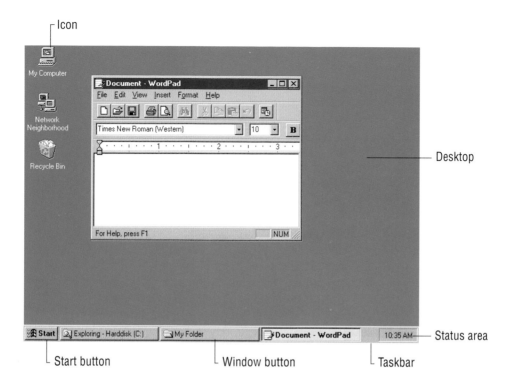

Figure 3.1 The desktop

The Taskbar

The taskbar is a special component of the desktop that can be used to switch between open windows and to access global commands and other frequently used objects. As a result, it provides a home base — an operational anchor for the interface.

Like most toolbars, the taskbar can be configured. For example, a user can move the taskbar from its default location and relocate it along another edge of the screen (as shown in Figure 3.2). The user can also configure display options of the taskbar. The taskbar can

For more information about integrating your application with the taskbar, see Chapter 10, "Integrating with the System."

provide the user access to your application. It can also be used to provide status information even when your application is not active. Because the taskbar is an interface shared across applications, be sure to follow the conventions and guidelines covered in this guide.

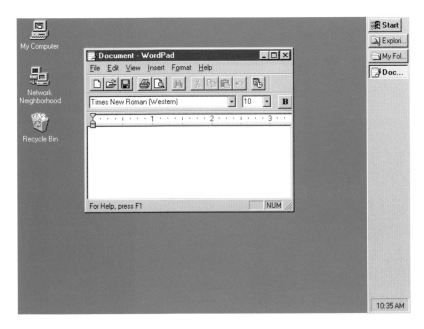

Fig 3.2 Showing the taskbar in another location

The Start Button

The Start button at the left side of the taskbar displays a special menu that includes commands for opening or finding files. The Program menu entry automatically includes the Program Manager entries when the system is installed over Windows 3.1. When installing your Windows-based application, you also can include an entry for your application by placing a shortcut icon in the system's Programs folder.

Window Buttons

Whenever the user opens a primary window, a button is placed on the taskbar for that window. This button provides the user access to the commands of that window and a convenient interface for switching to that window. The taskbar automatically adjusts the size of the buttons to accommodate as many buttons as possible. When the size of the button requires that the window's title be abbreviated, the taskbar also automatically supplies a small pop-up window (as shown in Figure 3.3) that displays the full title for the window.

— Full title of the window

Figure 3.3 Pop-up window with full title

When a window is minimized, the window's button remains on the taskbar, but is removed when the window is closed.

Taskbar buttons can also be used as drag and drop destinations. When the user drags over a taskbar button, the system activates the associated window, allowing the user to drop within that window.

> For more information about drag and drop, see Chapter 5, "General Interaction Techniques."

The Status Area

On the opposite side of the taskbar from the Start menu is a special status area. Your application can place special status or notification indicators here, even when it is not active.

Icons

Icons may appear on the desktop and in windows. *Icons* are pictorial representations of objects. This goes beyond the use of icons in Windows 3.1, which only represented minimized windows. Your software should provide and register icons for its application file and any of its associated document or data files.

> For more information about the use of icons, see Chapter 10, "Integrating with the System." For information about icon design, see Chapter 13, "Visual Design."

Windows includes a number of icons that represent basic objects, such as the following.

Table 3.1 Icons

Icon	Type	Function
My Computer	System Folder	Provides access to a user's private storage.
Network Neighborhood	System Folder	Provides access to the network.
Folder	Folder	Provides organization of files and folders.
Shortcut to My Favorite Folder	Shortcut	Provides access to other objects. A shortcut icon uses the icon of the type of file it is linked to, overlaid with the link symbol.
All Files	Saved Search	Locates files or folders.
Windows Explorer	Application	Allows browsing of the content of a user's computer or the network.
Recycle Bin	System Folder	Stores deleted icons.
Control Panel	System Folder	Provides access to properties of installed devices and resources (for example, fonts, displays, and keyboards).

Windows

You can open icons into windows. Windows provides a means of viewing and editing information, and viewing the content and properties of objects. You can also use windows to display parameters to complete commands, palettes of controls, or messages informing a user of a particular situation. Figure 3.4 demonstrates some of the different uses for windows.

For more information about windows, see Chapter 6, "Windows," and Chapter 8, "Secondary Windows."

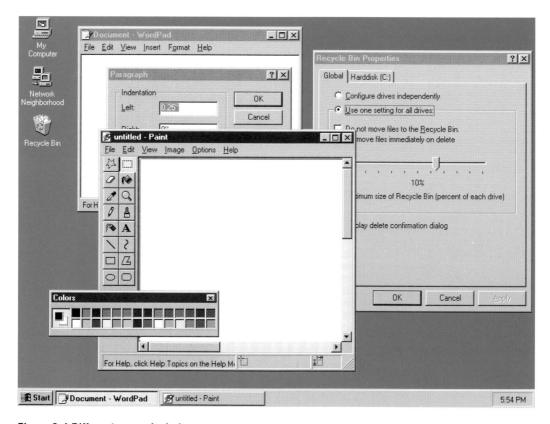

Figure 3.4 Different uses of windows

Input Basics

A user can interact with objects in the interface using different types of input devices. The most common input devices are the mouse, the keyboard, and the pen. This chapter covers the basic behavior for these devices; it does not exclude other forms of input.

Mouse Input

The mouse is a primary input device for interacting with objects in the Microsoft Windows interface. Other types of pointing devices that emulate a mouse, such as trackballs, fall under the general use of the term "mouse."

For more information about interactive techniques such as navigation, selection, viewing, editing, transfer, and creating new objects, see Chapter 5, "General Interaction Techniques."

Mouse Pointers

The mouse is operationally linked with a graphic on the screen called the *pointer* (also referred to as the *cursor*). By positioning the pointer and clicking the buttons on the mouse, a user can select objects and their operations.

As a user moves the pointer across the screen, its appearance can change to provide feedback about a particular location, operation, or state. Table 4.1 lists some common pointer shapes and their uses.

Table 4.1 Common Pointers

Shape	Screen location	Available or current action
	Over most objects	Pointing, selecting, or moving.
	Over text	Selecting text.
	Over any object or location	Processing an operation.
	Over any screen location	Processing in the background (application loading), but the pointer is still interactive.
	Over most objects	Context-sensitive Help mode.
	Inside a window	Zooming a view.
	Over a sizable edge	Resizing an edge vertically.
	Over a sizable edge	Resizing an edge horizontally.
	Over a sizable edge	Resizing an edge diagonally.
	Over a sizable edge	Resizing an edge diagonally.
	Along column gridlines	Resizing a column.
	Along row gridlines	Resizing a row.
	Over split box in vertical scroll bar	Splitting a window (or adjusting a split) horizontally.
	Over split box in horizontal scroll bar	Splitting a window (or adjusting a split) vertically.
	Over any object	Not available as a drop target.

The system does not provide all of these pointers. For more information about designing your own pointers, see Chapter 13, "Visual Design."

Each pointer has a particular point — called a *hot spot* — that defines the exact screen location of the mouse. The hot spot determines what object is affected by mouse actions. Screen objects can additionally define a hot zone; the *hot zone* defines the area the hot spot must be within to be considered over the object. Typically, the hot zone coincides with the borders of an object, but it may be larger, or smaller, to make user interaction easier.

Mouse Actions

Basic mouse actions in the interface use mouse button 1 or button 2. By default, button 1 is the leftmost mouse button and button 2 is the rightmost button. The system allows the user to swap the mapping of the buttons. Button 2 actions typically duplicate functions already accessible with button 1, but provide those functions more efficiently.

For a mouse with three buttons, button 2 is the *right-most* button, not the center button.

The following are the common behaviors performed with the mouse.

Action	Description
Pointing	Positioning the pointer so it "points to" a particular object on the screen without using the mouse button. Pointing is usually part of preparing for some other interaction. Pointing is often an opportunity to provide visual cues or other feedback to a user.
Clicking	Positioning the pointer over an object and then pressing and releasing the mouse button. Generally, the mouse is not moved during the click, and the mouse button is quickly released after it is pressed. Clicking identifies (selects) or activates objects.
Double-clicking	Positioning the pointer over an object and pressing and releasing the mouse button twice in rapid succession. Double-clicking an object typically invokes its default operation.
Pressing	Positioning the pointer over an object and then holding down the mouse button. Pressing is often the beginning of a click or drag operation.
Dragging	Positioning the pointer over an object, pressing down the mouse button while holding the mouse button down, and moving the mouse. Use dragging for actions such as selection and direct manipulation of an object.

For most mouse interactions, pressing the mouse button only identifies an operation. User feedback is usually provided at this point.
Releasing the mouse button activates (carries out) the operation. An
auto-repeat function — for example, pressing a scroll arrow to continuously scroll — is an exception.

This guide does not cover other mouse behaviors such as *chording*
(pressing multiple mouse buttons simultaneously) and multiple-
clicking (triple- or quadruple-clicking). Because these behaviors
require more user skill, they are not generally recommended for basic
operations. However, you can consider them for special shortcut
operations.

Because not every mouse has a third button, there is no basic action
defined for a third (middle) mouse button. It is best to limit the assignment of operations to this button to those environments where
the availability of a third mouse button can be assumed, and for
providing redundant or shortcut access to operations supported elsewhere in the interface. When assigning actions to the button, you
need to define the behaviors for the actions already described (pointing, clicking, dragging, and double-clicking) for this button.

Keyboard Input

The keyboard is a primary means of entering or editing text information. However, the Windows interface also supports the use of keyboard input to navigate, toggle modes, modify input, and, as a
shortcut, to invoke certain operations.

For more information about
using the keyboard for navigation, selection, and editing, see
Chapter 5, "General Interaction
Techniques."

Following are the common interactive behaviors performed with the keyboard.

Action	Description
Pressing	Pressing and releasing a key. Unlike mouse interaction, keyboard interaction occurs upon the down transition of the key. Pressing typically describes the keyboard interaction for invoking particular commands or for navigation.
Holding	Pressing and holding down a key. Holding typically describes interaction with keys such as ALT, SHIFT, and CTRL that modify the standard behavior of other input — for example, another key press or mouse action.
Typing	Typing input of text information from the keyboard.

Text Keys

Text keys include the following:

- Alphanumeric keys (a–z, A–Z, 0–9)

- Punctuation and symbol keys

- TAB and ENTER keys

- The SPACEBAR

In text-entry contexts, pressing a text key enters the corresponding character and typically displays that character on the screen. Except in special views, the characters produced by the TAB and ENTER keys are not usually visible. In some contexts, text keys can also be used for navigation or for invoking specific operations.

Most keyboards include two keys labeled ENTER: one on the main keyboard and one on the numeric keypad. Because these keys have the same label (and on some keyboards the latter may not be available), assign both keys the same functionality.

Access Keys

An access key is an alphanumeric key — sometimes referred to as a *mnemonic* — that when used in combination with the ALT key navigates to and activates a control. The access key matches one of the characters in the text label of the control. For example, pressing ALT+O activates a control whose label is "Open" and whose assigned access key is "O". Typically, access keys are not case sensitive. The effect of activating a control depends on the type of control.

Assign access key characters to controls using the following guidelines (in order of choice):

1. The first letter of the label for the control, unless another letter provides a better mnemonic association.

2. A distinctive consonant in the label.

3. A vowel in the label.

Avoid assigning a character where the visual indication of the access key cannot be distinguished from the character. Also, avoid using a character normally assigned to a common function. For example, when you include an Apply button, reserve the "A" — or its localized equivalent — as the access key for that button. In addition, do not assign access keys to the OK and Cancel commands when they map to the ENTER and ESC keys, respectively.

Nonunique access key assignments within the same scope access the first control. Depending on the control, if the user presses the access key a second time, it may or may not access another control with the same assignment. Therefore, define an access key to be unique within the scope of its interaction — that is, the area in which the control exists and to which keyboard input is currently being directed.

Controls without explicit labels can use static text controls to create labels with assigned access keys. Software that supports a nonroman writing system (such as Kanji), but that runs on a standard keyboard, can prefix each control label with an alphabetic (roman) character as its access key.

For more information about static text controls, see Chapter 7, "Menus, Controls, and Toolbars."

Mode Keys

Mode keys change the actions of other keys (or other input devices). There are two kinds of mode keys: toggle keys and modifier keys.

A toggle key turns a particular mode on or off each time it is pressed. For example, pressing the CAPS LOCK key toggles uppercase alphabetic keys; pressing the NUM LOCK key toggles between numeric and directional input using the keypad keys.

Like toggle keys, modifier keys change the actions of normal input. Unlike toggle keys, however, modifier keys establish modes that remain in effect only while the modifier key is held down. Modifier keys include the SHIFT, CTRL, and ALT keys. Such a "spring-loaded" mode is often preferable to a "locked" mode because it requires the user to continuously activate it, making it a conscious choice and allowing the user to easily cancel the mode by releasing the key.

Because it can be difficult for a user to remember multiple modifier assignments, avoid using multiple modifier keys as the primary means of access to basic operations. In some contexts, such as environments that are specific to pen input, the keyboard may not be available. Therefore, use modifier-based actions only for quick access to operations that are supported adequately elsewhere in the interface.

Shortcut Keys

Shortcut keys (also referred to as accelerator keys) are keys or key combinations that, when pressed, provide quick access to frequently performed operations. CTRL+*letter* combinations and function keys (F1 through F12) are usually the best choices for shortcut keys. By definition, a shortcut key is a keyboard equivalent of functionality that is supported adequately elsewhere in the interface. Therefore, avoid using a shortcut key as the only way to access a particular operation.

Function key and modified function key combinations may be easier for international users because they have no mnemonic relationship. However, there is a tradeoff because function keys are often more difficult to remember and to reach. For a list of the most common shortcut key assignments, see Appendix B, "Keyboard Interface Summary."

When defining shortcut keys, observe the following guidelines:

- Assign single keys where possible because these keys are the easiest for the user to perform.

- Make modified-letter key combinations case insensitive.

- Use SHIFT+*key* combinations for actions that extend or complement the actions of the key or key combination used without the SHIFT key. For example, ALT+TAB switches windows in a top-to-bottom order. SHIFT+ALT+TAB switches windows in reverse order. However, avoid SHIFT+*text* keys, because the effect of the SHIFT key may differ for some international keyboards.

- Use CTRL+*key* combinations for actions that represent a larger scale effect. For example, in text editing contexts, HOME moves to the beginning of a line, and CTRL+HOME moves to the beginning of the text. Use CTRL+*key* combinations for access to commands where a letter key is used — for example, CTRL+B for bold. Remember that such assignments may be meaningful only for English-speaking users.

- Avoid ALT+*key* combinations because they may conflict with the standard keyboard access for menus and controls. The ALT+*key* combinations — ALT+TAB, ALT+ESC, and ALT+SPACEBAR — are reserved for system use. ALT+*number* combinations enter special characters.

- Avoid assigning shortcut keys defined in this guide to other operations in your software. That is, if CTRL+C is the shortcut for the Copy command and your application supports the standard copy operation, don't assign CTRL+C to another operation.

- Provide support for allowing the user to change the shortcut key assignments in your software, when possible.

- Use the ESC key to stop a function in process or to cancel a direct manipulation operation. It is also usually interpreted as the shortcut key for a Cancel button.

Some keyboards also support three new keys, the Application key and the two Windows keys. The primary use for the Application key is to display the pop-up menu for current selection (same as SHIFT+F10). You may also use it with modifier keys for application-specific functions. Pressing either of the Windows keys — left or right — displays the Start menu. These keys are also used by the system as modifiers for system-specific functions. Do not use these keys as modifiers for nonsystem-level functions.

Windows key and Application key

Pen Input

 Systems with a Windows pen driver installed support user input using tapping or writing on the surface of the screen or a tablet with a pen, and in some cases with a finger.

Depending on the placement of the pen, you can use it for both pointing and writing. For example, if you move the pen over menus or most controls, it acts as a pointing device. Because of the pointing capabilities of the pen, the user can perform most mouse-based operations. When over a text entry or drawing area, the pen becomes a writing or drawing tool; the pointer changes to a pen shape to provide feedback to the user. When the tip of the pen touches the input surface, the pen starts *inking* — that is, tracing lines on the screen. The user can then draw shapes, characters, and other patterns; these patterns remain on the screen exactly as drawn or can be recognized, interpreted, and redisplayed.

The pen can retain the functionality of a pointing device (such as a mouse) even in contexts where it would normally function as a writing or drawing tool. For example, you can use timing to differentiate operations; that is, if the user holds the pen tip in the same location for a predetermined period of time, a different action may be inferred. However, this method is often unreliable or inefficient for many operations, so it may be better to use toolbar buttons to switch to different modes of operation. Choosing a particular button allows the user to define whether to use the pen for entering information (writing or drawing) or as a pointing device.

You can also provide the user with access to other operations using an action handle. An *action handle* is a special graphic displayed for a selection. An action handle can be used to support direct manipulation operations or to provide access to pop-up menus.

The **GetSystemMetrics** function provides access to the SM_PENWINDOWS constant that indicates when a pen is installed. For more information about this function, see the documentation included in the Microsoft Win32 Software Development Kit (SDK).

For more information about action handles, see Chapter 5, "General Interaction Techniques."

Following are the fundamental behaviors defined for a pen.

Action	Description
Pressing	Positioning and pressing the tip to the input surface. A pen press is equivalent to a mouse press and typically identifies a particular pen action.
Tapping	Pressing the pen tip on the input surface and lifting it without moving the pen. In general, tapping is equivalent to clicking mouse button 1. Therefore, this action typically selects an object, setting a text insertion point or activating a button
Double-tapping	Pressing and lifting the pen tip twice in rapid succession. Double-tapping is usually interpreted as the equivalent to double-clicking mouse button 1.
Dragging	Pressing the pen tip on the input surface and keeping it pressed while moving the pen. In inking contexts, you can use dragging for the input of pen strokes for writing, drawing, gestures, or for direct manipulation, depending on which is most appropriate for the context. In noninking contexts, it is the equivalent of a mouse drag.

A user may move the pen more between taps when double-tapping than a user double-clicking with a mouse. As a result, you may want to slightly increase your hot zones for detecting a double-tap when of a pen device has been installed.

Some pens include buttons on the pen barrel that can be pressed. For pens that support barrel buttons, the following behaviors may be supported.

Action	Description
Barrel-tapping	Holding down the barrel button of the pen while tapping. Barrel-tapping is equivalent to clicking with mouse button 2.
Barrel-dragging	Holding down the barrel button of the pen while dragging the pen. Barrel-dragging is equivalent to dragging with mouse button 2.

Because not all pens support barrel buttons, any behaviors that you support using a barrel button should also be supported by other techniques in the interface.

Pen input is delimited, by the lifting of the pen tip, an explicit termination tap (such as tapping the pen on another window or as the completion of a gesture), or a time-out without further input. You can also explicitly define an application-specific recognition time-out.

Proximity is the ability to detect the position of the pen without it touching the input surface. While Windows provides support for pen proximity, avoid depending on proximity as the exclusive means of access to basic functions, because not all pen hardware supports this feature. Even pen hardware that does support proximity may allow other non-pen input, such as touch input, where proximity cannot be supported.

Pen Pointers

For pen tablets, as with a mouse, pointers play an important part in visually indicating the user's location of interaction on the screen. When the input surface is actually a screen display, pointers may seem superfluous; however, they still have an important role to play. Pointers help the pen user select small targets faster. Moreover, changes from one pointer to another provide useful feedback about the actions supported by the object under the pen. For example, when the pen moves over a resizable border, the pointer can change from a pen (indicating that writing is possible) to a resizing pointer (indicating that the border can be dragged to resize the object). Whenever possible, include this type of feedback in pen-enabled applications to help users understand the kinds of supported actions.

Following are two common pointers used with the pen.

Table 4.2 Pen Pointers

Shape	Common usage
⌖	Pointing, selecting, moving, and resizing
✎	Writing and drawing

When the screen is the input surface — because a pointer may be partially obscured by the pen or by the user's hand — you may need to consider including additional forms of feedback, such as toolbar button states or status bar information, to indicate the pen's input state.

Pen Gestures

When using the pen for writing, certain ink patterns are interpreted as *gestures*. Using one of these specially drawn symbols invokes a particular operation, such as deleting text, or produces a nonprinting text character, such as a carriage return or a tab. For example, a circled X gesture is equivalent to the Cut command. After the system interprets a gesture, the gesture's ink is removed from the display.

All gestures include a circular stroke to distinguish them from ordinary characters. Most gestures also operate positionally; in other words, they act upon the objects on which they are drawn. Determining the position of the specific gesture depends on either the area surrounded by the gesture or a single point — the hot spot of the gesture.

Pen gestures usually cannot be combined with ink (writing or drawing actions) within the same recognition sequence. For example, the user cannot draw a few characters, immediately followed by a gesture, followed by more characters.

The rapidity of gestural commands is one of the key advantages of the pen. Do not rely on gestures as the only or primary way to perform commands, however, because gestures require memorization by users. Regard gestures as a quick access, shortcut method for operations adequately supported elsewhere in the interface, such as in menus or buttons. If the pen extensions are installed, you can optionally place a bitmap of the gesture next to the corresponding command (in place of the keyboard shortcut text) to help the user learn particular gestures.

In addition, avoid using gestures when they interfere with common functionality or make operations with parallel input devices, such as the mouse or keyboard, more cumbersome. For example, although writing a character gesture in a list box could be used as a way to

For more information about common gestures and their interpretation, see Chapter 5, "General Interaction Techniques."

scroll automatically within the list, it would interfere with the basic and more frequent user action of selecting an item in the list. A better technique is to provide a text input field where the user can write and, based on the letters entered, scroll the list.

Pen Recognition

Recognition is the interpretation of pen strokes into some standardized meaning. Consider recognition as a means to an end, not an end in itself. Do not use recognition if it is unnecessary or if it is not the best interface. For example, it may be more effective to provide a control that allows a user to select a date, rather than requiring the user to write it in just so your software can recognize it.

Accurate recognition is difficult to achieve, but you can greatly improve your recognition interface by providing a fast, easy means to correct errors. For example, if you allow users to overwrite characters or choose alternatives, they will be less frustrated and find recognition more useful. You can also improve recognition by using context and constraints. For example, a checkbook application can constrain certain fields to contain only numbers.

Ink Input

In some cases — for example, signatures — recognition of pen input may be unnecessary; the ink is a sufficient representation of information. Ink is a standard data type supported by the Clipboard. Consider supporting ink entries as input wherever your software accepts normal text input, unless the representation of that input needs to be interpreted for other operations, such as searching or sorting.

Targeting

Targeting, or determining where to direct pen input, is an important design factor for pen-enabled software. For example, if the user gestures over a set of objects, which objects should be affected? If the user writes text that spans several writing areas, which text should be placed in which area? In general, you use the context of the input to determine where to apply pen input. More specifically, use the following guidelines for targeting gestures on objects:

- If the user draws the gesture on any part of a selection, apply the gesture to the selection.

- If the user draws the gesture on an object that is not selected, select that object, and apply the gesture to that object.

- If the user does not draw the gesture on any object or selection, but there is a selection, apply the gesture to that selection.

If none of these guidelines applies, ignore the gesture.

For handwriting, you can also use context to determine where to direct the input. Figure 4.1 demonstrates how the proximity of the text to the text boxes determines the destination of the written text.

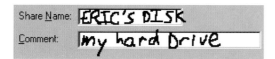

Figure 4.1 Targeting handwritten input

The system's pen services provide basic support for targeting, but your application can also provide additional support. For example, your application can define a larger inking rectangle than the control usually provides. In addition, because your application often knows the type of input to expect, it can use this information to better interpret where to target the input.

General Interaction Techniques

This chapter covers basic interaction techniques, such as navigation, selection, viewing, editing, and creation. Many of these techniques are based on an object-action paradigm in which a user identifies an object and an action to apply to that object. By maintaining these techniques consistently, you enable users to transfer their skills to new tasks.

Where applicable, support the basic interaction techniques for the mouse, keyboard, and pen. When adding or extending these basic techniques, consider how the feature or function can be supported across input devices. Techniques for a particular device need not be identical for all devices. Instead, tailor techniques to optimize the strengths of a particular device. In addition, make it easy for the user to switch between devices so that an interaction started with one device can be completed with another.

Navigation

One of the most common ways of identifying or accessing an object is by navigating to it. The following sections include information about mouse, pen, and keyboard techniques.

Mouse and Pen Navigation

Navigation with the mouse is simple; when a user moves the mouse left or right, the pointer moves in the corresponding direction on the screen. As the mouse moves away from or toward the user, the pointer moves up or down. By moving the mouse, the user can move the pointer to any location on the screen. Pen navigation is similar to mouse navigation, except that the user navigates by moving the pen without touching the input surface.

Keyboard Navigation

Keyboard navigation requires a user to press specific keys and key combinations to move the *input focus* — the indication of where the input is being directed — to a particular location. The appearance of the input focus varies by context; in text, it appears as a text cursor or insertion point.

For more information about displaying the input focus, see Chapter 13, "Visual Design."

Basic Navigation Keys

The navigation keys are the four arrow keys and the HOME, END, PAGE UP, PAGE DOWN, and TAB keys. Pressed in combination with the CTRL key, a navigation key increases the movement increment. For example, where pressing RIGHT ARROW moves right one *character* in a text field, pressing CTRL+RIGHT ARROW moves right one *word* in the text field. Table 5.1 lists the common navigation keys and their functions. You can define additional keys for navigation.

Table 5.1 Basic Navigation Keys

Key	Moves cursor to	CTRL+key moves cursor to
LEFT ARROW	Left one unit.	Left one (larger) unit.
RIGHT ARROW	Right one unit.	Right one (larger) unit.
UP ARROW	Up one unit or line.	Up one (larger) unit.
DOWN ARROW	Down one unit or line.	Down one (larger) unit.
HOME	Beginning of line.	Beginning of data or file (topmost position).
END	End of line.	End of data or file (bottommost position).
PAGE UP	Up one screen (previous screen, same position).	Left one screen (or previous unit, if left is not meaningful).
PAGE DOWN	Down one screen (next screen, same position).	Right one screen (or next unit, if right is not meaningful).
TAB	Next field. (SHIFT+TAB moves in reverse order).	Next larger field.

Unlike mouse and pen navigation, keyboard navigation typically affects existing selections. Optionally, you can support the SCROLL LOCK key to enable scrolling navigation without affecting existing selections. If you do so, the keys scroll the appropriate increment.

For more information about keyboard navigation in secondary windows, such as dialog boxes, see Chapter 8, "Secondary Windows."

Selection

Selection is the primary means by which the user identifies objects in the interface. Consequently, the basic model for selection is one of the most important aspects of the interface.

Selection typically involves an overt action by the user to identify an object. This is known as an *explicit selection*. Once the object is selected, the user can specify an action for the object.

There are also situations where the identification of an object can be derived by inference or implied by context. An *implicit selection* works most effectively where the association of object and action is simple and visible. For example, when the user drags a scroll box, the user establishes selection of the scroll box and the action of moving at the same time. Implicit selection may result from the relationships of a particular object. For example, selecting a character in a text document may implicitly select the paragraph of which the character is a part.

A selection can consist of a single object or multiple objects. Multiple selections can be *contiguous* — where the selection set is made up of objects that are logically adjacent to each other, also known as a *range selection*. A *disjoint selection* set is made up of objects that are spatially or logically separated.

Multiple selections may also be classified as *homogeneous* or *heterogeneous*, depending on the type or properties of the selected objects. Even a homogeneous selection might have certain aspects in which it is heterogeneous. For example, a text selection that includes bold and italic text can be considered homogeneous with respect to the basic object type (characters), but heterogeneous with respect to the values of its font properties. The homogeneity or heterogeneity of a selection affects the access of the operations or properties of the objects in the selection.

Selection Feedback

Always provide visual feedback for explicit selections as the user makes the selection, so that the user can tell the effect of the selection operation. Display the appropriate selection appearance for each object included in the selection set. The form of selection appearance depends on the object and its context.

For more information about how to visually render the selection appearance of an object, see Chapter 13, "Visual Design." For more information about how the context of an object can affect its selection appearance, see Chapter 11, "Working with OLE Embedded and OLE Linked Objects."

You may not need to provide immediate selection feedback for implicit selection; you can often indicate the effects of implicit selection in other ways. For example, when the user drags a scroll box, the scroll box moves with the pointer. Similarly, if the effect of selecting a word in a paragraph implicitly selects the paragraph, you would not use selection appearance on the entire paragraph, but rather reflect the implicit selection by including the paragraph's properties when the user chooses the Properties command.

Scope of Selection

The *scope* of a selection is the area, extent, or region in which, if other selections are made, they will be considered part of the same selection set. For example, you can select two document icons in the same folder window. However, the selection of these icons is independent of the selection of the window's scroll bar, a menu, the window itself, or selections made in other windows. So, the selection scope of the icons is the area viewed through that window. Selections in different scopes are independent of each other. For example, selections in one window are typically independent of selections in other windows. Their windows define the scope of each selection independently. The scope of a selection is important because you use it to define the available operations for the selected items and how the operations are applied.

Hierarchical Selection

Range selections typically include objects at the same level. However, you can also support a user's elevating a range selection to the next higher level if it extends beyond the immediate containment of the object (but within the same window). When the user adjusts the range back within the containment of the start of the range, return the selection to the original level. For example, extending a selection from within a cell in a table to the next cell, as shown in Figure 5.1, should elevate the selection from the character level to the cell level; adjusting the selection back within the cell should reset the selection to the character level.

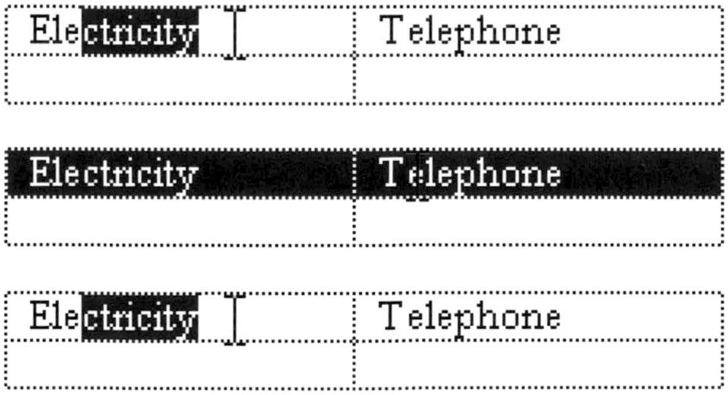

Figure 5.1 Hierarchical selection

Mouse Selection

Selection with the mouse relies on the basic actions of clicking and dragging. In general, clicking selects a single item or location, and dragging selects a single range consisting of all objects logically included from the button-down to the button-up location. If you also support dragging for object movement, use keyboard-modified mouse selection or region selection to support multiple selection.

Basic Selection

Support user selection using either mouse button. When the user presses the mouse button, establish the starting point, or *anchor point*, of a selection. If, while pressing the mouse button, the user drags the mouse, extend the selection to the object nearest the hot spot of the pointer. If, while continuing to hold the mouse button down, the user drags the mouse within the selection, reduce the selection to the object now nearest the pointer. Tracking the selection with the pointer while the mouse button continues to be held down allows the user to adjust a range selection dynamically. Use appropriate selection feedback to indicate the objects included in the selection.

For more information about the appearance of selection feedback, see Chapter 13, "Visual Design."

The release of the mouse button ends the selection operation and establishes the *active end* of the selection. If the user presses mouse button 2 to make a selection, display the contextual pop-up menu for the selected objects when the user releases the mouse button.

For more information about pop-up menus, see Chapter 7, "Menus, Controls, and Toolbars."

The most common form of selection optimizes for the selection of a single object or a single range of objects. In such a case, creating a new selection within the scope of an existing selection (for example, within the same area of the window) cancels the selection of the previously selected objects. This allows simple selections to be created quickly and easily.

When using this technique, reset the selection when the user presses the mouse button and the pointer (hot spot) is outside (not on) any existing selection. If the pointer is over a selected item, however, don't cancel the former selection. Instead, determine the appropriate result according to whether the user pressed mouse button 1 or 2.

If the user presses mouse button 1 and the pointer does not move from the button down point, the effect of the release of the mouse button is determined by the context of the selection. You can support whichever of the following best fits the nature of the user's task:

- The result may have no effect on the existing selection. This is the most common and safest effect.

- The object under the pointer may receive some special designation or distinction; for example, become the next anchor point or create a subselection.

- The selection can be reset to be only the object under the pointer.

If the user pressed mouse button 2, the selection is not affected, but you display a pop-up menu for selection.

Although selection is typically done by positioning the pointer over an object, it may be inferred based on the logical proximity of an object to a pointer. For example, when selecting text, the user can place the pointer on the blank area beyond the end of the line and the resulting selection is inferred as being the end of the line.

Selection Adjustment

Selections are adjusted (elements added to or removed from the selection) using keyboard modifiers with the mouse. The CTRL key is the disjoint, or toggle, modifier. If the user presses the CTRL key while making a new selection, preserve any existing selection within that scope and reset the anchor point to the new mouse button-down location. Toggle the selection state of the object under the pointer — that is, if it is not selected, select it; if it is already selected, unselect it.

Disjoint selection techniques may not apply to all situations where you support selection.

If a selection modified by the CTRL key is made by dragging, the selection state is applied for all objects included by the drag operation (from the anchor point to the current pointer location). This means if the first item included during the drag operation is not selected, select all objects included in the range. If the first item included was already selected, unselect it and all the objects included in the range regardless of their original state.

For example, the user can make an initial selection by dragging.

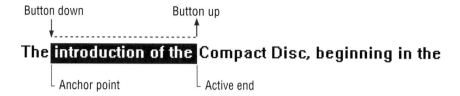

The user can then press the CTRL key and drag to create a disjoint selection, resetting the anchor point.

The user must press the CTRL key before using the mouse button for a disjoint (toggle) selection. After a disjoint selection is initiated, it continues until the user releases the mouse button (even if the user releases the CTRL key before the mouse button).

The SHIFT key adjusts (or extends) a single selection or range selection. When the user presses the mouse button while holding down the SHIFT key, reset the active end of a selection from the anchor point to the location of the pointer. Continue tracking the pointer, resetting the active end as the user drags, similar to a simple range drag selection. When the user releases the mouse button, the selection operation ends. You should then set the active end to the object nearest to the mouse button release point. Do not reset the anchor point. It should remain at its current location.

Only the selection made from the current anchor point is adjusted. Any other disjoint selections are not affected unless the extent of the selection overlaps an existing disjoint selection.

The effect on the selection state of a particular object is based on the first item included in the selection range. If the first item is already selected, select (not toggle the selection state of) all objects included in the range; otherwise, unselect (not toggle the selection state of) the objects included.

The user must press and hold down the SHIFT key before pressing the mouse button for the action to be interpreted as adjusting the selection. When the user begins adjusting a selection by pressing the SHIFT key, continue to track the pointer and adjust the selection (even if the user releases the modifier key) until the user releases the mouse button.

Pressing the SHIFT modifier key always adjusts the selection from the current anchor point. This means the user can always adjust the selection range of a single selection or CTRL key–modified disjoint selection. For example, the user can make a range selection by dragging.

The same result can be accomplished by making an initial selection.

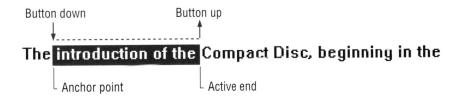

The user can adjust the selection with the SHIFT key and dragging.

The following sequence illustrates how the user can use the SHIFT key and dragging to adjust a disjoint selection. The user makes the initial selection by dragging.

The user presses the CTRL key and drags to create a disjoint selection.

The user can then extend the disjoint selection using the SHIFT key and dragging. This adjusts the selection from the anchor point to the button down point and tracks the pointer to the button up point.

Figure 5.2 shows how these same techniques can be applied within a spreadsheet.

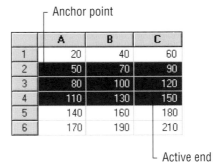

1. The user selects four cells by dragging from A2 to B3.

2. The user holds down the SHIFT key and clicks C4.

3. The user holds down the CTRL key and clicks A6.

4. The user holds down the SHIFT key and clicks C6.

Figure 5.2 Selection within a spreadsheet

The following summarizes the mouse selection operations.

Operation	Mouse action
Select object (range of objects)	Click (drag)
Disjoint selection state of noncontiguous object (range of objects)	CTRL+click (drag)
Adjust current selection to object (or range of objects)	SHIFT+click (drag)

For more information about the mouse interface, including selection behavior, see Appendix A, "Mouse Interface Summary."

Region Selection

In Z-ordered, or layered, contexts, in which objects may overlap, user selection can begin on the background (sometimes referred to as *white space*). To determine the range of the selection in such cases, a bounding outline (sometimes referred to as a marquee) is drawn. The outline is typically a rectangle, but other shapes (including freeform outline) are possible.

When the user presses the mouse button and moves the pointer (a form of selection by dragging), display the bounding outline, as shown in Figure 5.3. You set the selection state of objects included by the outline using the selection guidelines described in the previous sections, including operations that use the SHIFT and CTRL modifier keys.

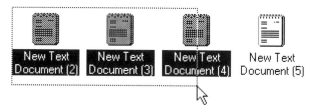

Figure 5.3 Region selection

You can use the context of your application and the user's task to determine whether an object must be totally enclosed or only intersected by the bounding region to be affected by the selection operation. Always provide good selection feedback during the operation to communicate to the user which method you support. When the user releases the mouse button, remove the bounding region, but retain the selection feedback.

Pen Selection

When the pen is being used as the pointing device, you can use the same selection techniques defined for the mouse. For example, in text input controls, you support user selection of text by dragging through it. Standard pen interfaces also support text selection using a special pen selection handle. In discrete object scenarios, like drawing programs, you support selection of individual objects by tapping or by performing region selection by dragging.

In some specialized contexts, you can also use a press-hold-drag technique or the *lasso-tap* gesture to support selection of individual objects or ranges of objects. However, avoid implementing these techniques when it might interfere with primary operations such as direct manipulation. In general, consider using a pen selection handle or pen controls that include the selection handles before you consider these methods.

For the press-hold-drag technique, you switch to a selection mode when the user holds the pen tip at the same location for a predefined time-out. Then the user can drag to make a selection.

Lasso-tap involves making a circular gesture around the object, then tapping within the gesture. For example, in Figure 5.4, making the lasso-tap gesture selects the word "controversial."

For more information about supporting selection in pen-enabled controls, see the "Pen-Specific Editing Techniques" section later in this chapter.

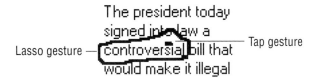

Lasso gesture

Tap gesture

Figure 5.4 A lasso-tap gesture

In text contexts, base the selection on the extent of the lasso gesture and the character-word-paragraph granularity of the text elements covered. For example, if the user draws the lasso around a single character, select only that character. If the user draws the lasso around multiple characters within a word, select the entire word. If the gesture encompasses characters in multiple words, select the range of words logically included by the gesture. This reduces the need for the user to be precise.

Keyboard Selection

Keyboard selection relies on the input focus to define selected objects. The input focus can be an insertion point, a dotted outline box, or some other cursor or visual indication of the location where the user is directing keyboard input.

For more information about input focus, see Chapter 13, "Visual Design."

In some contexts, selection may be implicit with navigation. When the user presses a navigation key, you move the input focus to the location (as defined by the key) and automatically select the object at that location.

In other contexts, it may be more appropriate to move the input focus and require the user to make an explicit selection with the Select key. The recommended keyboard Select key is the SPACEBAR, unless this assignment directly conflicts with the specific context — in which case, you can use CTRL+SPACEBAR. (If this conflicts with your software, define another key that best fits the context.) In some contexts, pressing the Select key may also unselect objects; in other words, it will toggle the selection state of an object.

Contiguous Selection

In text contexts, the user moves the insertion point to the desired location using the navigation keys. Set the anchor point at this location. When the user presses the SHIFT key with any navigation key (or navigation key combinations, such as CTRL+END), set that location as the active end of the selection and select all characters between the anchor point and the active end. (Do not move the anchor point.) If the user presses a subsequent navigation key, cancel the selection and move the insertion point to the appropriate location defined by the key. If the user presses LEFT ARROW or RIGHT ARROW keys, move the insertion point to the end of the former selection range. If UP ARROW or DOWN ARROW are used, move the insertion point to the previous or following line at the same relative location.

You can use this technique in other contexts, such as lists, where objects are logically contiguous. However, in such situations, the selection state of the objects logically included from the anchor point to the active end depend on the selection state of the object at, or first traversed from, the anchor point. For example, if the object at the anchor point is selected, then select all the objects in the range regardless of their current state. If the object at the anchor point is not selected, unselect all the items in the range.

Disjoint Selection

You use the Select key for supporting disjoint selections. The user uses navigation keys or navigation keys modified by the SHIFT key to establish the initial selection. The user can then use navigation keys to move to a new location and subsequently use the Select key to create an additional selection.

In some situations, you may prefer to optimize for selection of a single object or single range. In such cases, when the user presses a navigation key, reset the selection to the location defined by the navigation key. Creating a disjoint selection requires supporting the Add mode key (SHIFT+F8). In this mode, you move the insertion point when the user presses navigation keys without affecting the existing selections or the anchor point. When the user presses the Select key, toggle the selection state at the new location and reset the anchor point to that object. At any point, the user can use the SHIFT+navigation key combination to adjust the selection from the current anchor point.

When the user presses the Add mode key a second time, you toggle out of the mode, preserving the selections the user created in Add mode. But now, if the user makes any new selections within that selection scope, you return to the single selection optimization — canceling any existing selections — and reset the selection to be only the new selection.

Selection Shortcuts

Double-clicking with mouse button 1 and double-tapping — its pen equivalent — is a shortcut for the default operation of an object. In text contexts, it is commonly assigned as a shortcut to select a word. When supporting this shortcut, select the word and the space following the word, but not the punctuation marks.

Double-clicking as a shortcut for selection only applies to text. In other contexts, it may perform other operations.

You can define additional selection shortcuts or techniques for specialized contexts. For example, selecting a column label may select the entire column. Because shortcuts cannot be generalized across the user interface, however, do not use them as the only way to perform a selection.

Common Conventions for Supporting Operations

There are many ways to support operations for an object, including direct manipulation of the object or its control point (handle), menu commands, buttons, dialog boxes, tools, or programming. Support for a particular technique is not exclusive to other techniques. For example, the user can size a window by using the Size menu command and by dragging its border.

Design operations or commands to be *contextual*, or related to, the selected object to which they apply. That is, determine which commands or properties, or other aspects of an object, are made accessible by the characteristics of the object and its context (relationships). Often the context of an object may add to or suppress the traits of the object. For example, the menu for an object may include commands defined by the object's type and commands supplied by the object's current container.

Operations for a Multiple Selection

When determining which operations to display for a multiple selection, use an intersection of the operations that apply to the members of that selection. The selection's context may add to or filter out the available operations or commands displayed to the user.

It is also possible to determine the effect of an operation for a multiple selection based upon a particular member of that selection. For example, when the user selects a set of graphic objects and chooses an alignment command, you can make the operation relative to a particular item identified in the selection.

Limit operations on a multiple selection to the scope of the selected objects. For example, deleting a selected word in one window should not delete selections in other windows (unless the windows are viewing the same selected objects).

Default Operations and Shortcut Techniques

An object can have a default operation; a *default operation* is an operation that is assumed when the user employs a shortcut technique, such as double-clicking or drag and drop. For example, double-clicking a folder displays a window with the content of the folder. In text editing situations, double-clicking selects the word. The behavior differs because the default commands in each case differ: for a folder, the default command is Open; and for text, it is Select Word.

Similarly, when the user drags and drops an object at a new location with mouse button 1, there must be a default operation defined to determine the result of the operation. Dragging and dropping to some locations can be interpreted as a move, copy, link, or some other operation. In this case, the drop destination determines the default operation.

For more information about supporting default operations for drag and drop, see the "Transfer Operations" section later in this chapter; also see Chapter 11, "Working with OLE Embedded and OLE Linked Objects."

Shortcut techniques for default operations provide greater efficiency in the interface, an important factor for more experienced users. However, because they typically require more skill or experience and because not all objects may have a default operation defined, avoid shortcut techniques as the exclusive means of performing a basic operation. For example, even though double-clicking opens a folder icon, the Open command appears on its menu.

View Operations

Following are some of the common operations associated with viewing objects. Although these operations may not always be used with all objects, when supported, they should follow similar conventions.

Operation	Action
Open	Opens a primary window for an object. For container objects, such as folders and documents, this window displays the content of the object.
Close	Closes a window.
Properties	Displays the properties of an object in a window, typically in a property sheet window.
Help	Displays a window with the contextual Help information about an object.

When the user opens a new window, you should display it at the top of the Z order of its peer windows and activate it. Primary windows are typically peers with each other. Display supplemental or secondary windows belonging to a particular application at the top of their local Z order — that is, the Z order of the windows of that application, not the Z order of other primary windows.

For more information about opening windows, property sheets, and Help windows, see Chapter 6, "Windows," Chapter 8, "Secondary Windows," and Chapter 12, "User Assistance," respectively.

If the user interacts with another window before the new window opens, the new window does not appear on top; instead, it appears where it would usually be displayed if the user activated another window. For example, if the user opens window A, then opens window B, window B appears on top of window A. If the user clicks back in window A before window B is displayed, however, window A remains active and at the top of the Z order; window B appears behind window A.

Whether opening a window allows the user to also edit the information in that window's view depends on a number of factors. These factors can include who the user is, the type of view being used, and the content being viewed.

After the user opens a window, re-executing the command that opened the window should activate the existing window instead of opening another instance of the window. For example, if the user chooses the Properties command for a selected object whose property sheet is already open, the existing property sheet is activated, rather than a second window opened.

This guideline applies per user desktop. Two users opening a window for the same object on a network can each see separate windows for the object from their individual desktops.

Closing a window does not necessarily mean quitting the processes associated with the object being viewed. For example, closing a printer's window does not cancel the printing of documents in its queue. Quitting an application closes its windows, but closing a window does not necessarily quit an application. Similarly, you can use other commands in secondary windows which result in closing the window — for example, OK and Cancel. However, the effect of closing the window with a Close command depends on the context of the window. Avoid assuming that the Close command is the equivalent of the Cancel command.

If there are changes transacted in a window that have not yet been applied and the user chooses the Close command, and those changes will be lost if not applied, display a message asking whether the user wishes to apply or discard the changes or cancel the Close operation. If there are no outstanding changes or if pending changes are retained for the next time the window is opened, remove the window.

View Shortcuts

Following are the recommended shortcut techniques for the common viewing commands.

Shortcut	Operation
CTRL+O	Opens a primary window for an object. For container objects, such as folders and documents, this window displays the content of the object.
ALT+F4	Closes a window.
F1	Displays a window with contextual Help information.
SHIFT+F1	Starts context-sensitive Help mode.
Double-click (button 1) or ENTER	Carries out the default command.
ALT+double-click or ALT+ENTER	Displays the properties of an object in a window, typically in a property sheet window.

For more information on reserved and recommended shortcut keys, see Appendix B, "Keyboard Interface Summary."

Use double-clicking and the ENTER key to open a view of an object when that view command is the default command for the object. For example, double-clicking a folder opens the folder's primary window. But double-clicking a sound object plays the sound; this is because the Open command is the default command for folders, and the Play command is the default command for sound objects.

Editing Operations

Editing involves changing (adding, removing, replacing) some fundamental aspect about the composition of an object. Not all changes constitute editing of an object, though. For example, changing the view of a document to an outline or magnified view (which has no effect on the content of the document) is not editing. The following sections cover some of the common interface techniques for editing objects.

Editing Text

Editing text requires that you target the input focus at the text to be edited. For mouse input, the input focus always coincides with the pointer (button down) location. For the pen, it is the location of the pointer when the pen touches the input surface. For the keyboard, the input focus is determined with the navigation keys. In all cases, the visual indication that a text field has the input focus is the presence of the text cursor, or insertion point.

Inserting Text

Inserting text involves the user placing the insertion point at the appropriate location and then typing. For each character typed, your application should move the insertion point one character to the right (or left, depending on the language).

If the text field supports multiple lines, *wordwrap* the text; that is, automatically move text to the next line as the textual input exceeds the width of the text-entry area.

Overtype Mode

Overtype is an optional text-entry behavior that operates similarly to the insertion style of text entry, except that you replace existing characters as new text is entered — with one character being replaced for each new character entered.

Use a block cursor that appears at the current character position to support overtype mode, as shown in Figure 5.5. This looks the same as the selection of that character and provides the user with a visual cue about the difference between the text-entry modes.

The 1▊93 statistics are complete

Figure 5.5 An overtype cursor

Use the INSERT key to toggle between the normal insert text-entry convention and overtype mode.

Deleting Text

The DELETE and BACKSPACE keys support deleting text. The DE-LETE key deletes the character to the right of the text insertion point. BACKSPACE removes the character to the left. In either case, move text in the direction of the deletion to fill the gap — this is sometimes referred to as *auto-joining*. Do not place deleted text on the Clipboard. For this reason, include at least a single-level undo operation in these contexts.

For a text selection, when the user presses DELETE or BACKSPACE, remove the entire block of selected text. Delete text selections when new text is entered directly or by a transfer command. In this case, replace the selected text by the incoming input.

Handles

Objects may include special control points, called *handles*. You can use handles to facilitate certain types of operations, such as moving, sizing, scaling, cropping, shaping, or auto-filling. The type of handle you use depends on the type of object. For example, the title bar acts as a "move handle" for windows. The borders of the window act as "sizing handles." For icons, the selected icon acts as its own "move handle." In pen-enabled controls, special handles may appear for selection and access to the operations available for an object.

For more information about pen handles, see the "Pen-Specific Editing Techniques" section later in this chapter.

A common form of handle is a square box placed at the edge of an object, as shown in Figure 5.6.

Figure 5.6 A graphic object with handles

When the handle's interior is solid, the handle implies that it can perform a certain operation, such as sizing, cropping, or scaling. If the handle is "hollow," the handle does not currently support an operation. You can use such an appearance to indicate selection even when an operation is not available.

For more information about the design of handles, see Chapter 13, "Visual Design."

Transactions

A *transaction* is a unit of change to an object. The granularity of a transaction may span from the result of a single operation to that of a set of multiple operations. In an ideal model, transactions are applied immediately, and there is support for "rolling back," or undoing, transactions. Because there are times when this is not practical, specific interface conventions have been established for committing transactions. If there are pending transactions in a window when it is closed, always prompt the user to ask whether to apply or discard the transactions.

Transactions can be committed at different levels, and a commitment made at one level may not imply a permanent change. For example, the user may change font properties of a selection of text, but these text changes may require saving the document file before the changes are permanent.

Use the following commands for committing transactions at the file level.

Command	Function
Save	Saves all interim edits, or checkpoints, to disk and begins a new editing session.
Save As	Saves the file (with all interim edits) to a new filename and begins a new editing session.
Close	Prompts the user to save any uncommitted edits. If confirmed, the interim edits are saved and the window is removed.

Use the Save command in contexts where committing file transactions applies to transactions for an entire file, such as a document, and are committed at one time. It may not necessarily apply for transactions committed on an individual basis, such as record-oriented processing.

On a level with finer granularity, you can use the following commands for common handling transactions within a file.

Command	Function
Repeat	Duplicates the last/latest user transaction.
Undo	Reverses the last, or specified, transaction.
Redo	Restores the most recent, or specified, "undone" transaction.
OK	Commits any pending transactions and removes the window.
Apply	Commits any pending transactions, but does not remove the window.
Cancel	Discards any pending transactions and removes the window.

Following are the recommended commands for handling process transactions.

Command	Function
Pause	Suspends a process.
Resume	Resumes a suspended process.
Stop	Halts a process.

Although you can use the Cancel command to halt a process, Cancel implies that the state will be restored to what it was before the process was initiated.

Properties

Defining and organizing the properties of an application's components are a key part of evolving toward a more data-centered design. Commands such as Options, Info, Summary Info, and Format often describe features that can be redefined as properties of a particular object (or objects). The Properties command is the common command for accessing the properties of an object; when the user chooses this command, display a secondary window with the properties of the object.

For more information about property sheets, see Chapter 8, "Secondary Windows."

Defining how to provide access to properties for visible or easily identifiable objects, such as a selection of text, cells, or drawing objects, is straightforward. It may be more difficult to define how to access properties of less tangible objects, such as paragraphs. In some cases, you can include these properties by implication. For example, requesting the properties of a text selection can also provide access to the properties of the paragraph in which the text selection is included.

Another way to provide access to an object's properties is to create a representation of the object. For example, the properties of a page could be accessed through a graphic or other representation of the page in a special area (for example, the status bar) of the window.

Yet another technique to consider is to include specific property entries on the menu of a related object. For example, the pop-up menu of a text selection could include a menu entry for a paragraph. Or consider using the cascading submenu of the Properties command for individual menu entries, but only if the properties are not easily made accessible otherwise. Adding entries for individual properties can easily end up cluttering a menu.

The Properties command is not the exclusive means of providing access to the properties of an object. For example, folder views display certain properties of objects stored in the file system. In addition, you can use toolbar controls to display properties of selected objects.

Pen-Specific Editing Techniques

A pen is more than just a pointing device. When a standard pen device is installed, the system provides special interfaces and editing techniques.

Editing in Pen-Enabled Controls

If a pen is installed, the system automatically provides a special interface, called the *writing tool*, to make text editing as easy as possible, enhance recognition accuracy, and streamline correction of errors. The writing tool interface, as shown in Figure 5.7, adds a button to your standard text controls. Because this effectively reduces the visible area of the text box, take this into consideration when designing their size.

Writing tool button

Figure 5.7 A standard text box with writing tool button

Figure 5.8 shows how you can also add writing tool support for any special needs of your software, such as a multiline text box.

Figure 5.8 Adding the writing tool button

When the text box control has the focus, a selection handle appears, as shown in Figure 5.9. The user can drag this handle to make a selection.

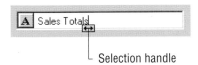

Selection handle

Figure 5.9 Text box displaying a pen selection handle

Tapping the writing tool button with a pen (or clicking it with a mouse) presents a special text editing window, as shown in Figure 5.10. Within this window, the user can write text that is recognized automatically.

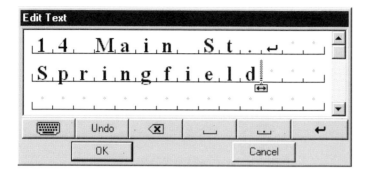

Figure 5.10 Single and multiline writing tool windows

In the writing tool editing window, each character is displayed
within a special cell. If the user selects text in the original text field,
the writing tool window reflects that selection. The user can reset the
selection to an insertion point by tapping between characters. This
also displays a selection handle that can be dragged to select multiple
characters, as shown in Figure 5.11.

Figure 5.11 Selecting text with the selection handle

The user can select a single character in its cell by tapping, or
double-tapping to select a word. When the user taps a single character, an action handle displays a list of alternative characters, as
shown in Figure 5.12.

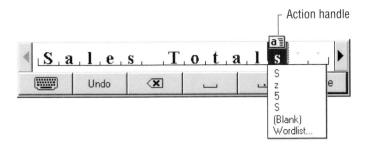

Action handle

Figure 5.12 An action handle with a list of alternatives

Choosing an alternative replaces the selected character and removes the list. Writing over a character or tapping elsewhere also removes the list. The new character replaces the existing one and resets the selection to an insertion point placed to the left of the new character.

The list also includes an item labeled Wordlist. When the user selects this choice, the word that contains the character becomes selected and a list of alternatives is displayed, as shown in Figure 5.13. This list also appears when the user selects a complete word by double-tapping. Choosing an alternative replaces the selected word.

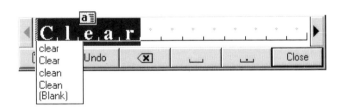

Figure 5.13 Tapping displays a list of alternatives

Whenever a selection exists in the window, an action handle appears; the user can use it to perform other operations on the selected items. For example, using the action handle moves or copies the selection by dragging, or the pop-up menu for the selection can be accessed by tapping on the handle, as shown in Figure 5.14.

For more information about pop-up menus, see Chapter 7, "Menus, Controls, and Toolbars."

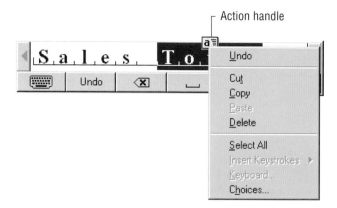

Figure 5.14 Tapping on the handle displays a pop-up menu

The buttons on the writing tool window provide for scrolling the text as well as common functions such as Undo, Backspace, Insert Space, Insert Period, and Close (for closing the text window). A multiline writing tool window includes Insert New Line.

The writing tool window also provides a button for access to an onscreen keyboard as an alternative to entering characters with the pen, as shown in Figure 5.15. The user taps the button with the corresponding keyboard glyph on it and the writing tool onscreen keyboard pop-up window replaces the normal writing tool window.

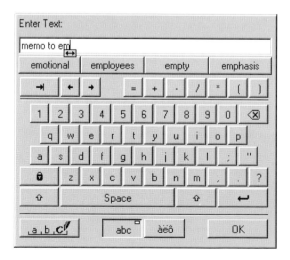

Figure 5.15 The writing tool onscreen keyboard window

The writing tool "remembers" its previous use — for text input or as an onscreen keyboard — and opens in the appropriate editing window when subsequently used. In addition, note that when the user displays a writing tool window, it gets the input focus, so avoid using the loss of input focus to a field as an indication that the user is finished with that field or that all text editing occurs directly within a text box.

Pen Editing Gestures

The pen, when used as a pointing device, supports editing techniques defined for the mouse. When used as a writing device, the pen supports gestures for editing. Gestures (except for Undo) operate positionally, acting upon the objects on which they are drawn. If the user draws a gesture on an unselected object, it applies to that object, even if a selection exists elsewhere within the same selection area. Any pending selections become unselected. If a user draws a gesture over both selected and unselected objects, however, it applies only to the selected ones. If a gesture is drawn over only one element of the selection, it applies to the entire selection. If the gesture is drawn in empty space (on the background), it applies to any existing selection within that selection scope. If no selection exists, the gesture has no effect.

For most gestures, the hot spot of the gesture determines specifically which object the gesture applies to. If the hot spot occurs on any part of a selection, it applies to the whole selection.

Table 5.2 lists the common pen editing gestures. For these gestures, the hot spot of the gesture is the area inside the circle stroke of the gesture.

Table 5.2 Pen Editing Gestures

Gesture	Name	Operation
	circled-check	Edit (displays the writing tool editing window) for text; Properties for all other objects.
	circled-c	Copy
	circled-d	Delete (or Clear)
	circled-m	Menu
	circled-n	New line
	circled-p	Paste
	circled-s	Insert space
	circled-t	Insert tab
	circled-u	Undo
	circled-x	Cut
	circled-^	Insert text

These gestures may be localized in certain international versions. In Japanese versions, the circled-k gesture is used to convert Kana to Kanji.

Transfer Operations

Transfer operations are operations that involve (or can be derived from) moving, copying, and linking objects from one location to another. For example, printing an object is a form of a transfer operation because it can be defined as copying an object to a printer.

Three components make up a transfer operation: the object to be transferred, the destination of the transfer, and the operation to be performed. You can define these components either explicitly or implicitly, depending on which interaction technique you use.

The operation defined by a transfer is determined by the destination. Because a transfer may have several possible interpretations, you can define a default operation and other optimal operations, based on information provided by the source of the transfer and the compatibility and capabilities of the destination. For example, attempting to transfer an object to a container can result in one of the following alternatives:

- Rejecting the object.

- Accepting the object.

- Accepting a subset or transformed form of the object (for example, extract its content or properties but discard its present containment, or convert the object into a new type).

Most transfers are based on one of the following three fundamental operations.

Operation	Description
Move	Relocates or repositions the selected object. Because it does not change the basic identity of an object, a move operation is not the same as copying an object and deleting the original.
Copy	Makes a duplicate of an object. The resulting object is independent of its original. Duplication does not always produce an identical clone. Some of the properties of a duplicated object may be different from the original. For example, copying an object may result in a different name or creation date. Similarly, if some component of the object restricts copying, then only the unrestricted elements may be copied.
Link	Creates a connection between two objects. The result is usually an object in the destination that provides access to the original.

There are two different methods for supporting the basic transfer interface: the command method and the direct manipulation method.

Command Method

The command method for transferring objects uses the Cut, Copy, and Paste commands. Place these commands on the Edit drop-down menu and on the pop-up menu for a selected object. You can also include toolbar buttons to support these commands.

To transfer an object, the user:

1. Makes a selection.

2. Chooses either Cut or Copy.

3. Navigates to the destination (and sets the insertion location, if appropriate).

4. Chooses a Paste operation.

Cut removes the selection and transfers it (or a reference to it) to the Clipboard. Copy duplicates the selection (or a reference to it) and transfers it to the Clipboard. Paste completes the transfer operation. For example, when the user chooses Cut and Paste, remove the selection from the source and relocate it to the destination. For Copy and Paste, insert an independent duplicate of the selection and leave the original unaffected. When the user chooses Copy and Paste Link or Paste Shortcut, insert an object at the destination that is linked to the source.

Choose a form of Paste command that indicates how the object will be transferred into the destination. Use the Paste command by itself to indicate that the object will be transferred as native content. You can also use alternative forms of the Paste command for other possible transfers, using the following general form.

Paste [*type name*] [**as** *type name* | **to** *object name*]

For example, Paste Cells as Word Table, where [*type name*] is Cells and Word Table is the converted type name.

The following summarizes common forms of the Paste command.

Command	Function
Paste	Inserts the object on the Clipboard as native content (data).
Paste [*type name*]	Inserts the object on the Clipboard as an OLE embedded object. The OLE embedded object can be activated directly within the destination.
Paste [*type name*] as Icon	Inserts the object on the Clipboard as an OLE embedded object. The OLE embedded object is displayed as an icon.
Paste Link	Inserts a data link to the object that was copied to the Clipboard. The object's value is integrated or transformed as native content within the destination, but remains linked to the original object so that changes to it are reflected in the destination.
Paste Link to [*object name*]	Inserts an OLE linked object, displayed as a picture of the object copied to the Clipboard. The representation is linked to the object copied to the Clipboard so that any changes to the original source object will be reflected in the destination.
Paste Shortcut	Inserts an OLE linked object, displayed as a shortcut icon, to the object that was copied to the Clipboard. The representation is linked to the object copied to the Clipboard so that any changes to the original source object will be reflected in the destination.
Paste Special	Displays a dialog box that gives the user explicit control over how to insert the object on the Clipboard.

For more information about object names, including their type name, see Chapter 10, "Integrating with the System."

For more information about these Paste command forms and the Paste Special dialog box, see Chapter 11, "Working with OLE Embedded and OLE Linked Objects."

Use the destination's context to determine what form(s) of the Paste operation to include based on what options it can offer to the user, which in turn may depend on the available forms of the object that its source location object provides. It can also be dependent on the nature or purpose of the destination. For example, a printer defines the context of transfers to it.

Typically, you will need only Paste and Paste Special commands. The Paste command can be dynamically modified to reflect the destination's default or preferred form by inserting the transferred object — for example, as native data or as an OLE embedded object. The Paste Special command can be used to handle any special forms of transfer. Although, if the destination's context makes it reasonable to provide fast access to another specialized form of transfer, such as Paste Link, you can also include that command.

Use the destination's context also to determine the appropriate side effects of the Paste operation. You may also need to consider the type of object being inserted by the Paste operation and the relationship of that type to the destination. The following are some common scenarios:

- When the user pastes into a destination that supports a specific insertion location, replace the selection in the destination with the transferred data. For example, in text or list contexts, where the selection represents a specific insertion location, replace the destination's active selection. In text contexts where there is an insertion location, but there is no existing selection, place the insertion point after the inserted object.

- For destinations with nonordered or Z-ordered contexts where there is no explicit insertion point, add the pasted object and make it the active selection. Also use the destination's context to determine where to place the pasted object. Consider any appropriate user contextual information. For example, if the user chooses the Paste command from a pop-up menu, you can use the pointer's location when the mouse button is clicked to place the incoming object. If the user supplies no contextual clues, place the object at the location that best fits the context of the destination — for example, at the next grid position.

- If the new object is automatically connected (linked) to the active selection (for example, table data and a graph), you may insert the new object in addition to the selection and make the inserted object the new selection.

You also use context to determine whether to display an OLE embedded or OLE linked object as content (view or picture of the object's internal data) or as an icon. For example, you can decide what presentation to display based on what Paste operation the user selects; Paste Shortcut implies pasting an OLE link as an icon. Similarly, the Paste Special command includes options that allow the user to specify how the transferred object should be displayed. If there is no user-supplied preference, the destination application defines the default. For documents, you typically display the inserted OLE object as in its content presentation. If icons better fit the context of your application, make the default Paste operation display the transferred OLE object as an icon.

The execution of a Paste command should not affect the content of the Clipboard. This allows data on the Clipboard to be pasted multiple times, although subsequent Paste operations should always result in copies of the original. However, a subsequent Cut or Copy command replaces the last entry on the Clipboard.

Direct Manipulation Method

The command method is useful when a transfer operation requires the user to navigate between source and destination. However, for many transfers, direct manipulation is a natural and quick method. In a direct manipulation transfer, the user selects and drags an object to the desired location, but because this method requires motor skills that may be difficult for some users to master, avoid using it as the exclusive transfer method. The best interfaces support the transfer command method for basic operations and direct manipulation transfer as a shortcut technique.

When a pen is being used as a pointing device, or when it drags an action handle, it follows the same conventions as dragging with mouse button 1. For pens with barrel buttons, use the barrel+drag action as the equivalent of dragging with mouse button 2. There is no keyboard interface for direct manipulation transfers.

You can support direct manipulation transfers to any visible object. The object (for example, a window or icon) need not be currently active. For example, the user can drop an object in an inactive window. The drop action activates the window. If an inactive object cannot accept a direct manipulation transfer, it (or its container) should provide feedback to the user.

How the transferred object is integrated and displayed in the drop destination is determined by the destination's context. A dropped object can be incorporated either as native data, an OLE object, a partial form of the object — such as its properties — or a transformed object. You determine whether to add to or replace an existing selection based on the context of the operation, using such factors as the formats available for the object, the destination's purpose, and any user-supplied information such as the specific location that the user drops or commands (or modes) that the user has selected. For example, an application can supply a particular type of tool for copying the properties of objects.

Default Drag and Drop

Default drag and drop transfers an object using mouse button 1. How the operation is interpreted is determined by what the destination defines as the appropriate default operation. As with the command method, the destination determines this based on information about the object (and the formats available for the object) and the context of the destination itself. Avoid defining a destructive operation as the default. When that is unavoidable, display a message box to confirm the intentions of the user.

Using this transfer technique, the user can directly transfer objects between documents defined by your application as well as to system resources, such as folders and printers. Support drag and drop following the same conventions the system supports: the user presses button 1 down on an object, moves the mouse while holding the button down, and then releases the button at the destination. For the pen, the destination is determined by the location where the user lifts the pen tip from the input surface.

The most common default transfer operation is Move, but the destination (dropped on object) can reinterpret the operation to be whatever is most appropriate. Therefore, you can define a default drag and drop operation to be another general transfer operation such as Copy or Link, a destination specific command such as Print or Send To, or even a specialized form of transfer such as Copy Properties.

Nondefault Drag and Drop

Nondefault drag and drop transfers an object using mouse button 2. In this case, rather than executing a default operation, the destination displays a pop-up menu when the user releases the mouse button, as shown in Figure 5.16. The pop-up menu contains the appropriate transfer completion commands.

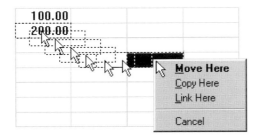

Figure 5.16 A nondefault drag and drop operation

The destination always determines which transfer completion commands to include on the resulting pop-up menu, usually factoring in information about the object supplied by the source location.

The form for nondefault drag and drop transfer completion verbs follows similar conventions as the Paste command. Use the common transfer completion verbs, Move Here, Copy Here, and Link Here, when the object being transferred is native data of the destination. When it is not, include the type name. You can also display alternative completion verbs that communicate the context of the destination; for example, a printer displays a Print Here command. For commands that support only a partial aspect or a transformation of an object, use more descriptive indicators — for example, Copy Properties Here, or Transpose Here.

Use the following general form for nondefault drag and drop transfer commands.

[*Command Name*] [*type name* | *object name*] **Here** [**as** *type name*]

The following summarizes common forms for nondefault transfer completion commands.

Command	Function
Move Here	Moves the selected object to the destination as native content (data).
Copy Here	Creates a copy of the selected object in the destination as native content.
Link Here	Creates a data link between the selected object and the destination. The original object's value is integrated or transformed as native data within the destination, but remains linked to the original object so that changes to it are reflected in the destination.
Move [*type name*] Here Copy [*type name*] Here	Moves or copies the selected object as an OLE embedded object. The OLE embedded object is displayed in its content presentation and can be activated directly within the destination.
Link [*type name*] Here	Creates an OLE linked object displayed as a picture of the selected object. The representation is linked to the selected object so that any changes to the original object will be reflected in the destination.

(Continued)

Command	Function
Move [*type name*] Here as Icon Copy [*type name*] Here as Icon	Moves or copies the selected object as an OLE embedded object and displays it as an icon.
Create Shortcut Here	Creates an OLE linked object to the selected object; displayed as a shortcut icon. The representation is linked to the selected object so that any changes to the original object will be reflected in the destination.

Define and appropriately display one of the commands in the pop-up menu to be the default drag and drop command. This is the command that corresponds to the effect of dragging and dropping with mouse button 1.

For more information about how to display default menu commands, see Chapter 13, "Visual Design."

Canceling a Drag and Drop Transfer

When a user drags and drops an object back on itself, interpret the action as cancellation of a direct manipulation transfer. Similarly, cancel the transfer if the user presses the ESC key during a drag transfer. In addition, include a Cancel command in the pop-up menu of a nondefault drag and drop action. When the user chooses this command, cancel the operation.

Differentiating Transfer and Selection When Dragging

Because dragging performs both selection and transfer operations, provide a convention that allows the user to differentiate between these operations. The convention you use depends on what is most appropriate in the current context of the object, or you can provide specialized handles for selection or transfer. The most common technique uses the location of the pointer at the beginning of the drag operation. If the pointer is within an existing selection, interpret the drag to be a transfer operation. If the drag begins outside of an existing selection, on the background's white space, interpret the drag as a selection operation.

Scrolling When Transferring by Dragging

When the user drags and drops an object from one scrollable area (such as a window, pane, or list box) to another, some tasks may require transferring the object outside the boundary of the area. Other tasks may involve dragging the object to a location not currently in view. In this latter case, it is convenient to automatically scroll the area (also known as *automatic scrolling* or autoscroll) when the user drags the object to the edge of that scrollable area. You can accommodate both these behaviors by using the velocity of the dragging action. For example, if the user is dragging the object slowly at the edge of the scrollable area, you scroll the area; if the object is being dragged quickly, do not scroll.

To support this technique during a drag operation, you sample the pointer's position at the beginning of the drag each time the mouse moves, and on an application-set timer (every 100 milliseconds recommended). If you use OLE drag and drop support, you need not set a timer. Store each value in an array large enough to hold at least three samples, replacing existing samples with later ones. Then calculate the pointer's velocity based on at least the last two locations of the pointer.

To calculate the velocity, sum the distance between the points in each adjacent sample and divide the total by the sum of the time elapsed between samples. Distance is the absolute value of the difference between the x and y locations, or (abs(x1 - x2) + abs(y1 - y2)). Multiply this by 1024 and divide it by the elapsed time to produce the velocity. The 1024 multiplier prevents the loss of accuracy caused by integer division.

> Distance as implemented in this algorithm is not true Cartesian distance. This implementation uses an approximation for purposes of efficiency, rather than using the square root of the sum of the squares, (sqrt((x1 - x2)^2 + (y1 - y2)^2)), which is more computationally expensive.

You also predefine a hot zone along the edges of the scrollable area and a scroll time-out value. Use twice the width of a vertical scroll bar or height of a horizontal scroll bar to determine the width of the hot zone.

During the drag operation, scroll the area if the following conditions are met: the user moves the pointer within the hot zone, the current velocity is below a certain threshold velocity, and the scrollable area is able to scroll in the direction associated with the hot zone it is in. The recommended threshold velocity is 20 pixels per second. These conventions are illustrated in Figure 5.17.

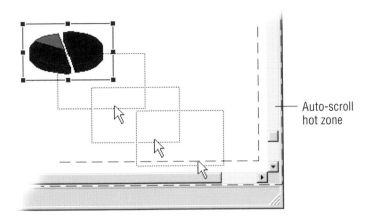

Figure 5.17 Automatic scrolling based on velocity of dragging

The amount you scroll depends on the type of information and reasonable scrolling distance. For example, for text, you typically scroll vertically one line at a time. Consider using the same scrolling granularity that is provided for the scroll bar arrows.

To support continuous scrolling, determine what the scroll frequency you want to support — for example, four lines per second. After using a velocity check to initiate auto-scrolling, set a timer — for example, 100 milliseconds. When the timer expires, determine how long it has been since the last time you scrolled. If the elapsed time is greater than your scrolling frequency, scroll another unit. If not, reset your timer and check again when the timer completes.

For more information about scrolling, see Chapter 6, "Windows."

Transfer Feedback

Because transferring objects is one of the most common user tasks, providing appropriate feedback is an important design factor. Inconsistent or insufficient feedback can result in user confusion.

For more information about designing transfer feedback, see Chapter 13, "Visual Design."

Command Method Transfers

For a command method transfer, remove the selected object visually when the user chooses the Cut command. If there are special circumstances that make removing the object's appearance impractical, you can instead display the selected object with a special appearance to inform the user that the Cut command was completed, but that the object's transfer is pending. For example, the system displays icons in a checkerboard dither to indicate this state. You will also need to restore the visual state of the object if the user chooses Cut or Copy for another object before choosing a Paste command, effectively canceling the pending Cut command. The user will expect Cut to remove a selected object, so carefully consider the impact of inconsistency if you choose this alternate feedback.

The Copy command requires no special feedback. A Paste operation also requires no further feedback than that already provided by the insertion of the transferred object. However, if you did not remove the display of the object and used an alternate representation when the user chose the Cut command, you must remove it now.

Direct Manipulation Transfers

During a direct manipulation transfer operation, provide visual feedback for the object, the pointer, and the destination. Specifically:

- Display the object with selected appearance while the view it appears in has the focus. To indicate that the object is in a transfer state, you can optionally display the object with some additional appearance characteristics. For example, for a move operation, you can use the checkerboard dithered appearance used by the system to indicate when an icon is Cut. Change this visual state based on the default completion operation supported by the destination the pointer is currently over. Retain the representation of the object at the original location until the user completes the transfer operation. This not only provides a visual cue to the nature of the transfer operation, it provides a convenient visual reference point.

- Display a representation of the object that moves with the pointer. Use a presentation that provides the user with information about how the information will appear in the destination and that does not obscure the context of the insertion location. For example, when transferring an object into a text context, it is important that the insertion point not be obscured during the drag operation. A translucent or outline representation, as shown in Figure 5.18, works well because it allows the underlying insertion location to be seen while also providing information about the size, position, and nature of the object being dragged.

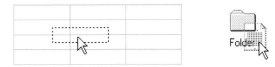

Figure 5.18 Outline and translucent representations for transfer operations

• The object's existing source location provides the transferred object's initial appearance, but any destination can change the appearance. Design the presentation of the object to provide feedback as to how the object will be integrated by that destination. For example, if an object will be embedded as an icon, display the object as an icon. If the object will be incorporated as part of the native content of the destination, then the presentation of the object that the destination displays should reflect that. For example, if a table being dragged into a document will be incorporated as a table, the representation could be an outline or translucent form of the table. On the other hand, if the table will be converted to text, display the table as a representation of text, such as a translucent presentation of the first few words in the table.

• Display the pointer appropriate to the context of the destination, usually used for inserting objects. For example, when dragging an object into a text editing context such that the object will be inserted between characters, display the usual text editing pointer (sometimes called the I-beam pointer).

• Display the interpretation of the transfer operation at the lower right corner of the pointer, as shown in Figure 5.19. No additional glyph is required for a move operation. Use a plus sign (+) when the transfer is a copy operation. Use the shortcut arrow graphic for linking.

Figure 5.19 Pointers - move, copy, and link operations

- Use visual feedback to indicate the receptivity of potential destinations. You can use selection highlighting and optionally animate or display a representation of the transfer object in the destination. Optionally, you can also indicate when a destination cannot accept an object by using the "no drop" pointer when the pointer is over it, as shown in Figure 5.20.

Figure 5.20 A "no drop " pointer

Specialized Transfer Commands

In some contexts, a particular form of a transfer operation may be so common, that introducing an additional specialized command is appropriate. For example, if copying existing objects is a frequent operation, you can include a Duplicate command. Following are some common specialized transfer commands.

Command	Function
Delete	Removes an object from its container. If the object is a file, the object is transferred to the Recycle Bin.
Clear	Removes the content of a container.
Duplicate	Copies the selected object.
Print	Prints the selected object on the default printer.
Send To	Displays a list of possible transfer destinations and transfers the selected object to the user selected destination.

Delete and Clear are often used synonymously. However, they are best differentiated by applying Delete to an object and Clear to the container of an object.

Shortcut Keys for Transfer Operations

Following are the defined shortcut techniques for transfer operations.

Shortcut	Operation
CTRL+X	Performs a Cut command.
CTRL+C	Performs a Copy command.
CTRL+V	Performs a Paste command.
CTRL+drag	Toggles the meaning of the default direct manipulation transfer operation to be a copy operation (provided the destination can support the copy operation). The modifier may be used with either mouse button.
ESC	Cancels a drag and drop transfer operation.

For more information about reserved and recommended shortcut key assignments, see Appendix B, "Keyboard Interface Summary."

Because of the wide use of these command shortcut keys throughout the interface, do not reassign them to other commands.

Creation Operations

Creating new objects is a common user action in the interface. Although applications can provide the context for object creation, avoid considering an application's interface as the exclusive means of creating new objects. Creation is typically based on some predefined object or specification and can be supported in the interface in a number of ways.

Copy Command

Making a copy of an existing object is the fundamental paradigm for creating new objects. Copied objects can be modified and serve as prototypes for the creation of other new objects. The transfer model conventions define the basic interaction techniques for copying objects. Copy and Paste commands and drag and drop manipulation provide this interface.

New Command

The New command facilitates the creation of new objects. New is a command applied to a specific object, automatically creating a new instance of the object's type. The New command differs from the Copy and Paste commands in that it is a single command that generates a new object.

Insert Command

The Insert command works similarly to the New command, except that it is applied to a container to create a new object, usually of a specified type, in that container. In addition to inserting native types of data, use the Insert command to insert objects of different types. By supporting OLE, you can support the creation of a wide range of objects. In addition, objects supported by your application can be inserted into data files created by other OLE applications.

For more information about inserting objects, see Chapter 11, "Working with OLE Embedded and OLE Linked Objects."

Using Controls

You can use controls to support the automatic creation of new objects. For example, in a drawing application, buttons are often used to specify tools or modes for the creation of new objects, such as drawing particular shapes or controls. Buttons can also be used to insert OLE objects.

For more information about using buttons to create new objects, see Chapter 11, "Working with OLE Embedded and OLE Linked Objects."

Using Templates

A *template* is an object that automates the creation of a new object. To distinguish its purpose, display a template icon as a pad with the small icon of the type of the object to be created, as shown in Figure 5.21.

Figure 5.21 A template icon

Define the New command as the default operation for a template object; this starts the creation process, which may either be automatic or request specific input from the user. Place the newly created object in the same location as the container of the template. If circumstances make that impractical, place the object in a common location, such as the desktop, or, during the creation process, include a prompt that allows a user to specify some other destination. In the former situation, display a message box informing the user where the object will appear.

Operations on Linked Objects

A *link* is a connection between two objects that represents or provides access to another object that is in another location in the same container or in a different, separate container. The components of this relationship include the link source (sometimes referred to as the referent) and the link or linked object (sometimes referred to as the reference). A linked object often has operations and properties independent of its source. For example, a linked object's properties can include attributes like update frequency, the path description of its link source, and the appearance of the linked object. The containers in which they reside provide access to and presentation of commands and properties of linked objects.

Links can be presented in various ways in the interface. For example, a *data link* propagates a value between two objects, such as between two cells in a worksheet or a series of data in a table and a chart. *Jumps* (also referred to as hyperlinks) provide navigational access to another object. An *OLE linked object* provides access to any operation available for its link source and also supplies a presentation of the link source. A shortcut icon is a link, displayed as an icon.

For more information about OLE linked objects, see Chapter 11, "Working with OLE Embedded and OLE Linked Objects." For more information about jumps, see Chapter 12, "User Assistance."

When the user transfers a linked object, store both the absolute and relative path to its link source. The absolute path is the precise description of its location, beginning at the root of its hierarchy. The relative path is the description of its location relative to its current container.

The destination of a transfer determines whether to use the absolute or relative path when the user accesses the link source through the linked object. The relative path is the most common default path. However, regardless of which path you use, if it fails, use the alternative path. For example, if the user copies a linked object and its link source to another location, the result is a duplicate of the linked object and the link source. The relative path for the duplicate linked object is the location of the duplicate of the link source. The absolute path for the duplicate linked object is the description of the location of the initial link source. Therefore, when the user accesses the duplicate of the linked object, its inferred connection should be with the duplicate of the link source. If that connection fails — for example, because the user deletes the duplicate of the linked source — use the absolute path, the connection to the original link source.

Optionally, you can make the preferred path for a linked object a field in the property sheet for linked object. This allows the user to choose whether to have a linked object make use of the absolute or relative path to its link source.

When the user applies a link operation to a linked object, link to the linked object rather than its linked source. That is, linking a linked object results in a linked object linked to a linked object. If such an operation is not valid or appropriate - for example, because the linked object provides no meaningful context - then disable any link commands or options when the user selects a linked object.

Activation of a linked object depends on the kind of link. For example, a single click can activates a jump. However, a single click only results in selecting a data link or an OLE linked object. If you use a single click to do anything other than select the linked object, distinguish the object by either presenting it as a button control, displaying the hand pointer (as shown in Figure 5.22) when the user moves the pointer over the linked object, or both. These techniques provide feedback to the user that the clicking involves more than selection.

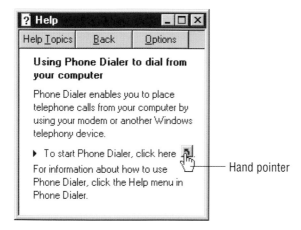

Figure 5.22 The hand pointer

Part II

Windows Interface Components

Windows

Windows provide the fundamental way a user views and interacts with data. Consistency in window design is particularly important because it enables users to easily transfer their learning skills and focus on their tasks rather than learn new conventions. This chapter describes the common window types and presents guidelines for general appearance and operation.

Common Types of Windows

Because windows provide access to different types of information, they are classified according to common usage. Interacting with objects typically involves a *primary window* in which most primary viewing and editing activity takes place. In addition, multiple supplemental *secondary windows* can be included to allow users to specify parameters or options, or to provide more specific details about the objects or actions included in the primary window.

For more information about secondary windows, see Chapter 8, "Secondary Windows."

Primary Window Components

A typical primary window consists of a frame (or border) which defines its extent, and a title bar which identifies what is being viewed in the window. If the viewable content of the window exceeds the current size of the window, scroll bars are used. The window can also include other components like menu bars, toolbars, and status bars.

Figure 6.1 shows the common components of a primary window.

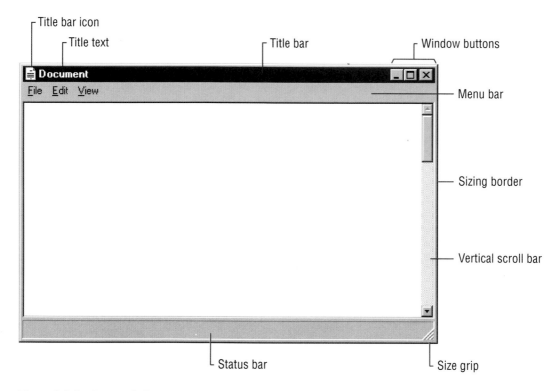

Figure 6.1 A primary window

Window Frames

Every window has a boundary that defines its shape. A sizable window has a distinct border that provides control points (handles) for resizing the window using direct manipulation. If the window cannot be resized, the border coincides with the edge of the window.

Title Bars

At the top edge of the window, inside its border, is the *title bar* (also referred to as the caption or caption bar), which extends across the width of the window. The title bar identifies what the window is viewing. It also serves as a control point for moving the window and an access point for commands that apply to the window and its associated view. For example, clicking on the title bar with mouse button 2 displays the pop-up menu for the window. Pressing the ALT+SPACEBAR key combination also displays the pop-up menu for the window.

Title Bar Icons

A primary window includes the small version of the object's icon. The small icon appears in the upper left corner of the title bar and represents the object being viewed in the window. If the window represents a "tool" or utility application (that is, an application that does not create, load, and save its own data files), use the small version of the application's icon in its title bar, as shown in Figure 6.2.

For information about how to register icons for your application and data file types, see Chapter 10, "Integrating with the System." For more information about designing icons, see Chapter 13, "Visual Design."

Application icon

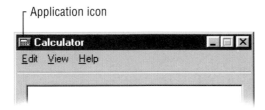

Figure 6.2 "Tool" title bar

If the application creates, loads and saves documents or data files and the window represents the view of one of its files, use the icon that represents its document or data file type in the title bar, as shown in Figure 6.3. Display the data file icon even if the user has not saved the file yet, rather than displaying the application icon and then the data file icon once the user saves the file.

Document icon

Figure 6.3 Document title bar

If an application uses the multiple document interface (MDI) design, place the application's icon in the parent window's title bar, and place an icon that reflects the application's data file type in the child window's title bar, as shown in Figure 6.4.

For more information about MDI, see Chapter 9, "Window Management."

Application icon

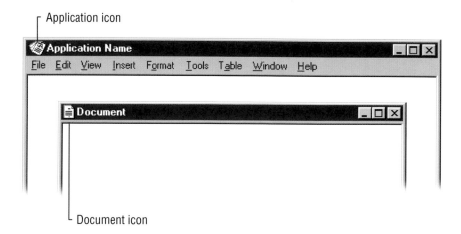

Document icon

Figure 6.4 MDI application and document title bars

However, when a user maximizes the child window, and you hide its title bar and merge its title information with the parent, display the icon from the child window's title bar in the menu bar of the parent window. If multiple child windows are open within the MDI parent window, display only the icon from the active (topmost) child window.

When the user clicks the title bar icon with mouse button 2, display the pop-up menu for the object. Typically, the menu contains a similar set of commands that are available for the icon from which the window was opened, except that Close replaces Open. Also define Close as the default command, so when the user double-clicks the title bar icon, the window closes. Clicking elsewhere with button 2 on the title bar displays the pop-up menu for the window.

When the user clicks the title bar icon with mouse button 1, the system also displays the pop-up menu for the window. However, this behavior is only supported for backward compatibility with Windows 3.1. Avoid documenting it as the primary way to access the pop-up menu for the window. Instead, document the use of button 2 as the correct way to display the pop-up menu for the window.

Title Text

The window title text identifies the name of the object being viewed in the window. It should always correspond to the icon of the type you display in the title bar. It should also match the label of the icon in the file system that represents the object. For example, if the user opens a data file named "My Document" in the resulting window, you display the icon for that document type followed by the name of the data file. You may also include the name of the application in use; however, if it is used, display the name of the data file first, followed by a dash and the application name, as shown in Figure 6.5.

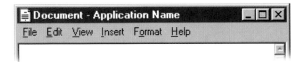

Figure 6.5 Title text order: document name — application name

If the window represents a "tool" application that does not create or edit its own data files, such as the Windows Calculator, display the application's name, as displayed for the application's icon label, in the title bar. If the tool application operates as a utility for other files created by other applications — such as a special viewer or browser application — where the view displayed is not the primary open view of the file, or where the "tool" application requires an additional specification to indicate its context — such as the Windows Explorer — place the name of the application first, then include a dash and the specification text. For example, the title text of the Windows Explorer includes the name of the current container displayed in the browser.

For an MDI application, use the application's name in the parent window and the data file's name in the child windows. When the user maximizes the file's child window, format the title text following the same convention as a tool application, with the application's name first, followed by the data filename, as shown in Figure 6.6.

The order of the document (or data) filename and application name differs from the Windows 3.1 guidelines. The new convention is better suited for the design of a data-centered interface.

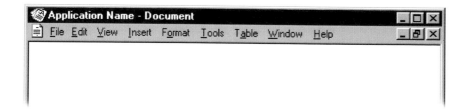

Figure 6.6 Document follows application name for maximized child window

When the user directly opens an application that displays a new data file, supply a name for the file and place it in the title bar, even if the user has not saved the file yet. Use the type name — for example Document (*n*), Sheet (*n*), Chart (*n*), where *n* is a number, as in Document (1). Make certain that the proposed name does not conflict with an existing name in the current directory. Also use this name as the proposed default filename for the object in the Save As dialog box. If it is impractical or inappropriate to supply a default name, display a placeholder in the title, such as (Untitled).

For more information about type names, see Chapter 10, "Integrating with the System." For more information about the Save As dialog box, see Chapter 8, "Secondary Windows."

Follow the same convention if your application includes a New command that creates new files. Avoid prompting the user for a name. Instead, you can supply a Save As dialog box that allows the user to confirm or change your proposed name when they save or close the file or attempt to create a new file.

Display a filename in the title bar exactly as it appears to the user in the file system, using both uppercase and lowercase letters. However, avoid displaying the file's extension or the path in the title bar. This information is not meaningful for most users and can make it more difficult for them to identify the file. However, because the system provides an option for users to display filename extensions, use the system-supplied functions to format a filename, which will display the filename appropriately based on the user's preference.

The **GetFileTitle** and **SHGet-FileInfo** functions automatically format names correctly. For more information about these functions, see the documentation included in the Microsoft Win32 Software Development Kit (SDK).

If your application supports multiple windows for viewing the same file, you may use the title text to distinguish between the views — but use a convention that will not be confused as part of the filename. For example, you may want to append :*n*, where *n* represents the instance of the window, as in Document:2. Make certain you do not include this view designation as part of the filename you supply in the Save As dialog box.

If the name of the displayed object in the window changes — for example, when the user edits the name in the object's property sheet — update the title text to reflect that change. Always try to maintain a clear association between an object and its open window.

The title text and title bar icon should always represent the outmost container — the object that was opened — even if the user selects an embedded object or navigates the internal hierarchy of the object being viewed in the window. If you need an additional specification to clarify what the user is viewing, place this specification after the filename and separate it clearly from the filename, such as enclosing it in parentheses — for example, My HardDisk (C:). Because the system now supports long filenames, avoid additional specification whenever possible. Complex or verbose additions to the title text also make it more difficult for the user to easily read and identify the window.

When the width of the window does not allow you to display the complete title text, you may abbreviate the title text, being careful to maintain the essential information that allows the user to quickly identify the window.

For more information about abbreviating names, see Chapter 10, "Integrating with the System."

Avoid drawing directly into the title bar or adding other controls. Such added items can make reading the name in the title difficult, particularly because the size of the title bar varies with the size of the window. In addition, the system uses this area for displaying special controls. For example, in some international versions of Windows, the title area provides information or controls associated with the input of certain languages.

Title Bar Buttons

Include command buttons associated with the common commands of the primary window in the title bar. These act as shortcuts to specific window commands. Clicking a title bar button with mouse button 1 invokes the command associated with the command button. Optionally, you can also support clicking a title bar command button with mouse button 2 to display the pop-up menu for the window. For the pen, tapping a window button invokes its associated command, and optionally you may support barrel-tapping it (or using the pen menu gesture) to display the pop-up menu for the window.

In a typical situation, one or more of the following buttons appear in a primary window (provided that the window supports the respective functions).

6.1 Title Bar Buttons

Button	Command	Operation
☒	Close	Closes the window.
▬	Minimize	Minimizes the window.
☐	Maximize	Maximizes the window.
▣	Restore	Restores the window.

When displaying these buttons, use the following guidelines:

- When a command is not supported by a window, do not display its corresponding button.

- The Close button always appears as the rightmost button. Leave a gap between it and any other buttons.

- The Minimize button always precedes the Maximize button.

- The Restore button always replaces the Maximize button or the Minimize button when that command is carried out.

The system does not support the inclusion of the context-sensitive Help button available for secondary windows. Applications wishing to provide this functionality can do so by including a Help toolbar button. Similarly, avoid including Maximize, Minimize, and Restore buttons in the title bars of secondary windows because those commands do not apply to those windows.

Basic Window Operations

The basic operations for a window include: activation and deactivation, opening and closing, moving, sizing, scrolling, and splitting. The following sections describe these operations.

Activating and Deactivating Windows

While the system supports the display of multiple windows, the user generally works within a single window at a time. This window is called the *active window*. The active window is typically at the top of the window Z order. It is also visually distinguished by its title bar that is displayed in the active window title color. All other windows are *inactive* with respect to the user's input; that is, while other windows can have ongoing processes, only the active window receives the user's input. The title bar of an inactive window displays the system inactive window color. Your application can query the system for the current values for the active title bar color and the inactive title bar color.

For more information about using the **GetSysColor** function to access the COLOR_ACTIVE-CAPTION and COLOR_INACTIVE-CAPTION constants, see the documentation included in the Win32 SDK.

The user activates a primary window by switching to it; this inactivates any other primary windows. To activate a window with the mouse or pen, the user clicks or taps on any part of the window, including its interior. If the window is minimized, the user clicks (taps) the button representing the window in the taskbar. From the keyboard, the system provides the ALT+TAB key combination for switching between primary windows. The SHIFT+ALT+TAB key also switches between windows, but in reverse order. (The system also supports ALT+ESC for switching between windows.) The reactivation of a window should not affect any pre-existing selection within it; the selection and focus are restored to the previously active state.

When the user reactivates a primary window, the window and all its secondary windows come to the top of the window order and maintain their relative positions. If the user activates a secondary window, its primary window comes to the top of the window order along with the primary window's other secondary windows.

When a window becomes inactive, hide the selection feedback (for example, display of highlighting or handles) of any selection within it to prevent confusion over which window is receiving keyboard input. A direct manipulation transfer (drag and drop) is an exception. Here, you can display transfer feedback if the pointer is over the window during the drag operation. Do not activate the window unless the user releases the mouse button (the pen tip is lifted) in that window.

Opening and Closing Windows

When the user opens a primary window, include an entry for it on the taskbar. If the window has been opened previously, restore the window to its size and position when it was last closed. If possible and appropriate, reinstate the other related view information, such as selection state, scroll position, and type of view. When opening a primary window for the first time, open it to a reasonable default size and position as best defined by the object or application. For details about storing state information in the system registry, see Chapter 10, "Integrating with the System."

> Only primary windows, not secondary windows, should include an entry on the taskbar.

Because display resolution and orientation varies, your software should not assume a fixed display size, but rather adapt to the shape and size defined by the system. If you use standard system interfaces the system automatically places your windows relative to the current display configuration.

> The **SetWindowPlacement** function is an example of a system interface that will automatically place windows correctly relative to the current display. For more information about this function, see the documentation included in the Win32 SDK.

Opening the primary window activates that window and places it at the top of the window order. If the use attempts to open a primary window that is already open within the same desktop, activate the existing window using the following recommendations. If the existing window is minimized, restore it when you activate it.

File type	Action when repeating an Open operation
Document or data file	Activates the existing window of the object and displays it at the top of the window Z order.
Application file	Displays a message box indicating that an open window of that application already exists and offers the user the option to switch to the open window or to open another window. Either choice activates the selected window and brings it to the top of the window Z order.
Document file that is already open in an MDI application window	Activates the existing window of the file. Its MDI parent window comes to the top of the window Z order, and the file appears at the top of the Z order within its MDI parent window.
Document file that is not already open, but its associated MDI application is already running (open)	Opens a new instance of the file's associated MDI application at the top of the window Z order and displays the child window for the file. Optionally, as an alternative, displays a message box indicating that an open window of that application already exists and offers the user the option to use the existing window or to open a new parent window.

For more information about MDI, see Chapter 9, "Window Management."

The user closes a primary window by clicking (for a pen, tapping the screen) the Close button in the title bar or choosing the Close command from the window's pop-up menu. Although the system supports double-clicking (with a pen, double-tapping the screen) on the title bar icon as a shortcut for closing the window for compatibility with previous versions of Windows, avoid documenting this as the primary way to close a primary window. Instead, document the Close button.

When the user chooses the Close command, if your application does not automatically save these changes and pending transactions or edits that have not yet been saved to file remain, display a message asking the user whether to save any changes, discard any changes, or cancel the Close operation before closing the window. If there are no pending transactions, just close the window. Follow this same convention for any other command that results in closing the primary window (for example, Exit or Shut Down).

For more information about supporting the Close command, see Chapter 5, "General Interaction Techniques."

When closing the primary window, close any of its dependent secondary windows as well. The design of your application determines whether closing the primary window also ends the application processes. For example, closing the window of a text document typically halts any application code or processes remaining for inputting or formatting text. However, closing the window of a printer has no effect on the jobs in the printer's queue. In both cases, closing the window removes its entry from the taskbar.

Moving Windows

The user can move a window either by dragging its title bar using the mouse or pen or by using the Move command on the window's pop-up menu. On most configurations, an outline representation moves with the pointer during the operation, and the window is redisplayed in the new location after the completion of the move. (The system also provides a display property setting that redraws the window dynamically as it is moved.) After choosing the Move command, the user can move the window with the keyboard interface by using arrow keys and pressing the ENTER key to end the operation and establish the window's new location. Never allow the user to reposition a window so that it cannot be accessed.

A window need not be active before the user can move it. The action of moving the window implicitly activates it.

Moving a window may clip or reveal information shown in the window. In addition, activation can affect the view state of the window — for example, the current selection can be displayed. However, when the user moves a window, avoid making any changes to the content being viewed in that window.

Resizing Windows

Make your primary windows resizable unless the information displayed in the window is fixed, such as in the Windows Calculator program. The system provides several conventions that support user resizing of a window.

Sizing Borders

The user resizes a primary window by dragging the sizing border with the mouse or pen at the edge of a window or by using the Size command on the window's menu. An outline representation of the window moves with the pointer. (On some configurations, the system may include a display option to dynamically redraw the window as it is sized.) After completing the size operation, the window assumes its new size. Using the keyboard, the user can size the window by choosing the Size command, using the arrow keys, and pressing the ENTER key.

A window does not need to be active before the user can resize it. The action of sizing the window implicitly makes it active, and it remains active after the sizing operation.

When the user resizes a window to be smaller, you must determine how to display the information viewed in that window. Use the context and type of information to help you choose your approach. The most common approach is to clip the information. However, in other situations where you want the user to see as much information as possible, you may want to consider using different methods, such as rewrapping or scaling the information. Use these variations carefully because they may not be consistent with the resizing behavior of most windows. In addition, avoid these methods when readability or maintaining the structural relationship of the information is important.

Although the size of a primary window can vary, based on the user's preference, you can define a window's maximum size. When defining this size, consider the reasonable usage within the window, and the size and orientation of the screen.

Maximizing Windows

Although the user may be able to directly resize a window to its maximum size, the Maximize command optimizes this operation. Include this command on a window's pop-up menu, and as the Maximize command button in the title bar of the window.

Maximizing a window increases the size of the window to its largest, optimum size. The system default setting for the maximum size is as large as the display, excluding the space used by the taskbar (or other application-defined desktop toolbars). For an MDI child window, the default maximize size fills the parent window. But, you can define the size to be less or, in some cases, more than the default dimensions.

When the user maximizes a window, replace the Maximize button with a Restore button. Then, disable the Maximize command and enable the Restore command on the pop-up menu for the window.

Minimizing Windows

Minimizing a window reduces it to its smallest size. To support this command, include it on the pop-up menu for the window and as the Minimize command button in the title bar of the window.

For primary windows, minimizing removes the window from the screen, but leaves its entry in the taskbar. For MDI child windows, the window resizes to a minimum size within its parent window. To minimize a window, the user chooses the Minimize command from the window's pop-up menu or the Minimize command button on the title bar.

Because the representation of minimized windows changed in Microsoft Windows 95, using an icon as the way to reflect state information may not be appropriate. As an alternative, you may want to consider creating a status indicator for the taskbar. For more information about status notification, see Chapter 10, "Integrating with the System."

When the user minimizes a window, disable the Minimize command on the pop-up menu and enable the Restore command.

Restoring Windows

Support the Restore command to restore a window to its previous size and position after the user has maximized or minimized the window. For maximized windows, enable this command on the window's pop-up menu and replace the Maximize button with the Restore button in the title bar of the window.

For minimized windows, also enable the Restore command in the pop-up menu of the window. The user restores a minimized primary window to its former size and position by clicking (for pens, tapping the screen) on its button in the taskbar that represents the window, selecting the Restore command on the pop-up menu of the window's taskbar button, or using the ALT+TAB (or the SHIFT+ALT+TAB) key combination.

Size Grip

When you define a sizable window, you may include a size grip. A *size grip* is a special handle for sizing a window. It is not exclusive to the sizing border. To size the window, the user drags the grip and the window resizes following the same conventions as the sizing border.

Always locate the size grip in the lower right corner of the window. Typically, this means you place the size grip at the right end of a horizontal scroll bar or the bottom of a vertical scroll bar. However, if you include a status bar in the window, display the size grip at the far corner of the status bar instead. Never display the size grip in both locations at the same time.

For more information about the use of the size grip in a status bar, see Chapter 7, "Menus, Controls, and Toolbars."

Scrolling Windows

When the information viewed in a window exceeds the size of that window, the window should support scrolling. Scrolling enables the user to view portions of the object that are not currently visible in a window. Scrolling is commonly supported through the use of a scroll bar. A *scroll bar* is a rectangular control consisting of *scroll arrows*, a *scroll box*, and a *scroll bar shaft*, as shown in Figure 6.7.

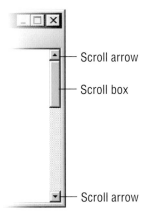

Figure 6.7 Scroll bar and its components

You can include a vertical scroll bar, a horizontal scroll bar, or both. Align a scroll bar with the vertical or horizontal edge of the window orientation it supports. If the content is never scrollable in a particular direction, do not include a scroll bar for that direction.

The common practice is to display scroll bars if the view requires some scrolling under any circumstances. If the window becomes inactive or resized so that its content does not require scrolling, you should continue to display the scroll bars. While removing the scroll bars when the window is inactive potentially allows the display of more information and feedback about the state of the window, it also requires the user to explicitly activate the window to scroll. Consistently displaying scroll bars provides a more stable environment.

Scroll bars are also available as separate window components. For more information about scroll bar controls, see Chapter 7, "Menus, Controls, and Toolbars."

Scroll Arrows

Scroll arrow buttons appear at each end of a scroll bar, pointing in opposite directions away from the center of the scroll bar. The scroll arrows point in the direction that the window "moves" over the data. When the user clicks (for pens, tapping the screen) a scroll arrow, the data in the window moves, revealing information in the direction of the arrow in appropriate increments. The granularity of the increment depends on the nature of the content and context, but it is typically based on the size of a standard element. For example, you can

The default system support for scroll bars does not disable the scroll arrow buttons when the region or area is no longer scrollable in this direction. However, it does provide support for you to disable the scroll arrow button under the appropriate conditions.

use one line of text for vertical scrolling, one row for spreadsheets. You can also use an increment based a fixed unit of measure. Whichever convention you choose, maintain the same scrolling increment throughout a window. The objective is to provide an increment that provides smooth but efficient scrolling. When a window cannot be scrolled any further in a particular direction, disable the scroll arrow corresponding to that direction.

When scroll arrow buttons are pressed and held, they exhibit a special auto-repeat behavior. This action causes the window to continue scrolling in the associated direction as long as the pointer remains over the arrow button. If the pointer is moved off the arrow button while the user presses the mouse button, the auto-repeat behavior stops and does not continue unless the pointer is moved back over the arrow button (also when the pen tip is moved off the control).

Scroll Box

The scroll box, sometimes referred to as the elevator, thumb, or slider, moves along the scroll bar to indicate how far the visible portion is from the top (for vertical scroll bars) or from the left edge (for horizontal scroll bars). For example, if the current view is in the middle of a document, the scroll box in the vertical scroll bar is displayed in the middle of the scroll bar.

The size of the scroll box can vary to reflect the difference between what is visible in the window and the entire content of the file, as shown in Figure 6.8.

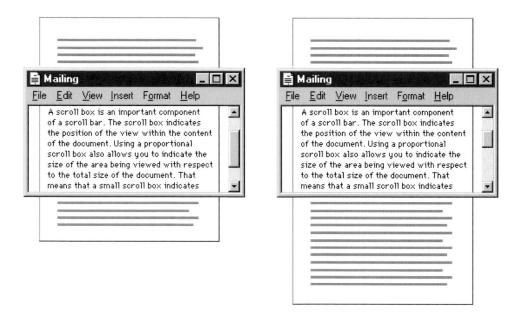

Figure 6.8 Proportional relationship between scroll box and content

For example, if the content of the entire document is visible in a window, the scroll box extends the entire length of the scroll bar, and the scroll arrows are disabled. Make the minimum size of the scroll box no smaller than the width of a window's sizing border.

The user can also scroll a window by dragging the scroll box. Update the view continuously as the user moves the scroll box. If you cannot support scrolling at a reasonable speed, you can scroll the information at the end of the drag operation as an alternative.

If the user starts dragging the scroll box and then moves the pointer outside of the scroll bar, the scroll box returns to its original position. The distance the user can move the pointer off the scroll bar before the scroll box snaps back to its original position is proportional to the width of the scroll bar. If dragging ends at this point, the scroll action is canceled — that is, no scrolling occurs. However, if the user moves the pointer back within the scroll-sensitive area, the scroll box returns to tracking the pointer movement. This behavior allows the user to scroll without having to remain within the scroll bar and to selectively cancel the initiation of a drag-scroll operation.

Dragging the scroll box to the end of the scroll bar implies scrolling to the end of that dimension; this does not always mean that the area cannot be scrolled further. If your application's document structure extends beyond the data itself, you can interpret dragging the scroll box to the end of its scroll bar as moving to the end of the data rather than the end of the structure. For example, a typical spreadsheet exceeds the data in it — that is, the spreadsheet may have 65,000 rows, with data only in the first 50 rows. This means you can implement the scroll bar so that dragging the scroll box to the bottom of the vertical scroll bar scrolls to the last row containing data rather than the last row of the spreadsheet. The user can use the scroll arrow buttons to scroll further to the end of the structure. This situation also illustrates why disabling the scroll arrow buttons can provide important feedback so that the user can distinguish between scrolling to the end of data from scrolling to the end of the extent or structure. In the example of the spreadsheet, when the user drags the scroll box to the end of the scroll bar, the arrow would still be shown as enabled because the user can still scroll further, but it would be disabled when the user scrolls to the end of the spreadsheet.

Scroll Bar Shaft

The scroll bar shaft not only provides a visual context for the scroll box, it also serves as part of the scrolling interface. Clicking in the scroll bar shaft should scroll the view an equivalent size of the visible area in the direction of the click. For example, if the user clicks in the shaft below the scroll box in a vertical scroll bar, scroll the view a distance equivalent to the height of the view. Where possible, allow overlap from the previous view, as shown in Figure 6.9. For example, if the user clicks below the scroll box, the bottom line becomes the top line of scrolled view. The same thing applies for clicking above the scroll box and horizontal scrolling. These conventions provide the user with a common reference point.

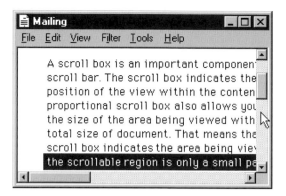 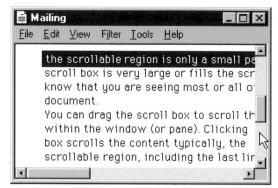

Figure 6.9 Scrolling with the scroll bar shaft by a screenful

Pressing and holding mouse button 1 with the pointer in the shaft auto-repeats the scrolling action. If the user moves the pointer outside the scroll-sensitive area while pressing the button, the scrolling action stops. The user can resume scrolling by moving the pointer back into the scroll bar area. (This behavior is similar to the effect of dragging the scroll box.)

Automatic Scrolling

The techniques previously summarized describe the explicit ways for scrolling. However, the user can also scroll as a secondary result of another user action. This type of scrolling is called *automatic scrolling*. The situations in which to support automatic scrolling are as follows:

- When the user begins or adjusts a selection and drags it past the edge of the scroll bar or window, scroll the area in the direction of the drag.

- When the user drags an object and approaches the edge of a scrollable area, scroll the area following the recommended auto-scroll conventions covered in Chapter 5, "General Interaction Techniques." Base the scrolling increment on the context of the destination and, if appropriate, on the size of the object being dragged.

- When the user enters text from the keyboard at the edge of a window or moves or copies an object into a location at the edge of a window, the view should scroll to allow the user to focus on the inserted information. The amount to scroll depends on context. For example, for text, vertically scroll a single line at a time. When scrolling horizontally, scroll in units greater than a single character to prevent continuous or uneven scrolling. Similarly, when the user transfers a graphic object near the edge of the view, base scrolling on the size of the object.

- If an operation results in a selection or moves the cursor, scroll the view to display the new selection. For example, for a Find command that selects a matching object, scroll the object into view because usually the user wants to focus on that location. In addition, other forms of navigation may cause scrolling. For example, completing an entry field in a form may result in navigating to the next field. In this case, if the field is not visible, the form can scroll to display it.

Keyboard Scrolling

Use navigation keys to support scrolling with the keyboard. When the user presses a navigation key, the cursor moves to the appropriate location. For example, in addition to moving the cursor, pressing arrow keys at the edge of a scrollable area scrolls in the corresponding direction. Similarly, the PAGE UP and PAGE DOWN keys are comparable to clicking in the scroll bar shaft, but they also move the cursor.

Optionally, you can use the SCROLL LOCK key to facilitate keyboard scrolling. In this case, when the SCROLL LOCK key is toggled on and the user presses a navigation key, scroll the view without affecting the cursor or selection.

Placing Adjacent Controls

It is sometimes convenient to locate controls or status bars adjacent to a scroll bar and position the end of the scroll bar to accommodate them. Take care when placing adjacent elements; too many can make it difficult for users to scroll, particularly if you reduce the scroll bar too much. If you need a large number of controls, consider using a conventional toolbar instead.

For more information about toolbars, see Chapter 7, "Menus, Controls, and Toolbars."

Splitting Windows

A window can be split into two or more separate viewing areas, which are called *panes*. For example, a split window allows the user to examine two parts of a document at the same time. You can also use a split window to display different, yet simultaneous, views of the same information, as shown in Figure 6.10.

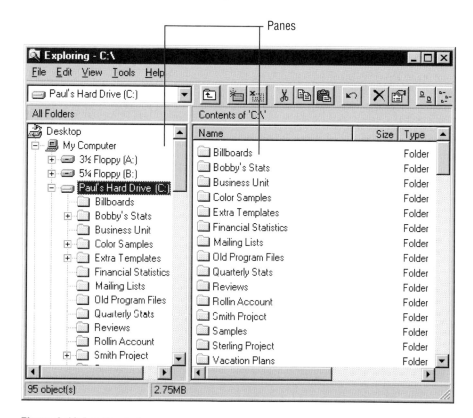

Figure 6.10 A split window

While you can use a split window pane to view the contents of multiple files or containers at the same time, displaying these in separate windows typically allows the user to better identify the files as individual elements. When you need to present views of multiple files as a single task, consider window management techniques, such as MDI.

The panes that appear in a split window can be implemented either as part of a window's basic design or as a user-configurable option. To support splitting a window that is not presplit by design, include a split box. A *split box* is a special control placed adjacent to the end of a scroll bar that splits or adjusts the split of a window. The size of the split box should be just large enough for the user to successfully target it with the pointer; the default size of a size handle, such as the window's sizing border, is a good guideline. Locate the split box at the top of the up arrow button of the vertical scroll bar, as shown in Figure 6.11, or to the left of the left arrow button of a horizontal scroll bar.

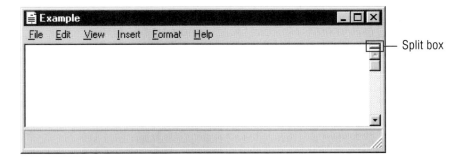

Figure 6.11 Split box location

The user splits a window by dragging the split box to the desired position. When the user positions the hot spot of the pointer over a split box, change the pointer's image to provide feedback and help the user target the split box. While the user drags the split box, move a representation of the split box and split bar with the pointer, as shown in Figure 6.12.

At the end of the drag, display a visual separator, called the *split bar*, that extends from one side of the window to the other, defining the edge between the resulting panes, as shown in Figure 6.12. Base the size for the split bar to be, at a minimum, the current setting for the size of window sizing borders. This allows you to appropriately adjust when a user adjusts size borders. If you display the split box after the split operation, place it adjacent to the split bar.

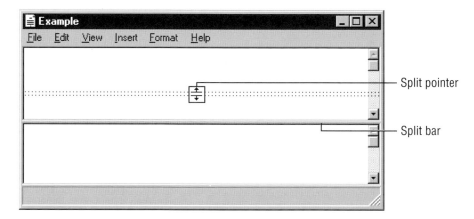

Figure 6.12 Moving the split bar

You can support dragging the split bar (or split box) to the end of the scroll bar to close the split. Optionally, you can also support double-clicking (or, for pens, double-tapping) as a shortcut technique for splitting the window at some default location (for example, in the middle of the window or at the last split location) or for removing the split. This technique works best when the resulting window panes display peer views. It may not be appropriate when the design of the window requires that it always be displayed as split or for some types of specialized views.

To provide a keyboard interface for splitting the window, include a Split command on the window or view's menu. When the user chooses the Split command, split the window in the middle or in a context-defined location. Support arrow keys for moving the split box up or down; pressing the ENTER key sets the split at the current location. Pressing the ESC key cancels the split mode.

You can also use other commands to create a split window. For example, you can define specialized views that, when selected by the user, split a window to a fixed or variable set of panes. Similarly, you can enable the user to remove the split of a window by closing a view pane or by selecting another view command.

When the user splits a window, add scroll bars if the resulting panes require scrolling. In addition, you may need to scroll the information in panes so that the split bar does not obscure the content over which it appears. Use a single scroll bar, at the appropriate side of the window, for a set of panes that scroll together. However, if the panes each require independent scrolling, a scroll bar should appear in each pane for that purpose. For example, the vertical scroll bars of a set of panes in a horizontally split window are typically controlled separately.

When you use split window panes to provide separate views, independently maintain each pane's view properties, such as view type and selection state. Display only the selection in the active pane. However, if the selection state is shared across the panes, display a selection in all panes and support selection adjustment across panes.

When a window is closed, save the window's split state (that is, the number of splits, the place where they appear, the scrolled position in each split, and its selection state) as part of the view state information for that window so that it can be restored the next time the window is opened.

Menus, Controls, and Toolbars

Microsoft Windows provides a number of interactive components that make it easy to provide interfaces to carry out commands and specify values. These components also provide a consistent structure and set of interface conventions. This chapter describes the interactive elements of menus, controls, and toolbars, and how to use them.

Menus

Menus list commands available to the user. By making commands visible, menus leverage user recognition rather than depending on user recollection of command names and syntax.

There are several types of menus, including drop-down menus, pop-up menus, and cascading menus. The following sections cover these menus in more detail.

The Menu Bar and Drop-down Menus

A *menu bar*, one of the most common forms of a menu interface, is a special area displayed across the top of a window directly below the title bar (as shown in Figure 7.1). A menu bar includes a set of entries called *menu titles*. Each menu title provides access to a *drop-down menu* composed of a collection of *menu items*, or choices.

Figure 7.1 A menu bar

The content of the menu bar and its drop-down menus are determined by the functionality of your application and the context of a user's interaction. You can also optionally provide user configuration of the menu structure, including hiding the menu bar. If you provide this kind of option, supplement the interface with other components such as pop-up menus, handles, and toolbars, so that a user can access the functionality typically provided by the menu bar.

When displayed, a drop-down menu appears as a panel with its menu items arranged in a column. While the system supports multiple columns for a drop-down menu, avoid this form of presentation because it adds complexity to browsing and interaction of the menu.

Drop-down Menu Interaction

When the user chooses a menu title, it displays its associated drop-down menu. To display a drop-down menu with the mouse, the user points to the menu title and presses or clicks mouse button 1. This action highlights the menu title and opens the menu. Tapping the menu title with a pen has the same effect as clicking the mouse.

If the user opens a menu by pressing the mouse button while the pointer is over the menu title, the user can drag the pointer over menu items in the drop-down menu. As the user drags, each menu item is highlighted, tracking the pointer as it moves through the menu. Releasing the mouse button with the pointer over a menu item chooses the command associated with that menu item and the system removes the drop-down menu. If the user moves the pointer off the menu and then releases the mouse button, the menu is "canceled" and the drop-down menu is removed. However, if the user moves the pointer back onto the menu before releasing the mouse button, the tracking resumes and the user can still select a menu item.

If the user opens a menu by clicking on the menu title, the menu title is highlighted and the drop-down menu remains displayed until the user clicks the mouse again. Clicking a menu item in the drop-down menu or dragging over and releasing the mouse button on a menu item chooses the command associated with the menu item and re moves the drop-down menu. When the system displays a drop-down menu, clicking its associated menu title again cancels the menu and removes the drop-down. Clicking another menu title also results in canceling any displayed drop-down menu, and displays the menu associated with that menu title.

The keyboard interface for drop-down menus uses the ALT key to activate the menu bar. When the user presses an alphanumeric key while holding the ALT key, or after the ALT key is released, the system displays the drop-down menu whose access key for the menu title matches the alphanumeric key (matching is not case sensitive). Pressing a subsequent alphanumeric key chooses the menu item in the drop-down menu with the matching access character.

The user can also use arrow keys to access drop-down menus from the keyboard. When the user presses the ALT key, but has not yet selected a drop-down menu, LEFT ARROW and RIGHT ARROW keys highlight the previous or next menu title, respectively. At the end of the menu bar, pressing another arrow key in the corresponding direction wraps the highlight around to the other end of the menu bar. Pressing the ENTER key displays the drop-down menu associated with the selected menu title. If a drop-down menu is already displayed on that menu bar, then pressing LEFT ARROW or RIGHT ARROW navigates the highlight to the next drop-down menu in that direction, unless the drop-down menu displays its content in multiple columns, in which case the arrow keys move the highlight to the next column in that direction, and then to the next drop-down menu.

Pressing UP ARROW or DOWN ARROW in the menu bar also displays a drop-down menu if none is currently open. In an open drop-down menu, pressing these keys moves to the next menu item in that direction, wrapping the highlight around at the top or bottom. If the drop-down menu has multiple columns, then pressing the arrow keys first wraps the highlight around to the next column.

The user can cancel a drop-down menu by pressing the ALT key whenever the menu bar is active. This not only closes the drop-down menu, it also deactivates the menu bar. Pressing the ESC key also cancels a drop-down menu. However, the ESC key cancels only the current menu level. For example, if a drop-down menu is open, pressing ESC closes the drop-down menu, but leaves its menu title highlighted. Pressing ESC a second time unhighlights the menu title and deactivates the menu bar, returning input focus to the content information in the window.

You can assign shortcut keys to commands in drop-down menus. When the user presses a shortcut key associated with a command in the menu, the command is carried out immediately. Optionally, you can also highlight its menu title, but do not display the drop-down.

Common Drop-down Menus

This section describes the conventions for drop-down menus commonly used in applications. While these menus are not required for all applications, apply these guidelines when including these menus in your software's interface.

The File Menu

The File menu provides an interface for the primary operations that apply to a file. Your application should include commands such as Open, Save, Send To, and Print. These commands are often also included on the pop-up menu of the icon displayed in the title bar of the window.

For more information about the commands in the pop-up menu for a title bar icon, see the section, "Icon Pop-up Menus," later in this chapter.

If your application supports an Exit command, place this command at the bottom of the File menu preceded by a menu separator. When the user chooses the Exit command, close any open windows and files, and stop any further processing. If the object remains active even when its window is closed — for example, like a folder or printer — then include the Close command instead of Exit.

The Edit Menu

Include general purpose editing commands on the Edit menu. These commands include the Cut, Copy, and Paste transfer commands, OLE object commands, and the following commands (if they are supported).

For more information about transfer commands, see Chapter 5, "General Interaction Techniques."

Command	Function
Undo	Reverses last action.
Repeat	Repeats last action.
Find and Replace	Searches for and substitutes text.
Delete	Removes the current selection.
Duplicate	Creates a copy of the current selection.

Include these commands on this menu and on the pop-up menu of the selected object.

The View Menu

Put commands on the View menu that change the user's view of data in the window. Include commands on this menu that affect the view and not the data itself — for example, Zoom or Outline. Also include commands for controlling the display of particular interface elements in the view — for example, Show Ruler. Also place these commands on the pop-up menu of the window or pane.

The Window Menu

Use the Window menu in multiple document interface-style (MDI) applications for commands associated with managing the windows within an MDI workspace. Also include these commands on the pop-up menu of the parent MDI window.

For more information about the design of MDI software, see Chapter 9, "Window Management."

The Help Menu

Use the Help menu for commands that provide access to Help information. Include a Help Topics command; this command provides access to the Help Topics browser, which displays topics included in your application's Help file. Alternatively, you can provide individual commands that access specific pages of the Help Topics browser, such as Contents, Index, and Find Topic. You can also include other user assistance commands on this drop-down menu.

For more information about the Help Topics browser and support for user assistance, see Chapter 12, "User Assistance."

If you provide access to copyright and version information for your application, include an About *application name* command on this menu. When the user chooses this command, display a window containing the application's name, version number, copyright information, and any other informational properties related to the application. Display this information in a dialog box or alternatively as a copyright page of the property sheet of the application's main executable file. Do not use an ellipsis at the end of this command, because the resulting window does not require the user to provide any further parameters.

Pop-up Menus

Even if you include a menu bar in your software's interface, you should also support pop-up menus. Pop-up menus provide an efficient way for the user to access the operations of objects, as shown in Figure 7.2. Because pop-up menus are displayed at the pointer's current location, they eliminate the need for the user to move the pointer to the menu bar or a toolbar. In addition, because you populate pop-up menus with commands specific to the object or its immediate context, they reduce the number of commands the user must browse through. Pop-up menus also minimize screen clutter because they are displayed only upon demand and do not require dedicated screen space.

Figure 7.2 A pop-up menu

While a pop-up menu looks similar to a drop-down menu, a pop-up menu should only contain commands that apply to the selected object or objects and its context, rather than commands grouped by function. For example, a pop-up menu for a text selection can include commands for moving and copying the text and access to the font properties of the text and the paragraph properties of which the selection is a part. However, keep the size of the pop-up menu as small as possible by limiting the items on the menu to common, frequent actions. It is better to include a single Properties command and allow the user to navigate among properties in the resulting property sheet than to list individual properties in the pop-up menu.

The container or the composition of which a selection is a part typically supplies the pop-up menu for the selection. Similarly, the commands included on a pop-up menu may not always be supplied by the object itself, but rather be a combination of those commands provided by the object and by its current container. For example, the pop-up menu for a file in a folder includes transfer commands. In this case, the folder (container) supplies the commands, not the files. Pop-up menus for OLE objects follow these same conventions.

Avoid using a pop-up menu as the exclusive means to a particular operation. At the same time, the items in a pop-up menu need not be limited only to commands that are provided in drop-down menus.

When ordering the commands in a pop-up menu, use the following guidelines:

- Place the object's primary commands first (for example, commands such as Open, Play, and Print), transfer commands, other commands supported by the object (whether provided by the object or by its context), and the What's This? command (when supported).

- Order the transfer commands as Cut, Copy, Paste, and other specialized Paste commands.

- Place the Properties command, when present, as the last command on the menu.

For more information about transfer commands and the Properties command, see Chapter 5, "General Interaction Techniques." For more information about the What's This? command, see Chapter 12, "User Assistance."

Pop-up Menu Interaction

With a mouse, the user displays a pop-up menu by clicking an object with button 2. The down transition of the mouse button selects the object. Upon the up transition, display the menu to the right and below the hot spot of the pointer adjusted to avoid the menu being clipped by the edge of the screen.

If the pointer is over an existing selection when the user invokes a pop-up menu, display the menu that applies to that selection. If the menu is outside a selection but within the same selection scope, then establish a new selection (usually resetting the current selection in that scope) at the button down point and display the menu for the new selection. Dismiss the pop-up menu when the user clicks outside the menu with button 1 or if the user presses the ESC key.

You can support pop-up menus for objects that are implicitly selected or cannot be directly selected, such as scroll bars or items in a status bar. When providing pop-up menus for objects such as controls, include commands for the object that the control represents, rather than for the control itself. For example, a scroll bar represents a navigational view of a document, so commands might include Beginning of Document, End of Document, Next Page, and Previous Page. But when a control represents itself as an object, as in a forms layout or window design environment, you can include commands that apply to the control—for example, commands to move or copy the control.

The pen interface uses an action handle in pen-enabled controls to access the pop-up menu for the selection. Tapping the action handle displays the pop-up menu, as shown in Figure 7.3.

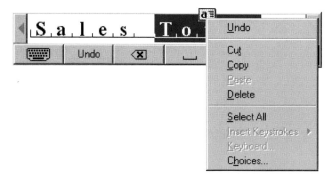

Figure 7.3 Using an action handle to provide pen access to pop-up menus

In addition, you can use techniques like barrel-tapping or the pop-up menu gesture to display a pop-up menu. This interaction is equivalent to a mouse button 2 click.

Use SHIFT+F10 and the Application key (for keyboards that support the Windows keys specification) to provide keyboard access for pop-up menus. In addition, menu access keys, arrow keys, ENTER, and ESC keys all operate in the same fashion in the menu as they do in drop-down menus. To enhance space and visual efficiency, avoid including shortcut keys in pop-up menus.

The system provides a message, WM_CONTEXTMENU, when the user presses a system defined pop-up menu key. For more information about this message, see documentation included in the Microsoft Win32 Software Development Kit (SDK).

Common Pop-up Menus

The pop-up menus included in any application depend on the objects and context supplied by that application. The following sections describe common pop-up menus for Windows-based applications.

The Window Pop-up Menu

The window pop-up menu is the pop-up menu associated with a window — do not confuse it with the Window drop-down menu found in MDI applications. The window pop-up menu replaces the Windows 3.1 Control menu, also referred to as the System menu. For example, a typical primary window includes Close, Restore, Move, Size, Minimize, and Maximize.

You can also include other commands on the window's menu that apply to the window or the view within the window. For example, an application can append a Split command to the menu to facilitate splitting the window into panes. Similarly, you can add commands that affect the view, such as Outline, commands that add, remove, or filter elements from the view, such as Show Ruler, or commands that open certain subordinate or special views in secondary windows, such as Show Color Palette.

A secondary window also includes a pop-up menu. Usually, because the range of operations are more limited than in a primary window, a secondary window's pop-up menu includes only Move and Close commands, or just Move. Palette windows can also include an Always on Top command that sets the window to always be on top of its parent window and secondary windows of its parent window.

The user displays a window's pop-up menu by clicking mouse button 2 anywhere in the title bar area, excluding the title bar icon. Clicking on the title bar icon with button 2 displays the pop-up menu for the object represented by the icon. To avoid confusing users, if you do not provide a pop-up menu for the title bar icon, do not display the pop-up for the window when the user clicks with button 2 on the title bar icon.

For the pen, performing barrel-tapping or the equivalent pop-up menu gesture on these areas displays the menu. Pressing ALT+ SPACEBAR also displays the menu. The pop-up for the window can also be accessed from the keyboard by the user pressing the ALT key and then using the arrow keys to navigate beyond the first or last entry in the menu bar. In MDI applications, the pop-up menu for a child window can also be accessed this way or directly using ALT+HYPHEN.

For compatibility with previous versions of Windows, the system also supports clicking button 1 on the icon in the title bar to access the pop-up menu of a window. However, do not document this as the primary method for accessing the pop-up menu for the window. Document only the button 2 technique.

Icon Pop-up Menus

Pop-up menus displayed for icons include operations of the objects represented by those icons. Accessing the pop-up menu of an application or document icon follows the standard conventions for pop-up menus, such as displaying the menus with a mouse button 2 click.

An icon's container application supplies the pop-up menu for the icon. For example, pop-up menus for icons placed in standard folders or on the desktop are automatically provided by the system. However, your application supplies the pop-up menus for OLE embedded or linked objects placed in it — that is, placed in the document or data files your application supports.

For more information about supporting pop-up menus for OLE objects, see Chapter 11, "Working with OLE Embedded and OLE Linked Objects."

The container populates the pop-up menu for an icon with commands the container supplies for its content, such as transfer commands and those registered by the object's type. For example, an application can register a New command that automatically generates a new data file of the type supported by the application.

The pop-up menu of an application's icon, for example, the Microsoft WordPad executable file, should include the commands listed in Table 7.1.

For more information about registering commands, see Chapter 10, "Integrating with the System."

Table 7.1 Application File Icon Pop-up Menu Commands

Command	Meaning
Open	Opens the application file.
Send To	Displays a submenu of destinations to which the file can be transferred. The content of the submenu is based on the content of the system's Send To folder.
Cut	Marks the file for moving. (Registers the file on the Clipboard.)
Copy	Marks the file for duplication. (Registers the file on the Clipboard.)
Paste	Attempts to open the file registered on the Clipboard with the application.
Create Shortcut	Creates a shortcut icon of the file.
Delete	Deletes the file.
Rename	Allows the user to edit the filename.
Properties	Displays the properties for the file.

An icon representing a document or data file typically includes the following common menu items for the pop-up menu for its icon.

Table 7.2 Document or Data File Icon Pop-up Menu Commands

Command	Meaning
Open	Opens the file's primary window.
Print	Prints the file on the current default printer.
Quick View	Displays the file using a special viewing tool window.
Send To	Displays a submenu of destinations to which the file can be transferred. The content of the submenu is based on the content of the system's Send To folder.
Cut	Marks the file for moving. (Registers the file on the Clipboard.)
Copy	Marks the file for duplication. (Registers the file on the Clipboard.)
Delete	Deletes the file.
Rename	Allows the user to edit the filename.
Properties	Displays the properties for the file.

With the exception of the Open and Print commands, the system automatically provides these commands for icons when they appear in system containers, such as the desktop or folders. If your application supplies its own containers for files, you need to supply these commands.

For the Open and Print commands to appear on the menu, your application must register these commands in the system registry. You can also register additional or replacement commands. For example, you can optionally register a Quick View command that displays the content of the file without running the application and a What's This? command that displays descriptive information for your data file types.

For more information about registering commands and the Quick View command, see Chapter 10, "Integrating with the System." For more information about the What's This? command, see Chapter 12, "User Assistance."

The icon in the title bar of a window represents the same object as the icon the user opens. As a result, the application associated with the icon also includes a pop-up menu with appropriate commands for the title bar's icon. When the icon of an application appears in the title bar, include the same commands on its pop-up menu as are included for the icon that the user opens, unless a particular command cannot be applied when the application's window is open. In addition, replace the Open command with Close.

Similarly, when the icon of the data or document file appears in the title bar, you also use the same commands as found on its file icon, with the following exceptions: replace the Open command with a Close command and add Save if the edits in the document require explicit saving to file.

For an MDI application, supply a pop-up menu for the application icon in the parent window, following the conventions for application title bar icons. Also consider including the following commands where they apply.

For more information about the design of MDI-style applications, see Chapter 9, "Window Management."

Table 7.3 Optional MDI Parent Window Title Bar Icon Pop-up Menu Commands

Command	Meaning
New	Creates a new data file or displays a list of data file types supported by the application from which the user can choose.
Save All	Saves all data files open in the MDI workspace, and the state of the MDI window.
Find	Displays a window that allows the user to specify criteria to locate a data file.

In addition, supply an appropriate pop-up menu for the title bar icon that appears in the child window's title bar. You can follow the same conventions for non-MDI data files.

Cascading Menus

A *cascading menu* (also referred to as a *hierarchical menu* or child menu) is a submenu of a menu item. The visual cue for a cascading menu is the inclusion of a triangular arrow display adjacent to the label of its parent menu item.

You can use cascading menus to provide user access to additional choices rather than taking up additional space in the parent menu. They may also be useful for displaying hierarchically related objects.

Be aware that cascading menus can add complexity to the menu interface by requiring the user to navigate further through the menu structure to get to a particular choice. Cascading menus also require more coordination to handle the changes in direction necessary to navigate through them.

In light of these design tradeoffs, use cascading menus sparingly. Minimize the number of levels for any given menu item, ideally limiting your design to a single submenu. Avoid using cascading menus for frequent, repetitive commands.

As an alternative, make choices available in a secondary window, particularly when the choices are independent settings; this allows the user to set multiple options in one invocation of a command. You can also support many common options as entries on a toolbar.

The user interaction for a cascading menu is similar to that of a drop-down menu from the menu bar, except a cascading menu displays after a short time-out. This avoids the unnecessary display of the menu if the user is browsing or navigating to another item in the parent menu. Once displayed, if the user moves the pointer to another menu item, the cascading menu is removed after a short time-out. This time-out enables the user to directly drag from the parent menu into an entry in its cascading menu.

Menu Titles

All drop-down and cascading menus have a menu title. For drop-down menus, the menu title is the entry that appears in the menu bar. For cascading menus, the menu title is the name of the parent menu item. Menu titles represent the entire menu and should communicate as clearly as possible the purpose of all items on the menu.

Use single words for menu bar menu titles. Multiple word titles or titles with spaces may be indistinguishable from two one-word titles. In addition, avoid uncommon compound words, such as Fontsize.

Define one character of each menu title as its access key. This character provides keyboard access to the menu. Windows displays the access key for a menu title as an underlined character, as shown in Figure 7.4.

For more information about keyboard input and defining access keys, see Chapter 4, "Input Basics."

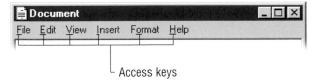

Figure 7.4 Access keys in a menu bar

Define unique access keys for each menu title. Using the same access key for more than one menu title may eliminate direct access to a menu.

Menu Items

Menu items are the individual choices that appear in a menu. Menu items can be text, graphics — such as icons — or graphics and text combinations that represent the actions presented in the menu. The format for a menu item provides the user with visual cues about the nature of the effect it represents, as shown in Figure 7.5.

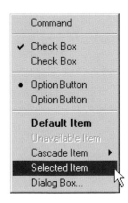

Figure 7.5 Formats for different menu items

Whenever a menu contains a set of related menu items, you can separate those sets with a grouping line known as a *separator*. The standard separator is a single line that spans the width of the menu. Avoid using menu items themselves as group separators, as shown in Figure 7.6.

— Don't use a menu item as a menu separator

Figure 7.6 Inappropriate separator

Always provide the user with a visual indication about which menu items can be applied. If a menu item is not appropriate or applicable in a particular context, then disable or remove it. Leaving the menu item enabled and presenting a message box when the user selects the menu item is a poor method for providing feedback.

In general, it is better to disable a menu item rather than remove it because this provides more stability in the interface. However, if the context is such that the menu item is no longer or never relevant, remove it. For example, if a menu displays a set of open files and one of those files is closed or deleted, it is appropriate to remove the corresponding menu item.

If all items in a menu are disabled, disable its menu title. If you disable a menu item or its title, it does not prevent the user from browsing or choosing it. If you provide status bar messages, you can display a message indicating that the command is unavailable and why.

The system provides a standard appearance for displaying disabled menu items. If you are supplying your own visuals for a disabled menu item, follow the visual design guidelines for how to display it with an unavailable appearance.

For more information about displaying commands with an unavailable appearance, see Chapter 13, "Visual Design."

Types of Menu Items

Many menu items take effect as soon as they are chosen. If the menu item is a command that requires additional information to complete its execution, follow the command with an *ellipsis* (...). The ellipsis informs the user that information is incomplete. When used with a command, it indicates that the user needs to provide more information to complete that command. Such commands usually result in the display of a dialog box. For example, the Save As command includes an ellipsis because the command is not complete until the user supplies or confirms a filename.

Not every command that produces a dialog box or other secondary window should include an ellipsis. For example, do not include an ellipsis with the Properties command because carrying out the Properties command displays a properties window. After completing the command, no further parameters or actions are required to fulfill the intent of the command. Similarly, do not include an ellipsis for a command that may result in the display of a message box.

While you can use menu items to carry out commands, you can also use menu items to switch a mode or set a state or property, rather than initiating a process. For example, choosing an item from a menu that contains a list of tools or views implies changing to that state. If the menu item represents a property value, when the user chooses the menu item, the property setting changes.

Menu items for state settings can be independent or interdependent:

- Independent settings are the menu equivalent of check boxes. For example, if a menu contains text properties, such as Bold and Italic, they form a group of independent settings. The user can change each setting without affecting the others, even though they both apply to a single text selection. Include a check mark to the left of an independent setting when that state applies.

- Interdependent settings are the menu equivalent of option buttons. For example, if a menu contains alignment properties — such as Left, Center, and Right — they form a group of interdependent settings. Because a particular paragraph can have only one type of alignment, choosing one resets the property to be the chosen menu item setting. When the user chooses an interdependent setting, place an option button mark to the left of that menu item.

When using the menu to represent the two states of a setting, if those states are obvious opposites, such as the presence or absence of a property value, you can use a check mark to indicate when the setting applies. For example, when reflecting the state of a text selection with a menu item labeled Bold, show a check mark next to the menu item when the text selection is bold and no check mark when it is not. If a selection contains mixed values for the same stat reflected in the menu, you also display the menu without the check mark.

However, if the two states of the setting are not obvious opposites, use a pair of alternating menu item names to indicate the two states. For example, a naive user might guess that the opposite of a menu item called Full Duplex is Empty Duplex. Because of this ambiguity, pair the command with the alternative name Half Duplex, rather using a mark to indicate the alternative states, and consider the following guidelines for how to display those alternatives:

- If there is room in a menu, include both alternatives as individual menu items and interdependent choices. This avoids confusion because the user can view both options simultaneously. You can also use menu separators to group the choices.

- If there is not sufficient room in the menu for the alternative choices, you can use a single menu item and change its name to the alternative action when selected. In this case, the menu item's name does not reflect the current state; it indicates the state after choosing the item. Where possible, define names that use the same access key. For example, the letter D could be used for a menu item that toggles between Full Duplex and Half Duplex.

Avoid defining menu items that change depending on the state of a modifier key. Such techniques hide functionality from a majority of users.

A menu can also have a default item. A default menu item reflects a choice that is also supported through a shortcut technique, such as double-clicking or drag and drop. For example, if the default command for an icon is Open, define this as the default menu item. Similarly, if the default command for a drag and drop operation is Copy, display this command as the default menu item in the pop-up menu that results from a nondefault drag and drop operation (button 2). The system designates a default menu item by displaying its label as bold text.

Menu Item Labels

Include descriptive text or a graphic label for each menu item. Even if you provide a graphic for the label, consider including text as well. The text allows you to provide more direct keyboard access to the user and provides support for a wider range of users.

Use the following guidelines for defining text menu names for
menu item labels:

- Define unique item names within a menu. However, item
  names can be repeated in different menus to represent similar or
  different actions.

- Use a single word or multiple words, but keep the wording brief
  and succinct. Verbose menu item names can make it harder for
  the user to scan the menu.

- Define unique access keys for each menu item within a menu.
  This provides the user direct keyboard access to the menu item.
  The guidelines for selecting an access key for menu items are
  the same as for menu titles, except that the access key for a menu
  item can also be a number included at the beginning of the menu
  item name. This is useful for menu items that vary, such as filenames. Where possible, also define consistent access keys for
  common commands.

- Follow book title capitalization rules for menu item names. For
  English language versions, capitalize the first letter of every word,
  except for articles, conjunctions, and prepositions that occur other
  than at the beginning or end of a multiple-word name. For example, the following menu names are correct: New Folder, Go To,
  Select All, and Table of Contents.

- Avoid formatting individual menu item names with different text
  properties. Even though these properties illustrate a particular text
  style, they also may make the menu cluttered, illegible, or confusing. For example, it may be difficult to indicate an access key if an
  entire menu entry is underlined.

> For more information about
> defining access keys, see
> Chapter 4, "Input Basics." For more
> information about common access
> key assignments, see Appendix B,
> "Keyboard Interface Summary."

Shortcut Keys in Menu Items

If you define a keyboard shortcut associated with a command in a
drop-down menu, display the shortcut in the menu. Display the
shortcut key next to the item and align shortcuts with other shortcuts
in the menu. Left align at the first tab position after the longest item
in the menu that has a shortcut. Do not use spaces for alignment
because they may not display properly in the proportional font used
by the system to display menu text or when the font setting menu
text changes.

You can match key names with those commonly inscribed on the keycap. Display CTRL and SHIFT key combinations as Ctrl+*key* (rather than Control+*key* or CONTROL+*key* or ^+*key*) and Shift+*key*. When using function keys for menu item shortcuts, display the name of the key as F*n*, where *n* is the function key number.

Avoid including shortcut keys in pop-up menus. Pop-up menus are already a shortcut form of interaction and are typically accessed with the mouse. In addition, excluding shortcut keys makes pop-up menus easier for users to scan.

For more information about the selection of shortcut keys, see Chapter 4, "Input Basics."

Controls

Controls are graphic objects that represent the properties or operations of other objects. Some controls display and allow editing of particular values. Other controls start an associated command.

Each control has a unique appearance and operation designed for a specific form of interaction. The system also provides support for designing your own controls. When defining your own controls, follow the conventions consistent with those provided by the system-supplied controls.

For more information about using standard controls and designing your own controls, see Chapter 13, "Visual Design."

Like most elements of the interface, controls provide feedback indicating when they have the input focus and when they are activated. For example, when the user interacts with controls using a mouse, each control indicates its selection upon the down transition of the mouse button, but does not activate until the user releases the button, unless the control supports auto-repeat.

Controls are generally interactive only when the pointer, actually the hot spot of the pointer, is over the control. If the user moves the pointer off the control while pressing a mouse button, the control no longer responds to the input device. If the user moves the pointer back onto the control, it once again responds to the input device. The hot zone, or boundary that defines whether a control responds to the pointer, depends on the type of control. For some controls, such as buttons, the hot zone coincides with the visible border of the control. For others, the hot zone may include the control's graphic and label (for example, check boxes) or some controls, such as scroll bars, as defined around the control's borders.

Many controls provide labels. Because labels help identify the purpose of a control, always label a control with which you want the user to directly interact. If a control does not have a label, you can provide a label using a static text field or a tooltip control. Define an access key for text labels to provide the user direct keyboard access to a control. Where possible, define consistent access keys for common commands.

For more information about defining access keys, see Chapter 4, "Input Basics."

While controls provide specific interfaces for user interaction, you can also include pop-up menus for controls. This can provide an effective way to transfer the value the control represents or to provide access to context-sensitive Help information. The interface to pop-up menus for controls follows the standard conventions for pop-up menus, except that it does not affect the state of the control; that is, clicking the control with button 2 does not trigger the action associated with the control when the user clicks it with button 1. The only action is the display of the pop-up menu.

A pop-up menu for a control is contextual to what the control represents, rather than the control itself. Therefore, avoid commands such as Set, Unset, Check, or Uncheck. The exception is in a forms design or window layout context, where the commands on the pop-up menu can apply to the control itself.

Buttons

Buttons are controls that start actions or change properties. There are three basic types of buttons: command buttons, option buttons, and check boxes.

Command Buttons

A *command button*, also referred to as a push button, is a control, commonly rectangular in shape, that includes a label (text, graphic, or sometimes both), as shown in Figure 7.7.

Figure 7.7 Command buttons

When the user chooses a command button with mouse button 1 (for pens, tapping), the command associated with the button is carried out. When the user presses the mouse button, the input focus moves to the button, and the button state changes to its pressed appearance. If the user moves the pointer off the command button while the mouse button remains pressed, the button returns to its original state. Moving the pointer back over the button while pressing the mouse button returns the button to its pressed state.

When the user releases the mouse button with the pointer on the command button, the command associated with the control starts. If the pointer is not on the control when the user releases the mouse button, no action occurs.

You can define access keys and shortcut keys for command buttons. In addition, you can use the TAB key and arrow keys to support user navigation to or between command buttons. The SPACEBAR activates a command button if the user moves the input focus to the button.

For more information about navigation and activation of controls, see Chapter 8, "Secondary Windows."

The effect of choosing a button is immediate with respect to its context. For example, in toolbars, clicking a button carries out the associated action. In a secondary window, such as a dialog box, activating a button may initiate a transaction within the window, or apply a transaction and close the window.

The command button's label represents the action the button starts. When using a text label, the text should follow the same capitalization conventions defined for menus. If the control is disabled, display the label of the button as unavailable.

Include an ellipsis (...) as a visual cue for buttons associated with commands that require additional information. Like menu items, the use of an ellipsis indicates that further information is needed, not simply that a window will appear. Some buttons, when clicked, can display a message box, but this does not imply that the command button's label should include an ellipsis.

You can use command buttons to enlarge a secondary window and display additional options, also known as an *unfold button*. An unfold button is not really a different type of control, but the use of a command button for this specific function. When using a command button for this purpose, include a pair of "greater than" (>>) characters as part of the button's label.

In some cases, a command button can represent an object and its default action. For example, the taskbar buttons represent an object's primary window and the Restore command. When the user clicks on the button with mouse button 1, the default command of the object is carried out. Clicking on a button with mouse button 2 displays a pop-up menu for the object the button represents.

You can also use command buttons to reflect a mode or property value similar to the use of option buttons or check boxes. While the typical interaction for a command button is to return to its normal "up" state, if you use it to represent a state, display the button in the option-set appearance, as shown in Table 7.4.

For more information about the appearance of different states of buttons, see Chapter 13, "Visual Design."

Table 7.4 Command Button Appearance

Appearance	Button state
	Normal appearance
	Pressed appearance
	Option-set appearance
	Unavailable appearance
	Option-set, unavailable appearance
	Mixed-value appearance
	Input focus appearance

You can also use command buttons to set tool modes — for example, in drawing or forms design programs for drawing out specific shapes or controls. In this case, design the button labels to reflect the tool's use. When the user chooses the tool (that is, clicks the button), display the button using the option-set appearance and change the pointer to indicate the change of the mode of interaction.

You can also use a command button to display a pop-up menu. This convention is known as a *menu button*. While this is not a specific control provided by the system, you can create this interface using the standard components.

A menu button looks just like a standard command button, except that, as a part of its label, it includes a triangular arrow similar to the one found in cascading menu titles, as shown in Figure 7.8.

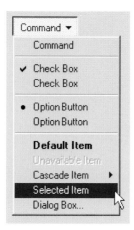

Figure 7.8 A menu button

A menu button supports the same type of interaction as a drop-down menu; the menu is displayed when the button is pressed and allows the user to drag into the menu from the button and make menu selections. Like any other menu, use highlighting to track the movement of the pointer.

Similarly, when the user clicks a menu button, the menu is displayed. At this point, interaction with the menu is the same as with any menu. For example, clicking a menu item carries out the associated command. Clicking outside the menu or on the menu button removes the menu.

When pressed, display the menu button with the pressed appearance. When the user releases the mouse button and the menu is displayed, use the option-set appearance. Otherwise, the menu button's appearance is the same as a typical command button. For example, if the button is disabled, display the button using the unavailable appearance.

Option Buttons

An *option button*, also referred to as a radio button, represents a single choice within a limited set of mutually exclusive choices — that is, in any group of option buttons, only one option in the group can be set. Accordingly, always group option buttons in sets of two or more, as shown in Figure 7.9.

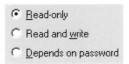

Figure 7.9 A set of option buttons

Option buttons appear as a set of small circles. When an option button choice is set, a dot appears in the middle of the circle. When the choice is not the current setting, the circle is empty. Avoid using option buttons to start an action other than the setting of a particular option or value represented by the option button. The only exception is that you can support double-clicking the option button as a short-cut for setting the value and carrying out the default command of the window in which the option buttons appear, if choosing an option button is the primary user action for the window.

You can use option buttons to represent a set of choices for a particular property. When the option buttons reflect a selection with mixed values for that property, display all the buttons in the group using the mixed-value appearance to indicate that multiple values exist for that property. The mixed-value appearance for a group of option buttons displays all buttons without a setting dot, as shown in Figure 7.10.

Figure 7.10 Option buttons with mixed-value appearance

If the user chooses any option button in a group with mixed-value appearance, that value becomes the setting for the group; the dot appears in that button and all the other buttons in the group remain empty.

Limit the use of option buttons to small sets of options, typically seven or less, but always at least two. If you need more choices, consider using another control, such as a single selection list box or drop-down list box.

Each option button includes a text label. (If you need graphic labels for a group of exclusive choices, consider using command buttons instead.) The standard control allows you to include multiple line labels. When implementing multiple line labels, use top alignment, unless the context requires an alternate orientation.

Define the option button's label to represent the value or effect for that choice. Also use the label to indicate when the choice is unavailable. Use sentence capitalization for an option button's label; only capitalize the first letter of the first word, unless it is a word in the label normally capitalized.

For more information about labeling or appearance states, see Chapter 13, "Visual Design."

Because option buttons appear as a group, you can use a group box control to visually define the group. You can label the option buttons to be relative to a group box's label. For example, for a group box labeled Alignment, you can label the option buttons as Left, Right, and Center.

As with command buttons, the mouse interface for choosing an option button uses a click with mouse button 1 (for pens, tapping) either on the button's circle or on the button's label. The input focus is moved to the option button's label when the user presses the mouse button, and the option button displays its pressed appearance. If the user moves the pointer off the option button before releasing the mouse button, the option button is returned to its original state. The option is not set until the user releases the mouse button while the pointer is over the control. Releasing the mouse button outside of the option button or its label has no effect on the current setting of the option button. In addition, successive mouse clicks on the same option button do not toggle the button's state; the user needs to explicitly select an alternative choice in the group to change or restore a former choice.

Assign access keys to option button labels to provide a keyboard interface to the buttons. You can also define the TAB or arrow keys to allow the user to navigate and choose a button. Access keys or arrow keys automatically set an option button and set the input focus to that button.

For more information about the guidelines for defining access keys, see Chapter 4, "Input Basics." For more information about navigation and interaction with option buttons, see Chapter 8, "Secondary Windows."

Check Boxes

Like option buttons, check boxes support options that are either on or off; check boxes differ from option buttons in that you typically use check boxes for independent or nonexclusive choices. As in the case of independent settings in menus, use check boxes only when both states of the choice are clearly opposite and unambiguous. If this is not the case, then use option buttons or some other form of single selection choice control instead.

A check box appears as a square box with an accompanying label. When the choice is set, a check mark appears in the box. When the choice is not set, the check box is empty, as shown in Figure 7.11.

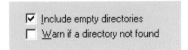

Figure 7.11 A set of check boxes

A check box's label is typically displayed as text and the standard control includes a label. (Use a command button instead of a check box when you need a nonexclusive choice with a graphic label.) Use a single line of text for the label as this makes the label easier to read. However, if you do use multiple lines, use top alignment, unless the context requires a different orientation.

Define a check box's label to appropriately express the value or effect of the choice. Use sentence capitalization for multiple word labels. The label also serves as an indication of when the control is unavailable.

Group related check box choices. If you group check boxes, it does not prevent the user from setting the check boxes on or off in any combination. While each check box's setting is typically independent of the others, you can use a check box's setting to affect other controls. For example, you can use the state of a check box to filter the content of a list. If you have a large number of choices or if the number of choices varies, use a multiple selection list box instead of check boxes.

When the user clicks a check box with mouse button 1 (for pens, tapping) either on the check box square or on the check box's label, that button is chosen and its state is toggled. When the user presses the mouse button, the input focus moves to the control and the check box assumes its pressed appearance. Like option buttons and other controls, if the user moves the pointer off the control while holding down the mouse button, the control's appearance returns to its original state. The setting state of the check box does not change until the mouse button is released. To change the control's setting, the pointer must be over the check box or its label when the user releases the mouse button.

Define access keys for check box labels to provide a keyboard interface for navigating to and choosing a check box. In addition, the TAB key and arrow keys can also be supported to provide user navigation to or between check boxes. In a dialog box, for example, the SPACEBAR toggles a check box when the input focus is on the check box.

For more information about guidelines for defining access keys, see Chapter 4, "Input Basics." For more information about navigation and supporting interaction for controls with the keyboard, see Chapter 8, "Secondary Windows."

If you use a check box to display the value for the property of a multiple selection whose values for that property differ (for example, for a text selection that is partly bold), display the check box in its mixed-value appearance, as shown in Figure 7.12.

Figure 7.12 A mixed-value check box (magnified)

If the user chooses a check box in the mixed-value state, the associated value is set and a check mark is placed in it. This implies that the property of all elements in the multiple selection will be set to this value when it is applied. If the user chooses the check box again, the setting to be unchecked is toggled. If applied to the selection, the value will not be set. If the user chooses the check box a third time, the value is toggled back to the mixed-value state. When the user applies the value, all elements in the selection retain their original value. This three-state toggling occurs only when the control represents a mixed set of values.

List Boxes

A *list box* is a convenient, preconstructed control for displaying a list of choices for the user. The choices can be text, color, icons, or other graphics. The purpose of a list box is to display a collection of items and, in most cases, support selection of a choice of an item or items in the list.

List boxes are best for displaying large numbers of choices that vary in number or content. If a particular choice is not available, omit the choice from the list. For example, if a point size is not available for the currently selected font, do not display that size in the list.

Order entries in a list using the most appropriate choice to represent the content in the list and to facilitate easy user browsing. For example, alphabetize a list of names, but put a list of dates in chronological order. If there is no natural or logical ordering for the content, use ascending or alphabetical ordering — for example, 0–9 or A–Z.

List box controls do not include their own labels. However, you can include a label using a static text field; the label enables you to provide a descriptive reference for the control and keyboard access to the control. Use sentence capitalization for multiple word labels and make certain that your support for keyboard access moves the input focus to the list box and not the static text field label.

For more information about navigation to controls in a secondary window, see Chapter 8, "Secondary Windows." For more information about defining access keys for control labels, see Chapter 4, "Input Basics." For more information about static text fields, see the section, "Static Text Fields," later in this chapter.

When a list box is disabled, display its label using an unavailable appearance. If possible, display all of the entries in the list as unavailable to avoid confusing the user as to whether the control is enabled or not.

The width of the list box should be sufficient to display the average width of an entry in the list. If that is not practical because of space or the variability of what the list might include, consider one or more of the following options:

- Make the list box wide enough to allow the entries in the list to be sufficiently distinguished.

- Use an ellipsis (...) in the middle or at the end of long text entries to shorten them, while preserving the important characteristics needed to distinguish them. For example, for long paths, usually the beginning and end of the path are the most critical; you can use an ellipsis to shorten the entire name: \Sample\...\Example.

- Include a horizontal scroll bar. However, this option reduces some usability, because adding the scroll bar reduces the number of entries the user can view at one time. In addition, if most entries in the list box do not need to be horizontally scrolled, including a horizontal scroll bar accommodates the infrequent case.

When the user clicks an item in a list box, it becomes selected. Support for multiple selection depends on the type of list box you use. List boxes also include scroll bars when the number of items in the list exceeds the visible area of the control.

Arrow keys also provide support for selection and scrolling a list box. In addition, list boxes include support for keyboard selection using text keys. When the user presses a text key, the list navigates and selects the matching item in the list, scrolling the list if necessary to keep the user's selection visible. Subsequent key presses continue the matching process. Some list boxes support sequential matches based on timing; each time the user presses a key, the control matches the next character in a word if the user presses the key within the system's time-out setting. If the time-out elapses, the control is reset to matching based on the first character. Other list box controls, such as combo boxes and drop-down combo boxes, do sequential character matching based on the characters typed into the text box component of the control. These controls may be preferable because they do not require the user to master the timing sequence. However, they do take up more space and potentially allow the user to type in entries that do not exist in the list box.

When the list is scrolled to the beginning or end of data, disable the corresponding scroll bar arrow button. If all items in the list are visible, disable both scroll arrows. If the list box never includes more items that can be shown in the list box, so that the user will not need to scroll the list, you may remove the scroll bar.

When incorporating a list box into a window's design, consider supporting both command (Cut, Copy, and Paste) and direct manipulation (drag and drop) transfers for the list box. For example, if the list displays icons or values that the user can move or copy to other locations, such as another list box, support transfer operations for the list. The list view control automatically supports this; however, the system provides support for you to enable this for other list boxes as well.

For more information about disabling scroll bar arrows, see Chapter 6, "Windows."

List boxes can be classified by how they display a list and by the type of selection they support.

Single Selection List Boxes

A *single selection list box* is designed for the selection of only one item in a list. Therefore, the control provides a mutually exclusive operation similar to a group of option buttons, except that a list box can more efficiently handle a large number of items.

Define a single selection list box to be tall enough to show at least three to eight choices, as shown in Figure 7.13 — depending on the design constraints of where the list box is used. Always include a vertical scroll bar. If all the items in the list are visible, then follow the window scroll bar guidelines for disabling the scroll arrows and enlarging the scroll box to fill the scroll bar shaft.

Figure 7.13 A single selection list box

The currently selected item in a single selection list box is highlighted using selection appearance.

The user can select an entry in a single selection list box by clicking on it with mouse button 1 (for pens, tapping). This also sets the input focus on that item in the list. Because this type of list box supports only single selection, when the user chooses another entry any other selected item in the list becomes unselected. The scroll bar in the list box allows the mouse user to scroll through the list of entries, following the interaction defined for scroll bars.

For more information about the interaction techniques of scroll bars, see Chapter 6, "Windows."

The keyboard interface uses navigation keys, such as the arrow keys, HOME, END, PAGE UP, and PAGE DOWN. It also uses text keys, with matches based on timing; for example, when the user presses a text key, an entry matching that character scrolls to the top of the list and becomes selected. These keys not only navigate to an entry in the list, but also select it. If no item in the list is currently selected, when the user chooses a list navigation key, the first item in the list that corresponds to that key is selected. For example, if the user presses the DOWN ARROW key, the first entry in the list is selected, instead of navigating to the second item in the list.

If the choices in the list box represent values for the property of a selection, then make the current value visible and highlighted when displaying the list. If the list box reflects mixed values for a multiple selection, then no entry in the list should be selected.

Drop-down List Boxes

Like a single selection list box, a *drop-down list box* provides for the selection of a single item from a list of items; the difference is that the list is displayed upon demand. In its closed state, the control displays the current value for the control. The user opens the list to change the value. Figure 7.14 shows the drop-down list box in its closed and opened state.

Figure 7.14 A drop-down list box (closed and opened state)

While drop-down list boxes are an effective way to conserve space and reduce clutter, they require more user interaction for browsing and selecting an item than a single selection list box.

Make the width of a closed drop-down list box a few spaces larger than the average width of the items in its list. The open list component of the control should be tall enough to show three to eight items, following the same conventions of a single selection list box. The width of the list should be wide enough not only to display the choices in the list, but also to allow the user to drag directly into the list.

The interface for drop-down list boxes is similar to that for menus. For example, the user can press the mouse button on the current setting portion of the control or on the control's menu button to display the list. Choosing an item in the list automatically closes the list.

If the user navigates to the control using an access key, the TAB key or arrow keys, an UP ARROW or DOWN ARROW, or ALT+UP ARROW or ALT+DOWN ARROW displays the list. Arrow keys or text keys navigate and select items in the list. If the user presses ALT+UP ARROW, ALT+DOWN ARROW, a navigation key, or an access key to move to another control, the list automatically closes. When the list is closed, preserve any selection made while the list was open. The ESC key also closes the list.

If the choices in a drop-down list represent values for the property of a multiple selection and the values for that property are mixed, then display no value in the current setting component of the control.

Extended and Multiple Selection List Boxes

Although most list boxes are single selection lists, some contexts require the user to choose more than one item. *Extended selection list boxes* and *multiple selection list boxes* support this functionality.

Extended and multiple selection list boxes follow the same conventions for height and width as single selection list boxes. The height should display no less than three items and generally no more than eight, unless the size of the list varies with the size of the window. Base the width of the box on the average width of the entries in the list.

Extended selection list boxes support conventional navigation, and contiguous and disjoint selection techniques. That is, extended selection list boxes are optimized for selecting a single item or a single range, while still providing for disjoint selections.

When you want to support user selection of several disjoint entries from a list, but an extended selection list box is too cumbersome, you can define a multiple selection list box. Whereas extended selection list boxes are optimized for individual item or range selection, multiple selection list boxes are optimized for independent selection. However, because simple multiple selection list boxes are not visually distinct from extended selection list boxes, consider designing them to appear similar to a scrollable list of check boxes, as shown in Figure 7.15. This requires providing your own graphics for the items in the list (using the owner-drawn list box style). This appearance helps the user to distinguish the difference in the interface of the list box with a familiar convention. It also serves to differentiate keyboard navigation from the state of a choice. Because the check box controls are nested, you use the flat appearance style for the check boxes. You may also create this kind of a list box using a list view control.

For more information about contiguous and disjoint selection techniques, see Chapter 5, "General Interaction Techniques."

For more information about the flat appearance style for controls in a list box, see Chapter 13, "Visual Design."

Figure 7.15 A multiple selection list box

List View Controls

A *list view control* is a special extended selection list box that displays a collection of items, each item consisting of an icon and a label. List view controls can display content in four different views.

View	Description
Icon	Each item appears as a full-sized icon with a label below it. The user can drag the icons to any location within the view.
Small Icon	Each item appears as a small icon with its label to the right. The user can drag the icons to any location within the view.
List	Each item appears as a small icon with its label to the right. The icons appear in a columnar, sorted layout.
Report	Each item appears as a line in a multicolumn format with the leftmost column including the icon and its label. The subsequent columns contain information supplied by the application displaying the list view control.

The control also supports options for alignment of icons, selection of icons, sorting of icons, and editing of the icon's labels. It also supports drag and drop interaction.

Use this control where the representation of objects as icons is appropriate. In addition, provide pop-up menus on the icons displayed in the views. This provides a consistent paradigm for how the user interacts with icons elsewhere in the Windows interface.

Selection and navigation in this control work similarly to that in folder windows. For example, clicking on an icon selects it. After selecting the icon, the user can use extended selection techniques, including region selection, for contiguous or disjoint selections. Arrow keys and text keys (time-out based matching) support keyboard navigation and selection.

As an option, the standard control also supports the display of graphics that can be used to represent state information. For example, you can use this functionality to include check boxes next to items in a list.

Tree View Controls

A *tree view control* is a special list box control that displays a set of objects as an indented outline based on their logical hierarchical relationship. The control includes buttons that allow the outline to be expanded and collapsed, as shown in Figure 7.16. You can use a tree view control to display the relationship between a set of containers or other hierarchical elements.

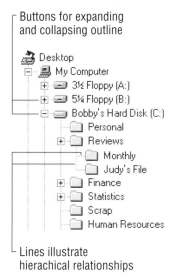

Buttons for expanding
and collapsing outline

Lines illustrate
hierachical relationships

Figure 7.16 A tree view control

You can optionally include icons with the text label of each item in the tree. Different icons can be displayed when the user expands or collapses the item in the tree. In addition, you can also include a graphic, such as a check box, that can be used to reflect state information about the item.

The control also supports drawing lines that define the hierarchical relationship of the items in the list and buttons for expanding and collapsing the outline. It is best to include these features (even though they are optional) because they make it easier for the user to interpret the outline.

Arrow keys provide keyboard support for navigation through the control; the user presses UP ARROW and DOWN ARROW to move between items and LEFT ARROW and RIGHT ARROW to move along a particular branch of the outline. Pressing RIGHT ARROW can also expand the outline at a branch if it is not currently displayed. Text keys can also be used to navigate and select items in the list, using the matching technique based on timing.

When you use this control in a dialog box, if you use the ENTER key or use double-clicking to carry out the default command for an item in the list, make certain that the default command button in your dialog box matches. For example, if you use double-clicking an entry in the outline to display the item's properties, then define a Properties button to be the default command button in the dialog box when the tree view control has the input focus.

Text Fields

Windows includes a number of controls that facilitate the display, entry, or editing of a text value. Some of these controls combine a basic text-entry field with other types of controls.

Text fields do not include labels as a part of the control. However, you can add one using a static text field. Including a label helps identify the purpose of a text field and provides a means of indicating when the field is disabled. Use sentence capitalization for multiple word labels. You can also define access keys for the text label to provide keyboard access to the text field. When using a static text label, define keyboard access to move the input focus to the text field with which the label is associated rather than the static text field itself. You can also support keyboard navigation to text fields by using the TAB key (and, optionally, arrow keys).

For more information about static text fields, see the section, "Static Text Fields," later in this chapter.

When using a text field for input of a restricted set of possible values, for example, a field where only numbers are appropriate, validate user input immediately, either by ignoring inappropriate characters or by providing feedback indicating that the value is invalid or both.

For more information about validation of input, see Chapter 8, "Secondary Windows."

Text Boxes

A *text box* (also referred to as an edit control) is a rectangular control where the user enters or edits text, as shown in Figure 7.17. It can be defined to support a single line or multiple lines of text. The outline border of the control is optional, although the border is typically included when displaying the control in a toolbar or a secondary window.

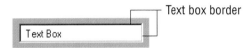

Figure 7.17 A standard text box

The standard text box control provides basic text input and editing support. Editing includes the insertion or deletion of characters and the option of text wrapping. Although individual font or paragraph properties are not supported, the entire control can support a specific font setting.

You can also use text boxes to display read-only text that is not editable, but still selectable. When setting this option with the standard control, the system automatically changes the background color of the field to indicate to the user the difference in behavior.

A text box supports standard interactive techniques for navigation and contiguous selection. Horizontal scrolling is available for single line text boxes, and horizontal and vertical scroll bars are supported for multiple line text boxes.

You can limit the number of characters accepted as input for a text box to whatever is appropriate for the context. In addition, you can support *auto-exit* for text boxes defined for fixed-length input; that is, as soon as the last character is typed in the text box, the focus moves to the next control. For example, you can define a five-character auto-exit text box to facilitate the entry of zip code, or three two-character auto-exit text boxes to support the entry of a date. Use auto-exit text boxes sparingly; the automatic shift of focus can surprise the user. They are best limited to situations involving extensive data entry.

Rich-Text Boxes

A *rich-text box*, as shown in Figure 7.18, provides the same basic text editing support as a standard text box. In addition, a rich-text box supports font properties, such as typeface, size, color, bold, and italic format, for each character and paragraph format property, such as alignment, tabs, indents, and numbering. The control also supports printing of its content and embedding of OLE objects.

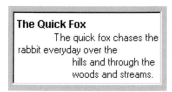

Figure 7.18 A rich-text box

Combo Boxes

A *combo box* is a control that combines a text box with a list box, as shown in Figure 7.19. This allows the user to type in an entry or choose one from the list.

Figure 7.19 A combo box

The text box and its associated list box have a dependent relationship. As text is typed into the text box, the list scrolls to the nearest match. In addition, when the user selects an item in the list box, it automatically uses that entry to replace the content of the text box and selects the text.

The interface for the control follows the conventions supported for each component, except that the UP ARROW and DOWN ARROW keys move only in the list box. LEFT ARROW and RIGHT ARROW keys operate solely in the text box.

Drop-down Combo Boxes

A *drop-down combo box*, as shown in Figure 7.20, combines the characteristics of a text box with a drop-down list box. A drop-down combo box is more compact than a regular combo box; it can be used to conserve space, but requires additional user interaction required to display the list.

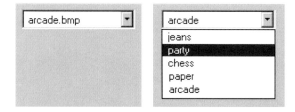

Figure 7.20 A drop-down combo box (closed and opened state)

The closed state of a drop-down combo box is similar to that of a drop-down list, except that the text box is interactive. When the user clicks the control's menu button the list is opened. Clicking the menu button a second time, choosing an item in the list, or clicking another control closes the list.

Provide a static text field label for the control and assign an access key. Use the access key so the user can navigate to the control. You can also support the TAB key or arrow keys for navigation to the control. When the control has the input focus, when the user presses the UP ARROW or DOWN ARROW or ALT+UP ARROW or ALT+DOWN ARROW key, the list is displayed.

When the control has the input focus, pressing a navigation key, such as the TAB key, or an access key or ALT+UP ARROW or ALT+DOWN ARROW to navigate to another control closes the list. When the list is closed, preserve any selection made while the list was open, unless the user presses a Cancel command button. The ESC key also closes the list.

When the list is displayed, the interdependent relationship between the text box and list is the same as it is for standard combo boxes when the user types text into the text box. When the user chooses an item in the list, the interaction is the same as for drop-down lists — the selected item becomes the entry in the text box.

Spin Boxes

Spin boxes are text boxes that accept a limited set of discrete ordered input values that make up a circular loop. A spin box is a combination of a text box and a special control that incorporates a pair of buttons (also known as an up-down control), as shown in Figure 7.21.

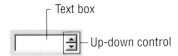

Figure 7.21 A spin box

When the user clicks on the text box or the buttons, the input focus is set to the text box component of the control. The user can type a text value directly into the control or use the buttons to increment or decrement the value. The unit of change depends on what you define the control to represent.

Use caution when using the control in situations where the meaning of the buttons may be ambiguous. For example, with numeric values, such as dates, it may not be clear whether the top button increments the date or changes to the previous date. Define the top button to increase the value by one unit and the bottom button to decrease the value by one unit. Typically, wrap around at either end of the set of values. You may need to provide some additional information to communicate how the buttons apply.

By including a static text field as a label for the spin box and defining an associated access key, you can provide direct keyboard access to the control. You can also support keyboard access using the TAB key (or, optionally, arrow keys). Once the control has the input focus, the user can change the value by pressing UP ARROW or DOWN ARROW.

You can also use a single set of spin box buttons to edit a sequence of related text boxes, for example, time as expressed in hours, minutes, and seconds. The buttons affect only the text box that currently has the input focus.

Static Text Fields

You can use static text fields to present read-only text information. Unlike read-only text box controls, the text is not selectable. However, your application can still alter read-only static text to reflect a change in state. For example, you can use static text to display the current directory path or the status information, such as page number, key states, or time and date. Figure 7.22 illustrates a static text field.

Static Text Field

Figure 7.22 A static text field

You can also use static text fields to provide labels or descriptive information for other controls. Using static text fields as labels for other controls allows you to provide access-key activation for the control with which it is associated. Make certain that the input focus moves to its associated control and not to the static field. Also remember to include a colon at the end of the text. Not only does this help communicate that the text represents the label for a control, it is also used by screen review utilities.

For more information about the layout of static text fields, see Chapter 13, "Visual Design." For information about the use of static text fields as labels and screen review utilities, see Chapter 14, "Special Design Considerations."

Shortcut Key Input Controls

A *shortcut key input control* (also known as a hot key control) is a special kind of text box to support user input of a key or key combination to define a shortcut key assignment. Use it when you provide an interface for the user to customize shortcut keys supported by your application. Because shortcut keys carry out a command directly, they provide a more efficient interface for common or frequently used actions.

The control allows you to define invalid keys or key combinations to ensure valid user input; the control will only access valid keys. You also supply a default modifier to use when the user enters an invalid key. The control displays the valid key or key combination including any modifier keys.

When the user clicks a shortcut key input control, the input focus is set to the control. Like most text boxes, the control does not include its own label, so use a static text field to provide a label and assign an appropriate access key. You can also support the TAB key to provide keyboard access to the control.

For more information about the use of shortcut keys, see Chapter 4, "Input Basics."

Other General Controls

The system also provides support for controls designed to organize other controls and controls for special types of interfaces.

Group Boxes

A *group box* is a special control you can use to organize a set of controls. A group box is a rectangular frame with an optional label that surrounds a set of controls, as shown in Figure 7.23. Group boxes generally do not directly process any input. However, you can provide navigational access to items in the group using the TAB key or by assigning an access key to the group label.

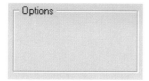

Figure 7.23 A group box

You can make the label for controls that you place in a group box relative to the group box's label. For example, a group labeled Alignment can have option buttons labeled Left, Right, and Center. Use sentence capitalization for a multiple word label.

Column Headings

Using a *column heading* control, also known as a header control, you can display a heading above columns of text or numbers. You can divide the control into two or more parts to provide headings for multiple columns, as shown in Figure 7.24. The list view control also provides support for a column heading control.

┌ Column heading

Name	Size	Type	Modified	
11-12.bmp	233KB	Bitmap Image	1/23/95 3:00 PM	
11-13.bmp	470KB	Bitmap Image	1/23/95 3:01 PM	
11-14.bmp	151KB	Bitmap Image	1/17/95 5:05 PM	
11-15.bmp	151KB	Bitmap Image	1/17/95 5:06 PM	

Column part

Figure 7.24 A column heading divided into four parts

Each header part label can include text and a graphic image. Use the graphic image to show information such as the sort direction. You can align the title elements left, right, or centered.

You can configure each part to behave like a command button to support a specific function when the user clicks on it. For example, consider supporting sorting the list by clicking on a particular header part. Also, you can support clicking on the part with button 2 to display a pop-up menu containing specific commands, such as Sort Ascending and Sort Descending.

The control also supports the user dragging on the divisions that separate header parts to set the width of each column. As an option, you can support double-clicking on a division as a shortcut to a command that applies to formatting the column, such as automatically sizing the column to the largest value in that column.

Tabs

A *tab* control is analogous to a divider in a file cabinet or notebook, as shown in Figure 7.25. You can use this control to define multiple logical pages or sections of information within the same window.

Figure 7.25 A tab control

Tab labels can include text or graphic information, or both. Usually, the control automatically sizes the tab to the size of its label; however, you can define your tabs to have a fixed width. Use the system font for the text labels of your tabs and use the same capitalization for multiple word labels as you use for menus and command buttons (in English versions, book title capitalization). If you use only graphics as your tab label, support tooltips for your tabs.

By default, a tab control displays only one row of tabs. While the control supports multiple rows or scrolling a single row of tabs, avoid these alternatives because they add complexity to the interface by making it harder to read and access a particular tab. You may want to consider alternatives such as separating the tabbed pages into sets and using another control to move between the sets. However, if scrolling the tabs seems appropriate, follow the conventions documented in this guide.

When the user clicks a tab with mouse button 1, the input focus moves and switches to that tab. When a tab has the input focus, LEFT ARROW or RIGHT ARROW keys move between tabs. CTRL+TAB also switches between tabs. Optionally, you can also define access keys for navigating between tabs. If the user switches pages using the tab, you can place the input focus on the particular control on that page. If there is no appropriate control or field in which to place the tab, leave the input focus on the tab itself.

Property Sheet Controls

A *property sheet control* provides the basic framework for defining a property sheet. It provides the common controls used in a property sheet and accepts modeless dialog box layout definitions to automatically create tabbed property pages.

The property sheet control also includes support for creating wizards. Wizards are a special form of user assistance that guide the user through a sequence of steps in a specific operation or process. When using the control as a wizard, tabs are not included, and the standard OK, Cancel, and Apply buttons are replaced with a Back, Next, or Finish button, and a Cancel button.

> For more information about property sheets, see Chapter 8, "Secondary Windows." For more information about wizards, see Chapter 12, "User Assistance."

Scroll Bars

Scroll bars are horizontal or vertical scrolling controls you can use to create scrollable areas other than on the window frame or list box where they can be automatically included. Use scroll bar controls only for supporting scrolling contexts. For contexts where you want to provide an interface for setting or adjusting values, use a slider or other control, such as a spin box. Because scroll bars are designed for scrolling information, using a scroll bar to set values may confuse the user as to the purpose or interaction of the control.

When using scroll bar controls, follow the recommended conventions for disabling the scroll bar arrows. Disable a scroll bar arrow button when the user scrolls the information to the beginning or end of the data, unless the structure permits the user to scroll beyond the data. For more information about scroll bar conventions, see Chapter 6, "Windows."

While scroll bar controls can support the input focus, avoid defining this type of interface. Instead, define the keyboard interface of your scrollable area so that it can scroll without requiring the user to move the input focus to a scroll bar. This makes your scrolling interface more consistent with the user interaction for window and list box scroll bars.

Sliders

Use a slider for setting or adjusting values on a continuous range of values, such as volume or brightness. A *slider* is a control, sometimes called a trackbar control, that consists of a bar that defines the extent or range of the adjustment, and an indicator that both shows the current value for the control and provides the means for changing the value, as shown in Figure 7.26.

Figure 7.26 A slider

Because a slider does not include its own label, use a static text field to create one. You can also add text and graphics to the control to help the user interpret the scale and range of the control.

Sliders support a number of options. You can set the slider orientation as vertical or horizontal, define the length and height of the slide indicator and the slide bar component, define the increments of the slider, and whether to display tick marks for the control.

The user moves the slide indicator by dragging to a particular location or clicking in the hot zone area of the bar, which moves the slide indicator directly to that location. To provide keyboard interaction, support the TAB key and define an access key for the static text field you use for its label. When the control has the input focus, arrow keys can be used to move the slide indicator in the respective direction represented by the key.

Progress Indicators

A *progress indicator* is a control, also known as a progress bar control, you can use to show the percentage of completion of a lengthy operation. It consists of a rectangular bar that "fills" from left to right, as shown in Figure 7.27.

Figure 7.27 A progress indicator

Because a progress indicator only displays information, it is typically noninteractive. However, it may be useful to add static text or other information to help communicate the purpose of the progress indicator. If you do include text, place it outside of the progress indicator control.

Use the control as feedback for long operations or background processes as a supplement to changing the pointer. The control provides more visual feedback to the user about the progress of the process. You can also use the control to reflect the progression of a background process, leaving the pointer's image to reflect interactivity for foreground activities. When determining whether to use a progress indicator in message box or status bar, consider how modal the operation or process the progress indicator represents.

For more information about message boxes, see Chapter 9, "Secondary Windows." For more information about status bars, see the section, "Toolbars and Status Bars," later in this chapter.

Tooltip Controls

A tooltip control provides the basic functionality of a tooltip. A tooltip is a small pop-up window that includes descriptive text displayed when the user moves the pointer over a control, as shown in Figure 7.28. The tooltip appears after a short time-out and is automatically removed when the user clicks the control or moves the pointer off the control.

For more information about the use of tooltips, see Chapter 12, "User Assistance." For more information about the use of tooltips in toolbars, see the section, "Toolbars and Status Bars," later in this chapter.

Figure 7.28 A tooltip control

The system displays a tooltip control at the lower right of the pointer, but automatically adjusts the tooltip to avoid displaying it offscreen. However for text boxes, the tooltip should be displayed centered under the control it identifies. The control supports an option to support this behavior.

Wells

A *well* is a special field similar to a group of option buttons, but facilitates user selection of graphic values such as a color, pattern, or images, as shown in Figure 7.29. This control is not currently provided by the system; however, its purpose and interaction guidelines are described here to provide a consistent interface.

Figure 7.29 A well control for selection colors

Like option buttons, use well controls for values that have two or more choices and group the choices to form a logical arrangement. When the control is interactive, use the same border pattern as a check box or text box. When the user chooses a particular value in the group, indicate the set value with a special selection border drawn around the edge of the control.

For more information about how to display well controls, see Chapter 13, "Visual Design."

Follow the same interaction techniques as option buttons. When the user clicks a well in the group the value is set to that choice. Provide a group box or static text to label the group and define an access key for that label and supporting the TAB key to navigate to a group. Use arrow keys to move between values in the group.

Pen-Specific Controls

When the user installs a pen input device, single line text boxes and combo boxes automatically display a writing tool button described in Chapter 5, "General Interaction Techniques." In addition, the system provides special controls for supporting pen input.

Boxed Edit Controls

A *boxed edit* control provides the user with a discrete area for entering characters. It looks and operates similarly to a writing tool window without some of the writing tool window's buttons, as shown in Figure 7.30.

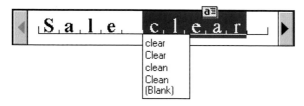

Figure 7.30 A single line boxed edit control

Both single and multiple line boxed edit controls are supported. Figure 7.31 shows a multiple line boxed edit control.

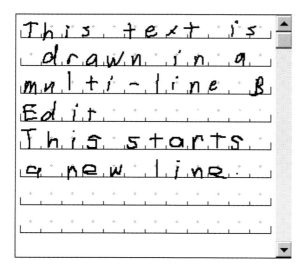

Figure 7.31 A multiple line boxed edit control

Like the writing tool window, these controls provide a pen selection handle for selection of text and an action handle for operations on a selection. They also provide easy correction by overwriting and selecting alternative choices.

Ink Edit Controls

The *ink edit* is a pen control in which the user can create and edit lines drawn as ink; no recognition occurs here. It is a drawing area designed for ink input, as shown in Figure 7.32.

Action handle

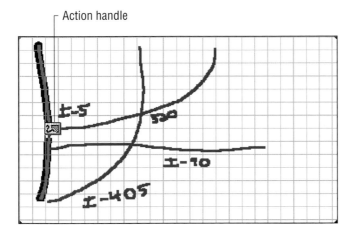

Figure 7.32 An ink edit control

The control provides support for an optional grid, optional scroll bars, and optional display of a frame border. Selection is supported using tapping to select a particular stroke; lasso-tapping is also supported for selecting single or multiple strokes. After the user makes a selection, an action handle is displayed. Tapping on the action handle displays a pop-up menu that includes commands for Undo, Cut, Copy, Paste, Delete, Use Eraser, Resize, What's This?, and Properties. Choosing the Properties command displays a property sheet associated with the selection — this allows the user to change the stroke width and color.

If you use an ink edit control, you may also want to include some controls for special functions. For example, a good addition is an Eraser button, as shown in Figure 7.33.

Figure 7.33 The eraser toolbar button

Implement the Eraser button to operate as a "spring-loaded" mode; that is, choosing the button causes the pen to act as an eraser while the user presses the pen to the screen. As soon as it is lifted, the pen reverts to its drawing mode.

Toolbars and Status Bars

Like menu bars, toolbars and status bar are special interface constructs for managing sets of controls. A *toolbar* is a panel that contains a set of controls, as shown in Figure 7.34, designed to provide quick access to specific commands or options. Specialized toolbars are sometimes called ribbons, tool boxes, and palettes.

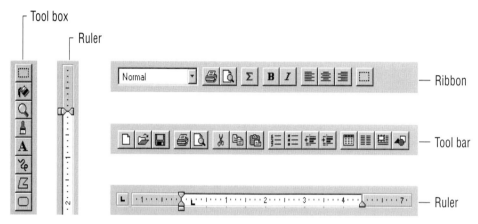

Figure 7.34 Examples of toolbars

A *status bar*, shown in Figure 7.35, is a special area within a window, typically the bottom, that displays information about the current state of what is being viewed in the window or any other contextual information, such as keyboard state. You can also use the status bar to provide descriptive messages about a selected menu or toolbar button. Like a toolbar, a status bar can contain controls; however, typically include read-only or noninteractive information.

For more information about status bar messages, see Chapter 12, "User Assistance."

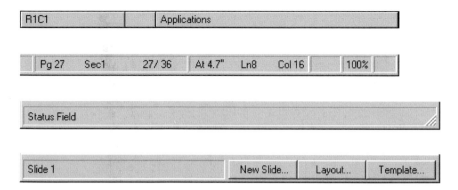

Figure 7.35 Examples of status bars

Interaction with Controls in Toolbars and Status Bars

The user can access the controls included in a toolbar or status bar with the mouse or pen through the usual means of interaction for those controls. You can provide keyboard access using either shortcut keys or access keys. If a control in a toolbar or status bar does not have a text label, access keys may not be as effective. Furthermore, if a particular access key is already in use in the primary window, it may not be available for accessing the control in the toolbar. For example, if the menu bar of the primary window is already using a particular access key, then the menu bar receives the key event.

When the user interacts with controls in a toolbar or status bar that reflect properties, any change is directly applied to the current selection. For example, if a button in a toolbar changes the property of text to bold, choosing that button immediately changes the text to bold; no further confirmation or transaction action is required. The only exception is if the control, such as a button, requires additional input from the user; then the effect may not be realized until the user provides the information for those parameters. An example of such an exception would be the selection of an object or a set of input values through a dialog box.

Always provide a tooltip for controls you include in a toolbar or status bar that do not have a text label. The system provides support for tooltips in the standard toolbar control and a tooltip control for use in other contexts.

Support for User Options

To provide maximum flexibility for users and their tasks, design your toolbars and status bars to be user configurable. Providing the user with the option to display or hide toolbars and status bars is one way to do this. You can also include options that allow the user to change or rearrange the elements included in toolbars and status bars.

Provide toolbar buttons in at least two sizes: 24 by 22 and 32 by 30 pixels. To fit a graphic label in these button sizes, design the images no larger than 16 by 16 and 24 by 24 pixels, respectively. In addition, support the user's the option to change between sizes by providing a property sheet for the toolbar (or status bar).

For more information about designing toolbar buttons, see Chapter 13, "Visual Design."

Consider also making the location of toolbars user adjustable. While toolbars are typically *docked* by default — aligned to the edge of a window or pane to which they apply — design your toolbars to be moveable so that the user can dock them along another edge or display them as a palette window.

For more information about palette windows, see Chapter 8, "Secondary Windows."

To undock a toolbar from its present location, the user must be able to click anywhere in the "blank" area of the toolbar and drag it to its new location. If the new location is within the hot zone of an edge, your application should dock the toolbar at the new edge when the user releases the mouse button. If the new location is not within the hot zone of an edge, redisplay the toolbar in a palette window. To redock the window with an edge, the user drags the window by its title bar until the pointer enters the hot zone of an edge. Return the toolbar to a docked state when the user releases the mouse button.

As the user drags the toolbar, provide visual feedback, such as a dotted outline of the toolbar. When the user moves the pointer into a hot zone of a dockable location, display the outline in its docked configuration to provide a cue to the user about what will happen when the drag operation is complete. You can also support user options such as resizing the toolbar by dragging its border or docking multiple toolbars side by side, reconfiguring their arrangement and size as necessary.

When supporting toolbar and status bar configuration options, avoid including controls whose functionality is not available elsewhere in the interface. In addition, always preserve the current position and size, and other state information, of toolbar and status bar configuration so that they can be restored to their state when the user reopens the window.

Toolbar and Status Bar Controls

The system includes toolbar and status bar controls that you can use to implement these interfaces in your applications. The toolbar control supports docking and windowing functionality. It also supports a dialog box for allowing the user to customize the toolbar. You define whether the customization features are available to the user and what features the user can customize. The system also supports creation of desktop toolbars. For more information about desktop toolbars, see Chapter 10, "Integrating with the System."

The standard status bar control also includes the option of including a size grip control for sizing the window, described in Chapter 6, "Windows." When the status bar size grip is displayed, if the window displays a size grip at the junction of the horizontal and vertical scroll bars of a window, that grip should be hidden so that it does not appear in both locations at the same time. Similarly, if the user hides the status bar, restore the size grip at the corner of the scroll bars.

Common Toolbar Buttons

Table 7.5 illustrates the button images that you can use for common functions.

Table 7.5 Common Toolbar Buttons

16 x 16 button	24 x 24 button	Function
		New
		Open
		Save
		Print
		Print Preview
		Undo
		Redo
		Cut
		Copy

(Continued)

16 x 16 button	24 x 24 button	Function
		Paste
		Delete
		Find
		Replace
		Properties
		Bold
		Italic
		Underline
		What's This? (context-sensitive Help mode)
		Show Help Topics

(Continued)

16 x 16 button	24 x 24 button	Function
		Open parent folder
		View as large icons
		View as small icons
		View as list
		View as details
		Region selection tool
		Writing tool (pen)
		Eraser tool (pen)

Use these images only for the function described. Consistent use of these common tool images allows the user to transfer their learning and skills from product to product. If you use one of the standard images for a different function, you may confuse the user. When designing your own toolbar buttons, follow the conventions supported by the standard system controls.

For more information about the design of toolbar buttons, see Chapter 13, "Visual Design."

Secondary Windows

Most primary windows require a set of secondary windows to support and supplement a user's activities in the primary windows. Secondary windows are similar to primary windows but differ in some fundamental aspects. This chapter covers the common uses of secondary windows, such as property sheets, dialog boxes, palette windows, and message boxes.

Characteristics of Secondary Windows

Although secondary windows share some characteristics with primary windows, they also differ from primary windows in their behavior and use. For example, secondary windows should not appear on the taskbar. Secondary windows obtain or display supplemental information which is often related to the objects that appear in a primary window.

Appearance and Behavior

A typical secondary window, as shown in Figure 8.1, includes a title bar and frame; a user can move it by dragging its title bar. However, a secondary window does not include Maximize and Minimize buttons because these sizing operations typically do not apply to a secondary window. A Close button can be included to dismiss the window. The title text is a label that describes the purpose of the window; the content of the label depends on the use of the window. The title bar does not include icons.

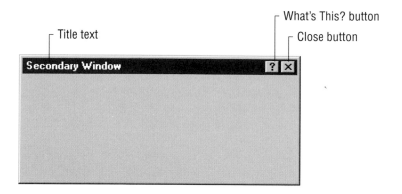

Figure 8.1 A secondary window

You can include status information in secondary windows, but avoid including a status bar control used in primary windows.

Like a primary window, a secondary window includes a pop-up menu with commands that apply to the window. A user can access the pop-up menu for the window using the same interaction techniques as primary windows.

A secondary window can also include a What's This? button in its title bar. This button allows a user to display context-sensitive Help information about the components displayed in the window.

Interaction with Other Windows

Secondary windows that are displayed because of commands chosen within a primary window depend on the state of the primary window; that is, when the primary window is closed or minimized, its secondary windows are also closed or hidden. When the user re-opens or restores the primary window, restore the secondary windows to their former positions and states. However, if opening a secondary window is the result of an action outside of the object's primary window — for example, if the user chooses the Properties command on an icon in a folder or on the desktop — then the property sheet window is independent and appears as a peer with any primary windows, though it should not appear in the taskbar.

When the user opens or switches to a secondary window, it is activated or deactivated like any other window. With the mouse or pen, the user activates a secondary window in the same way as a primary window. With the keyboard, the ALT+F6 key combination switches between a secondary window and its primary window, or other peer secondary windows that are related to its primary window. A secondary window must be modeless to support this form of switching.

When the user activates a primary window, bringing it to the top of the window Z order, all of its dependent secondary windows also come to the top, maintaining their same respective order. Similarly, activating a dependent secondary window brings its primary window and related peer windows to the top.

A dependent secondary window always appears on top of its associated primary window, layered with any related window that is a peer secondary window. When activated, the secondary window appears on top of its peers. When a peer is activated, the secondary window appears on top of its primary window, but behind the newly activated secondary window that is a peer.

You can design a secondary window to always appear at the top of its peer secondary windows. Typically, you should use this technique only for palette windows and, even in this situation, make this feature configurable by the user by providing an Always On Top property setting for the window. If you support this technique for multiple secondary windows, then the windows are managed in their own Z order within the collection of windows of which they are a part.

Avoid having a secondary window with the Always On Top behavior appear on top of another application's primary window (or any of the other application's dependent secondary windows) when the user activates a window of that application, unless the Always On Top window can also be applied to that application's windows.

When the user chooses a command that opens a secondary window, use the context of the operation to determine how to present information in that window. In property sheets, for example, set the values of the properties in that window to represent the selection.

In general, display the window in the same state as the user last accessed it. For example, an Open dialog box should preserve the current directory setting between the openings of a window. Similarly, if you use tabbed pages for navigating through information in a secondary window, display the last page the user was viewing when the user closed the window. This makes it easier for the user to repeat an operation that is associated with the window. It also provides more stability in the interface.

However, if a command or task implies or requires that the user begin a process in a particular sequence or state, such as with a wizard window, you should present the secondary window using a fixed or consistent presentation. For example, entering a record into a database may require the user to enter the data in a particular sequence. Therefore, it may be more appropriate to present the input window always displaying the first entry field.

Unfolding Secondary Windows

Except for palette windows, avoid defining secondary windows to be resizable because their purpose is to provide concise, predefined information. However, you can use an unfold button to expand a window to reveal additional options as a form of progressive disclosure. An *unfold button* is a command button with a label that includes two "greater than" characters (>>). When the user chooses the button, the secondary window expands to its alternative fixed size. As an option, you can use the button to "refold" the additional part of the window.

Cascading Secondary Windows

You can also provide the user access to additional options by including a command button that opens another secondary window. If the resulting window is independent in its operation, close the secondary window from which the user opened it and display only the new window. However, if the intent of the subsequent window is to obtain information for a field in the original secondary window, then the original should remain displayed and the dependent window should appear on top, offset slightly to the right and below the original secondary window. When using this latter method, limit the number of secondary windows to a single level to avoid creating a cluttered cascading chain of hierarchical windows.

Window Placement

When determining where to place a secondary window consider a number of factors, including the use of the window, the overall display dimensions, and the reason for the appearance of the window. In general, display a secondary window where it last appeared. If the user has not yet established a location for the window, place the window in a location that is convenient for the user to navigate to and that fully displays the window. If neither of these guidelines apply, horizontally center the secondary window within the primary window, just below the title bar, menu bar, and any docked toolbars.

Modeless vs. Modal

A secondary window can be modeless or modal. A *modeless* secondary window allows the user to interact with either the secondary window or the primary window, just as the user can switch between primary windows. It is also well suited to situations where the user wants to repeat an action — for example, finding the occurrence of a word or formatting the properties of text.

A *modal* secondary window requires the user to complete interaction within the secondary window and close it before continuing with any further interaction outside the window. A secondary window can be modal in respect to its primary window or the system. In the latter case, the user must respond and close the window before interacting with any other windows or applications.

Because modal secondary windows restrict the user's choice, use them sparingly. Limit their use to situations when additional information is required to complete a command or when it is important to prevent any further interaction until satisfying a condition. Avoid using system modal secondary windows unless your application operates as a system level utility and then only use them in severe situations — for example, when an impending fatal system error or unrecoverable condition occurs.

Default Buttons

When defining a secondary window, you can assign the ENTER key to activate a particular command button, called the *default button*, in the window. The system distinguishes the default button from other command buttons with a bold outline that appears around the button.

Define the default button to be the most likely action, such as a confirmation action or an action that applies transactions made in the secondary window. Avoid making a command button the default button if its action is irreversible or destructive. For example, in a text search and substitution window, do not use a Replace All button as the default button for the window.

You can change the default button as the user interacts with the window. For example, if the user navigates to a command button that is not the default button, the new button temporarily becomes the default. In such a case, the new default button takes on the default appearance, and the former default button loses the default appearance. Similarly, if the user moves the input focus to another control within the window that is not a command button, the original default button resumes being the default button.

The assignment of a default button is a common convention. However, when there is no appropriate button to designate as the default button or another control requires the ENTER key (for example, entering new lines in a multiline text control), you cannot define a default button for the window. In addition, when a particular control has the input focus and requires use of the ENTER key, you can temporarily have no button defined as the default. Then when the user moves the input focus out of the control, you can restore the default button.

Optionally, you can use double-clicking on single selection control, such as an option button or single selection list, as a shortcut technique to set or select the option and carry out the default button of the secondary window.

Navigation in Secondary Windows

With the mouse and pen, navigation to a particular field or control involves the user pointing to the field and clicking or tapping it. For button controls, this action also activates that button. For example, for check boxes, it toggles the check box setting and for command buttons, it carries out the command associated with that button.

The keyboard interface for navigation in secondary windows uses the TAB and SHIFT+TAB keys to move between controls, to the next and previous control, respectively. Each control has a property that determines its place in the navigation order. Set this property such that the user can move through the secondary window following the usual conventions for reading: in western countries, left-to-right and top-to-bottom, with the primary control the user interacts with located in the upper left area of the window. Order controls such that the user can progress through the window in a logical sequence, proceeding through groups of related controls. Command buttons for handling overall window transactions are usually at the end of the order sequence.

You need not provide TAB key access to every control in the window. When using static text as a label, set the control you associated with it as the appropriate navigational destination, not the static text field itself. In addition, combination controls such as combo boxes, drop-down combo boxes, and spin boxes are considered single controls for navigational purposes. Because option buttons typically appear as a group, use the TAB key for moving the input focus to the current set choice in that group, but not between individual options — use arrow keys for this purpose. For a group of check boxes, provide TAB navigation to each control because their settings are independent of each other.

Optionally, you can also use arrow keys to support keyboard navigation between controls in addition to the TAB navigation technique wherever the interface does not require those keys. For example, you can use the UP ARROW and DOWN ARROW keys to navigate between single-line text boxes or within a group of check boxes or command buttons. Always use arrow keys to navigate between option button choices and within list box controls.

You can also use access keys to provide navigation to controls within a secondary window. This allows the user to access a control by pressing and holding the ALT key and an alphanumeric key that matches the access key character designated in the label of the control.

For more information about guidelines for selecting access keys, see Chapter 4, "Input Basics."

Unmodified alphanumeric keys also support navigation if the control that currently has the input focus does not use these keys for input. For example, if the input focus is currently on a check box control and the user presses an alphanumeric key, the input focus moves to the control with the matching access key. However, if the input focus is in a text box or list box, an alphanumeric key is used as text input for that control so the user cannot use it for navigation within the window without modifying it with the ALT key.

Access keys not only allow the user to navigate to the matching control, they have the same effect as clicking the control with the mouse. For example, pressing the access key for a command button carries out the action associated with that button. To ensure the user direct access to all controls, select unique access keys within a secondary window.

You can also use access keys to support navigation to a control, but then return the input focus to the control from which the user navigated. For example, when the user presses the access key for a specific command button that modifies the content of a list box, you can return the input focus to the list box after the command has been carried out.

OK and Cancel command buttons are typically not assigned access keys if they are the primary transaction keys for a secondary window. In this case, the ENTER and ESC keys, respectively, provide access to these buttons.

Pressing ENTER always navigates to the default command button, if one exists, and invokes the action associated with that button. If there is no current default command button, then a control can use the ENTER key for its own use.

Validation of Input

Validate the user's input for a field or control in a secondary window as closely to the point of input as possible. Ideally, input is validated when it is entered for a particular field. You can either disallow the input, or use audio and visual feedback to alert the user that the data is not appropriate. You can also display a message box, particularly if the user repeatedly tries to enter invalid input. You can also reduce invalid feedback by using controls that limit selection to a specific set of choices — for example, check boxes, option buttons, drop-down lists — or preset the field with a reasonable default value.

If it is not possible to validate input at the point of entry, consider validating the input when the user navigates away from the control. If this is not feasible, then validate it when the transaction is committed, or whenever the user attempts to close the window. At that time, leave the window open and display a message; after the user dismisses the message, set the input focus to the control with the inappropriate data.

Property Sheets and Inspectors

You can display the properties of an object in the interface in a number of ways. For example, some folder views display certain file system properties of an object. The image and name of an icon on the desktop also reflect specific properties of that object. You can also use other interface conventions, such as toolbars, status bars, or even scroll bars, to reflect certain properties. The most common presentation of an object's properties is a secondary window, called a property sheet. A *property sheet* is a modeless secondary window that displays the user-accessible properties of an object — that is, viewable, but not necessarily editable properties. Display a property sheet when the user chooses the Properties command for an object.

A *property inspector* is different from a property sheet — even when a property sheet window is modeless, the window is typically modal with respect to the object for which it displays properties. If the user selects another object, the property sheet continues to display the properties of the original object. A property inspector always reflects the current selection.

Property Sheet Interface

The title bar text of the property sheet identifies the displayed object. If the object has a name, use its name and the word "Properties". If the combination of the name plus "Properties" exceeds the width of the title bar, the system truncates the name and adds an ellipsis. If the object has no name, use the object's type name. If the property sheet represents several objects, then also use the objects' type name. Where the type name cannot be applied — for example, because the selection includes heterogeneous types — substitute the word "Selection" for the type name.

Because there can be numerous properties for an object and its context, you may need to categorize and group properties as sets within the property window. There are two techniques for supporting navigation to groups of properties in a property sheet. The first is a tabbed *property page*. Each set of properties is presented within the window as a page with a tab labeled with the name of the set. Use tabbed property pages for grouping peer-related property sets, as shown in Figure 8.2.

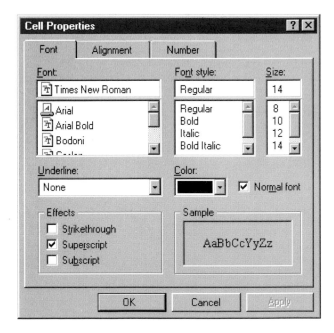

Figure 8.2 A property sheet with tabbed pages

When displaying the property sheet of an object, you can also provide access to the properties of the object's immediate context or hierarchically related properties in the property sheet. For example, if the user selects text, you may want to provide access to the properties of the paragraph of that text in the same property sheet. Similarly, if the user selects a cell in a spreadsheet, you may want to provide access to its related row and column properties in the same property sheet. Although you can support this with additional tabbed pages, better access may be facilitated using another control — such as a drop-down list — to switch between groups of tabbed pages, as shown in Figure 8.3. This technique can also be used instead of multiple rows of tabs.

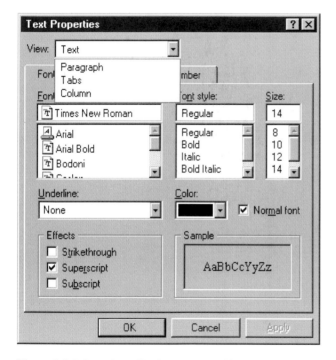

Figure 8.3 A drop-down list for access to hierarchical property sets

Where possible, make the values for properties found in property sheets transferable. You can support special transfer completion commands to enable copying only the properties of an object to another object. For example, you may want to support transferring data for text boxes or items in a list box.

For more details on transfer operations, see Chapter 5, "General Interaction Techniques."

Property Sheet Commands

Property sheets typically allow the user to change the values for a property and then apply those transactions. Include the following common command buttons for handling the application of property changes.

Command	Action
OK	Applies all pending changes and closes the property sheet window.
Apply	Applies all pending changes but leaves the property sheet window open.
Cancel	Discards any pending changes and closes the property sheet window. Does not cancel or undo changes that have already been applied.

Optionally, you can also support a Reset command for canceling pending changes without closing the window.

You can also include other command buttons in property sheets. However, the location of command buttons within the property sheet window is very important. If you place a button on a property page, apply the action associated with the button to that page. For command buttons placed outside the page but still inside the window, apply the command to the entire window.

For the common property sheet transaction buttons — OK, Cancel, and Apply — it is best to place the buttons outside the pages because users consider the pages to be just a simple grouping or navigation technique. This means that if the user makes a change on one page, the change is not applied when the user switches pages. However, if the user makes a change on the new page and then chooses the OK or Apply command buttons, both changes are applied — or, in the case of Cancel, discarded.

If your design requires groups of properties to be applied on a page-by-page basis, then place OK, Cancel, and Apply command buttons on the property pages, always in the same location on each page. When the user switches pages, any property value changes for that page are applied, or you can prompt the user with a message box whether to apply or discard the changes.

You can include a sample in a property sheet window to illustrate a property value change that affects the object when the user applies the property sheet. Where possible, include the aspect of the object that will be affected in the sample. For example, if the user selects text and displays the property sheet for the text, include part of the text selection in the property sheets sample. If displaying the actual object — or a portion of it — in the sample is not practical, use an illustration that represents the object's type.

Closing a Property Sheet

If the user closes a property sheet window, follow the same convention as closing the content view of an object, such as a document. Avoid interpreting the Close button as Cancel. If there are pending changes that have not been committed, prompt the user to apply or discard the changes through a message box, as shown in Figure 8.4. If there are no unsaved changes, just close the window.

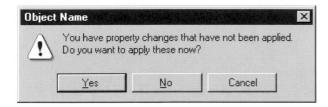

Figure 8.4 Prompting for pending property changes

If the user chooses the Yes button, the properties are applied and the message box window and the property sheet window are removed. If the user chooses the No button, the pending changes are discarded and the message box and property sheet windows are closed. Include a Cancel button in the message box, to allow the user to cancel the closing of the property sheet window.

Property Inspectors

You can also display properties of an object using a dynamic viewer or browser that reflects the properties of the current selection. Such a property window is called a property inspector. When designing a property inspector, use a toolbar or palette window, or preferably a toolbar that the user can configure as a docked toolbar or palette window, as shown in Figure 8.5.

For more information about supporting docked and windowed toolbars, see Chapter 7, "Menus, Controls, and Toolbars." For more information about palette windows, see the section, "Palette Windows," later in this chapter.

Figure 8.5 A property inspector

Apply property transactions that the user makes in a property inspector dynamically. That is, change the property value in the selected object as soon as the user makes the change in the control reflecting that property value.

Property inspectors and property sheets are not exclusive interfaces; you can include both. Each has its advantages. You can choose to display only the most common or frequently accessed properties in a property inspector and the complete set in the property sheet. You also can include multiple property inspectors, each optimized for managing certain types of objects.

As an option, you also can provide an interface for the user to change the behavior between a property sheet and a property inspector form of interaction. For example, you can provide a control on a property inspector that "locks" its view to be modal to the current object rather than tracking the selection.

Properties of a Multiple Selection

When a user selects multiple objects and requests the properties for the selection, reflect the properties of all the objects in a single property sheet or property inspector rather than opening multiple windows. Where the property values differ, display the controls associated with those values using the mixed value appearance — sometimes referred to as the indeterminate state. However, also support the display of multiple property sheets when the user displays the property sheet of the objects individually. This convention provides the user with sufficient flexibility. If your design still requires access to individual properties when the user displays the property sheet of a multiple selection, include a control such as a list box or drop-down list in the property window for switching between the properties of the objects in the set.

Properties of a Heterogeneous Selection

When a multiple selection includes different types of objects, include the intersection of the properties between the objects in the resulting property sheet. If the container of those selected objects treats the objects as if they were of a single type, the property sheet includes properties for that type only. For example, if the user selects text and an embedded object, such as a circle, and in that context an embedded object is treated as an element within the text stream, present only the text properties in the resulting property sheet.

Properties of Grouped Items

When displaying properties, do not equate a multiple selection with a grouped set of objects. A group is a stronger relationship than a simple selection, because the aggregate resulting from the grouping can itself be considered an object, potentially with its own properties and operations. Therefore, if the user requests the properties of a grouped set of items, display the properties of the group or composite object. The properties of its individual members may or may not be included, depending on what is most appropriate.

Dialog Boxes

A *dialog box* provides an exchange of information or dialog between the user and the application. Use a dialog box to obtain additional information from the user — information needed to carry out a particular command or task.

Because dialog boxes generally appear after choosing a particular menu item (including pop-up or cascading menu items) or a command button, define the title text for the dialog box window to be the name of the associated command. Do not include an ellipsis in the title text, even if the command menu name may have included one. Also, avoid including the command's menu title unless necessary to compose a reasonable title for the dialog box. For example, for a Print command on the File menu, define the dialog box window's title text as Print, not Print... or File Print. However, for an Object... command on an Insert menu, you can title the dialog box as Insert Object.

Dialog Box Commands

Like property sheets, dialog boxes commonly include OK and Cancel command buttons. Use OK to apply the values in the dialog box
and close the window. If the user chooses Cancel, the changes are
ignored and the window is closed, canceling the operation the user
chose. OK and Cancel buttons work best for dialog boxes that allow
the user to set the parameters for a particular command. Typically,
define OK to be the default command button when the dialog box
window opens.

You can include other command buttons in a dialog box in addition
to or replacing the OK and Cancel buttons. Label your command
buttons to clearly define the button's purpose, but be as concise as
possible. Long, wordy labels make it difficult for the user to easily
scan and interpret a dialog box's purpose. Follow the design conventions for command buttons.

For more information about
command buttons, see Chapter 7, "Menus, Controls, and
Toolbars," and Chapter 13, "Visual
Design."

Layout

Orient controls in dialog boxes in the direction people read. In countries where roman alphabets are used, this means left to right, top to
bottom. Locate the primary field with which the user interacts as
close to the upper left corner as possible. Follow similar guidelines
for orienting controls within a group in the dialog box.

Lay out the major command buttons either stacked along the upper
right border of the dialog box or lined up across the bottom of the
dialog box. Position the most important button — typically the default command — as the first button in the set. If you use the OK
and Cancel buttons, group them together. You can use other arrange-
ments if there is a compelling reason, such as a natural mapping
relationship. For example, it makes sense to place buttons labeled
North, South, East, and West in a compass-like layout. Similarly, a
command button that modifies or provides direct support for another
control may be grouped or placed next to those controls. However,
avoid making that button the default button because the user will
expect the default button to be in the conventional location.

Common Dialog Box Interfaces

The system provides prebuilt interfaces for many common operations. Use these interfaces where appropriate. They can save you time while providing a high degree of consistency. If you customize or provide your own interfaces, maintain consistency with the basic functionality supported in these interfaces and the guidelines for their use. For example, if you provide your own property sheet for font properties, model your design to be similar in appearance and design to the common Font dialog box. Consistent visual and operational styles will allow users to more easily transfer their knowledge and skills.

The common dialog box interfaces have been revised from the ones provided in previous releases of Microsoft Windows.

Open Dialog Box

The Open dialog box, as shown in Figure 8.6, allows the user to browse the file system, including direct browsing of the network, and includes controls to open a specified file. Use this dialog box to open files or browse for a filename, such as the File Open menu command or a Browse command button. Always set the title text to correctly reflect the command that displays the dialog box.

Figure 8.6 The Open dialog box

The system-supplied dialog box automatically handles the display of long filenames, direct manipulation transfers — such as drag and drop — and access to an icon's pop-up menus. The dialog box only displays filename extensions for files of registered types when the user selects this viewing option.

To open a file, the user selects a file from the list in the dialog box, or types a name in the File Name field and then chooses the Open command. The user can also display the pop-up menu for the file and choose its Open command. As a shortcut, double-clicking also opens the file. Choosing the Cancel button closes the window without opening the file.

When the user opens a shortcut icon, the dialog box opens the file of the object to which the link refers. In other words, the effect is the same as if the user directly opened the original file. Therefore, the name of the original file — not the name of the file link — should appear in the primary window's title bar.

The files listed in the dialog box reflect the current directory path and the type filter set in the Files Of Type drop-down list box. The list of files also includes shortcut icons in the current directory; these shortcut icons refer to file types that match the type filter.

The Look In drop-down list box displays the current directory. Displaying the list allows the user to view the hierarchy of the directory path and to navigate up the path tree. Tool buttons that are adjacent to this control provide the user with easy access to common functions. The dialog box also supports pop-up menus for the icons, the view in the list of files box, and the other controls in the window.

Set the default directory based on context. If the user opened the file directly, either from its location from the file system or using the Open dialog box, set the directory path to that location. If the user opened the application directly, then you can set the path as best fits the application. For example, an application may set up a default directory for its data files.

The user can change the directory path by selecting a different item in the Look In list, selecting a file system container (such as a folder) in the list of files, or entering a valid path in the File Name field and choosing the Open button. Choosing the Cancel button should not change the path. Always preserve the latest directory path between subsequent openings of the dialog box. If the application supports opening multiple files, such as in MDI design, set the directory path to the last file opened, not the currently active child window. However, for multiple instances of an application, maintain the path separately for each instance.

Your application determines the default Files Of Type filter for the Open dialog box. This can be based on the last file opened, the last file type set by the user, or always a specific type, based on what most appropriately fits the context of the application.

The user can change the type filter by selecting a different type in the Files Of Type drop-down list box or by typing a filter into the File Name text box and choosing the Open button. Filters can include filename extensions. For example, if the user types in *.*txt* and chooses the Open button, the list displays only files with the type extension of .TXT. Typing an extension into this text box also changes the respective type setting for the Files Of Type drop-down list box. If the application does not support that type, display the Files Of Type control with the mixed-case (indeterminate) appearance.

Include the types of files your application supports in the Files Of Type drop-down list box. For each item in the list, use a type description preferably based on the registered type names for the file types. For example, for text files, the type descriptor should be "Text Documents". You can also include an "All Files" entry to display all files in the current directory, regardless of type.

When the user types a filename into the Open dialog box and chooses the Open button, the following conventions apply:

- The string includes no extension: the system attempts to use your application's default extension or the current setting in the Files Of Type drop-down list box. For example, if the user types in *My Document*, and the application's default extension is .DOC, then the system attempts to open My Document.doc. (The extension is not displayed.) If the user changes the type setting to Text Documents (*.txt), the file specification is interpreted as My Document.txt. If using the application's default type or the type setting fails to find a matching file, the system attempts to open a file that appears in the list of files with the same name (regardless of extension). If more than one file matches, the first will be selected and the system displays a message box indicating multiple files match.

- The string includes an extension: the system first checks to see if it matches the application's default type, any other registered types, or any extension in the Files Of Type drop-down list box. If it does not match, the system attempts to open it using the application's default type or the current type setting in the Files Of Type drop-down list box. For example, Microsoft WordPad will open the file A Letter to Dr. Jones provided that: the file's type matches the .DOC extension or the current type setting, and because the characters Jones (after the period) do not constitute a registered type. If this fails, the system follows the same behavior as for a file without an extension, checking for a match among the files that appear in the list of files.

- The string includes double-quotes at the beginning and end: the system interprets the string exactly, without the quotes and without appending any extension. For example, "My Document" is interpreted as My Document.

- The system fails to find a file: when the system cannot find a file, it displays a message box indicating that the file could not be found and advises the user to check the filename and path specified. However, your application may chose to handle this condition itself.

- The string the user types in includes invalid characters for a filename: the system displays a message box advising the user of this condition.

The Open dialog only handles the matching of a name to a file. It is your application's responsibility to ensure the format of the file is valid, and if not, to appropriately notify the user.

Save As Dialog Box

The Save As dialog box, as shown in Figure 8.7, is designed to save a file using a particular name, location, type, and format. Typically, applications that support the creation of multiple user files provide this command. However, if your application maintains only private data files and automatically updates those files, this dialog box may not be appropriate.

Display this dialog box when the user chooses the Save As command or file-oriented commands with a similar function, such as the Export File command. Also display the Save As dialog box when the user chooses the Save command, and has not supplied or confirmed a filename. If you use this dialog box for other tasks that require saving files, define the title text of the dialog box to appropriately reflect that command.

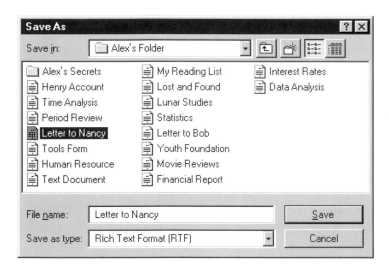

Figure 8.7 The Save As dialog box

The appearance and operation of the Save As dialog box is similar to the Open dialog box, except that the type field — the Save As Type drop-down list box — defines the default type for the saved file; it also filters the list of files displayed in the window.

To save a file, the user chooses the Save button and saves the file with the name that appears in the File Name text box. Although the user can type in a name or select a file from the list of files, your application should preset the field to the current name of the file. If the file has not been named yet, propose a name based on the registered type name for the file — for example, Text Document (2).

For more information about naming files, see Chapter 6, "Windows," and Chapter 10, "Integrating with the System."

The Save In drop-down list box indicates the immediate container in the directory path (or folder). The user can change the path using this control and the list of files box. If the file already exists, always save the file to its original location. This means that the current path for the Save As dialog box should always be set to the path where the file was last saved. If the file has never been saved, save the file with your application's default path setting or to the location defined by the user, either by typing in the path or by using the controls in the dialog box.

If the user chooses the Cancel button in the Save As dialog box, do not save the file or other settings. Restore the path to its original setting.

Include the file types supported by your application in the Save As Type drop-down list box. You may need to include a format description as part of a type name description. Although a file's format can be related to its type, a format and a type are not the same thing. For example, a bitmap file can be stored in monochrome, 16 , 256 or 24-bit color format, but the file's type is the same for all of them. Consider using the following convention for the items you include as type descriptions in the Save As Type drop-down list box.

Type Name [*Format Description*]

When the user supplies a name of the file, the Save As dialog box follows conventions similar to the Open dialog box. If the user does not include an extension, the system uses the setting in the Save As Type drop-down list or your application's default file type. If the user includes an extension, the system checks to see if the extension matches your application's default extension or a registered extension. If it does, the system saves the file as the type matching that extension. (The extension is hidden unless the system is set to display extensions.) Otherwise, the system interprets the user-supplied extension as part of the filename and appends the extension set in the Save As Type field. Note that this only means that the type (extension) is set. The format may not be correct for that type. It is your application's responsibility to write out the correct format.

Make certain you preserve the creation date for files that the user opens and saves. If your application saves files by creating a temporary file then deletes the original, renaming the temporary file to the original filename, be certain you copy the creation date from the original file. Certain system file management functionality may depend on preserving the identity of the original file.

If the user types in a filename beginning and ending with double quotes, the system saves the file without appending any extension. If the string includes a registered extension, the file appears as that type. If the user supplies a filename with invalid characters or the specified path does not exist, the system displays a message box, unless your application handles these conditions.

Here are some examples of how the system saves user supplied filenames. Examples assume .TXT as the application's default type or the Save As Type setting.

What the user types	How system saves the file	Description
My File	My File.txt	Type is based on the file type established in Save As Type drop-down list box or the application's default type.
My File.txt	My File.txt	Type must match the application's default type or a registered type.
My File for Mr. Jones	My File for Mr. Jones.txt	. Jones does not qualify as a registered type or a type included in the Save As Type drop-down list box, so the type is appended based on the Save As Type setting or the application's default type.
My File for Mr. Jones.txt	My File for Mr. Jones.txt	Type must match a registered type or a type included in the Save As Type drop-down list box.
"My File"	My File	Type will be unknown. The file is saved exactly as the string between the quotes appears.
"My File.txt"	My File.txt	No type is appended. The file is saved exactly as the string between the quotes appears.
My File.	My File..txt	Type is based on the Save As Type drop-down list box or the application's default type.
"My File."	My File.	Type will be unknown.
"My" File	File is not saved.	System (or application) displays a message box notifying the user of invalid filename.

Find and Replace Dialog Boxes

The Find and Replace dialog boxes provide controls that search for a text string specified by the user and optionally replace it with a second text string specified by the user. These dialog boxes are shown in Figure 8.8.

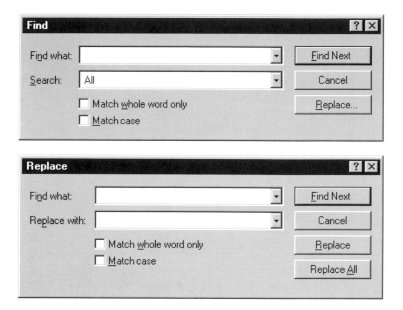

Figure 8.8 The Find and Replace dialog boxes

Print Dialog Box

The Print dialog box, shown in Figure 8.9, allows the user to select what to print, the number of copies to print, and the collation sequence for printing. It also allows the user to choose a printer and provides a command button that provides shortcut access to that printer's properties.

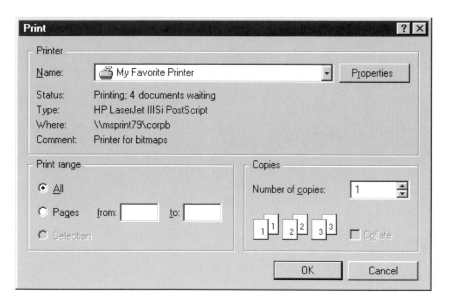

Figure 8.9 The Print dialog box

Print Setup Dialog Box

The Print Setup dialog box displays the list of available printers and provides controls for selecting a printer and setting paper orientation, size, source, and other printer properties.

Do not include this dialog box if you are creating or updating your application for Microsoft Windows 95 or later releases.

Page Setup Dialog Box

The Page Setup dialog box, as shown in Figure 8.10, provides controls for specifying properties about the page elements and layout.

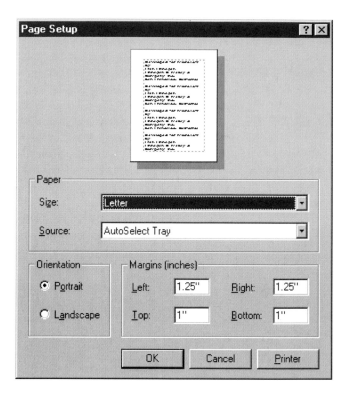

Figure 8.10 Page Setup interface used as a dialog box

In this context, page orientation refers to the orientation of the page and not the printer, which may also have these properties. Generally, the page's properties override those set by the printer, but only for the printing of that page or document.

The Printer button in the dialog box displays a supplemental dialog box (as shown in Figure 8.11) that provides information on the current default printer. Similarly to the Print dialog box, it displays the current property settings for the default printer and a button for access to the printer's property sheet.

Figure 8.11 The supplemental Printer dialog box

Font Dialog Box

This dialog box displays the available fonts and point sizes of the available fonts installed in the system. Your application can filter this list to show only the fonts applicable to your application. You can use the Font dialog box to display or set the font properties of a selection of text. Figure 8.12 shows the Font dialog box.

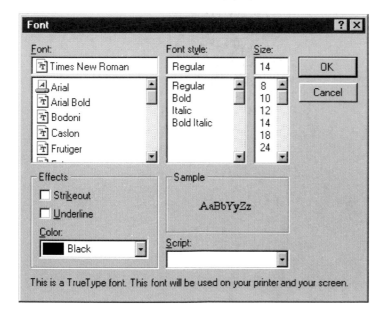

Figure 8.12 The Font dialog box

Color Dialog Box

The Color dialog box (as shown in Figure 8.13) displays the available colors and includes controls that allow the user to define custom colors. You can use this control to provide an interface for users to select colors for an object.

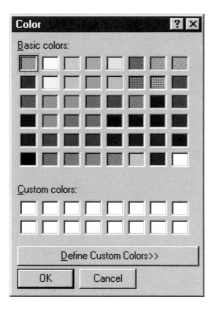

Figure 8.13 The Color dialog box (unexpanded appearance)

The Basic Colors control displays a default set of colors. The number of colors displayed here is determined by the installed display driver. The Custom Colors control allows the user to define more colors using the various color selection controls provided in the window.

Initially, you can display the dialog box as a smaller window with only the Basic Colors and Custom Colors controls and allow the user to expand the dialog box to define additional colors (as shown in Figure 8.14).

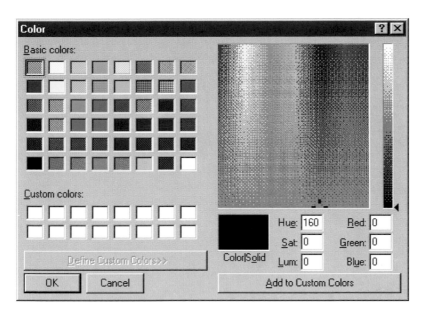

Figure 8.14 The Color dialog box (expanded)

Palette Windows

Palette windows are modeless secondary windows that present a set of controls. For example, when toolbar controls appear as a window, they appear in a palette window. Palette windows are distinguished by their visual appearance. The height of the title bar for a palette window is shorter, but it still includes only a Close button in the title area, as shown in 8.15.

For more information about toolbars and palette windows, see Chapter 7, "Menus, Controls, and Toolbars."

Figure 8.15 A palette window

Make the title text for a palette window the name of the command that displays the window or the name of the toolbar it represents. The system supplies default size and font settings for the title bar and title bar text for palette windows.

You can define palette windows as a fixed size, or, more typically, sizable by the user. Two visual cues indicate when the window is sizable: changing the pointer image to the size pointer, and placing a Size command in the window's pop-up menu. Preserve the window's size and position so the window can be restored if it, or its associated primary window, is closed.

Like other windows, the title bar and the border areas provide an access point for the window's pop-up menu. Commands on a palette window's pop-up menu can include Close, Move, Size (if sizable), Always On Top, and Properties, as shown in Figure 8.16.

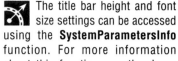 The title bar height and font size settings can be accessed using the **SystemParametersInfo** function. For more information about this function, see the documentation included in the Microsoft Win32 Software Development Kit (SDK).

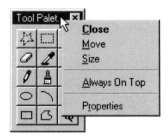

Figure 8.16 A pop-up menu for a palette window

Including the Always On Top command or property in the window's property sheet allows the user to configure the palette window to always stay at the top of the Z order of the window set of which it is a part. Turning off this option keeps the palette window within its set of related windows, but allows the user to have other windows of the set appear on top of the palette window. This feature allows the user to configure preferred access to the palette window.

You can also include a Properties command on the palette window's pop-up menu to provide an interface for allowing the user to edit properties of the window, such as the Always On Top property, or a means of customizing the content of the palette window.

Message Boxes

A message box is a secondary window that displays a message; information about a particular situation or condition. Messages are an important part of the interface for any software product. Messages that are too generic or poorly written frustrate users, increase support costs, and ultimately reflect on the quality of the product. Therefore, it is worthwhile to design effective message boxes.

However, it is even better to avoid creating situations that require you to display a message. For example, if there may be insufficient disk space to perform an operation, rather than assuming that you will display a message box, check before the user attempts the operation and disable the command.

Title Bar Text

Use the title bar of a message box to appropriately identify the context in which the message is displayed — usually the name of the object. For example, if the message results from editing a document, the title text is the name of that document, optionally followed by the application name. If the message results from a nondocument object, then use the application name. Providing an appropriate identifier for the message is particularly important in the Windows multitasking environment, because message boxes might not always be the result of current user interaction. In addition, because OLE technology allows objects to be embedded, different application code may be running when the user activates the object for visual editing. Therefore, the title bar text of a message box provides an important role in communicating the source of a message. Do not use descriptive text for message box title text such as "warning" or "caution." The message symbol conveys the nature of the message. Never use the word "error" in the title text.

Message Box Types

Message boxes typically include a graphical symbol that indicates what kind of message is being presented. Most messages can be classified in one of the categories shown in Table 8.1.

Table 8.1 Message Types and Associated Symbols

Symbol	Message type	Description
	Information	Provides information about the results of a command. Offers no user choices; the user acknowledges the message by clicking the OK button.

	Warning	Alerts the user to a condition or situation that requires the user's decision and input before proceeding, such as an impending action with potentially destructive, irreversible consequences. The message can be in the form of a question — for example, "Save changes to MyReport?".

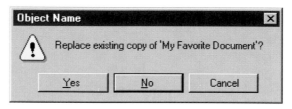

	Critical	Informs the user of a serious problem that requires intervention or correction before work can continue.

The system also includes a question mark message symbol. This message symbol (as shown in Figure 8.17) was used in earlier versions of Windows for cautionary messages that were phrased as a question.

Figure 8. 17 Inappropriate message symbol

However, the message icon is no longer recommended as it does not clearly represent a type of message and the phrasing of a message as a question could apply to any message type. In addition, users can confuse the message symbol question mark with Help information. Therefore, do not use this question mark message symbol in your message boxes. The system continues to support its inclusion only for backward compatibility.

You can include your own graphics or animation in message boxes. However, limit your use of these types of message boxes and avoid defining new graphics to replace the symbols for the existing standard types.

Because a message box disrupts the user's current task, it is best to display a message box only when the window of the application displaying the message box is active. If it is not active, then the application uses its entry in the taskbar to alert the user. Once the user activates the application, the message box can be displayed. Display only one message box for a specific condition. Displaying a sequential set of message boxes tends to confuse users.

For more information about how to use the taskbar to notify the user when the application may not be active, see Chapter 10, "Integrating with the System."

You can also use message boxes to provide information or status without requiring direct user interaction to dismiss them. For example, message boxes that provide a visual representation of the progress of a particular process automatically disappear when the process is complete, as shown in Figure 8.18. Similarly, product start-up windows that identify the product name and copyright information when the application starts can be automatically removed once the application has loaded. In these situations, you do not need to include a message symbol. Use this technique only for noncritical, informational messages, as some users may not be able to read the message within the short time it is displayed.

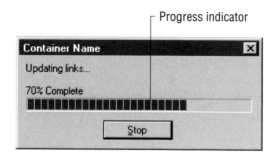

Figure 8.18 A progress message box

Command Buttons in Message Boxes

Typically, message boxes contain only command buttons as the appropriate responses or choices offered to the user. Designate the most frequent or least destructive option as the default command button. Command buttons allow the message box interaction to be simple and efficient. If you need to add other types of controls, always consider the potential increase in complexity.

If a message requires no choices to be made but only acknowledgment, use an OK button — and, optionally, a Help button. If the message requires the user to make a choice, include a command button for each option. The clearest way to present the choices is to state the message in the form of a question and provide a button for each response. When possible, phrase the question to permit Yes or No answers, represented by Yes and No command buttons. If these choices are too ambiguous, label the command buttons with the names of specific actions — for example, "Save" and "Delete."

You can include command buttons in a message box that correct the action that caused the message box to be displayed. For example, if the message box indicates that the user must switch to another application window to take corrective action, you can include a button that switches the user to that application window. Be sure, however, to make the result of any such button's action very clear.

Some situations may require offering the user not only a choice between performing or not performing an action, but an opportunity to cancel the process altogether. In such situations, use a Cancel button, as shown in Figure 8.19. Be sure, however, to make the result of any such button's action very clear.

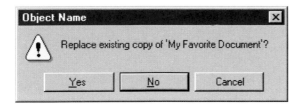

Figure 8.19 Message box choices

When using Cancel as a command button in a message box, remember that to users, Cancel implies restoring the state of the process or task that started the message. If you use Cancel to interrupt a process and the state cannot be restored, use Stop instead.

Message Box Text

The message text you include in a message box should be clear, concise, and in terms that the user understands. This usually means using no technical jargon or system-oriented information.

In addition, observe the following guidelines for your message text:

- State the problem, its probable cause (if possible), and what the user can do about it — no matter how obvious the solution may seem to be. For example, instead of "Insufficient disk space," use "'Sample Document' could not be saved, because the disk is full. Try saving to another disk or freeing up space on this disk."

- Consider making the solution an option offered in the message. For example, instead of "One or more of your lines are too long. The text can only be a maximum of 60 characters wide," you might say, "One or more of your lines are too long. Text can be a maximum of 60 characters in Portrait mode or 90 characters wide in Landscape. Do you want to switch to Landscape mode now?" Offer Yes and No as the choices.

- Avoid using unnecessary technical terminology and overly complex sentences. For example, "picture" can be understood in context, whereas "picture metafile" is a rather technical concept.

- Avoid phrasing that blames the user or implies user error. For example, use "Cannot find filename" instead of "Filename error." Avoid the word "error" altogether.

- Make messages as specific as possible. Avoid mapping more than two or three conditions to a single message. For example, there may be several reasons why a file cannot be opened; provide a specific message for each condition.

- Avoid relying on default system-supplied messages, such as MS-DOS® extended error messages and Kernel INT 24 messages; instead, supply your own specific messages wherever possible.

- Be brief, but complete. Provide only as much background information as necessary. A good rule of thumb is to limit the message to two or three lines. If further explanation is necessary, provide this through a command button that opens a Help window.

You may also include a message identification number as part of the message text for each message for support purposes. However, to avoid interrupting the user's ability to quickly read a message, place such a designation at the end of the message text and not in the title bar text.

Pop-up Windows

Use pop-up windows to display additional information when an abbreviated form of the information is the main presentation. For example, you could use a pop-up window to display the full path for a field or control, when an entire path cannot be presented and must be abbreviated. Pop-up windows are also used to provide context-sensitive Help information, as shown in Figure 8.20.

For more information about using pop-up windows for Help information, see Chapter 12, "User Assistance."

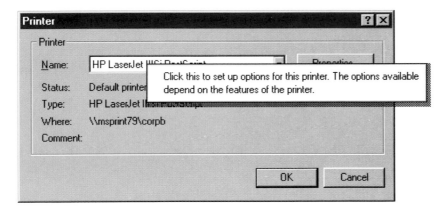

Figure 8.20 A context-sensitive Help pop-up window

Tooltips are another example of a pop-up window used to display contextual information, by providing the names for controls in toolbars. The writing tool is also another example of the use of a pop-up window.

How pop-up windows are displayed depends on their use, but the typical means is by the user either pointing or clicking with mouse button 1 (for pens, tapping), or an explicit command. If you use pointing as the technique to display a pop-up window, display the window after a time-out. The system automatically handles time-outs if you use the standard tooltip controls. If you are providing your own implementation, you can use the current double-click speed setting as a metric for displaying and removing the pop-up window.

If you use clicking to display a pop-up window, change the pointer as feedback to the user indicating that the pop-up window exists and requires a click. From the keyboard, you can use the Select key (SPACEBAR) to open and close the window.

Part III

Design
Specifications
and Guidelines

Window Management

User tasks can often involve working with different types of information, contained in more than one window or view. There are different techniques that you can use to manage a set of windows or views. This chapter covers some common techniques and the factors to consider for selecting a particular model.

Single Document Window Interface

In many cases, the interface of an object or application can be expressed using a single primary window with a set of supplemental secondary windows. The desktop and taskbar provide management of primary windows. Opening a window puts it at the top of the Z order and places an entry on the taskbar, making it easier for users to switch between windows without having to shuffle or reposition them.

By supporting a single instance model where you activate an existing window (within the same desktop) if the user reopens the object, you make single primary windows more manageable, and reduce the potential confusion for the user. This also provides a data-centered, one-to-one relationship between an object and its window.

In addition, Microsoft OLE supports the creation of compound documents or other types of information containers. Using these constructs, the user can assemble a set of different types of objects for a specific purpose within a single primary window, eliminating the necessity of displaying or editing information in separate windows.

For more information about OLE, see Chapter 11, "Working with OLE Embedded and OLE Linked Objects."

Some types of objects, such as device objects, may not even require a primary window and use only a secondary window for viewing and editing their properties. When this occurs, do not include the Open command in the menu for the object; instead, replace it with a Properties command, defined as the object's default command.

It is also possible for an object to have no windows; an icon is its sole representation. In this very rare case, make certain that you provide an adequate set of menu commands to allow a user to control its activity.

Multiple Document Interface

For some tasks, the taskbar may not be sufficient for managing a set of related windows; for example, it can be more effective to present multiple views of the same data or multiple views of related data in windows that share interface elements. You can use *multiple document interface* (MDI) for this kind of situation.

The MDI technique uses a single primary window, called a *parent window*, to visually contain a set of related *document* or *child windows*, as shown in Figure 9.1. Each child window is essentially a primary window, but is constrained to appear only within the parent window instead of on the desktop. The parent window also provides a visual and operational framework for its child windows. For example, child windows typically share the menu bar of the parent window and can also share other parts of the parent's interface, such as a toolbar or status bar. You can change these to reflect the commands and attributes of the active child window.

Figure 9.1 An MDI parent and child window

Secondary windows — such as dialog boxes, message boxes, or property sheets — displayed as a result of interaction within the MDI parent or child, are typically not contained or clipped by the parent window. These windows should be activated and displayed following the common conventions for secondary windows associated with a primary window, even if they apply to individual child windows.

For more information about the interaction between a primary window and its secondary windows, see Chapter 6, "Windows," and Chapter 8, "Secondary Windows."

For the title bar of an MDI parent window, include the icon and name of the application or the object that represents the work area displayed in the parent window. For the title bar of a child window, include the icon representing the document or data file type and its filename. Also support pop-up menus for the window and the title bar icon for both the parent window and any child windows.

Opening and Closing MDI Windows

The user starts an MDI application either by directly opening the application or by opening a document (or data file) of the type supported by the MDI application. If directly opening an MDI document, the MDI parent window opens first and then the child window for the file opens within it. To support the user opening other documents associated with the application, include an interface, such as an Open dialog box.

When the user directly opens an MDI document outside the interface of its MDI parent window — for example, by double-clicking the file — if the parent window for the application is already open, open another instance of the MDI parent window rather than the document's window in the existing MDI parent window. Although the opening of the child window within the existing parent window can be more efficient, the opening of the new window can disrupt the task environment already set up in that parent window. For example, if the newly opened file is a macro, opening it in the opened parent window could inadvertently affect other documents open in that window. If the user wishes to open a file as part of the set in a particular parent MDI window, the commands within that window provide that support.

Because MDI child windows are primary windows, support closing them following the same conventions for primary windows by including a Close button in their title bars and a Close command in their pop-up menu for the windows. When the user closes a child window, any unsaved changes are processed following these common conventions for primary windows. Do not close its parent window, unless the parent window does not provide context or operations without an open child window.

When the user closes the parent window, close all of its child windows. Where possible, preserve the state of a child window, such as its size and position within the parent window; restore the state when the user reopens the file.

Moving and Sizing MDI Windows

MDI allows the user to move or hide the child windows as a set by moving or minimizing the parent window. When the user moves an MDI parent window, maintain the relative positions of the open child windows within the parent window. Moving a child window constrains it to its parent window; in some cases, the size of the parent window's interior area may result in clipping a child window. Optionally, you can support automatic resizing of the parent window when the user moves or resizes a child window either toward or away from the edge of the parent window.

The recommended visual appearance of a minimized child window in Microsoft Windows is now that of a window that has been sized down to display only part of its title area and its border. This avoids potential confusion between minimized child window icons and icons that represent objects.

Although an MDI parent window minimizes as an entry on the taskbar, MDI child windows minimize within their parent window, as shown in Figure 9.2.

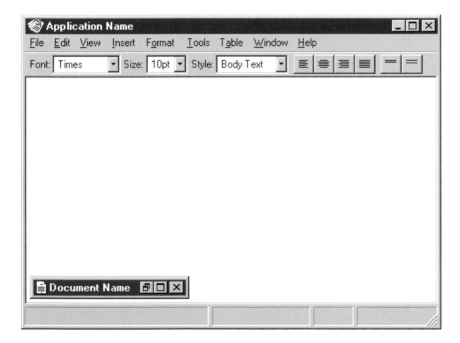

Figure 9.2 A minimized MDI child window

When the user maximizes an MDI parent window, expand the window to its maximum size, like any other primary window. When the user maximizes an MDI child window, also expand it to its maximum size. When this size exceeds the interior of its parent window, merge the child window with its parent window. The child window's title bar icon, Restore button, Close button, and Minimize button (if supported) are placed in the menu bar of the parent window in the same relative position as in the title bar of the child window, as shown in Figure 9.3. Append the child window title text to the parent window's title text.

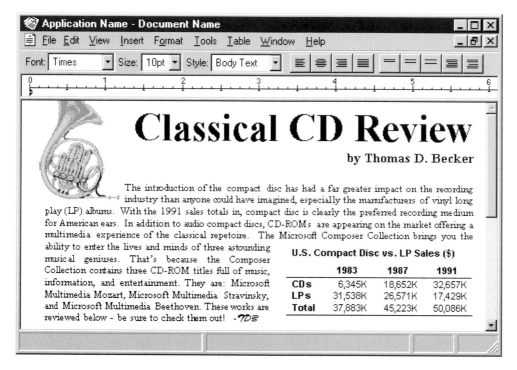

Figure 9.3 A maximized MDI child window

If the user maximizes one child window and it merges with the parent window and then switches to another, display that window as maximized. Similarly, when the user restores one child window from its maximized state, restore all other child windows to their previous sizes.

Switching Between MDI Child Windows

Apply the same common mouse conventions for activating and switching between primary windows for MDI child windows. CTRL+F6 and CTRL+TAB (and SHIFT+ modified combinations to cycle backwards) are the recommended keyboard shortcuts for switching between child windows. In addition, include a Window menu on the menu bar of the parent window with commands for switching between child windows and managing or arranging the windows within the MDI parent window — such as Tile or Cascade.

When the user switches child windows, you can change the interface of the parent window — such as its menu bar, toolbar, or status bar — to appropriately reflect the commands that apply to that child window. However, provide as much consistency as possible, keeping constant any menus that represent the document files and control the application or overall parent window environment, such as the File menu or the Window menu.

MDI Alternatives

MDI does have its limitations. MDI reinforces the visibility of the application as the primary focus for the user. Although the user can start an MDI application by directly opening one of its document or data files, to work with multiple documents within the same MDI parent window, the user uses the application's interface for opening those documents.

When the user opens multiple files within the same MDI parent window, the storage relationship between the child windows and the objects being viewed in those windows is not consistent. That is, although the parent window provides visual containment for a set of child windows, it does not provide containment for the files those windows represent. This makes the relationship between the files and their windows more abstract, making MDI more challenging for beginning users to learn.

Similarly, because the MDI parent window does not actually contain the objects opened within it, MDI cannot support an effective design for persistence. When the user closes the parent window and then reopens it, the context cannot be restored because the application state must be maintained independently from that of the files last opened in it.

MDI can make some aspects of the OLE interface unintentionally more complex. For example, if the user opens a text document in an MDI application and then opens a worksheet embedded in that text document, the task relationship and window management breaks down, because the embedded worksheet's window does not appear in the same MDI parent window.

Finally, the MDI technique of managing windows by confining child windows to the parent window can be inconvenient or inappropriate for some tasks, such as designing with window or form layout tools. Similarly, the nested nature of child windows may make it difficult for the user to differentiate between a child window in a parent window versus a primary window that is a peer with the parent window, but positioned on top.

Although MDI provides useful conventions for managing a set of related windows, it is not the only means of supporting task management. Some of its window management techniques can be applied in some alternative designs. The following — workspaces, workbooks, and projects — are examples of some possible design alternatives. They present a single window design model, but in such a way that preserves some of the window and task management benefits found in MDI.

Although these examples suggest a form of containment of multiple objects, you can also apply some of these designs to display multiple views of the same data. Similarly, these alternatives may provide greater flexibility with respect to the types of objects that they contain. However, as with any container, you can define your implementation to hold and manage only certain types of objects. For example, an appointment book and an index card file are both containers that organize a set of information but may differ in the way they display that information and the type of information they manage. Whether you define a container to hold the same or different types of objects depends on the design and purpose of the container.

The following examples illustrate alternatives of data-centered window or task management. They are not exclusive of other possible designs. They are intended only as suggestive possibilities, rather than standard constructs. As a result, the system does not include these constructs and provides no explicit programming interfaces. In addition, some specific details are left to you to define.

Workspaces

A *workspace* shares many of the characteristics of MDI, including the association and management of a set of related windows within a parent window, and the sharing of the parent window's interface elements, such as menus, toolbars, and status bar. Figure 9.4 shows an example of a workspace.

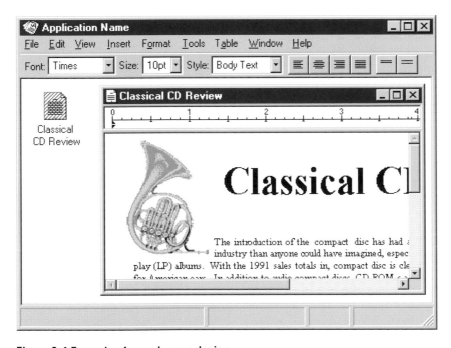

Figure 9.4 Example of a workspace design

Workspaces as a Container

Based on the metaphor of a work area, like a table, desktop, or office, a workspace differs from an MDI by including the concept of containment. Objects contained or stored in the workspace can be presented in the same way files appear in folders. However, objects within a workspace open as child windows within the workspace parent window. In this way, a workspace's behavior is similar to that of the desktop, except that a workspace itself is an object that can be displayed as an icon and opened into a window. To have an object's window appear in the workspace, the object must reside there.

The actual storage mechanism you use depends on the type of container you implement. The content of the parent window can represent a single file, or you can devise your own mechanism to map the content into the file system. Consider using OLE in your implementation to facilitate interaction between your workspace, the shell, and other applications. For example, you may want to support the user moving objects from the workspace into other containers, such as the desktop and folders. However, if you do, when the user opens the object, it should appear in its own window, not the workspace window — with its interface elements, such as a menu bar — also appearing within its own window.

The workspace is an object itself and therefore you should define its specific commands and properties. You can also include commands for creating new objects within the workspace and, optionally, a Save All command that saves the state of all the objects opened in the workspace.

Workspaces for Task Grouping

Because a workspace visually contains and constrains the icons and windows of the objects placed in it, you can define workspaces to allow the user to organize a set of objects for particular tasks. Like MDI, this makes it easy for the user to move or switch to a set of related windows as a set.

Also similar to MDI, the child windows of objects opened in the workspace can share the interface of the parent window. For example, if the workspace includes a menu bar, the windows of any objects contained within the workspace share the menu bar. If the workspace does not have a menu bar, or if you provide an option for the user to hide the menu bar, the menu bar should appear within the document's child window. The parent window can also provide a framework for sharing toolbars and status bars.

Window Management in a Workspace

A workspace manages windows using the same conventions as MDI. When a workspace closes, all the windows within it close. You should retain the state of these windows, for example, their size and position within the workspace, so you can restore them when the user reopens the workspace.

Like most primary windows, when the user minimizes the workspace window, the window disappears from the screen but its entry remains on the taskbar. Minimized windows of icons opened within the workspace have the same behavior and appearance as minimized MDI child windows. Similarly, maximizing a window within a workspace can follow the MDI technique: if the window's maximized size exceeds the size of the workspace window, the child window merges with the workspace window and its title bar icon and window buttons appear in the menu bar of the workspace window.

A workspace should provide a means of navigating between the child windows within a workspace, such as listing the open child windows on a Window drop-down menu and on the pop-up menu for the parent window, in addition to direct window activation.

Workbooks

A *workbook* is another alternative for managing a set of views — one which uses the metaphor of a book or notebook instead of a work area. Within the workbook, you present views of objects as sections within the workbook's primary window rather than in individual child windows. Figure 9.5 illustrates one possible way of presenting a workbook.

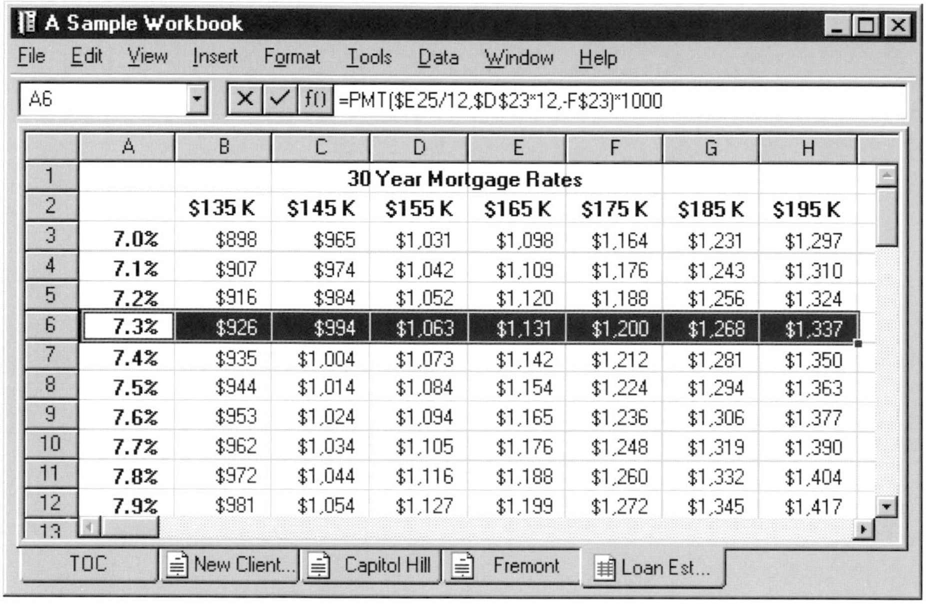

Figure 9.5 Example of a workbook design

For a workbook, you can use tabs to serve as a navigational interface to move between different sections. Locate the tabs as best fits the content and organization of the information you present. Each section represents a view of data, which could be an individual document. Unlike a folder or workspace, a workbook may be better suited for ordered content; that is, where the order of the sections has significance. In addition, you can optionally include a special section listing the content of the workbook, like a table of contents. This view can also be included as part of the navigational interface for the workbook.

A workbook shares an interface similar to an MDI parent window with all of its child windows maximized. The sections can share the parent window's interface elements, such as the menu bar and status bar. When the user switches sections within the workbook, you can change the menu bar so that it applies to the current object. When the user closes a workbook, follow the common conventions for handling unsaved edits or unapplied transactions when any primary window closes.

Consider supporting OLE to support transfer operations so the user can move, copy, and link objects into the workbook. You may also want to provide an Insert command that allows the user to create new objects, including a new tabbed section in the workbook. You can also include a Save All command, which saves any uncommitted changes or prompts the user to save or discard those changes.

Projects

A *project* is another window management technique that provides for association of a set of objects and their windows, but without visually containing the windows. A project is similar to a folder in that the icons contained within it can be opened into windows that are peers with the parent window. As a result, each child window can also have its own entry on the taskbar. Unlike a folder, a project provides window management for the windows of its content. For example, when the user opens a document in a folder and then closes the folder, it has no effect on the window of the opened document. However, when the user closes a project window, all the child windows of objects contained in the project also close. In addition, when the user opens a project window, this action should restore the windows of objects contained within it to their previous state.

Similarly, to facilitate window management, when the user minimizes a project window, you may want to minimize any windows of the objects the project contains. Taskbar entries for these windows remain. Allow the user to restore a specific child window without restoring the project window or other windows within the project. In addition, support the user independently minimizing any child window without affecting the project window. Figure 9.6 shows an example of a project.

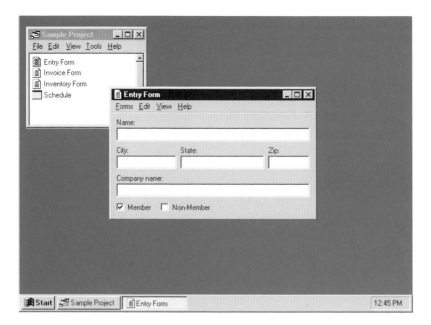

Figure 9.6 Example of a project design

The windows of objects stored in the project do not share the menu bar or other areas within the project window. Instead, include the interface elements for each object in its own window. However, you can provide toolbar palette windows that can be shared among the windows of the objects in the project.

Just as in workspaces and workbooks, a project should include commands for creating new objects within the project, for transferring objects in and out of the project, and for saving any changes for the objects stored in the project. In addition, a project should include commands and properties for the project object itself.

Selecting a Window Model

Deciding how to present your application's collection of related tasks or processes requires considering a number of design factors: your intended audience and their skill level, the presentation of object or task, effective use of the space on the display, and evolution towards data-centered design.

Presentation of Object or Task

What an object represents and how it is used and relates to other objects influences how you present its view. Simple objects that are self-contained may not require a primary window, or only require a set of menu commands and a property sheet to edit their properties.

An object with user-accessible content in addition to properties, such as a document, only requires a primary window. The single document window interface can be sufficient when the object's primary presentation or use is as a single unit, even when containing different types. Alternative views can easily be supported with controls that allow the user to change the view. Simple, simultaneous views of the same data can even be supported by splitting the window into panes. The system uses the single document window style of interface for most of the components it includes, such as folders.

MDI, workspaces, workbooks, and projects are more effective when the composition of an object requires multiple views or the nature of the user's tasks requires views of multiple objects. These constructs provide a grouping and focus for a set of specific user activities, within the larger environment of the desktop.

MDI is best suited for viewing homogeneous types. The user cannot mix different objects within the same MDI parent windows unless you supply them as part of the application. On the other hand, you can use MDI to support simultaneous views of different objects.

Use a workbook when you want to optimize quick user navigation of multiple views. A workbook simplifies the task by eliminating the management of child windows, but in doing so, it limits the user's ability to see simultaneous views.

Workspaces and projects provide flexibility for viewing and mixing of objects and their windows. Use a workspace as you would MDI, when you want to clearly segregate the icons and their windows used in a task. Use a project when you do not want to constrain any child windows.

A project provides the greatest flexibility for user placement and arrangement of its windows. It does so, however, at the expense of an increase in complexity because it may be more difficult for a user to differentiate the child window of a project from windows of other applications.

Display Layout

Consider the requirements for layout of information. For very high resolution displays, the use of menu bars, toolbars, and status bars poses little problem for providing adequate display of the information being viewed in a window. Similarly, the appearance of these common interface elements in each window has little impact on the overall presentation. At VGA resolution, however, this can be an issue. The interface components for a set of windows should not so dominate the user's work area that the user cannot easily view or manipulate their data.

MDI, workspaces, workbooks, and projects all allow some interface components to be shared among multiple views. Within shared elements, it must be clear when a particular interface component applies. Although you can automatically switch the content of those components, consider what functions are common across views or child windows and present them in a consistent way to provide for stability in the interface. For example, if multiple views share a Print toolbar button, present that button in a consistent location. If the button's placement constantly shifts when the user switches the view, the user's efficiency in performing the task may decrease. Note that shared interfaces may make user customization of interface components more complex because you need to indicate whether the customization applies to the current context or across all views.

Regardless of the window model you chose, always consider allowing users to determine which interface components they wish to have displayed. Doing so means that you also need to consider how to make basic functionality available if the user hides a particular component. For example, pop-up menus can often supplement the interface when the user hides the menu bar.

Data-Centered Design

A single document window interface provides the best support for a simple, data-centered design and may be the easiest for users to learn; MDI supports a more conventional application-centered design. It is best suited to multiple views of the same data or contexts where the application does not represent views of user data. You can use workspaces, workbooks, and projects to provide single document window interfaces while preserving some of the management techniques provided by MDI.

Combination of Alternatives

Single document window interfaces, MDIs, workspaces, workbooks, and projects are not exclusive design techniques. It may be advantageous to combine these techniques. For example, documents can be presented within a workspace. You can also design workbooks and projects as objects within a workspace. In similar fashion, a project might contain a workbook as one of its objects.

Integrating with the System

Users appreciate seamless integration between the system and their applications. This chapter covers information about integrating your software with the system and how to extend its features, including using the registry to store information about your application, installing your application, using appropriate naming conventions, and supporting shell features, such as the taskbar, Control Panel, and Recycle Bin.

This chapter is only intended to provide an overview. Details required for some conventions go beyond the scope of this guide. For information about these conventions, see the documentation included in the Microsoft Win32 Software Development Kit (SDK). In addition, some of these conventions and features may not be supported in all releases. For more information about specific releases, see Appendix D, "Supporting Specific Versions of Windows."

The Registry

Windows provides a special repository called the *registry* that serves as a central configuration database for user-, application-, and computer-specific information. Although the registry is not intended for direct user access, the information placed in it affects your application's user interface. Registered information determines the icons, commands, and other features displayed for files. The registry also makes it easier to manage and support configuration information used by your application and eliminates redundant information stored in different locations.

The registry is a hierarchical structure. Each node in the tree is called a key. Each key can contain subkeys and data entries called values. Key names cannot include a space, backslash (\), or wildcard character (* or ?). In the **HKEY_CLASSES_ROOT** key, names beginning with a period (**.**) are reserved for special syntax (filename extensions), but you can include a period within a key name. The name of a subkey must be unique with respect to its parent key. Key names are not localized into other languages, although their values may be.

A key can have any number of values. A value entry has three parts: the name of the value, its data type, and the value itself. Value entries larger than 2048 bytes should be stored as files with their filenames stored in the registry.

When the user installs your application, register keys for where application data is stored, for filename extensions, icons, shell commands, OLE registration data, and for any special extensions. To register your application's information, you can create a registration file and use the Registry Editor to merge this file into the system registry. You can also use other utilities that support this function, or use the system-supplied registry functions to access or manipulate registry data.

The example registry entries in this chapter represent only the hierarchical relationship of the keys. For more information about the registry and registry file formats, see the documentation included in the Win32 SDK.

To use memory most efficiently, the system stores only the registry entries that have been installed and that are required for operation. Applications should never fail to write a registry entry because it is not already installed. To ensure this happens, use registry creation functions when adding an entry.

Registering Application State Information

Use the registry to store state information for your application. Typically, the data you store here will be information you may have stored in initialization (.INI) files in previous releases of Windows. Create subkeys under the **Software** subkey in the **HKEY_LOCAL_MACHINE** and **HKEY_CURRENT_USER** keys that include information about your application.

HKEY_LOCAL_MACHINE
    Software
        CompanyName
            ProductName
                Version
...
HKEY_CURRENT_USER
    Software
        CompanyName
            ProductName
                Version

Use your application's **HKEY_LOCAL_MACHINE** entry as the location to store computer-specific data and the **HKEY_CURRENT _USER** entry to store user-specific data. The latter key allows you to store settings to tailor your application for individual users working with the same computer. Under your application's subkey, you can define your own structure for the information. Although the system still supports initialization files for backward compatibility, use the registry wherever possible to store your application's state information instead.

Use these keys to save your application's state whenever appropriate, such as when the user closes its primary window. In most cases, it is best to restore a window to its previous state when the user reopens it.

When the user shuts down the system with your application's window open, you may optionally store information in the registry so that the application's state is restored when the user starts up Windows. (The system does this for folders.) To have your application's state restored, store your window and application state information under its registry entries when the system notifies your application that it is shutting down. Store the state information in your application's entries under **HKEY_CURRENT_USER** and add a value name–value pair to the **RunOnce** subkey that corresponds to your application. When the user restarts the system, it runs the command line you supply. Once your application runs, you can use the data you stored to restore its state.

HKEY_CURRENT_USER
    Software
        Microsoft
            Windows
                CurrentVersion
                    RunOnce *application identifier = command line*

If you have multiple instances open, you can include value name entries for each or consolidate them as a single entry and use command-line switches that are most appropriate for your application. For example, you can include entries like the following.

WordPad Document 1 = C:\Program Files\Wordpad.exe Letter to Bill /restore
WordPad Document 2 = C:\Program Files\Wordpad.exe Letter to Paul /restore
Paint = C:\Program Files\Paint.exe Abstract.bmp Cubist.bmp

As long as you provide a valid command-line string that your application can process, you can format the entry in a way that best fits your application.

You can also include a **RunOnce** entry under the **HKEY_LOCAL_ MACHINE** key. When using this entry, however, the system runs the application before starting up. You can use this entry for applications that may need to query the user for information that affects how Windows starts. Just remember that any entry here will affect all users of the computer.

RunOnce entries are automatically removed from the registry once the system starts up. Therefore, you need not remove or update the entries, but your application must always save its state when the user shuts down the system. The system also supports a **Run** subkey in both the **HKEY_CURRENT_USER** and **HKEY_LOCAL_ MACHINE** keys. The system runs any value name entries under this subkey after the system starts up, but does not remove those entries from the registry. For example, a virus check program can be installed to run automatically after the system starts up. You can also support this functionality by placing a file or shortcut to a file in the Startup folder. The registry stores the location of the Startup folder, as a value in **HKEY_CURRENT_USER \Software\Microsoft\ Windows\CurrentVersion\Explorer\Shell Folders**.

The system's ability to restore an application's state depends on the availability of the application and its data files. If they have been deleted or the user has logged in over the network where the same files are not available, the system may not be able to restore the state.

Registering Application Path Information

The system supports "per application" paths. If you register a path, Windows sets the PATH environment variable to be the registered path when it starts your application. You set your application's path in the **App Paths** subkey under the **HKEY_LOCAL_MACHINE** key. Create a new key using your application's executable filename as its name. Set this key's Default value to the path of your executable file. The system uses this entry to locate your application if it fails to find it in the current path; for example, if the user chooses the Run command on the Start menu and only includes the filename of the application, or if a shortcut icon doesn't include a path setting. To identify the location of dynamic-link libraries placed in a separate directory, you can also include another value entry called Path and set its value to the path of your dynamic-link libraries.

HKEY_LOCAL_MACHINE
    Software
        Microsoft
            Windows
                CurrentVersion
                    App Paths
                        Application Executable Filename *= path*
                                Path = *path*

The system will automatically update the path and default entries if the user moves or renames the application's executable file using the system shell user interface.

Register any system-wide shared dynamic-link libraries in a subkey under a **SharedDLLs** subkey of **HKEY_LOCAL_MACHINE** key. If the file already exists, increment the entry's usage count index. For more information about the usage count index, see the section, "Installation," later in this chapter.

HKEY_LOCAL_MACHINE
    Software
        Microsoft
            Windows
                CurrentVersion
                    SharedDLLs *filename* [*= usage count index*]

Registering File Extensions

If your application creates and maintains files, register entries for the file types that you expose directly to users and that you want users to be able to easily differentiate. For every file type you register, include at least two entries: a filename-extension key entry and an application (class) identification key entry.

If you do not register an extension for a file type, it will be displayed with the system's generic file object icon, as shown in Figure 10.1, and its extension will always be displayed. In addition, the user will not be able to double-click the file to open it. (Open With will be the icon's default command.)

Figure 10.1 System-generated icons for unregistered types

The Filename Extension Key

The filename extension entry maps a filename extension to an application identifier. To register an extension, create a subkey in the **HKEY_CLASSES_ROOT** key using the three-letter extension (including a period) and set its value to an application identifier.

HKEY_CLASSES_ROOT
   .ext = *ApplicationIdentifier*

For the value of the application identifier (also known as programmatic identifier or Prog ID), use a string that uniquely identifies a given class. This string is used internally by the system and is not exposed directly to users (unless explicitly exported with a special registry utility); therefore, you need not localize this entry.

Avoid assigning multiple extensions to the same application identifier. To ensure that each file type can be distinguished by the user,
define each extension such that each has a unique application identifier. If you have utility files that the user does not interact with directly, you should still register an extension (and icon) for them,
preferably the same extension so that they can be identified. In addition, mark them with the hidden file attribute.

The system provides no arbitration for applications that use the same
extensions. So define unique identifiers and check the registry to
avoid writing over and replacing existing extension entries, a practice which may seriously affect the user's existing files. More specifically, avoid registering an extension that conflicts or redefines the
common filename extensions used by the system. Examples of these
extensions are shown in Table 10.1.

Table 10.1 Common Filename Extensions Supported by Windows

Extension	Type description
386	Windows virtual device driver
3GR	Screen grabber for MS-DOS–based applications
ACM	Audio compression manager driver
ADF	Administration configuration files
ANI	Animated pointer
AVI	Video clip
AWD	FAX viewer document
AWP	FAX key viewer
AWS	FAX signature viewer
BAK	Backed-up file
BAT	MS-DOS batch file
BFC	Briefcase
BIN	Binary data file
BMP	Picture (Windows bitmap)
CAB	Windows Setup file
CAL	Windows Calendar file
CDA	CD audio track
CFG	Configuration file

(Continued)

Extension	Type description
CNT	Help contents
COM	MS-DOS – based application
CPD	FAX cover page
CPE	FAX cover page
CPI	International code page
CPL	Control Panel extension
CRD	Windows Cardfile document
CSV	Command-separated data file
CUR	Cursor (pointer)
DAT	System data file
DCX	FAX viewer document
DLL	Application extension (dynamic-link library)
DOC	WordPad document
DOS	MS-DOS file (also extension for NDIS2 net card and protocol drivers)
DRV	Device driver
EXE	Application
FND	Saved search
FON	Font file
FOT	Shortcut to font
GR3	Windows 3.0 screen grabber
GRP	Program group file
HLP	Help file
HT	HyperTerminal™ file
ICM	ICM profile
ICO	Icon
IDF	MIDI instrument definition
INF	Setup information
INI	Initialization file (configuration settings)

(Continued)

Extension	Type description
KBD	Keyboard layout
LGO	Windows logo driver
LIB	Static-link library
LNK	Shortcut
LOG	Log file
MCI	MCI command set
MDB	File viewer extension
MID	MIDI sequence
MIF	MIDI instrument file
MMF	Microsoft Mail message file
MMM	Animation
MPD	Mini-port driver
MSG	Microsoft® Exchange mail document
MSN	Microsoft Network home base
NLS	Natural language services driver
PAB	Microsoft Exchange personal address book
PCX	Bitmap picture (PCX format)
PDR	Port driver
PF	ICM profile
PIF	Shortcut to MS-DOS–based application
PPD	PostScript® printer description file
PRT	Printer formatted file (result of Print to File option)
PST	Microsoft Exchange personal information store
PWL	Password list
QIC	Backup set for Microsoft Backup
REC	Windows Recorder file
REG	Application registration file
RLE	Picture (RLE format)
RMI	MIDI sequence

(Continued)

Extension	Type description
RTF	Document (rich-text format)
SCR	Screen saver
SET	File set for Microsoft Backup
SHB	Shortcut into a document
SHS	Scrap
SPD	PostScript printer description file
SWP	Virtual memory storage
SYS	System file
TIF	Picture (TIFF® format)
TMP	Temporary file
TRN	Translation file
TSP	Windows telephony service provider
TTF	TrueType® font
TXT	Text document
VBX	Microsoft Visual Basic® control file
VER	Version description file
VXD	Virtual device driver
WAV	Sound wave
WPC	WordPad file converter
WRI	Windows Write document

It is a good idea to investigate extensions commonly used by popular applications so you can avoid creating a new extension that might conflict with them, unless you intend to replace or superset the functionality of those applications.

The Application Identifier Key

The second registry entry you create for a file type is its class-definition (Prog ID) key. Using the same string as the application identifier you used for the extension's value, create a key, and assign a type name as the value of the key.

HKEY_CLASSES_ROOT
> **.ext** = *ApplicationIdentifier*
> **ApplicationIdentifier** = *Type Name*

Under this key, you specify shell and OLE properties of the class. Provide this entry even if you do not have any extra information to place under this key; doing so provides a label for users to identify the file type. In addition, you use this entry to register the icon for the file type.

Define the type name (also known as the MainUserTypeName) as the human-readable form of its application identifier or class name. It should convey to the user the object's name, behavior, or capability. A type name can include all of the following elements:

1. *Company Name*
   Communicates product identity.

2. *Application Name*
   Indicates which application is responsible for activating a data object.

3. *Data Type*
   Indicates the basic category of the object (for example, drawing, spreadsheet, or sound). Limit the number of characters to a maximum of 15.

4. *Version*
   When there are multiple versions of the same basic type, for upgrading purposes, you may want to include a version number to distinguish types.

When defining your type name, use title capitalization. The name can include up to a maximum of 40 characters. Use one of the following three recommended forms:

1. *Company Name Application Name* [*Version*] *Data Type*
   For example, Microsoft Excel Worksheet.

2. *Company Name-Application Name* [*Version*] *Data Type*
   For cases when the company name and application are the same
   — for example, ExampleWare 2.0 Document.

3. *Company Name Application Name* [*Version*]
   When the application sufficiently describes the data type — for
   example, Microsoft Graph.

These type names provide the user with a precise language for referring to objects. Because object type names appear throughout the
interface, the user becomes conscious of an object's type and its
associated behavior. However, because of their length, you may also
want to include a short type name. A *short type name* is the data
type portion of the full type name. Applications that support OLE
always include a short type name entry in the registry. Use the short
type name in drop-down and pop-up menus. For example, a
Microsoft® Excel Worksheet is simply referred to as a "Worksheet"
in menus.

To provide a short type name, add an **AuxUserType** subkey under
the application's registered **CLSID** subkey (which is under the
CLSID key).

For more information about
registering type names and
other information you should include under the **CLSID** key, see the
OLE documentation included in the
Win32 SDK.

HKEY_CLASSES_ROOT
    .ext = *ApplicationIdentifier*
...
    ApplicationIdentifier = *Type Name*
       CLSID = {***CLSID identifier***}
...
    CLSID
       {***CLSID identifier***}
          AuxUserType
             2 = *Short Type Name*

If a short type name is not available for an object because the string
was not registered, use the full type name instead. All controls that
display the full type name must allocate enough space for 40 characters in width. By comparison, controls need only accommodate 15
characters when using the short type name.

Supporting Creation

The system supports the creation of new objects in system containers, such as folders and the desktop. Register information for each file type that you want the system to include. The registered type will appear on the New command that the system includes on menus for the desktop, folders, and the Open and Save As common dialog boxes. This provides a more data-centered design because the user can create a new object without having to locate and run the associated application.

To register a file type for inclusion, create a subkey using the Application Identifier under the extension's subkey in **HKEY_ CLASSES_ROOT**. Under it, also create the **ShellNew** subkey.

HKEY_CLASSES_ROOT
    .ext = *ApplicationIdentifier*
        ApplicationIdentifier
            ShellNew *Value Name = Value*

Assign a value entry to the **ShellNew** subkey with one of the four methods for creating a file with this extension.

Value name	Value	Result
NullFile	" "	Creates a new file of this type as a null (empty) file.
Data	*binary data*	Creates a new file containing the binary data.
FileName	*path*	Creates a new file by copying the specified file.
Command	*filename*	Carries out the command. Use this to run your own application code to create a new file (for example, run a wizard).

The system also will automatically provide a unique filename for the new file using the type name you register.

When using a Command value, place your application file (that creates the new file) in the directory that the system uses to store these files. To determine the path for that directory, check the setting for the Templates value in the **Shell Folders** subkey found in **HKEY_CURRENT_USER\Software\Microsoft\Windows\ CurrentVersion\Explorer**. Then you need only register the filename for the command.

Registering Icons

The system uses the registry to determine which icon to display for a specific file. You register an icon for every data file type that your application supports and that you want the user to be able to distinguish easily. Create a **DefaultIcon** subkey entry under the application identifier subkey you created and define its value as the filename containing the icon. Typically, you use the application's executable filename and the index of the icon within the file. The index value corresponds to the icon resource within the file. A positive number represents the icon's position in the file. A negative number corresponds to the inverse of the resource ID number of the icon. The icon for your application should always be the first icon resource in your executable file. The system always uses the first icon resource to represent executable files. This means the index value for your data files will be a number greater than 0.

```
HKEY_CLASSES_ROOT
        ApplicationIdentifier = Type Name
            DefaultIcon = path [,index]
```

Instead of registering the application's executable file, you can register the name of a dynamic link library file (.DLL), an icon file (.ICO), or bitmap file (.BMP) to supply your data file icons. If an icon does not exist or is not registered, the system supplies an icon derived from the icon of the file type's registered application. If no icon is available for the application, the system supplies a generic icon. These icons do not make your files uniquely identifiable, so design and register icons for both your application and its data file types. Include the following sizes: 16 x 16 pixel (16 color), 32 x 32 pixel (16 color), and 48 x 48 pixel (256 color).

For more information about designing icons, see Chapter 13, "Visual Design."

Registering Commands

Many of the commands found on icons, including Send To, Cut, Copy, Paste, Create Shortcut, Delete, Rename, and Properties, are provided by their container — that is, their containing folder or the desktop. But you must provide support for the icon's primary commands, also referred to as verbs, such as Open, Edit, Play, and Print. You can also register additional commands that apply to your file types, such as a What's This? command and even commands for other file types.

To add these commands, in the **HKEY_CLASSES_ROOT** key, you register a **shell** subkey and a subkey for each verb, and a **command** subkey for each menu command name.

HKEY_CLASSES_ROOT
    ApplicationIdentifier = *Type Name*
        shell [= *default verb* [,*verb2* [,..]]
            verb [= *Menu Command Name*]
                command = *pathname* [*parameters*]

You can also register a DDE command string for a DDE command.

HKEY_CLASSES_ROOT
    ApplicationIdentifier = *Type Name*
        shell [= *default verb* [,*verb2* [,..]]
            verb [= *Menu Command Name*]
                ddeexec = *DDE command string*
                    Application = *DDE Application Name*
                    Topic = *DDE topic name*

A verb is a language-independent name of the command. Applications may use it to invoke a specific command programmatically. The system defines Open, Print, Find, and Explore as standard verbs and automatically provides menu command names and appropriate access key assignments, localized in each international version of Windows. When you supply verbs other than these, provide menu command names localized for the specific version of Windows on which the application is installed. To assign a menu command name for a verb, make it the default value of the verb subkey.

The menu command names corresponding to the verbs for a file type are displayed to the user, either on a folder's File drop-down menu or pop-up menu for a file's icon. These appear at the top of the menu. You define the order of the menu commands by ordering the verbs in the value of the **shell** key. The first verb becomes the default command in the menu.

By default, capitalization follows how you enter format the menu command name value of the verb subkey. Although the system automatically capitalizes the standard commands (Open, Print, Explore, and Find), you can use the value of the menu command name to format the capitalization differently. Similarly, you use the menu command name value to set the access key for the menu command following normal menu conventions, prefixing the character in the name with an ampersand (&). Otherwise, the system sets the first letter of the command as the access key for that command.

To support user execution of a verb, provide the path for the application or a DDE command string. You can include command-line switches. For paths, include a %1 parameter. This parameter is an operational placeholder for whatever file the user selects.

For example, to register an Analyze command for an application that manages stock market information, the registry entries might look like the following.

HKEY_CLASSES_ROOT
      stockfile = Stock Data
          shell = analyze
              analyze = &Analyze
                  command = C:\Program Files\Stock Analysis\Stock.exe /A

You may have different values for each command. You may assign one application to carry out the Open command and another to carry out the Print command, or use the same application for all commands.

Enabling Printing

If your file types are printable, include a Print verb entry in the **shell** subkey under **HKEY_CLASSES_ROOT**, following the conventions described in the previous section. This will display the Print command on the pop-up menu for the icon and on the File menu of the folder in which the icon resides when the user selects the icon. When the user chooses the Print command, the system uses the registry entry to determine what application to run to print the file.

Also register a Print To registry entry for the file types your application supports. This entry enables dragging and dropping of a file onto a printer icon. Although a Print To command is not displayed on any menu, the printer includes Print Here as the default command on the pop-up menu displayed when the user drag and drops a file on the printer using button 2.

In both cases, print the file, preferably, without opening the application's primary window. One way to do this is to provide a command-line switch that runs the application for handling the printing operation only (for example, WordPad.exe /p). In addition, display some form of user feedback that indicates whether a printing process has been initiated and, if so, its progress. For example, this feedback could be a modeless message box that displays, "Printing page *m* of *n* on *printer name*" and a Cancel button. You may also include a progress indicator control.

Registering OLE

Applications that support OLE use the registry as the primary means of defining class types, operations, and properties for data types supported by those applications. You store OLE registration information in the **HKEY_CLASSES_ROOT** key in subkeys under the **CLSID** subkey and in the class description's (Prog ID) subkey.

For more information about the specific registration entries for OLE, see the OLE documentation included in the Win32 SDK.

Registering Shell Extensions

Your application can extend the functionality of the operational environment provided by the system, also known as the shell, in a number of ways. A shell extension enhances the system by providing additional ways to manipulate file objects, by simplifying the task of browsing through the file system, or by giving the user easier access to tools that manipulate objects in the file system.

Support for shell extensions may depend on the version of Windows installed. For more information about specific releases, see Appendix D, "Supporting Specific Versions of Windows."

Every shell extension requires a *handler*, special application code (32-bit OLE InProc server implemented as a dynamic-link library) that implements subordinate functions. The types of handlers you can provide include:

- Pop-up (context) menu handlers: these add menu items to the pop-up menu for a particular file type.

- Drag handlers: these allow you to support the OLE data transfer conventions for drag and drop operations of a specific file type.

- Drop handlers: these allow you to carry out some action when the user drops objects on a specific type of file.

- Nondefault drag and drop handlers: these are pop-up menu handlers that the system calls when the user drags and drops an object by using mouse button 2.

- Icon handlers: these can be used to add per-instance icons for file objects or to supply icons for all files of a specific type.

- Property sheet handlers: these add pages to a property sheet that the shell displays for a file object. The pages can be specific to a class of files or to a particular file object.

- Copy-hook handlers: these are called when a folder or printer object is about to be moved, copied, deleted, or renamed by the user. The handler can be used to allow or prevent the operation.

You register the handler for a shell extension in the **HKEY_ CLASSES_ROOT** key. The **CLSID** subkey contains a list of class identifier key values such as {00030000-0000-0000-C000-000000000046}. Each class identifier must also be a globally unique identifier.

You must also create a **shellex** subkey under the application's class identification entry in the **HKEY_CLASSES_ROOT** key.

For more information about creating handlers and class identifiers, see the OLE documentation included in the Win32 SDK.

HKEY_CLASSES_ROOT
    ApplicationIdentifier = *Type Name*
      Shell [= *default verb* [,*verb2* [,..]]
        ...
        shellex
          HandlerType
            {*CLSID identifier*} = *Handler Name*
        ...
        HandlerType = {*CLSID identifier*}

The shell also uses several other special keys, such as *****, **Folder**, **Drives**, and **Printers**, under **HKEY_CLASSES_ROOT**. You can use these keys to register extensions for system-supplied objects. For example, you may use the * key to register handlers that the shell calls whenever it creates a pop-up menu or property sheet for a file object, as in the following example.

HKEY_CLASSES_ROOT
    * = *
      shellex
        ContextMenuHandlers
          {00000000-1111-2222-3333-0000000001}
        PropertySheetHandlers = SummaryInfo
          {00000000-1111-2222-3333-0000000002}
        IconHandler = {00000000-1111-2222-3333-000000003}

The shell would use these handlers to add to the pop-up menus and property sheets of every file object. (The entries are intended only as examples, not literal entries.)

A pop-up menu handler may add commands to the pop-up menu of a file type, but it may not delete or modify existing menu commands. You can register multiple pop-up menu handlers for a file type. The order of the subkey entries determines the order of the items in the context menu. Handler-supplied menu items always follow registered command names.

Keep in mind that if you want to include a command on the pop-up menu of every file of a particular type, you do not need to create and register a pop-up menu handler. You can just use the normal means of registering commands for that type. Create a pop-up menu handler only when you want to provide a command only under specific conditions, such as the length of the file or its timestamp.

When registering an icon handler for providing per-instance icons for a file type, set the value for the **DefaultIcon** key to %1. This denotes that each file instance of this type can have a different icon.

Supporting the Quick View Command

The system includes support for fast, read-only views of many file types when the user chooses the Quick View command from the file object's menu. This allows the user to view files without opening the application.

For more information about supporting the Quick View command and creating file viewers, see the documentation included in the Win32 SDK.

If your file type is not supported, you can install a file parser that translates your file type into a format the system file viewer can read. Although this approach allows you to easily support viewers for your data file types, it limits the interaction options for your file types to those provided by the system. Alternatively, you can create your own file viewer, using the system-supplied interfaces. You can also register a file viewer for a file type already registered.

You can also support the Quick View command for data objects stored within your application's interface, either by supplying a specific viewer for your data types or by writing the data to a temporary file and then executing a file viewer and passing the temporary file as a parameter.

Registering Sound Events

Your application can register specific events to which the user can assign sound files so that when those events are triggered, the assigned sound file is played. To register a sound event, create a key under the **HKEY_CURRENT_USER** key.

HKEY_CURRENT_USER
    AppEvents
        Event Labels
            EventName = *Event Name*

Set the value for EventName to a human-readable name.

Registering a sound event only makes it available in Control Panel so the user can assign a sound file. Your application must provide the code to process that event.

Installation

The following sections provide guidelines for installing your application's files. Applying these guidelines will help you reduce the clutter of irrelevant files when the user browses for a file. In addition, you'll reduce the redundancy of common files and make it easier for the user to update applications or the system software.

Copying Files

When the user installs your software, avoid copying files into the Windows directory (folder) or its System subdirectory. Doing so clutters the directory and may degrade system performance. Instead, create a single directory, preferably using the application's name, in the Program Files directory (or the location that the user chooses). In this directory, place the executable file. For example, if a program is named My Application, create a My Application subdirectory and place My Application.exe in that directory.

To locate the Program Files directory, check the ProgramFilesDir value in the **CurrentVersion** subkey under **HKEY_LOCAL_ MACHINE\Software\Microsoft\Windows**. The actual directory may not literally be named Program Files. For example, in international versions of Microsoft Windows, the directory name is appropriately localized. For networks that do not support the Windows long filename conventions, MS-DOS names may be used instead.

In your application's directory, create a subdirectory named System and place all support files that the user does not directly access in it, such as dynamic-link libraries and Help files. For example, place a support file called My Application.dll in the subdirectory Program Files\My Application\System. Hide the support files and your application's System directory and register its location using a Path value in the **App Paths** subkey under **HKEY_LOCAL_MACHINE \Software\Microsoft\Windows\CurrentVersion**. Although you may place support files in the same directory as your application, placing them in a subdirectory helps avoid confusing the user and makes files easier to manage.

Applications can share common support files to reduce the amount of disk space consumed by duplication. If some non-user-accessed files of your application are shared as systemwide components (such as Visual Basic's Vbrun300.dll), place them in the System subdirectory of the directory where the user installs Windows. The process for installing shared files includes these logical steps:

1. Before copying the file, verify that it is not already present.

2. If the file is already present, compare its date and size to determine whether it is the same version as the one you are installing. If it is, increment the usage count in its corresponding registry entry.

3. If the file you are installing is not more recent, do not overwrite the existing version.

4. If the file is not present, copy it to the directory.

The system provides support services in Ver.dll for assisting you to do version verification. For more information about this utility, see the documentation included in the Win32 SDK.

If you store a new file in the System directory installed by Windows, register a corresponding entry in the **SharedDLL** subkey under the **HKEY_LOCAL_MACHINE** key.

If a file is shared, but only among your applications, create a subdirectory using your application's name in the Common Files subdirectory of the Program Files subdirectory and place the file there. To locate the Common Files directory, check the Common-FilesDir value in the **CurrentVersion** subkey of **HKEY_LOCAL_MACHINE\Software\Microsoft\Windows**. Alternatively, for "suite" style when multiple applications are bundled together, you can create a suite subdirectory in Program Files, where you place your executable files, and within that a System subdirectory with the support files shared only within the suite. In either case, register the path using the **Path** subkey under the **App Paths** subkey

When installing an updated version of the shared file, ensure that it is upwardly compatible before replacing the existing file. Alternatively, you can create a separate entry with a different filename (for example, Vbrun301.dll).

Name your executable file, dynamic-link libraries, and any other files that the user does not directly use, but that may be shared on a network, using conventional MS-DOS (8.3) names rather than long filenames. This will provide better support for users operating in environments where these files may need to be installed on network services that do not support the Windows long filename conventions.

Windows no longer requires Autoexec.bat and Config.sys files. Ensure that your application also does not require these files. Consider converting any MS-DOS device drivers to Windows virtual device drivers. The system supports dynamic loading of this type of device drivers, unlike MS-DOS device drivers which need to be loaded through Config.sys when starting the system. Similarly, because the registry allows you to register your application paths, your application does not require path information in Autoexec.bat.

In addition, do not make entries in Win.ini. Storing information in this file can make it difficult for the user to update or move your application. Also, avoid maintaining your application's own initialization file. Instead, use the registry. The registry provides conventions for storing most application and user settings. The registry provides greater flexibility allowing you to store information on a per machine or per user basis. It also supports accessing this infomation across a network.

Make certain you register the types supported by your application and the icons for these types along with your application's icons. In addition, register other application information, such as information required to enable printing.

Providing Access to Your Application

To provide easy user access to your application, place a shortcut icon to the application in the Programs folder. You can determine the path for this folder in **Shell Folders** subkey under **HKEY_CURRENT_ USER\Software\Microsoft\Windows\CurrentVersion\Explorer**. This adds the entry to the submenu of the Programs menu of the Start button. Avoid adding entries for every application you might include in your software; this quickly overloads the menu. Optionally, you can allow the user to choose which icons to place in the menu. Avoid using a folder as your entry in the Programs menu, because this creates a multilevel hierarchy. Including a single entry makes it easier and simpler for a user to access your application.

You can create a "program group" entry in the Programs folder using the Windows 3.1 dynamic date exchange application programming interface (API). However, it is not recommended for applications installed with Microsoft Windows 95 and later releases, configured with the new shell user interface.

Also consider the layout of files you provide with your application. Folders in Windows 95 and later releases provide much greater flexibility for file organization than did the Windows Program Manager. In addition to the recommended structure for your main executable file and its support files, you may want to create special folders for documents, templates, conversion tools, or other files that the user accesses directly.

Designing Your Installation Program

Your installation program should offer the user different installation options such as:

- Typical Setup: installation that proceeds with the common defaults set, copying only the most common files. Make this the default setup option.

- Compact Setup: installation of the minimum files necessary to operate your application. This option is best for situations where disk space must be conserved — for example, on laptop computers. You can optionally add a Portable setup option for additional functionality designed especially for configurations on laptops, portables, and portables used with docking stations.

- Custom Setup: installation for the experienced user. This option allows the user to choose where to copy files and which options or features to include. This can include options or components not available for compact or typical setup.

- CD-ROM Setup: installation from a CD-ROM. This option allows users to select what files to install from the CD and allows them to run the remaining files directly from the CD.

- Silent Setup: installation using a command-line switch. This allows your setup program to run with a batch file

In addition to these setup options, your installation program should be a well-designed, Windows-based application and follow the conventions detailed in this guide and in the following guidelines:

- Supply a common response to every option so that the user can step through the installation process by confirming the default settings (that is, by pressing the ENTER key).

- Tell users how much disk space they will need before proceeding with installation. In the custom setup option, adjust the figure as the user chooses to include or exclude certain options. If there is not sufficient disk space, let the user know, but also give the user the option to override.

- Offer the user the option to quit the installation before it is finished. Keep a log of the files copied and the settings made so the canceled installation can be cleaned up easily.

- Ask the user to insert a disk only once during the installation. Lay out your files on disk so that the user does not have to reinsert the same disk multiple times.

- Provide a visual prompt and an audio cue when the user needs to insert the next disk.

- Support installation from any location. Do not assume that installation must be done from a logical MS-DOS drive (such as drive A). Design your installation program to support any valid universal naming convention (UNC) path.

- Provide a progress indicator message box to inform the user how far they are through the installation process.

If you are creating your own installation program, consider using the wizard control. Using this control and following the guidelines for wizards will result in a consistent interface for users.

For more information about designing wizards, see Chapter 12, "User Assistance."

Naming your installation program Setup.exe or Install.exe (or localized equivalent) will allow the system to recognize the file. Place the file in the root directory of the disk the user inserts. This allows the system to automatically run your installation program when the user chooses the Install button in the Add/Remove Programs utility in Control Panel.

Installing Fonts

When installing fonts with your application on a local system, determine whether the font is already present. If it is, rename your font file — for example, by appending a number to the end of its filename. After copying a font file, register the font in the **Fonts** subkey.

Installing Your Application on a Network

If you create a client-server application so that multiple users access it from a network server, create separate installation programs: an installation program that allows the network administrator to prepare the server component of the application, and a client installation program that installs the client component files and sets up the settings to connect to the server. Design your client software so that an administrator can deploy it over the network and have it automatically configure itself when the user starts it.

For more information about designing client-server applications, see Chapter 14, "Special Design Considerations." Additional information can also be found in the documentation included in Win32 SDK.

Because Windows may itself be configured to be shared on a server, do not assume that your installation program can store information in the main Windows directory on the server. In addition, shared application files should not be stored in the "home" directory provided for the user.

Design your installation program to support UNC paths. Also, use UNC paths for any shortcut icons you install in the Start Menu folder.

Uninstalling Your Application

The user may need to remove your application to recover disk space or to move the application to another location. To facilitate this, provide an uninstall program with your application that removes its files and settings. Remember to remove registry entries and shortcuts your application may have placed in the Start menu hierarchy. However, be careful when removing your application's directory structure not to delete any user files (unless you confirm their removal with the user).

Your uninstall program should follow the conventions detailed in this guide and in the following guidelines:

- Display a window that provides the user with information about the progress of the uninstall process. You can also provide an option to allow the program to uninstall "silently" — that is, without displaying any information so that it can be used in batch files.

- Display clear and helpful messages for any errors your uninstall program encounters during the uninstall process.

- When uninstalling an application, decrement the usage count in the registry for any shared component — for example, a dynamic-link library. If the result is zero, give the user the option to delete the shared component with the warning that other applications may use this file and will not work if it is missing.

Registering your uninstall program will display your application in the list of the Uninstall page of the Add/Remove Program utility included with Windows. To register your uninstall program, add entries for your application to the **Uninstall** subkey.

HKEY_LOCAL_MACHINE
    Software
        Microsoft
            Windows
                CurrentVersion
                    Uninstall
                        ApplicationName DisplayName = *Application Name*
                                      UninstallString = *path* [*switches*]

Both the **DisplayName** and **UninstallString** values must be supplied and be complete for your uninstall program to appear in the Add/Remove Program utility. The path you supply to **Uninstall-String** must be the complete command line used to carry out your uninstall program. The command line you supply should carry out the uninstall program directly rather than from a batch file or subprocess.

Supporting AutoPlay

Windows supports the ability to automatically run a file when the user inserts removable media that support insertion notification, such as CD-ROM, PCMCIA hard disks, or flash ROM cards. To support this feature, include a file named Autorun.inf in the root directory of the removable media. In this file, include the filename of the file to run, using the following syntax.

```
[autorun]
open = filename
```

Unless you specify a path, the system looks for the file in the root of the inserted media. If you want to run a file located in a subdirectory, include a path relative to the root; include that path with the file as in the following example.

```
open = My Directory\My File.exe
```

Running the file from a subdirectory does not change the current directory setting. The command-line string you supply can also include parameters or switches.

Because the autoplay feature is intended to provide automatic operation, design the file you specify in the Autorun.inf file to provide visual feedback quickly to confirm the successful insertion of the media. Consider using a startup up window with a graphic or animated sequence. If the process you are automating requires a long load time or requires user input, offer the user the option to cancel the process.

Although you can use this feature to install an application, avoid writing files to the user's local disk without the user's confirmation. Even when you get the user's confirmation, minimize the file storage requirements, particularly for CD-ROM games or educational applications. Consuming a large amount of local file space defeats some of the benefits of the turnkey operation that the autoplay feature provides. Also, because a network administrator or the user can disable this feature, avoid depending on it for any required operations.

You can define the icon that the system displays for the media by including an entry in the Autorun.inf file that includes the filename (and optionally the path) including the icon using the following form.

icon = *filename*

The filename can specify an icon, a bitmap, an executable, or a dynamic-link library file. If the file contains more than one icon resource, specify the resource with a number after the filename — for example, My File.exe, 1. The numbering follows the same conventions as the registry. The default path for the file will be relative to the Autorun.inf file. If you want to specify an absolute path for an icon, use the following form.

defaulticon = *path*

The system automatically provides a pop-up menu for the icon and includes AutoPlay as the default command on that menu, so that double-clicking the icon will run the Open = line. You can include additional commands on the menu for the icon by adding entries for them in the Autorun.inf file, using the following form.

shell\verb\command = *filename*
shell\verb = *Menu Item Name*

To define an access key assignment for the command, precede the character with an ampersand (&). For example, to add the command Read Me First to the menu of the icon, include the following in the Autorun.inf file.

shell\readme\command = Notepad.exe My Directory\Readme.txt
shell\readme = Read &Me First

Although AutoPlay is typically the default menu item, you can define a different command to be the default by including the following line.

```
shell = verb
```

When the user double-clicks on the icon, the command associated with this entry will be carried out.

System Naming Conventions

Windows provides support for filenames up to 255 characters long. Use the long filename when displaying the name of a file. Avoid displaying the filename extension unless the user chooses the option to display extensions or when the file type is not registered.

The system automatically formats a filename correctly if you use the **SHGetFileInfo** or **Get-FileTitle** function. For more information about these functions, see the documentation included in the Win32 SDK.

Because the system uses three-letter extensions to describe a file type, do not use extensions to distinguish different forms of the same file type. For example, if your application has a function that automatically backs up a file, name the backup file Backup of *filename.ext* (using its existing extension) or some reasonable equivalent, not *filename*.bak. The latter implies a change of the file's type. Similarly, do not use a Windows filename extension unless your file fits the type description.

Long filenames can include any character, except the following.

\ / : * ? < > | "

When your application automatically supplies a filename, use a name that communicates information about its creation. For example, files created by a particular application should use either the application-supplied type name or the short type name as a proposed name — for example, worksheet or document. When that file exists already in the target directory, add a number to the end of the proposed name — for example, Document (2). When adding numbers to the end of a proposed filename, use the first number of an ordinal sequence that does not conflict with an existing name in that directory.

When saving a file, make certain you preserve the creation date of the file. For simple applications that open and save a file, this happens automatically. However, more sophisticated applications may create temporary files, delete the original file, and rename the temporary file to the original filename. In this case, the application needs to copy the creation date as well from the old file to the new, using the standard system functions. Certain system file management functionality may depend on the correct creation date.

When you create a filename, the system automatically creates an MS-DOS filename (alias) for a file. The system displays both the long filename and the MS-DOS filename in the property sheet for the file.

When a file is copied, use the words "Copy of" as part of the generated filename — for example, "Copy of Sample" for a file named "Sample." If the prefix "Copy of" is already assigned to a file, include a number in parentheses — for example, "Copy (2) of Sample". You can apply the same naming scheme to links, except the prefix is "Link to" or "Shortcut to."

It is also important to support UNC paths for identifying the location of files and folders. UNC paths and filenames have the following form.

\\Server\Share\Directory\Filename.ext

Using UNC names enables the user to directly browse the network and open files without having to make explicit network connections.

Wherever possible, display the full name of a file (without the extension). The number of characters you'll be able to display depends somewhat on the font used and the context in which the name is displayed. In any case, supply enough characters such that the user can reasonably distinguish between names. Take into account common prefixes such as "Copy of" or "Shortcut to". If you don't display the full name, indicate that it has been truncated by appending an ellipsis to the end of the name.

You can use an ellipsis to abbreviate path names, in a displayable, but noneditable situation. In this case, include at least the first two entries of the beginning and the end of the path, using ellipses as notation for the names in between, as in the following example.

\\My Server\My Share\...\My Folder\My File

When using an icon to represent a network resource, label the icon with the name of the resource. If you need to show the network context rather than using a UNC path, label the resource using the following format.

Resource Name on *Computer Name*

Taskbar Integration

The system provides support for integrating your application's interface with the taskbar. The following sections provide information on some of the capabilities and appropriate guidelines.

Taskbar Window Buttons

When an application creates a primary window, the system automatically adds a taskbar button for that window and removes it when that window closes. For some specialized types of applications that run in the background, a primary window may not be necessary. In such cases, make certain you provide reasonable support for controlling the application using the commands available on the application's icon; it should not appear as an entry on the taskbar, however. Similarly, the secondary windows of an application should also not appear as a taskbar button.

The taskbar window buttons support drag and drop, but not in the conventional way. When the user drags an object over a taskbar window button, the system automatically restores the window. The user can then drop the object in the window.

Status Notification

The system allows you to add status or notification information to the taskbar. Because the taskbar is a shared resource, add information to it that is of a global nature only or that needs monitoring by the user while working with other applications.

Present status notification information in the form of a graphic supplied by your application, as shown in Figure 10.2.

The **Shell_NotifyIcon** function provides support for adding a status item in the taskbar. For more information about this function, see the documentation included in the Win32 SDK.

Figure 10.2 Status indicator in the taskbar

When adding a status indicator to the taskbar, also support the following interactions:

- Provide a pop-up window that displays further information or controls for the object represented by the status indicator when the user clicks with button 1. For example, the audio (speaker) status indicator displays a volume control. Use a pop-up window to supply for further information rather than a dialog box, because the user can dismiss the window by clicking elsewhere. Position the pop-up window near the status indicator so the user can navigate to it quickly and easily. Avoid displaying other types of secondary windows because they require explicit user interaction to dismiss them. If there is no information or control that applies, do not display anything.

- Display a pop-up menu for the object represented by the status indicator when the user clicks on the status indicator with button 2. On this menu, include commands that bring up property sheets or other windows related to the status indicator. For example, the audio status indicator provides commands that display the audio properties as well as the Volume Control mixer application.

- Carry out the default command defined in the pop-up menu for the status indicator when the user double-clicks.

- Display a tooltip that indicates what the status indicator represents. For example, this could include the name of the indicator, a value, or both.

- Provide the user an option to not display the status indicator, preferably in the property sheet for the object displaying the status indicator. This allows the user to determine which indicator to include in this shared space. You may need to provide an alternate means of conveying this status information when the user turns off the status indicator.

Message Notification

When your application's window is inactive but must display a message, rather than displaying a message box on top of the currently active window and switching the input focus, flash your application's title bar and taskbar window button to notify the user of the pending message. This avoids interfering with the user's current activity but lets the user know a message is waiting. When the user activates your application's window, the application can display a message box.

The **FlashWindow** function supports flashing your title bar and taskbar window button. For more information about this function, see the documentation included in the Win32 SDK.

Use the system setting for the cursor blink rate for your flash rate. This allows the user to control the flash rate to a comfortable frequency.

The **GetCaretBlinkTime** function provides access to the current cursor blink rate setting. For more information about this function, see the documentation included in the Win32 SDK.

Rather than flashing the button continually, you can flash the window button only a limited number of times (for example, three), then leave the button in the highlighted state, as shown in Figure 10.3. This lets the user know there is still a pending message.

Figure 10.3 Flashing a taskbar button to notify a user of a pending message

This cooperative means of notification is preferable unless a message relates to the system integrity of the user's data, in which case your application may immediately display a system modal message box. In such cases, flush the input queue so that the user does not inadvertently select a choice in that message box.

Application Desktop Toolbars

The system supports applications supplying their own desktop toolbars, also referred to as access bars or appbars, that operate similarly to the Windows taskbar. These may be docked to the edges of a screen and provide access to controls, such as buttons, for specific functions.

The system supports the same auto-hide behavior for application desktop toolbars as it does for the taskbar. This allows the desktop toolbar to only be visible when the user moves the pointer to the edge of the screen. The system also provides the "always on top" behavior used by the taskbar. When the user sets this property, the taskbar always appears on top (in the Z order) of any windows and also acts as a boundary for windows set to maximize to the display screen size.

Desktop toolbars can also be undocked and displayed as a palette window or redocked at a different edge of the screen. In the undocked, displayed as a palette window state, the toolbar no longer constrains other windows. However, if it supports the Always on Top property, it remains on top of other application windows.

For more information on the recommended behavior for undocking and redocking toolbars, see Chapter 7, "Menus, Controls, and Toolbars."

Before designing a desktop toolbar, consider whether your application's tasks really require one. Remember that a desktop toolbar will potentially affect the visible area for all applications. Only provide one for frequently used interfaces that can be applied across applications and always design it to be an optional interface, allowing the user to close it or otherwise configure it not to appear. You may also want to consider removing it when a specific application or applications are closed.

When creating your own desktop toolbar, model its behavior on the taskbar. Consider using the system's notification of when the taskbar's auto-hide or Always on Top property changes to apply a desktop toolbar you provide. If this does not fit your design, be certain to provide your own property sheet for setting these attributes for your desktop toolbar. Note that the system only supports auto-hide functionality for one desktop toolbar on each edge of the display. In addition, always provide a pop-up menu to access commands that apply to your desktop toolbar, such as Close, Move, Size, and Properties (but not the commands included on the desktop toolbar).

You can choose to display a desktop toolbar when the user runs a specific application, or by creating a separate application and including a shortcut icon to it in the system's Startup folder. Preferably set the initial size and position of your desktop toolbar so that it does not interfere with other desktop toolbars or the taskbar. However, the system does support multiple desktop toolbars to be docked along the same edge of the display screen. When docking on the same edge as the taskbar, the system places the taskbar on the outermost edge.

Your desktop toolbar can include any type of control. A desktop toolbar can also be a drag and drop target. Follow the recommendations outlined in this guide for supporting appropriate interaction.

Full-Screen Display

Although the taskbar and application desktop toolbars normally constrain or clip windows displayed on the screen, you can define a window to the full extent of the display screen. Because this is not the typical form of interaction, only consider using full-screen display for very special circumstances, such as a slide presentation, and only when the user explicitly chooses a command for this purpose. Make certain you provide an easy way for the user to return to normal display viewing. For example, you can display an on-screen button when the user moves the pointer that restores the display when the user clicks it. In addition, keyboard interfaces, like ALT+TAB and ESC, should automatically restore the display.

Remember that desktop toolbars, including the taskbar, should support auto-hide options that allow the user to configure them to reduce their visual impact on the screen. Consider whether this auto-hide capability may be sufficient before designing your application to require a full-screen presentation. Advising the user to close or hide desktop toolbars may provide you with sufficient space without having to use the full display screen.

Recycle Bin Integration

The Recycle Bin provides a repository for deleted files. If your application includes a facility for deleting files, support the Recycle Bin interface. You can also support deletion to the Recycle Bin for nonfile objects by first formatting the deleted data as a file by writing it to a temporary file and then calling the system functions that support the Recycle Bin.

The **SHFileOperation** function supports deletion using the Recycle Bin interface. For more information about this function, see the documentation included in the Win32 SDK.

Control Panel Integration

The Windows Control Panel includes special objects that let users configure aspects of the system. Your application can add Control Panel objects or add property pages to the property sheets of existing Control Panel objects.

Adding Control Panel Objects

You can create your own Control Panel objects. Most Control Panel objects supply only a single secondary window, typically a property sheet. Define your Control Panel object to represent a concrete object rather than an abstract idea.

Every Control Panel object is a dynamic-link library. To ensure that the dynamic-link library can be automatically loaded by the system, set the file's extension to .CPL and install it in the Windows System directory.

The system automatically caches information about Control Panel objects in order to provide quick user access, provided that the Control Panel object supports the correct system interfaces. For more information about developing Control Panel objects, see the documentation included in the Win32 SDK.

Adding to the Passwords Object

The Passwords object in Control Panel supplies a property sheet that allows the user to set security options and manage passwords for all password-protected services in the system. The Passwords object also allows you to add the name of a password-protected service to the object's list of services and use the Windows login password for all password-protected services in the system.

When you add your service to the Passwords object, the name of the service appears in the Select Password dialog box that appears when the user chooses Change Other Passwords. The user can then change the password for the service by selecting the name and filling in the resulting dialog box. The name of your service also appears in the Change Windows Password dialog box; the name appears with a check box next to it. By setting the check box option, the user chooses to keep the password for the service identical to the Windows login password. Similarly, the user can disassociate the service from the Windows login password by toggling the check box setting off.

To add your service to the Passwords object, register your service under the **HKEY_LOCAL_MACHINE** key.

For more information about registering your password service, see the documentation included in the Win32 SDK.

HKEY_LOCAL_MACHINE
 System
  CurrentControlSet
   Control
    PwdProvider
     Provider Name *Value Name = Value*

You can also add a page to the property sheet of the Passwords object to support other security-related services that the user can set as property values. Add a property page if your application provides security-related functionality beyond simple activation and changing of passwords. To add a property page, follow the conventions for adding shell extensions.

Plug and Play Support

Plug and Play is a feature of Windows that, with little or no user intervention, automatically installs and configures drivers when their corresponding hardware peripherals are plugged into a PC. This feature applies to peripherals designed according to the Plug and Play specification. Supporting and appropriately adapting to Plug and Play hardware change can make your application easier to use. Following are some examples of supporting Plug and Play:

- Resizing your windows and toolbars relevant to screen size changes.

- Prompting users to shut down and save their data when the system issues a low power warning.

- Warning users about open network files when undocking their computers.

- Saving and closing files appropriately when users eject or remove removable media or storage devices or when network connections are broken.

System Settings and Notification

The system provides standard metrics and settings for user interface aspects, such as colors, fonts, border width, and drag rectangle (used to detect the start of a drag operation). The system also notifies running applications when its settings change. When your application starts up, query the system to set your application's user interface to match the system parameters to ensure visual and operational consistency. Also, design your application to adjust itself appropriately when the system notifies it of changes to these settings.

The **GetSystemMetrics**, **Get-SysColor**, and **SystemParametersInfo** functions and the WM_SETTINGCHANGE message are important to consider when supporting standard system settings. For more information about these system interfaces, see the documentation included in the Win32 SDK.

Modeless Interaction

When designing your application, try to ensure that it is as interactive and nonmodal as possible. Here are some suggested ways of doing this:

- Use modeless secondary windows wherever possible.

- Segment processes, like printing, so you do not need to load the entire application to perform the operation.

- Make long processes run in the background, keeping the foreground interactive. For example, when something is printing, it should be possible to minimize the window even if the document cannot be altered. The multitasking support of Windows provides for defining separate processes, or *threads*, in the background.

For more information about threads, see the documentation included in the Win32 SDK.

Working with OLE Embedded and OLE Linked Objects

Microsoft OLE provides a set of system interfaces that enables users to combine objects supported by different applications. This chapter outlines guidelines for the interface for OLE embedded and OLE linked objects; you can apply many of these guidelines to any implementation of containers and their components.

The Interaction Model

As data becomes the major focus of interface design, its content is what occupies the user's attention, not the application managing it. In such a design, data is not limited to its native creation and editing environment; that is, the user is not limited to creating or editing data only within its associated application window. Instead, data can be transferred to other types of containers while maintaining its viewing and editing capability in the new container. Compound documents are a common example and illustration of the interaction between containers and their components, but they are not the only expression of this kind of object relationship that OLE can support.

Figure 11.1 shows an example of a compound document. The document includes word-processing text, tabular data from a spreadsheet, a sound recording, and pictures created in other applications.

Classical CD Review

by Thomas D. Becker

The introduction of the compact disc has had a far greater impact on the recording industry than anyone could have imagined, especially the manufacturers of vinyl long play (LP) albums. With the 1991 sales totals in, compact disc is clearly the preferred recording medium for American ears. In addition to audio compact discs, CD-ROMs are appearing on the market offering a multimedia experience of the classical repertoire. The Microsoft Composer Collection brings you the ability to enter the lives and minds of three astounding musical geniuses. That's because the Composer Collection contains three CD-ROM titles full of music, information, and entertainment. They are: Microsoft Multimedia Mozart, Microsoft Multimedia Stravinsky, and Microsoft Multimedia Beethoven. These works are reviewed below — be sure to check them out! *–TDB*

U.S. Compact Disc vs LP Sales ($)

	1983	1987	1991
CDs	6,345K	18,652K	32,657K
LPs	31,538K	26,571K	17,429K
Total	37,883K	45,223K	50,086K

Multimedia Mozart: The Dissonant Quartet

The Voyager Company
Microsoft

In the words of author and music scholar Robert Winter, the string quartet in the eighteenth century was regarded as one of the "most sublime forms of communication." The String Quartet in C Major is no exception. Discover the power and the beauty of this music with Microsoft Multimedia Mozart: *The Dissonant Quartet,* and enter the world in which Mozart created his most memorable masterpieces. Sit back and enjoy *The Dissonant Quartet* in its entirety, or browse around, exploring its themes and emotional dynamics in depth. View the entire piece in a single-screen overview with the *Pocket Audio Guide.*

Multimedia Stravinsky: The Rite of Spring

The Voyager Company
Microsoft

Multimedia Stravinsky: *The Rite of Spring* offers you an in-depth look at this controversial composition. Author Robert

Winter provides a fascinating commentary that follows the music, giving you greater understanding of the subtle dynamics of the instruments and powerful techniques of Stravinsky. You'll also have the opportunity to discover the ballet that accompanied *The Rite of Spring* in performance. Choreographed by Sergei Diaghilev, the ballet was as unusual for its time as the music. To whet your appetite, play this audio clip.

Multimedia Beethoven: The Ninth Symphony

The Voyager Company
Microsoft

Multimedia Beethoven: *The Ninth Symphony* is one of a series of engaging, informative, and interactive musical explorations from Microsoft. It enables you to examine Beethoven's world and life, and explore the form and beauty of one of his foremost compositions. You can compare musical themes, hear selected orchestral instruments, and see the symphonic score come alive. Multimedia Beethoven: *The Ninth Symphony* is an extraordinary opportunity to learn while you listen to one of the world's musical treasures. Explore this inspiring work at your own pace in *A Close Reading.* As you listen to a superb performance of Beethoven's

The Audiophile Journal, June 1994   12

Figure 11.1 A compound document

How was this music review created? First, a user created a document and typed the text, then moved, copied, or linked content from other documents. Data objects that, when moved or copied, retain their native, full-featured editing and operating capabilities in their new container are called *OLE embedded objects*.

A user can also link information. An *OLE linked object* represents or provides access to another object that is in another location in the same container or in a different, separate container.

Generally, containers support any level of nested OLE embedded and linked objects. For example, a user can embed a chart in a worksheet, which, in turn, can be embedded in a word-processing document. The model for interaction is consistent at each level of nesting.

Creating OLE Embedded and OLE Linked Objects

OLE embedded and linked objects are the result of transferring existing objects or creating new objects of a particular type.

Transferring Objects

Transferring objects into a document follows basic command and direct manipulation interaction methods. The following sections provide additional guidelines for these commands when you use them to create OLE embedded or linked objects.

For more information about command transfer and direct manipulation transfer methods, see Chapter 5, "General Interaction Techniques."

The Paste Command

As a general rule, using the Paste command should result in the most complete representation of a transferred object; that is, the object is embedded. However, containers that directly handle the transferred object can accept it optionally as native data instead of embedding it as a separate object, or as a partial or transformed form of the object if that is more appropriate for the destination container.

Use the format of the Paste command to indicate to the user how a transferred object is incorporated by a container. When the user copies a file object, if the container can embed the object, include the object's filename as a suffix to the Paste command. If the object is only a portion of a file, use the short type name — for example, Paste Worksheet or Paste Recording — as shown in Figure 11.2. A short type name can be derived from information stored in the registry. A Paste command with no name implies that the data will be pasted as native information.

For more information about type names and the system registry, see Chapter 10, "Integrating with the System," and the OLE documentation included in the Microsoft Win32 Software Development Kit (SDK).

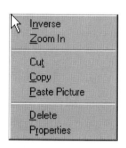

Figure 11.2 The Paste command with short type name

The Paste Special Command

Supply the Paste Special command to give the user explicit control over pasting in the data as native information, an OLE embedded object, or an OLE linked object. The Paste Special command displays its associated dialog box, as shown in Figure 11.3. This dialog box includes a list box with the possible formats that the data can assume in the destination container.

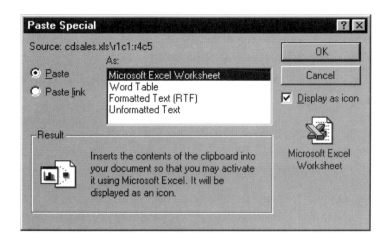

The Win32 SDK includes the Paste Special dialog box and other OLE-related dialog boxes that are described in this chapter.

Figure 11.3 The Paste Special dialog box

In the formats listed in the Paste Special dialog box, include the object's full type name first, followed by other appropriate native data forms. When a linked object has been cut or copied, precede its object type by the word "Linked" in the format list. For example, if the user copies a linked Microsoft Excel worksheet, the Paste Special dialog box shows "Linked Microsoft Excel Worksheet" in the list of format options because it inserts an exact duplicate of the original linked worksheet. Native data formats begin with the destination application's name and can be expressed in the same terms the destination identifies in its own menus. The initially selected format in the list corresponds to the format that the Paste command uses. For example, if the Paste command is displayed as Paste *Object Filename* or Paste *Short Type Name* because the data to be embedded is a file or portion of a file, this is the format that is initially selected in the Paste Special list box.

To support creation of a linked object, the Paste Special dialog box includes a Paste Link option. Figure 11.4 shows this option.

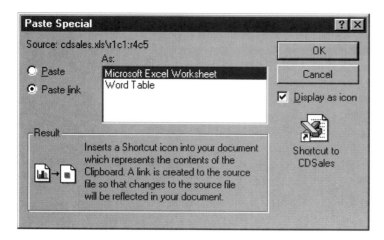

Figure 11.4 Paste Special dialog box with Paste Link option set

A Display As Icon check box allows the user to choose displaying the OLE embedded or linked object as an icon. At the bottom of the dialog box is a section that includes text and pictures that describe the result of the operation. Table 11.1 lists the descriptive text for use in the Paste Special dialog box.

Table 11.1 Descriptive Text for Paste Special Command

Function	Resulting text
Paste as an OLE embedded object.	"Inserts the contents of the Clipboard into your document so you that you may activate it using *CompanyName ApplicationName*."
Paste as an OLE embedded object so that it appears as an icon.	"Inserts the contents of the Clipboard into your document so you that you may activate it using *CompanyName ApplicationName* application. It will be displayed as an icon."
Paste as native data.	"Inserts the contents of the Clipboard into your document as *Native Type Name*. [*Optional additional Help sentence.*]"
Paste as an OLE linked object.	"Inserts a picture of the contents of the Clipboard into your document. Paste Link creates a link to the source file so that changes to the source file will be reflected in your document."

(Continued)

Function	Resulting text
Paste as an OLE linked object so that it appears as a shortcut icon.	"Inserts a Shortcut icon into your document which represents the contents of the Clipboard. A link is created to the source file so that changes to the source file will be reflected in your document."
Paste as linked native data.	"Inserts the contents of the Clipboard into your document as *Native Type Name*. A link is created to the source file so that changes to the source file will be reflected in your document."

The Paste Link, Paste Shortcut, and Create Shortcut Commands

If linking is a common function in your application, you can optionally include a command that optimizes this process. Use a Paste Link command to support creating a linked object or linked native data. When using the command to create a linked object, include the name of the object preceded by the word "to" — for example, "Paste Link to Latest Sales." Omitting the name implies that the operation results in linked native data.

Use a Paste Shortcut command to support creation of a linked object that appears as a shortcut icon. You can also include a Create Shortcut command that creates a shortcut icon in the container. Apply these commands to containers where icons are commonly used.

Direct Manipulation

You should also support direct manipulation interaction techniques, such as drag and drop, for creating OLE embedded or linked objects. When the user drags a selection into a container, the container application interprets the operation using information supplied by the source, such as the selection's type and format, and by the destination container's own context, such as the container's type and its default transfer operation. For example, dragging a spreadsheet cell selection into a word-processing document can result in an OLE embedded table object. Dragging the same cell selection within the

For more information about using direct manipulation for moving, copying, and linking objects, see Chapter 5, "General Interaction Techniques."

spreadsheet, however, would likely result in simply transferring the data in the cells. Similarly, the destination container in which the user drops the selection can also determine whether the dragging operation results in an OLE linked object.

For nondefault OLE drag and drop, the container application displays a pop-up menu with appropriate transfer commands at the end of the drag. The choices may include multiple commands that transfer the data in a different format or presentation. For example, as shown in Figure 11.5, a container application could offer the following choices for creating links: Link Here, Link *Short Type Name* Here, and Create Shortcut Here, respectively resulting in a native data link, an OLE linked object displayed as content, and an OLE linked object displayed as an icon. The choices depend on what the container can support.

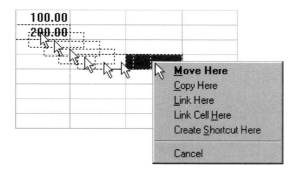

Figure 11.5 Containers can offer different OLE link options

The default appearance of a transferred object also depends on the destination container application. For most types of documents, make the default command one that results in the data or content presentation of the object (or in the case of an OLE linked object, a representation of the content), rather than as an icon. If the user chooses Create Shortcut Here as the transfer operation, display the transferred object as an icon. If the object cannot be displayed as content — for example, because it does not support OLE — always display the object as an icon.

Transfer of Data to Desktop

The system allows the user to transfer data selection within a file to the desktop or folders providing that the application supports the OLE transfer protocol. For move or copy operations — using the Cut, Copy, and Paste commands or direct manipulation — the transfer operation results in a file icon called a *scrap*. A link operation also results in a shortcut icon that represents a shortcut into a document.

When the user transfers a scrap into a container supported by your application, integrate it as if it were being transferred from its original source. For example, if the user transfers a selected range of cells from a spreadsheet to the desktop, it becomes a scrap. If the user transfers the resulting scrap into a word-processing document, the document should incorporate the scrap as if the cells were transferred directly from the spreadsheet. Similarly, if the user transfers the scrap back into the spreadsheet, the spreadsheet should integrate the cells as if they had been transferred within that spreadsheet. (Typically, internal transfers of native data within a container result in repositioning the data rather than transforming it.)

Inserting New Objects

In addition to transferring objects, you can support user creation of OLE embedded or linked objects by generating a new object based on an existing object or object type and inserting the new object into the target container.

The Insert Object Command

Include an Insert Object command on the menu responsible for creating or importing new objects into a container, such as an Insert menu. If no such menu exists, use the Edit menu. When the user selects this command, display the Insert Object dialog box, as shown in Figure 11.6. This dialog box allows the user to generate new objects based on their object type or an existing file.

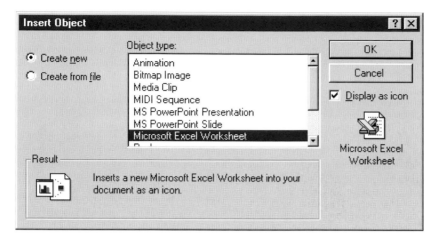

Figure 11.6 The Insert Object dialog box

The type list is composed of the type names of registered types. When the user selects a type from the list box and chooses the OK button, an object of the selected type is created and embedded.

For more information about type names and the registry, see Chapter 10, "Integrating with the System."

The user can also create an OLE embedded or linked object from an existing file, using the Create From File and Link options. When the user sets these options and chooses the OK button, the result is the same as directly copying or linking the selected file.

When the user chooses the Create From File option button, the Object Type list is removed, and a text box and Browse button appear in its place, as shown in Figure 11.7. Ignore any selection formerly displayed in the Object Type list box (shown in Figure 11.6).

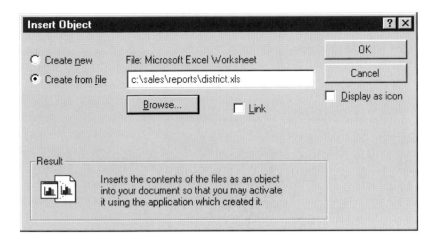

Figure 11.7 Creating an OLE embedded object from an existing file

The text box initially includes the current directory as the selection. The user can edit the current directory path when specifying a file. As an alternative, the Browse button displays an Open dialog box that allows the user to navigate through the file system to select a file. Use the file's type to determine the type of the resulting OLE object.

Use the Link check box to support the creation of an OLE linked object to the file specified. The Insert Object dialog box displays this option only when the user chooses the Create From File option. This means that a user cannot insert an OLE linked object when choosing the Create New option button, because linked objects can be created only from existing files.

The Display As Icon check box in the Insert Object dialog box enables the user to specify whether to display the OLE object as an icon. When this option is set, the icon appears beneath the check box. An OLE linked object displayed as an icon is the equivalent of a shortcut icon. It should appear with the link symbol over the icon.

At the bottom of the Insert Object dialog box, text and pictures describe the final outcome of the insertion. Table 11.2 outlines the syntax of descriptive text to use within the Insert Object dialog box.

If the user chooses a non-OLE file for insertion, it can be inserted only as an icon. The result is an OLE package. A *package* is an OLE encapsulation of a file so that it can be embedded in an OLE container. Because packages support limited editing and viewing capabilities, support OLE for all your object types so they will not be converted into packages.

Table 11.2 Descriptive Text for Insert Object Dialog Box

Function	Resulting text
Create a new OLE embedded object based on the selected type.	"Inserts a new *Type Name* into your document."
Create a new OLE embedded object based on the selected type and display it as an icon.	"Inserts a new *Type Name* into your document as an icon."
Create a new OLE embedded object based on a selected file.	"Inserts the contents of the file as an object into your document so that you may activate it using the application which created it."
Create a new OLE embedded object based on a selected file (copies the file) and display it as an icon.	"Inserts the contents of the file as an object into your document so that you may activate it using the application which created it. It will be displayed as an icon."
Create an OLE linked object that is linked to a selected file.	"Inserts a picture of the file contents into your document. The picture will be linked to the file so that changes to the file will be reflected in your document."
Create an OLE linked object that is linked to a selected file and display it as a Shortcut icon.	"Inserts a Shortcut icon into your document which represents the file. The Shortcut icon will be linked to the original file, so that you can quickly open the original from inside your document."

You can also use the context of the current selection in the container to determine the format of the newly created object and the effect of it being inserted into the container. For example, an inserted graph can automatically reflect the data in a selected table. Use the following guidelines to support predictable insertion:

- If an inserted object is not based on the current selection, follow the same conventions as for a Paste command and add or replace the selection depending on the context. For example, in text or list contexts, where the selection represents a specific insertion location, replace the active selection. For nonordered or Z-ordered contexts, where the selection does not represent an explicit insertion point, add the object, using the destination's context to determine where to place the object.

- If the new object is automatically connected (linked) to the selection (for example, an inserted graph based on selected table data), insert the new object in addition to the selection and make the inserted object the new selection.

After inserting an OLE embedded object, activate it for editing. However, if the user inserts an OLE linked object, do not activate the object.

For more information about the guidelines for inserting an object with a Paste command, see Chapter 5, "General Interaction Techniques."

Other Techniques for Inserting Objects

The Insert Object command provides support for inserting all registered OLE objects. You can include additional commands tailored to provide access to common or frequently used object types. You can implement these as additional menu commands or as toolbar buttons or other controls. These buttons provide the same functionality as the Insert Object dialog box, but perform more efficiently. Figure 11.8 illustrates two examples. The drawing button inserts a new blank drawing object; the graph button creates a new graph that uses the data values from a currently selected table.

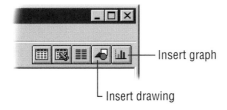

Insert graph

Insert drawing

Figure 11.8 Using toolbar buttons for creating new objects

Displaying Objects

While a container can control whether to display an OLE embedded or linked object in its content or icon presentation, the container requests the object to display itself. In the content presentation, the object may be visually indistinguishable from native objects, as shown in Figure 11.9.

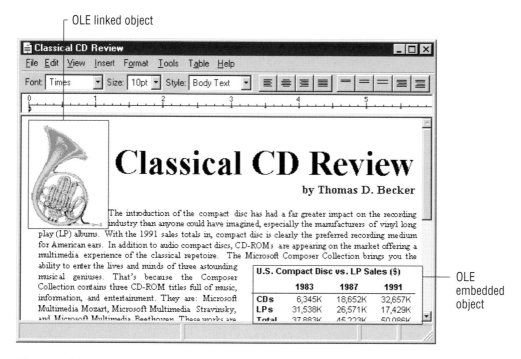

Figure 11.9 A compound document containing OLE objects

You may find it preferable to enable the user to visually identify OLE embedded or linked objects without interacting with them. To do so, you can include a Show Objects command that, when chosen, displays a solid border, one pixel wide, drawn in the window text color around the extent of an OLE embedded object and a dotted border around OLE linked objects (shown in Figure 11.10). If the container application cannot guarantee that an OLE linked object is up-to-date with its source because of an unsuccessful automatic update or a manual link, the system should draw a dotted border using the system grayed text color to suggest that the OLE linked object is out of date. The border should be drawn around a container's first-level objects only, not objects nested below this level.

The **GetSysColor** function provides the current settings for window text color (COLOR_WINDOWTEXT) and grayed text color (COLOR_GRAYTEXT). For more information about this function, see the documentation included in the Win32 SDK.

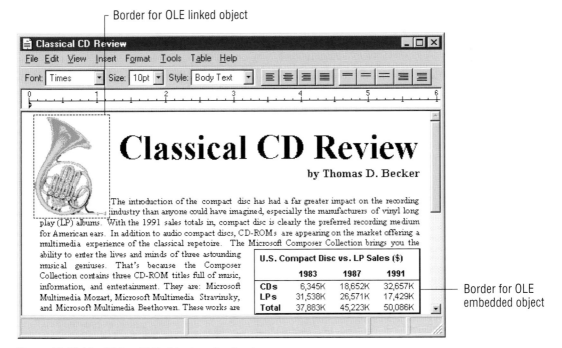

Border for OLE linked object

Border for OLE embedded object

Figure 11.10 Identifying OLE objects using borders

If these border conventions are not adequate to distinguish OLE embedded and linked objects, you can optionally include additional distinctions; however, make them clearly distinct from the appearance for any standard visual states and distinguish OLE embedded from OLE linked objects.

Whenever the user creates an OLE linked or embedded object with the Display As Icon check box set, display the icon using the icon of its type, unless the user explicitly changes it. A linked icon also includes the shortcut graphic. If an icon is not registered in the registry for the object, use the system-generated icon.

An icon includes a label. When the user creates an OLE embedded object, define the icon's label to be one of the following, based on availability:

- The name of the object, if the object has an existing human-readable name such as a filename without its extension.

- The object's registered short type name (for example, Picture, Worksheet, and so on), if the object does not have a name.

- The object's registered full type name (for example, a bitmap image, a Microsoft Excel Worksheet), if the object has no name or registered short type name.

- "Document" if an object has no name, a short type name, or a registered type name.

When an OLE linked object is displayed as an icon, define the label using the source filename as it appears in the file system, preceded by the words "Shortcut to" — for example, "Shortcut to Annual Report." The path of the source is not included. Avoid displaying the filename extension unless the user chooses the system option to display extensions or the file type is not registered.

> The system provides support to automatically format the name correctly if you use the **GetIconOfFile** function. For more information about this function, see the OLE documentation included in the Win32 SDK.

When the user creates an OLE object linked to only a portion of a document (file), follow the same conventions for labeling the shortcut icon. However, because a container can include multiple links to different portions of the same file, you may want to provide further identification to differentiate linked objects. You can do this by appending a portion of the end of the link path (moniker). For example, you may want to include everything from the end of the path up to the last or next to last occurrence of a link path delimiter. OLE applications should use the exclamation point (!) character for identifying a data range. However, the link path may include other types of delimiters. Be careful when deriving an identifier from the link path to format the additional information using only valid filename characters so that if the user transfers the shortcut icon to a folder or the desktop, the name can still be used.

Selecting Objects

An OLE embedded or linked object follows the selection behavior and appearance techniques supported by its container; the container application supplies the specific appearance of the object. For example, Figure 11.11 shows how the linked drawing of a horn is handled as part of a contiguous selection in the document.

For information about selection, see Chapter 5, "General Interaction Techniques." For information about selection appearance, see Chapter 13, "Visual Design."

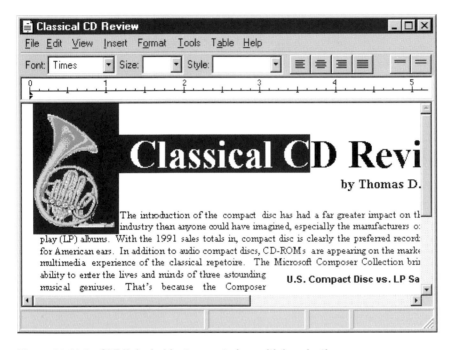

Figure 11.11 An OLE linked object as part of a multiple selection

When the user individually selects the object, display the object with an appropriate selection appearance. For example, for the content view of an object, display it with handles, as shown in Figure 11.12. For OLE linked objects, overlay the content view's lower left corner with the shortcut graphic. In addition, if your application's window includes a status bar that displays messages, display an appropriate description of how to activate the object (see Table 11.3 later in this chapter).

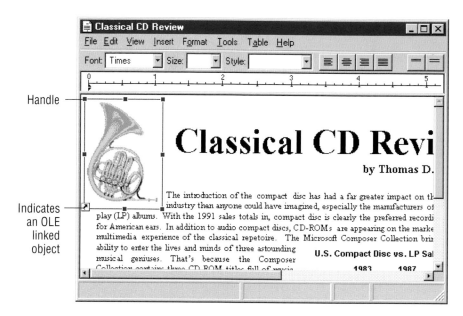

Handle

Indicates an OLE linked object

Figure 11.12 An individually selected OLE linked object

When the object is displayed as an icon, use the same selection appearance as for selected icons in folders and on the desktop, as shown in Figure 11.13.

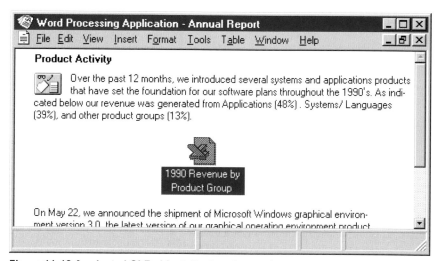

Figure 11.13 A selected OLE object displayed as an icon

Accessing Commands for Selected Objects

A container application always displays the commands that can be applied to its objects. When the user selects an OLE embedded or linked object as part of the selection of native data in a container, enable commands that apply to the selection as a whole. When the user individually selects the object, enable only commands that apply specifically to the object. The container application retrieves these commands from what has been registered by the object's type in the registry and displays these commands in the menus that are supplied for the object. If your application includes a menu bar, include the selected object's commands on a submenu of the Edit menu, or as a separate menu on the menu bar. Use the name of the object as the text for the menu item. If you use the short type name as the name of the object, add the word "Object." For an OLE linked object, use the short type name, preceded by the word "Linked." Figure 11.14 shows these variations.

You can also support operations based on the selection appearance. For example, you can support operations, such as resizing, using the handles you supply. When the user resizes a selected OLE object, however, scale the presentation of the object, because there is no method by which another operation, such as cropping, can be applied to the OLE object.

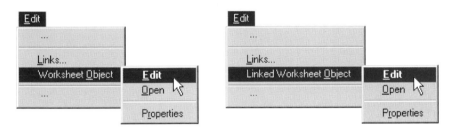

Figure 11.14 Drop-down menus for selected OLE object

Define the first letter of the word "Object", or its localized equivalent, as the access character for keyboard users. When no object is selected, display the command with just the text, "Object", and disable it.

A container application should also provide a pop-up menu for a selected OLE object (shown in Figure 11.15), displayed using the standard interaction techniques for pop-up menus (clicking with mouse button 2). Include on this menu the commands that apply to the object as a whole as a unit of content, such as transfer commands and the object's registered commands. In the pop-up menu, display the object's registered commands as individual menu items rather than in a cascading menu. It is not necessary to include the object's name or the word "Object" as part of the menu item text.

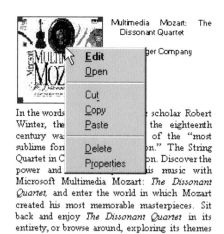

Multimedia Mozart: The Dissonant Quartet

...ger Company

Edit
Open

Cut
Copy
Paste

Delete
Properties

In the words ... scholar Robert Winter, the ... the eighteenth century wa... of the "most sublime for... ...n." The String Quartet in C ... ...n. Discover the power and ... ...is music with Microsoft Multimedia Mozart: *The Dissonant Quartet*, and enter the world in which Mozart created his most memorable masterpieces. Sit back and enjoy *The Dissonant Quartet* in its entirety, or browse around, exploring its themes and emotional dynamics in depth. View the entire piece in a single-screen overview with the *Pocket Audio Guide*.

Winter provides a fascinating commentary that follows the music, giving you greater understanding of the subtle dynamics of the instruments and powerful techniques of Stravinsky. You'll also have the opportunity to discover the ballet that accompanied *The Rite of Spring* in performance. Choreographed by Sergei Diaghilev, the ballet was as unusual for its time as the music. To whet your appetite, play this audio clip.

Multimedia Beethoven: The Ninth Symphony

The Voyager Company
Microsoft

Figure 11.15 Pop-up menu for an OLE embedded picture

In the drop-down menu and the pop-up menu, include a Properties command. You can also include commands that depend on the state of the object. For example, a media object that uses Play and Rewind as operations disables Rewind when the object is at the beginning of the media object.

If an object's type is not registered, you still supply any commands that can be appropriately applied to the object as content, such as transfer commands, alignment commands, and an Edit and Properties command. When the user chooses the Edit command, display the system-supplied message box, as shown in Figure 11.41. This message box provides access to a dialog box that enables the user to choose from a list of applications that can operate on the type or convert the object's type.

Activating Objects

Although selecting an object provides access to commands applicable to the object as a whole, it does not provide access to editing the content of the object. The object must be activated in order to provide user interaction with the internal content of the object. There are two basic models for activating objects: outside-in activation and inside-out activation.

Outside-in Activation

Outside-in activation requires that the user choose an explicit activation command. Clicking, or some other selection operation, performed on an object that is already selected simply reselects that object and does not constitute an explicit action. The user activates the object by using a particular command such as Edit or Play, usually the object's default command. Shortcut actions that correspond to these commands, such as double-clicking or pressing a shortcut key, can also activate the object. Most OLE container applications employ this model because it allows the user to easily select objects and reduces the risk of inadvertently activating an object whose underlying code may take a significant amount of time to load and dismiss.

When supporting outside-in activation, display the standard pointer (northwest arrow) over an outside-in activated object within your container when the object is selected, but inactive. This indicates to the user that the outside-in object behaves as a single, opaque object. When the user activates the object, the object's application displays the appropriate pointer for its content. Use the registry to determine the object's activation command.

Inside-out Activation

With *inside-out activation*, interaction with an object is direct; that is, the object is activated as the user moves the pointer over the extent of the object. From the user's perspective, inside-out objects are indistinguishable from native data because the content of the object is directly interactive and no additional action is necessary. Use this method for the design of objects that benefit from direct interaction, or when activating the object has little effect on performance or use of system resources.

Inside-out activation requires closer cooperation between the container and the object. For example, when the user begins a selection within an inside-out object, the container must clear its own selection so that the behavior is consistent with normal selection interaction. An object supporting inside-out activation controls the appearance of the pointer as it moves over its extent and responds immediately to input. Therefore, to select the object as a whole, the user selects the border, or some other handle, provided by the object or its container. For example, the container application can support selection techniques, such as region selection that select the object.

Although the default behavior for an OLE embedded object is outside-in activation, you can store information in the registry that indicates that an object's type (application class) is capable of inside-out activation (OLEMISC_INSIDEOUT) and prefers inside-out behavior (OLEMISC_ACTIVATEWHENVISIBLE). You can set these values in a **MiscStatus** subkey, under the **CLSID** subkey of the **HKEY_CLASSES_ROOT** key.

For more information about how to access OLEMISC_ INSIDEOUT and OLEMISC_ACTIVATE-WHENVISIBLE and the **IOleObject:: GetMiscStatus** function, see the OLE documentation included in the Win32 SDK.

Container Control of Activation

The container application determines how to activate its component objects: either it allows the inside-out objects to handle events directly or it intercedes and only activates them upon an explicit action. This is true regardless of the capability or preference setting of the object. That is, even though an object may register inside-out activation, it can be treated by a particular container as outside-in. Use an activation style for your container that is most appropriate for its specific use and is in keeping with its own native style of activation so that objects can be easily assimilated.

Regardless of the activation capability of the object, a container should always activate its content objects of the same type consistently. Otherwise, the unpredictability of the interface is likely to impair its usability. Following are four potential container activation methods and when to use them.

Activation method	When to use
Outside-in throughout	This is the most common design for containers that often embed large OLE objects and deal with them as whole units. Because many available OLE objects are not yet inside-out capable, most compound document editors support outside-in throughout to preserve uniformity.
Inside-out throughout	Ultimately, OLE containers will blend embedded objects with native data so seamlessly that the distinction dissolves. Inside-out throughout containers will become more feasible as increasing numbers of OLE objects support inside-out activation.
Outside-in plus inside-out preferred objects	Some containers may use an outside-in model for large, foreign embeddings but also include some inside-out preferred objects as though they were native objects (by supporting OLEMISC_ACTIVATE-WHENVISIBLE). For example, an OLE document might present form control objects as inside-out native data while activating larger spreadsheet and chart objects as outside-in.
Switch between inside-out throughout and outside-in throughout	Visual programming and forms layout design applications may include design and run modes. In this type of environment, a container typically holds an object that is capable of inside-out activation (if not preferable) and alternates between outside-in throughout when designing and inside-out throughout when running.

OLE Visual Editing of OLE Embedded Objects

One of the most common uses for activating an object is editing its content in its current location. Supporting this type of in-place interaction is called *OLE visual editing*, because the user can edit the object within the visual context of its container.

Unless the container and the object both support inside-out activation, the user activates an embedded object for visual editing by selecting the object and choosing its Edit command, either from a drop-down or pop-up menu. You can also support shortcut techniques. For example, by making Edit the object's default operation, the user can double-click to activate the object for editing. Similarly, you can support pressing the ENTER key as a shortcut for activating the object.

Although earlier versions of OLE user interface documentation suggested the ALT+ENTER key combination to activate an object if the ENTER key was already assigned, this key combination is now the recommended shortcut key for the Properties command. Instead, support the pop-up menu shortcut key. This enables the user to activate the object by selecting the command from the pop-up menu.

When the user activates an OLE embedded object for visual editing, the user interface for its content becomes available and blended into its container application's interface. The object can display its frame *adornments*, such as row or column headers, handles, or scroll bars, outside the extent of the object and temporarily cover neighboring material. The object's application can also change the menu interface, which can range from adding menu items to existing drop-down menus to replacing entire drop-down menus. The object can also add toolbars, status bars, supplemental palette windows, and provide pop-up menus for selected content.

The degree of interface blending varies based on the nature of the OLE embedded object. Some OLE embedded objects may require extensive support and consequently result in dramatic changes to the container application's interface. Finer grain objects that emulate the native components of a container may have little or no need to make changes in the container's user interface. The container always determines the degree to which an OLE embedded object's interface can be blended with its own, regardless of the capability or preference of the OLE embedded object. A container application that provides its own interface for an OLE embedded object can suppress an OLE embedded object's own interface. Figure 11.16 shows how the interface might appear when its embedded worksheet is active.

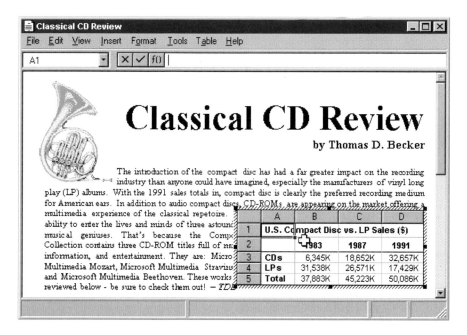

Figure 11.16 An embedded worksheet activated for OLE visual editing

When the user activates an OLE embedded object, avoid changing the view and position of the rest of the content in the window. Although it may seem reasonable to scroll the window and thereby preserve the content's position, doing so can disturb the user's focus, because the active object shifts down to accommodate a new toolbar and shifts back up when it is deactivated. An exception may be when the activation exposes an area in which the container has nothing to display. However, even in this situation, you may wish to render a visible region or filled area that corresponds to the background area outside the visible edge of the container so that activation keeps the presentation stable.

Activation does not affect the title bar. Always display the top-level container's name. For example, when the worksheet shown in Figure 11.16 is activated, the title bar continues to display the name of the document in which the worksheet is embedded and not the name of the worksheet. You can provide access to the name of the worksheet by supporting property sheets for your OLE embedded objects.

A container can contain multiply nested OLE embedded objects. However, only a single level is active at any one time. Figure 11.17 shows a document containing an active embedded worksheet with an embedded graph of its own. Clicking on the graph merely selects it as an object within the worksheet.

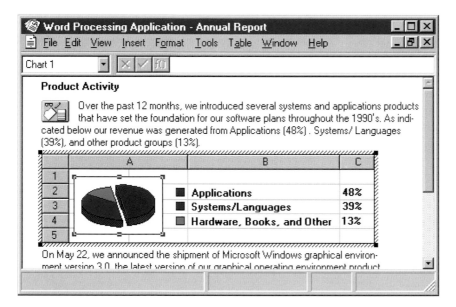

Figure 11.17 A selected graph within an active worksheet

Activating the embedded graph, for example, by choosing the graph's Edit command, activates the object for OLE visual editing, displaying the graph's menus in the document's menu bar. This is shown in Figure 11.18. At any given time, only the interface for the currently active object and the topmost container are presented; intervening parent objects do not remain visibly active.

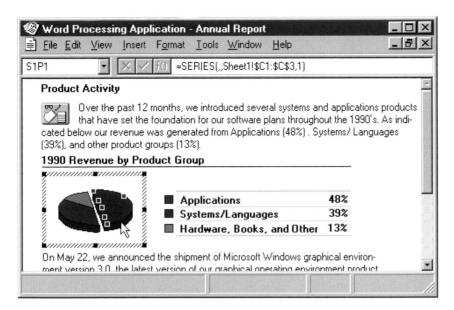

Figure 11.18 An active graph within a worksheet

An OLE embedded object should support OLE visual editing at any view magnification level because its container's view can be scaled arbitrarily. If an object cannot accommodate OLE visual editing in its container's current view scale, or if its container does not support OLE visual editing, open the object into a separate window for editing. For more information about opening OLE embedded objects, see the section, "Opening Embedded Objects," later in this chapter.

For any user interaction outside the extent of an active object, such as when the user selects or activates another object in the container, deactivate the current object and give the focus to the new object. This is also true for an object that is nested in the currently active object. An OLE embedded object application should also support user deactivation when the user presses the ESC key, after which it becomes the selected object of its container. If the object uses the ESC key at all times for its internal operation, the SHIFT+ESC key should deactivate the object.

Edits made to an active object become part of the container immediately and automatically, just like edits made to native data. Consequently, do not display an "Update changes?" message box when the object is deactivated. Remember that the user can abandon changes to the entire container, embedded or otherwise, if the topmost container includes an explicit command that prompts the user to save or discard changes to the container's file.

While Edit is the most common command for activating an OLE embedded object for OLE visual editing, other commands can also create such activation. For example, when the user carries out a Play command on a video clip, you can display a set of commands that allow the user to control the clip (Rewind, Stop, and Fast Forward). In this case, the Play command provides a form of OLE visual editing.

> OLE embedded objects participate in the undo stack of the window in which they are activated. For more information about embedded objects and the undo stack, see the section, "Undo Operations for Active and Open Objects," later in this chapter.

The Active Hatched Border

If a container allows an OLE embedded object's user interface to change its user interface, then the active object's application displays a hatched border around itself to show the extent of the OLE visual editing context (shown in Figure 11.19). For example, if an active object places its menus in the topmost container's menu bar, display the active hatched border. The object's request to display its menus in the container's menu bar must be granted by the container application. If the object's menus do not appear in the menu bar (because the object did not require menus or the container refused its request for menu display), or the object is otherwise accommodated by the container's user interface, you need not display the hatched border. The hatched pattern is made up of 45-degree diagonal lines.

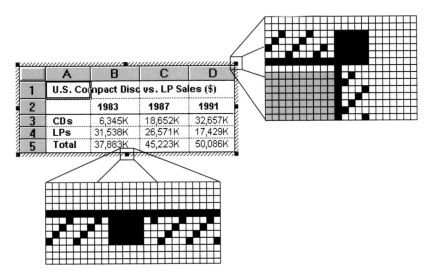

Figure 11.19 Hatched border around active OLE embedded objects

The active object takes on the appearance that is best suited for its own editing; for example, the object may display frame adornments, table gridlines, handles, and other editing aids. Because the hatched border is part of the object's territory, the active object defines the pointer that appears when the user moves the mouse over the border.

Clicking in the hatched pattern (and not on the handles) is interpreted by the object as clicking just inside the edge of the border of the active object. The hatched area is effectively a hot zone that prevents inadvertent deactivations and makes it easier to select the content of the embedded object.

Menu Integration

As the user activates different objects, different commands need to be accessed in the window's user interface. The following classification of menus — primary container menu, workspace menu, and active object menus — separates the interface based on menu groupings. This classification enhances the usability of the interface by defining the interface changes as the user activates or deactivates different objects.

Primary Container Menu

The topmost or primary container viewed in a primary window controls the work area of that window. If the primary container includes a menu bar, it supplies at least one menu that includes commands that apply to the primary container as an entire unit. For example, for document file objects, use a File menu for this purpose, as shown in Figure 11.20. This menu includes document and file level commands such as Open, Save, and Print. Always display the primary container menu in the menu bar at all times, regardless of which object is active.

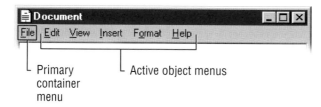

Figure 11.20 OLE visual editing menu layout

Workspace Menu

An MDI-style application also includes a workspace menu (typically labeled "Window") on its menu bar that provides commands for managing the document windows displayed within it, as shown in Figure 11.21. Like the primary container menu, the workspace menu should always be displayed, independent of object activation.

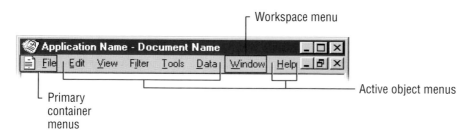

Figure 11.21 OLE visual editing menu layout for MDI

Active Object Menus

Active objects can define menus that appear on the primary container's menu bar that operate on their content. Place commands for moving, deleting, searching and replacing, creating new items, applying tools, styles, and Help on these menus. As the name suggests, active object commands are executed by the currently active object and apply only within the extent of that object. If no embedded objects are active, but the window is active, the primary container should be considered the active object.

An active object's menus typically occupy the majority of the menu bar. Organize these menus following the same order and grouping that you display when the user opens the object into its own window. Avoid naming your active object menus File or Window, because primary containers often use those titles. Objects that use direct manipulation as their sole interface need not provide active object menus or alter the menu bar when activated.

The active object can display a View menu. However, when the object is active, include only commands that apply to the object. If the object's container requires its document or window-level "viewing" commands to be available while an object is active, place them on a menu that represents the primary container window's pop-up menu and on the Window menu — if present.

When designing the interface of selected objects within an active object, follow the same guidelines as that of a primary container and one of its selected OLE embedded objects; that is, the active object displays the commands of the selected object (as registered in the registry) either as submenus of its menus or as separate menus.

An active object also has the responsibility for defining and displaying pop-up menus for its content, with commands appropriate to apply to any selection within it. Figure 11.22 shows an example of a pop-up menu for a selection within an active bitmap image.

Selection within the active object

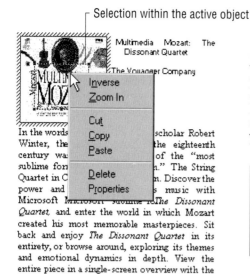

Multimedia Mozart: The Dissonant Quartet

The Voyager Company

Inverse
Zoom In

Cut
Copy
Paste

Delete
Properties

In the words [...] scholar Robert Winter, the [...] the eighteenth century wa [...] of the "most sublime for [...] ." The String Quartet in C [...] . Discover the power and [...] s music with Microsoft [...] *The Dissonant Quartet*, and enter the world in which Mozart created his most memorable masterpieces. Sit back and enjoy *The Dissonant Quartet* in its entirety, or browse around, exploring its themes and emotional dynamics in depth. View the entire piece in a single-screen overview with the *Pocket Audio Guide.*

Winter provides a fascinating commentary that follows the music, giving you greater understanding of the subtle dynamics of the instruments and powerful techniques of Stravinsky. You'll also have the opportunity to discover the ballet that accompanied *The Rite of Spring* in performance. Choreographed by Sergei Diaghilev, the ballet was as unusual for its time as the music. To whet your appetite, play this audio clip.

Multimedia Beethoven: The Ninth Symphony

The Voyager Company
Microsoft

Figure 11.22 Example of pop-up menu for a selection in an active object

Keyboard Interface Integration

In addition to integrating the menus, you must also integrate the access keys and shortcut keys used in these menus.

Access Keys

The access keys assigned to the primary container's menu, an active object's menus, and MDI workspace menus should be unique. Following are guidelines for defining access keys for integrating these menu names:

- Use the first letter of the menu of the primary container as its access key character. Typically, this is "F" for File. Use "W" for a workspace's Window menu. Localized versions should use the appropriate equivalent.

- Use characters other than those assigned to the primary container and workspace menus for the menu titles of active OLE embedded objects. (If an OLE embedded object has previously existed as a standalone document, its corresponding application avoids these characters already.)

- Define unique access keys for an object's registered commands and avoid characters that are potential access keys for common container-supplied commands, such as Cut, Copy, Paste, Delete, and Properties.

Despite these guidelines, if the same access character is used more than once, pressing an ALT+*letter* combination cycles through each command, selecting the next match each time it is pressed. To carry out the command, the user must press the ENTER key when it is selected. This is standard system behavior for menus.

Shortcut Keys

For primary containers and active objects, follow the shortcut key guidelines covered in this guide. In addition, avoid defining shortcut keys for active objects that are likely to be assigned to the container. For example, include the standard editing and transfer (Cut, Copy, and Paste) shortcut keys, but avoid File menu or system-assigned shortcut keys. There is no provision for registering shortcut keys for a selected object's commands.

For more information about defining shortcut keys, see Chapter 4, "Input Basics," and Appendix B, "Keyboard Interface Summary."

If a container and an active object share a common shortcut key, the active object captures the event. That is, if the user activates an OLE embedded object, its application code directly processes the shortcut key. If the active object does not process the key event, it is available to the container, which has the option to process it or not. This applies to any level of nested OLE embedded objects. If there is duplication between shortcut keys, the user can always direct the key based on where the active focus is by activating that object. To direct a shortcut key to the container, the user deactivates an OLE embedded object — for example, by selecting in the container — but outside the OLE embedded object. Activation, not selection, of an OLE embedded object allows it to receive the keyboard events. The exception is inside-out activation, where activation results from selection.

Toolbars, Frame Adornments, and Palette Windows

Integrating drop-down and pop-up menus is straightforward because they are confined within a particular area and follow standard conventions. Toolbars, frame adornments (as shown in Figure 11.23), and palette windows can be constructed less predictably, so it is best to follow a replacement strategy when integrating these elements for active objects. That is, toolbars, frame adornments, and palette windows are displayed and removed as entire sets rather than integrated at the individual control level — just like menu titles on the menu bar.

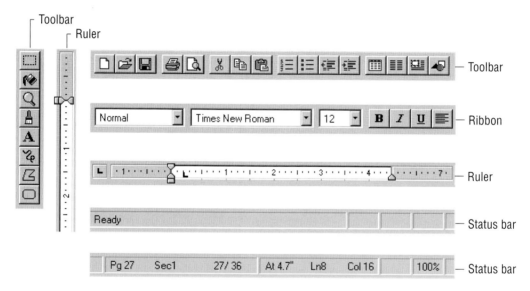

Figure 11.23 Examples of toolbars, status bars, and frame adornments

When the user activates an object, the object application requests a specific area from its container in which to post its tools. The container application determines whether to:

- Replace its tool (or tools) with the tools of the object, if the requested space is already occupied by a container tool.

- Add the object's tool (or tools), if a container tool does not occupy the requested space.

- Refuse to display the tool (or tools) at all. This is the least desirable method.

Toolbars, frame adornments, and palette windows are all basically the same interfaces — they differ primarily in their location and the degree of shared control between container and object. There are four locations in the interface where these types of controls reside, and you determine their location by their scope. Figure 11.24 shows possible positions for interface controls.

Location	Description
Object frame	Place object-specific controls, such as a table header or a local coordinate ruler, directly adjacent to the object itself for tightly coupled interaction between the object and its interface. An object (such as a spreadsheet) can include scrollbars if its content extends beyond the boundaries of its frame.
Pane frame	Locate view-specific controls at the pane level. Rulers and viewing tools are common examples.
Document (primary container) window frame	Attach tools that apply to the entire document (or documents in the case of an MDI window) just inside any edge of its primary window frame. Popular examples include ribbons, drawing tools, and status lines.
Windowed	Display tools in a palette window — this allows the user to place them as desired. A palette window typically floats above the primary window and any other windows of which it is part.

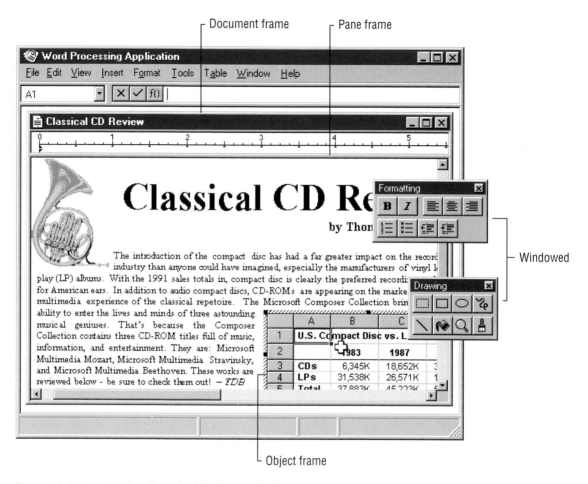

Figure 11.24 Possible locations for interface controls

When determining where to locate a tool area, avoid situations that cause the view to shift up and down as different-sized tool areas are displayed or removed as the user activates different objects. This can be disruptive to the user's task.

Because container tool areas can remain visible while an object is active, they are available to the user simply by interacting with them — this can reactivate the container application. The container determines whether to activate or leave the object active. If toolbar buttons of an active object represent a primary container or workspace commands, such as Save, Print, or Open, disable them.

For more information about the negotiation protocols used for activation, see the OLE documentation included in the Win32 SDK.

As the user resizes or scrolls its container's area, an active object and its toolbar or frame adornments placed on the object frame are clipped, as is all container content. These interface control areas lie in the same plane as the object. Even when the object is clipped, the user can still edit the visible part of the object in place and while the visible frame adornments are operational.

Some container applications scroll at certain increments that may prevent portions of an OLE embedded object from being visually edited. For example, consider a large picture embedded in a worksheet cell. The worksheet scrolls vertically in complete row increments; the top of the pane is always aligned with the top edge of a row. If the embedded picture is too large to fit within the pane at one time, its bottom portion is clipped and consequently never viewed or edited in place. In cases like this, the user can open the picture into its own window for editing.

Window panes clip frame adornments of nested embedded objects, but not by the extent of any parent object. Objects at the very edge of their container's extent or boundary potentially display adornments that extend beyond the bounds of the container's defined area. In this case, if the container displays items that extend beyond the edge, display all the adornments; otherwise, clip the adornments at the edge of the container. Do not temporarily move the object within its container just to accommodate the appearance of an active embedded object's adornments. A pane-level control can potentially be clipped by the primary (or parent, in the case of MDI) window frame, and a primary window adornment or control is clipped by other primary windows.

Opening OLE Embedded Objects

The previous sections have focused on OLE visual editing — editing an OLE embedded object in place; that is, its current location is within its container. Alternatively, the user can also open embedded objects into their own window. This gives the user the opportunity of seeing more of the object or seeing the object in a different view state. Support this operation by registering an Open command for the object. When the user chooses the Open command of an object, it opens it into a separate window for editing, as shown in Figure 11.25.

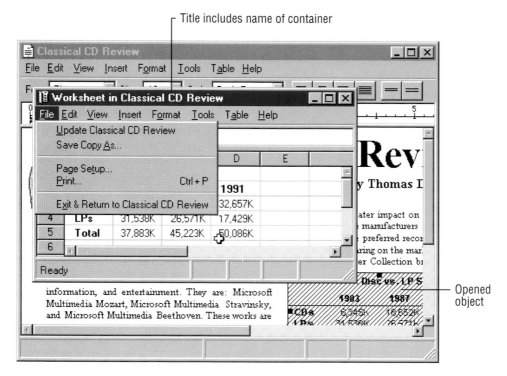

Figure 11.25 An opened OLE embedded worksheet

After opening an object, the container displays it masked with an "open" hatched (lines at a 45-degree angle) pattern that indicates the object is open in another window, as shown in Figure 11.26.

Figure 11.26 An opened OLE embedded object

Format the title text for the open object's window as "*Object Name* in *Container Name*" (for example, "Sales Worksheet in Classical CD Review"). Including the container's name emphasizes that the object in the container and the object in the open window are considered the same object.

This convention for the title bar text applies only when the user opens an OLE embedded object. When the user activates an OLE embedded object for visual editing, do not change the title bar text.

An open OLE embedded object represents an alternate window onto the same object within the container as opposed to a separate application that updates changes to the container document. Therefore, reflect edits immediately and automatically in the object in the window of its container. There is no need to display an update confirmation message upon exiting the open window. Nevertheless, you can still include an Update *Container Filename* command in the window of the open object to allow the user to request an update explicitly. This is useful if you cannot support frequent "real-time" image updates because of operational performance. In addition, when the user closes an open object's window, automatically update its presentation in the container's window. Provide a Close & Return To *Container Filename* or Exit & Return To *Container Filename* on the File menu replacing the Close or Exit command, as shown in Figure 11.25.

You can also include Import File and similar commands in the window of the open object. Treat importing a file into the window of the open embedded object the same as any change to the object.

If it has file operations, such as New or Open, remove these in the resulting window or replace them with commands, such as Import, to avoid severing the object's connection with its container. The objective is to present a consistent conceptual model; the object in the opened window is always the same as the one in the container. You can replace the Save As command with a Save Copy As command that displays the Save As dialog box, but unlike Save As, Save Copy As does not make the copied file the active file.

When the user opens an object, it is the selected object in the container; however, the user can change the selection in the container afterwards. Like any selected OLE embedded object, the container supplies the appropriate selection appearance together with the open appearance, as shown in Figure 11.27.

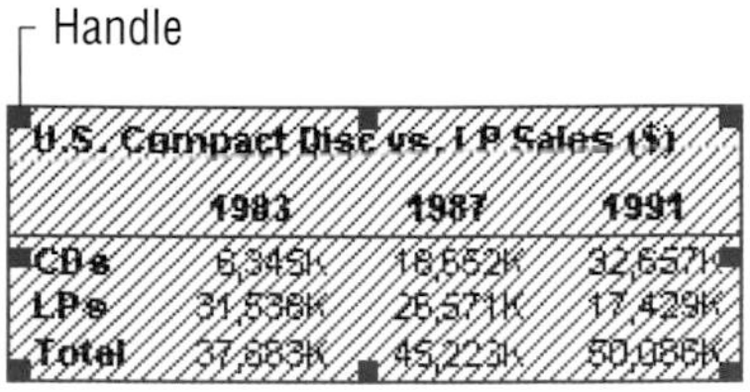

Figure 11.27 A selected open OLE embedded object

The selected and open appearances apply only to the object's appearance on the display. If the user chooses to print the container while an OLE embedded object is open or active, use the presentation form of objects; neither the open nor active hatched pattern should appear in the printed document because neither pattern is part of the content.

While an OLE embedded object is open, it is still a functioning member of its container. It can still be selected or unselected, and can respond to appropriate container commands. At any time, the user may open any number of OLE embedded objects. When the user closes its container window, deactivate and close the windows for any open OLE embedded objects.

Editing an OLE Linked Object

An OLE linked object can be stored in a particular location, moved or copied, and has its own properties. Container actions can be applied to the OLE linked object as a unit of content. So an OLE container supplies commands, such as Cut, Copy, Delete, and Properties, and interface elements such as handles, drop-down and pop-up menu items, and property sheets, for the OLE linked objects it contains.

The container also provides access to the commands that activate the OLE linked object, including the commands that provide access to content represented by the OLE linked object. These commands are the same as those that have been registered for the link source's type. Because an OLE linked object represents and provides access to another object that resides elsewhere, editing an OLE linked object always takes the user back to the link source. Therefore, the command used to edit an OLE linked object is the same as the command of its linked source object. For example, the menu of a linked object can include both Open and Edit if its link source is an OLE embedded object. The Open command opens the embedded object, just as carrying out the command on the OLE embedded object does. The Edit command opens the container window of the OLE embedded object and activates the object for OLE visual editing.

Figure 11.28 shows the result of opening a linked bitmap image of a horn. The image appears in its own window for editing. Note that changes made to the horn are reflected not only in its host container, the "Classical CD Review" document, but in every other document that contains an OLE linked object linked to that same portion of the "Horns" document. This illustrates both the power and the potential danger of using links in documents.

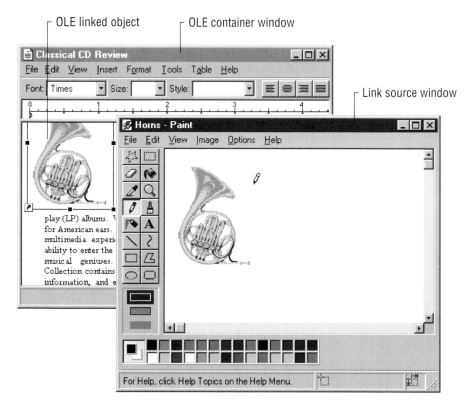

Figure 11.28 Editing a link source

At first glance, editing an OLE linked object seems to appear similar to an opened OLE embedded object; a separate primary window opens displaying the data. However, the container of an OLE linked object does not render the link representation using the open hatched pattern because the link source does not reside at this location. The

OLE linked object is not the real object, only a stand-in that enables the source to be visually present in other locations. Editing the linked object is functionally identical to opening the link source. Similarly, the title bar text of the link source's window does not use the convention as an open OLE embedded object because the link source is an independent object. Therefore, the windows operate and close independently of each other. If the link source's window is already visible, the OLE linked object notifies the link source to activate, bringing the existing window to the top of the Z order.

Note that the container of the OLE linked object does display messages related to opening the link source. For example, the container displays a message if the link source cannot be accessed.

Automatic and Manual Updating

When the user creates an OLE link, by default it is an automatic link; that is, whenever the source data changes, the link's visual representation changes without requiring any additional information from the user. Therefore, do not display an "Update Automatic Links Now?" message box. If the update takes a significant time to complete, you can display a message box indicating the progress of the update.

If users wish to exercise control over when links are updated, they can set the linked object's update property to manual. Doing so requires that the user choose an explicit command to update the link representation. The link can also be updated as a part of the link container's "update fields" or "recalc" action or other command that implies updating the presentation in the container's window.

Operations and Links

The operations available for an OLE linked object are supplied by its container and its source. When the user chooses a command supplied by its container, the container application handles the operation. For example, the container processes commands such as Cut, Copy, or Properties. When the user chooses a command supplied (registered) by its source, the operation is conceptually passed back to the linked source object for processing. In this sense, activating an OLE linked object activates its source object.

In certain cases, the linked object exhibits the result of an operation; in other cases, the linked source object can be brought to the top of the Z order to handle the operation. For example, carrying out commands, such as Play or Rewind, on a link to a sound recording appear to operate on the linked object in place. However, if the user chooses a command to alter the link's representation of its source's content (such as Edit or Open), the link source is exposed and responds to the operation instead of the linked object itself.

A link can play a sound in place, but cannot support editing in place. For a link source to properly respond to editing operations, fully activate the source object (with all of its containing objects and its container). For example, when the user double-clicks a linked object whose default operation is Edit, the source (or its container) opens, displaying the linked source object ready for editing. If the source is already open, the window displaying the source becomes active. This follows the standard convention for activating a window already open; that is, the window comes to the top of the Z order. You can adjust the view in the window, scrolling or changing focus within the window, as necessary, to present the source object for easy user interaction. The linked source window and linked object window operate and close independently of each other.

If a link source is contained within a read-only document, display a message box advising the user that edits cannot be saved to the source file.

Types and Links

An OLE linked object includes a cached copy of its source's type at the time of the last update. When the type of a linked source object changes, all links derived from that source object contain the old type and operations until either an update occurs or the linked source is activated. Because out-of-date links can potentially display obsolete operations to the user, a mismatch can occur. When the user chooses a command for an OLE linked object, the linked object compares the cached type with the current type of the linked source. If they are the same, the OLE linked object forwards the operation on to the source. If they are different, the linked object informs its container. In response, the container can either:

- Carry out the new type's operation, if the operation issued from the old link is syntactically identical to one of the operations registered for the source's new type.

- Display a message box, if the issued operation is no longer supported by the link source's new type (as shown in Figure 11.44).

In either case, the OLE linked object adopts the source's new type, and subsequently the container displays the new type's operations in the OLE linked object's menu.

Link Management

An OLE linked object includes properties such as: the name of its source, its source's type, and the link's updating basis, which is either automatic or manual. An OLE linked object also has a set of commands related to these properties. It is the responsibility of the container of the linked object to provide the user access to these commands and properties. To support this, an OLE container provides a property sheet for all of its OLE objects. You can optionally also include a Links dialog box for viewing and altering the properties of several links simultaneously.

Accessing Properties of OLE Objects

Like other types of objects, OLE embedded and linked objects have properties. The container of an OLE object is responsible for providing the user interface for access to the object's properties. The following sections describe how to provide user access to the properties of OLE objects.

The Properties Command

Design OLE containers to include a Properties command and property sheets for any OLE objects it contains. If the container application already includes a Properties command for its own native data, you can also use it to support selected OLE embedded or linked objects. Otherwise, add the command to the drop-down and pop-up menu you provide for accessing the other commands for the object, preceded by a menu separator, as shown in Figure 11.29.

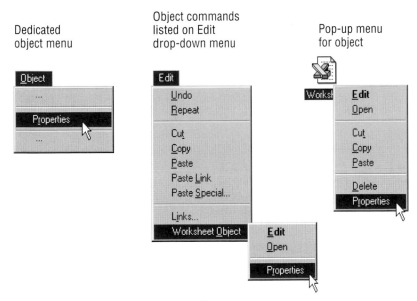

Figure 11.29 The Properties command

When the user chooses the Properties command, the container displays a property sheet containing all the salient properties and values, organized by category, for the selected object. Figure 11.30 shows examples property sheet pages for an OLE object.

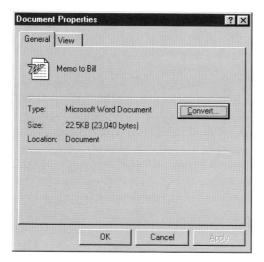
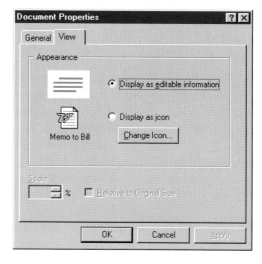

Figure 11.30 OLE embedded object property sheet

Follow the format the system uses for property sheets and the conventions outlined in this guide. Use the short type name in the title bar; for an OLE linked object, precede the name with the word "Linked," as in "Linked Worksheet." Include a General property page displaying the icon, name, type, size, and location of the object. Also include a Convert command button to provide access to the type conversion dialog box. On a View page, display properties associated with the view and presentation of the OLE object within the container. These include scaling or position properties and whether to display the object in its content presentation or as an icon. The Display As Icon field includes a Change Icon command button that allows the user to customize the icon presentation of the object. The Change Icon dialog box is shown in Figure 11.31.

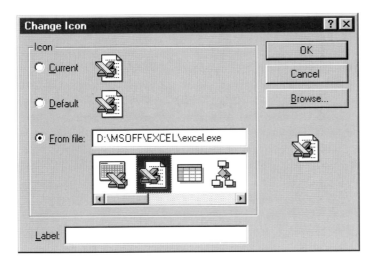

Figure 11.31 The Change Icon dialog box

For OLE linked objects, also include a Link page in its property
sheet containing the essential link parameters and commands, as
shown in Figure 11.32.

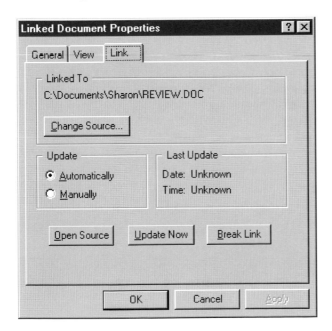

Figure 11.32 The Link page for the property sheet of an OLE linked object

For the typical OLE link, include the source name, the Update setting (automatic or manual), the Last Update timestamp, and command buttons that provide the following link operations:

- Break Link effectively disconnects the selected link.

- Update Now forces the selected link to connect to its sources and retrieve the latest information.

- Open Source opens the link source for the selected link.

- Change Source invokes a dialog box similar to the common Open dialog box to allow the user to respecify the link source.

The Links Command

In addition to property sheets, OLE containers can optionally include a Links command that provides access to a dialog box for displaying and managing multiple links. Figure 11.33 shows the Links dialog box. The list box in the dialog box displays the links in the container. Each line in the list contains the link source's name, the link source's object type (short type name), and whether the link updates automatically or manually. If a link source cannot be found, "Unavailable" appears in the update status column.

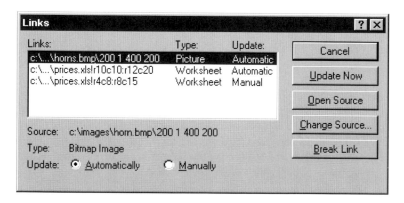

Figure 11.33 The Links dialog box

If the user chooses the Links command when the current selection includes a linked object (or objects), display that link (or links) as selected in the Links dialog box and scroll the list to display the first selected link at the top of the list box.

Allow 15 characters for the short type name field, and enough space for Automatic and Manual to appear completely. As the user selects each link in the list, its type, name, and updating basis appear in their entirety at the bottom of the dialog box. The dialog box also includes link management command buttons included in the Link page of OLE linked object property sheets: Break Link, Update Now, Open Source, and Change Source.

Define the Open Source button to be the default command button when the input focus is within the list of links. Support double-clicking an item in the list as a shortcut for opening that link source.

Clicking the Change Source button displays a version of the Open dialog box that allows the user to change the source of a link by selecting a file or typing a filename. If the user enters a source name that does not exist and chooses the default button, a message box is displayed with the following message, as shown in Figure 11.34.

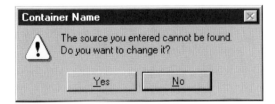

Figure 11.34 A message box for an invalid source

If the user chooses Yes, display the Change Source dialog box to correct the string. If the user chooses No, store the unparsed display name of the link source until the user links successfully to a newly created object that satisfies the dangling reference. The container application can also choose to allow the user to connect only to valid links.

If the user changes a link source or its directory, and other linked objects in the same container are connected to the same original link source, the container may offer the user the option to make the changes for the other references. To support this option, use the message box, as shown in Figure 11.35.

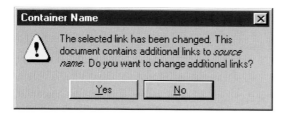

Figure 11.35 Changing additional links with the same source

Converting Types

Users may want to convert an object's type, so they can edit the object with a different application. To support the user's converting an OLE object from its current type to another registered type, provide a Convert dialog box, as shown in Figure 11.36. The user accesses the Convert dialog box by including a Convert button beside the Type field in an object's property sheet.

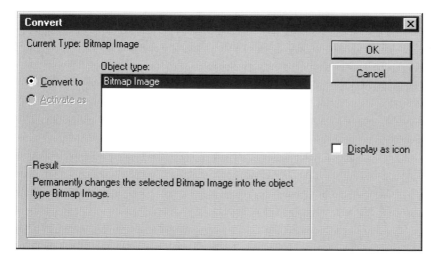

Figure 11.36 The Convert dialog box

This dialog box displays the current type of the object and a list box with all possible conversions. This list is composed of all types registered as capable of reading the selected object's format, but this does not necessarily guarantee the possibility of reverse conversion. If the user selects a new type from the list and chooses the OK button, the selected object is converted immediately to the new type. If the object is open, the container closes it before beginning the conversion.

Previous guidelines recommended including a Convert command on the menu for a selected OLE object. You may continue to support this; however, providing access through a button in the property sheet of the object is the preferred method.

Make sure the application that supplies the conversion does so with minimal impact in the user interface. That is, avoid displaying the application's primary window, but do provide a progress indicator message box with appropriate controls so that the user can monitor or interrupt the conversion process.

If the conversion of the type could result in any lost data or information, the application you use to support the type conversion should display a warning message box indicating that data will be lost and request confirmation by the user before continuing. Make the message as specific as possible about the nature of the information that might be lost; for example, "Text properties will not be preserved." If the conversion will result in no data loss, the warning message is not necessary.

In addition to converting a type, the Convert dialog box offers the user the option to change the type association for the object by choosing the Activate As option. When the user chooses this option, selects a type from the list, and chooses the OK button, the object's type is now treated as the new type. This differs from type conversion in that the object's type remains the same, but its activation command is now handled by a different application. It also differs in that converting a type only affects the object that is converted. Changing the activation association of a single object of the type, changes it for all OLE embedded objects of that type. For example, converting a rich-text format document to a text document only affects the converted document. However, if the user chooses the Activate As option to change the association for the rich-text format object so they will be activated as a text object (that is, by the same application registered for editing text objects), all OLE embedded rich-text format objects will be also be activated this way.

At the bottom of the Convert dialog box, text describes the outcome of the choices the user selects. Table 11.3 outlines the syntax of the descriptive text to use within the Convert dialog box.

Table 11.3 Descriptive Text for Convert Dialog Box

Function	Resulting text
Convert the selected object's type to a new type.	"Permanently changes the selected *Existing Type Name* object to a *New Type Name* object."
Convert the selected object's type to a new type and display the object as an icon.	"Permanently changes the selected *Existing Type Name* object to a *New Type Name* object. The object will be displayed as an icon."
No type change (the selected type is the same as its existing type).	"The *New Type Name* you selected is the same as the type of the selected object, so its type will not be converted."
Change the activation association for the selected object's type.	"Every *Existing Type Name* object will be activated as a *New Type Name* object, but not be converted to the new type."
Change the activation association for the selected object's type and display the object as an icon.	"Every *Existing Type Name* object will be activated as a *New Type Name* object, but converted to the new type. The selected object will be displayed as an icon.

Disable the Convert option for a linked object because conversion for a link must occur on the link source. Also disable Activate As option if no types are registered for alternative activation. If the user can neither convert nor change the activation association, disable the Convert command that displays this dialog box.

Using Handles

A container displays handles for an OLE embedded or linked object when the object is selected individually. When an object is selected and not active, only the scaling of the object (its cached metafile) can be supported. If a container uses handles for indicating selection but does not support scaling of the image, use the hollow form of handles.

For more information about the appearance of handles, see Chapter 13, "Visual Design."

When an OLE embedded object is activated for OLE visual editing, it displays its own handles. Display the handles within the active hatched pattern, as shown in Figure 11.37.

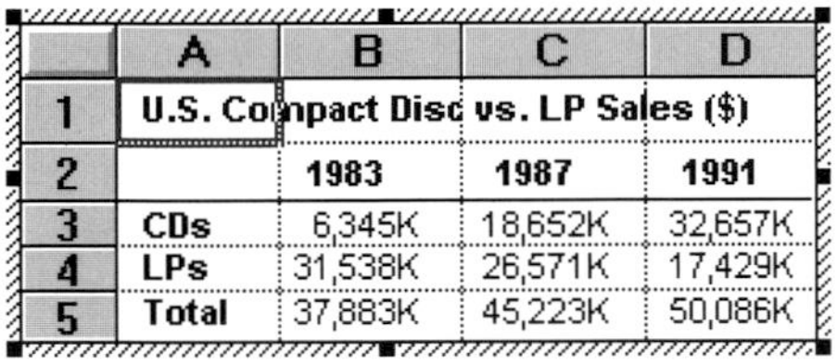

	A	B	C	D
1	U.S. Compact Disc vs. LP Sales ($)			
2		1983	1987	1991
3	CDs	6,345K	18,652K	32,657K
4	LPs	31,538K	26,571K	17,429K
5	Total	37,883K	45,223K	50,086K

Figure 11.37 An active OLE embedded object with handles

The interpretation of dragging the handle is defined by the OLE embedded object's application. The recommended operation is cropping, where you expose more or less of the OLE embedded object's content and adjust the viewport. If cropping is inappropriate or unsupportable, use an operation that better fits the context of the object or simply support scaling of the object. If no operation is meaningful, but handles are required to indicate selection while activated, use the hollow handle appearance.

Undo Operations for Active and Open Objects

Because different objects (that is, different underlying applications) take control of a window during OLE visual editing, managing commands like Undo or Redo present a question: how are the actions performed within an edited OLE embedded object reconciled with actions performed on the native data of the container with the Undo command? The recommended undo model is a single undo stack per open window — that is, all actions that can be reversed, whether generated by OLE embedded objects or their container, accumulate on the same undo state sequence. Therefore, choosing Undo from either the container's menus or an active object's menus reverses the last undoable action performed in that open window, regardless of whether it occurred inside or outside the OLE embedded object. If the container has the focus and the last action in the window occurred within an OLE embedded object, when the user chooses Undo, activate the embedded object, reverse the action, and leave the embedded object active.

The same rule applies to open objects — that is, objects that have been opened into their own window. Because each open window manages a single stack of undoable states, actions performed in an open object are local to that object's window and consequently must be undone from there; actions performed in the open object (even if they create updates in the container) do not contribute to the undo state of the container.

Carrying out a registered command of a selected, but inactive, object (or using a shortcut equivalent) is not a reversible action; therefore, it does not add to a container's undo stack. For example, if the user opens an object, this action cannot be undone from its container. The resulting window must be closed directly to remove it.

Figure 11.38 shows two windows: container Window A, which has an active OLE embedded object, and an open embedded object in Window B. Between the two windows, nine actions have been performed in the order and at the location indicated by the numbers. The resulting undo stacks are displayed beneath the windows.

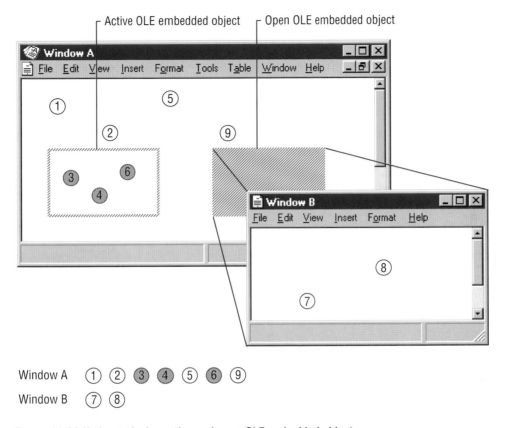

Window A ① ② ③ ④ ⑤ ⑥ ⑨
Window B ⑦ ⑧

Figure 11.38 Undo stacks for active and open OLE embedded objects

The sequence of undo states shown in Figure 11.38 does not necessarily imply an n-level undo. It is merely a timeline of actions that can be undone at 0, 1, or more levels, depending on what the container-object cooperation supports.

The active object actions and native data actions within Window A have been serialized into the same stack, while the actions in Window B have accumulated onto its own separate stack.

The actions discussed so far apply to a single window, not to actions that span multiple windows, such as OLE drag and drop. For a single action that spans multiple windows, the ideal design allows the user to undo the action from the last window involved. This is because, in most cases, the user focuses on that window when desiring to reverse the action. So if the user drags and drops an item from Window A into Window B, the action appends to Window B's undo thread, and undoing it undoes the entire OLE drag and drop operation. Unfortunately, the system does not support multiple window undo coordination. So for a multiple window action, create independent undo actions in each window involved in the action.

Displaying Messages

This section includes recommendations about other messages to display for OLE interaction using message boxes and status line messages. Use the following messages in addition to those described earlier in this chapter.

> The system supplies most of the message boxes described in this chapter. For more information about how to support these, see the OLE documentation included in the Win32 SDK.

Object Application Messages

Display the following messages to notify the user about situations where an OLE object's application is not accessible.

Object's Application Cannot Run Standalone

Some OLE objects are designed to be used only as components within a container and have no value in being opened directly. If the user attempts to open or run an OLE object's application that cannot run as a standalone application, display the message box shown in Figure 11.39.

Figure 11.39 Object's application cannot be run standalone message

Object's Application Busy

An object's application can be running, but busy for several reasons. For example, it can be busy printing, waiting for user input to a modal message box, or the application has stopped responding to the system. If the object's application is busy, display the message box shown in Figure 11.40.

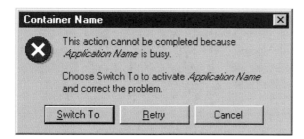

Figure 11.40 Object's application is busy message

Object's Application Unavailable

If the user attempts to activate an object and the container cannot locate the requested object's application, for example, because the object's type is not registered or because the network server where the application resides is unavailable, display the message box shown in Figure 11.41.

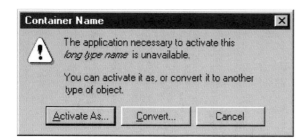

Figure 11.41 Object's application is unavailable message

Choosing the Activate As button displays the Convert dialog box preset with the Activate As option and a list of current types the user can use to associate with activating the object. Choosing the Convert button displays the Convert dialog box with the Convert option set, and the list of types the user can choose to change the type of the object. Ideally, an application that registers the type should be able to read and write that format without any loss of information. If it cannot preserve the information of the original type, the application handling the type emulation displays a message box warning the user about what information it cannot preserve and optionally allows the user to convert the object's type.

If a container supports inside-out activation for an object, display this message when the user tries to interact with that object, not when its container is opened. This avoids the display of the message to the user who only intends to view the content.

OLE Linked Object Messages

Display the following messages to notify the user about situations related to interaction with OLE linked objects.

Link Source Files Unavailable

When a container requests an update for its OLE linked objects, either because the user chooses an explicit Update command or as the result of another action such as a Recalc operation that forces an update, if the link source files for some OLE links are unavailable to provide the update, display the message box shown in Figure 11.42.

Figure 11.42 Link source files are unavailable message

When the user chooses the OK button, close the dialog box without updating the links.

Optionally, if you want to support the user changing the source, you supply your own message box that also includes a Properties button, a Links button, or both in the message box. Choosing the Properties button displays the property sheet for the link (see Figure 11.32) with "Unavailable" in the Update field. The user can then use the

Change Source button to search for the file or choose other commands related to the link. When the user chooses this Links button, display your Links dialog box, following the same conventions as for the property sheet.

Similarly, if the user issues a command to an OLE linked object with an unavailable source, display the warning message shown in Figure 11.43.

Figure 11.43 Selected link source is unavailable message

You can also supply your own message if you want to provide a Properties or Links button that enables the user to change the source. Display the OLE linked object's update status as "Unavailable."

Link Source Type Changed

If a link source's type has changed, but it is not yet reflected for an OLE linked object, and the user chooses a command that does not support the new type, display the message box shown in Figure 11.44.

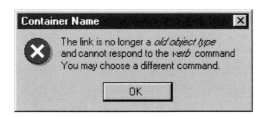

Figure 11.44 Link source's type has changed message

Link Updating

While links are updating, display the progress indicator message box shown in Figure 11.45. The Stop button interrupts the update process and prevents any updating of additional links.

Figure 11.45 Progress indicator while links update message

Status Line Messages

Table 11.4 lists suggested status line messages for commands on the primary container menu (commonly the File menu) of an opened object.

Table 11.4 Primary Container Menu Status Line Messages

Command	Status line message
Update *Container-Document*	Updates the appearance of this *Type Name* in *Container-Document*.
Close & Return to *Container-Document*	Closes *Object Name* and returns to *Container-Document*.
Save Copy As	Saves a copy of *Type Name* in a separate file.
Exit & Return to *Container-Document*	Exits *Object Application* and returns to *Container-Document*.

If the open object is within an MDI application with other open documents, the Exit & Return To command should simply be "Exit". There is no guarantee of a successful Return To *Container-Document* after exiting, because the container might be one of the other documents in that MDI instance.

Table 11.5 lists the recommended status line messages for the Edit menu of containers of OLE embedded and linked objects.

Table 11.5 Edit Menu Status Line Messages

Command	Status line message
Paste *Object Name*[1]	Inserts the content of the Clipboard as O*bject Name*.
Paste Special	Inserts the content of the Clipboard with format options.
Paste Link [to *Object Name*[1]]	Inserts a link to *Object Name*.
Paste Shortcut [to O*bject Name*[1]]	Inserts a shortcut icon to *Object Name*.
Insert Object	Inserts a new object.
[Linked] *Object Name*[1] [Object] ▶	Applies the following commands to *Object Name*.
[Linked] O*bject Name*[1] [Object] ▶ *Command*	Varies based on command.
[Linked] *Object Name*[1] [Object] ▶ Properties	Allows properties of *Object Name* to be viewed or modified.
Links	Allows links to be viewed, updated, opened, or removed.

[1]*Object Name* may be either the object's short type name or its filename.

Table 11.6 lists other related status messages.

Table 11.6 Other Status Line Messages

Command	Status line message
Show Objects	Displays the borders around objects (toggle).
Select Object (when the user selects an object)	Double-click or press ENTER to *Default Command Object Name*.

The default command stored in the registry contains an ampersand character (&) and the access key indicator; these must be stripped out before the verb is displayed on the status line.

User Assistance

Online user assistance is an important part of a product's design and can be supported in a variety of ways, from automatic display of information based on context to commands that require explicit user selection. Its content can be composed of contextual, procedural, explanatory, reference, or tutorial information. But user assistance should always be simple, efficient, and relevant so that a user can obtain it without becoming lost in the interface. This chapter provides a description of the system support to create common online forms of user assistance support and guidelines for implementation. For more information about authoring Help files, see the documentation included in the Microsoft Win32 Software Development Kit (SDK).

Contextual User Assistance

A contextual form of user assistance provides information about a particular object and its context. It answers questions such as "What is this?" and "Why would I use it?" This section covers some of the basic ways to support contextual user assistance in your application.

Context-Sensitive Help

The What's This? command supports a user obtaining contextual information about any object on the screen, including controls in property sheets and dialog boxes. This form of contextual user assistance is referred to as *context-sensitive Help.* As shown in Figure 12.1, you can support user access to this command by including:

- A What's This? command from the Help drop-down menu of a primary window.

- A What's This? button on a toolbar.

- A What's This? button on the title bar of a secondary window.

- A What's This? command included on the pop-up menu for the specific object.

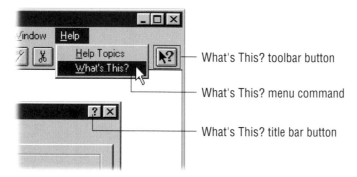

Figure 12.1 Different methods of accessing What's This?

Design your application so that when the user chooses the What's This? command from the Help drop-down menu or clicks a What's This? button, the system is set to a temporary mode. Change the pointer's shape to reflect this mode change, as shown in Figure 12.2. The SHIFT+F1 combination is the shortcut key for this mode.

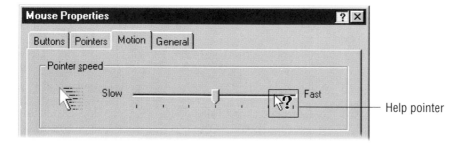

Figure 12.2 A context-sensitive Help pointer

Display the context-sensitive Help pointer only over the window that provides context-sensitive Help; that is, only over the active window from which the What's This? command was chosen.

In this mode, when the user clicks an object with mouse button 1 (for pens, tapping), display a context-sensitive Help pop-up window for that object. The context-sensitive Help window provides a brief explanation about the object and how to use it, as shown in Figure 12.3. Once the context-sensitive Help window is displayed, return the pointer and pointer operation to its usual state.

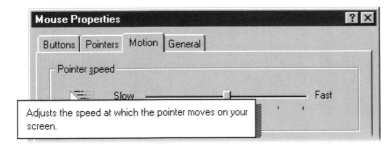

Figure 12.3 A pop-up window for context-sensitive Help

If the user presses a shortcut key that applies to a window that is in contextual Help mode, you can display a contextual Help pop-up window for the command associated with that shortcut key.

However, there are some exceptions to this interaction. First, if the user chooses a menu title, either in the menu bar or a cascading menu, maintain the mode until the user chooses a menu item and then display the context-sensitive Help window. Second, if the user clicks the item with mouse button 2 and the object supports a pop-up menu, maintain the mode until the user chooses a menu item or cancels the menu. If the object does not support a pop-up menu, the interaction should be the same as clicking it with mouse button 1. Finally, if the chosen object or location does not support context-sensitive Help or is otherwise an inappropriate target for context-sensitive Help, cancel the context-sensitive Help mode.

If the user chooses the What's This? command a second time, clicks outside the window, or presses the ESC key, cancel the context-sensitive Help mode. Restore the pointer to its usual image and operation in that context.

When the user chooses the What's This? command from a pop-up menu (as shown in Figure 12.4), the interaction is slightly different. Because the user has identified the object by clicking mouse button 2, there is no need for entering the context-sensitive Help mode. Instead, immediately display the context-sensitive Help pop-up window for that object.

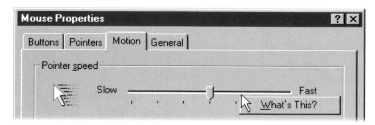

Figure 12.4 A pop-up menu for a control

The F1 key is the shortcut key for this form of interaction; that is, pressing F1 displays a context-sensitive Help window for the object that has the input focus.

Guidelines for Writing Context-Sensitive Help

When authoring context-sensitive Help information, you are answering the question "What is this?" Indicate the action associated with the item. In English versions, begin the description with a verb; for example, "Adjusts the speed of your mouse," or "Provides a place for you to type in a name for your document." For command buttons, you may use an imperative form — for example, "Click this to close the window." When describing a function or object, use words that explain the function or object in common terms instead of technical terminology or jargon. For example, instead of "Undoes the last action," say "Reverses the last action."

In the explanation, you might want to include "why" information. You can also include "how to" information, but if the procedure requires multiple steps, consider supporting this information using task-oriented Help. Keep your information brief, but as complete as possible so that the Help window is easy and quick to read.

As an option, you can provide context-sensitive Help information for your supported file types by registering a What's This? command for the type, as shown in Figure 12.5. This allows the user to choose the "What's This?" command from the file icon's pop-up menu to get information about an icon representing that type. When defining this Help information, include the type name and a brief description of its function, using the previously described guidelines.

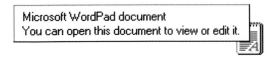

For more information about registering commands for file types and about type names, see Chapter 10, "Integrating with the System."

Figure 12.5 Context-sensitive Help information for an icon

Tooltips

Another form of contextual user assistance are tooltips. *Tooltips* are small pop-up windows that display the name of a control when the control has no text label. The most common use of tooltips is for toolbar buttons that have graphic labels, as shown in Figure 12.6, but they can be used for any control.

Figure 12.6 A tooltip for a toolbar button

Display a tooltip after the pointer, or pointing device, remains over the button for a short period of time. The tooltip remains displayed until the user presses the button or moves off of the control, or after another time-out. If the user moves the pointer directly to another control supporting a tooltip, ignore the time-out and display the new tooltip immediately, replacing the former one.

If you use the standard toolbar control, the system automatically provides support for tootips. It also includes a tooltip control that can be used in other contexts. If you create your own tooltip controls, make them consistent with the system-supplied controls.

For more information about toolbars and tooltip controls, see Chapter 7, "Menus, Controls, and Toolbars."

Status Bar Messages

You can also use a status bar to provide contextual user assistance. However, if you support the user's choice of displaying a status bar, avoid using it for displaying information or access to functions that are essential to basic operation and not provided elsewhere in the application's interface. In addition, because the status bar's location may not be near the user area of activity, the user may not always notice a status bar message. As a result, it is best to consider status bar messages as a secondary or supplemental form of user assistance.

In addition to displaying state information about the context of the activity in the window, you can display descriptive messages about menu and toolbar buttons, as shown in Figure 12.7. Like tooltips, the window typically must be active to support these messages. When the user moves the pointer over a toolbar button or presses the mouse button on a menu or button, display a short message the describing use of the associated command.

Selected menu item

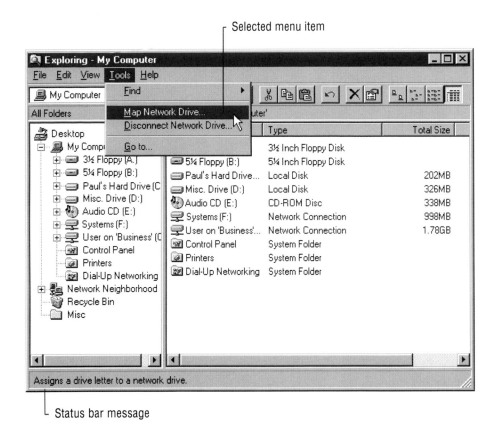

Status bar message

Figure 12.7 A status bar message for a selected menu command

A status bar message can include a progress indicator control or other forms of feedback about an ongoing process, such as printing or saving a file, that the user initiated in the window. Although you can display progress information in a message box, you may want to use the status bar for background processes so that the window's interface is not obscured by the message box.

Guidelines for Writing Status Bar Messages

When writing status bar messages, begin the text with a verb in the present tense and use familiar terms—avoiding jargon. For example, say "Cuts the selection and puts it on the Clipboard." Try to be as brief as possible so the text can be easily read, but avoid truncation.

Be constructive, not just descriptive, informing the user about the purpose of the command. When describing a command with a specific function, use words specific to the command. If the scope of the command has multiple functions, try to summarize. For example, say "Contains commands for editing and formatting your document."

When defining messages for your menu and toolbar buttons, don't forget their unavailable, or disabled, state. Provide an appropriate message to explain why the item is not currently available. For example, when the user selects a disabled Cut command you could display "This command is not available because no text is selected."

The Help Command Button

You can also provide contextual Help for a property sheet, dialog box, or message box by including a Help button in that window, as shown in Figure 12.8. When the user chooses the Help command button, display the Help information in a Help secondary window, rather than a context-sensitive Help pop-up window.

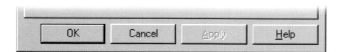

Figure 12.8 A Help button in a secondary window

The user assistance provided by a Help command button differs from the "What's This?" form of Help. Command button Help should provide an overview, summary assistance, or explanatory information for that window. For example, for a message box, it can provide more information about causes and remedies for the reason the message was displayed. Consider the Help command an optional, secondary form of contextual user assistance, not a substitute for context-sensitive, "What's This?" Help. Don't use it as a substitute for clear, understandable designs for your secondary windows.

Task-Oriented Help

Task-oriented help provides the steps for carrying out a task. It can involve a number of procedures. You present task-oriented Help in task Help topic windows.

Task Topic Windows

Task Help topic windows are displayed as primary windows. The user can size this window like any other primary window.

You provide primary access to task Help topics through the Help Topics browser, described later in this chapter. You can also include access to specific topics through other interfaces, such as navigation links placed in other Help topics.

Task topic windows include a set of command buttons at the top of the window (as shown in Figure 12.9) that provide the user access to the Help Topics browser, the previously selected topic, and other Help commands, such as copying and printing a topic. You can define which buttons appear by defining them in your Help files.

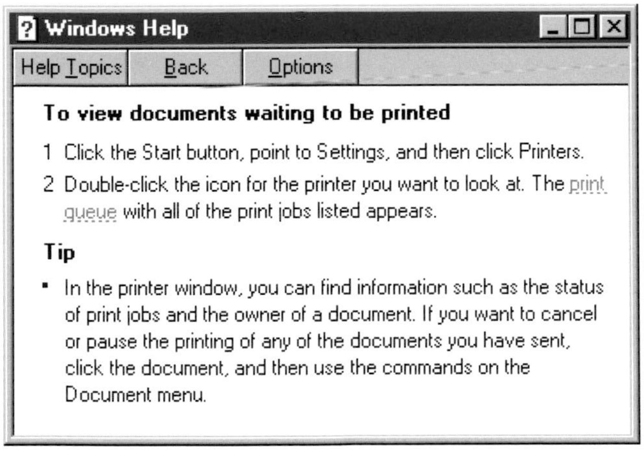

The window style is referred to as a primary window because of its appearance and operation. In technical documentation, this window style is sometimes referred to as a Help secondary window.

To view documents waiting to be printed

1 Click the Start button, point to Settings, and then click Printers.
2 Double-click the icon for the printer you want to look at. The print queue with all of the print jobs listed appears.

Tip

* In the printer window, you can find information such as the status of print jobs and the owner of a document. If you want to cancel or pause the printing of any of the documents you have sent, click the document, and then use the commands on the Document menu.

Figure 12.9 A window for a task Help topic

Although you can define the size and location of a task Help topic window to the specific requirements of your application, it is best to size and position the window so as to cover the minimum of space, but make it large enough to allow the user to read the topic, preferably without having to scroll the window. This makes it easier for the novice user who may be unfamiliar with scrolling.

The title bar text of the Help topic identifies the context supplying the topic window. Consider naming the Help file to also match. Include a topic title as part of the body of the topic. Define the topic title to correspond to the entries you include in the Help Topics browser that provide direct access to the topic. This does not mean that you must use the same wording as those entries, but they should be similar enough to allow the user to recognize their relationship.

Like tooltips, the default interior color of a task topic window should use the system color setting for Help windows. This allows the user to more easily distinguish the Help topic from their other windows. However, for specialized topics, you can set the color of a task topic window.

Guidelines for Writing Task Help Topics

The buttons that appear at the top of a task Help topic window are defined by your Help file. At a minimum, you should provide a button that displays the Help Topics browser dialog box, a Back button to return the user to the previous topic, and buttons that provide access to other functions, such as Copy and Print.

To provide access to the Help Topics browser dialog box, include a Help Topics button. This displays the Help Topics browser window on the tabbed page that the user was viewing when the window was last displayed. Although this is the most common form of access to the Help Topics browser window, alternatively you can include buttons, such as Contents and Index, that correspond to the tabbed pages to provide the user with direct access to those pages when the dialog box is displayed.

As with context-sensitive Help, when writing task Help information topics, make them complete, but brief. However, in task Help topics, focus on "how" information rather than "what" or "why." Task Help should assist the user in completing a task, not try to document everything there is to know about a topic. If there are multiple alternatives, pick one method — usually the simplest, most common method for a specific procedure. If you want to include information on alternative methods, provide access to them through other choices or commands.

If you keep the procedure to four or fewer steps, the user will not need to scroll the window. Avoid introductory, conceptual, or reference material in the procedure.

Also, take advantage of the context of a procedure. For example, if a property sheet includes a slider control that is labeled "Slow" at one end and "Fast" at the other, be concise. Say "Move the slider to adjust the speed" instead of "To increase the speed, move the slider to the right. To decrease the speed, move the slider to the left." If you refer to a control by its label, capitalize each word in the label, even though the label has only the first word capitalized. This helps distinguish the label from the rest of your text.

Optionally, you can include a Related Topics button in your topic window to provide access to other topics. When the user chooses this button, display the Topics Found dialog box (as shown in Figure 12.14).

Shortcut Buttons

Task Help topic windows can also include a shortcut or "do it" button that provides the user with a shortcut or automated form of performing a particular step, as shown in Figure 12.10. For example, use this to automatically open a particular dialog box, property sheet, or other object so that the user does not have to search for it.

Shortcut button

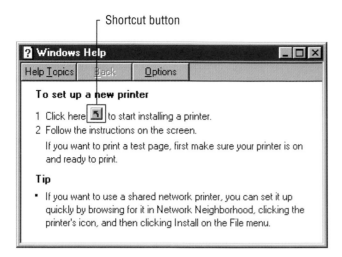

Figure 12.10 A task Help topic with a shortcut button

Shortcut buttons not only provide efficiency for the user, they also reduce the amount of information you may need to present and the user needs to read. However, you need not use the buttons as a substitute for doing the task or a specific step in the task; particularly if you want to support the user being able to accomplish the task without using Help. For common tasks, you may want a balance, including information that tells the user how to do the task, and shortcut buttons that make stepping through the task easier. For example, you might include text that reads "Click here to display the Display properties" and a shortcut button.

Reference Help

Reference Help is a form of Help information that serves more as online documentation. Use reference Help to document the features of a product or as a user's guide to a product. Often the use determines the balance of text and graphics used in the Help file. Reference-oriented documentation typically includes more text and follows a consistent presentation of information. User's guide documentation typically organizes information by specific tasks and may include more illustrations.

The Reference Help Window

When designing reference Help, use a Help primary window style (sometimes called a "main" Help window), as shown in Figure 12.11, rather than the context-sensitive Help pop-up windows or task Help topic windows.

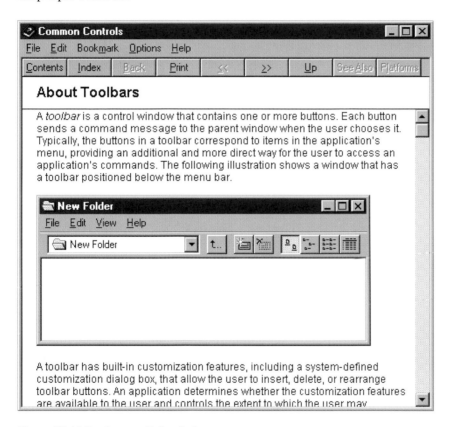

Figure 12.11 A reference Help window

You can provide access to reference Help in a variety of ways. The most common is as an explicit menu command in the Help drop-down menu, but you can also provide access using a toolbar button, or even as a specific file object (icon).

A reference Help window includes a menu bar, with File, Edit, Bookmark, Options, and Help entries and a toolbar with Contents, Index, Back, and Print buttons. The system provides these features by default for a "main" Help window. These features support user functions, such as opening a specific Help file (using the Help Topics browser), copying and printing topics, creating annotations and bookmarks for specific topics, and setting the Help window's properties. You can add other buttons to this window to tailor your online documentation to fit your particular user needs.

Although the reference Help style can provide information similar to that provided in contextual Help and task Help, these forms of Help are not exclusive of each other. Often the combination of all these items provides the best solution for user assistance. They can also be supplemented with other forms of user assistance.

Guidelines for Writing Reference Help

Reference Help topics can include text, graphics, animations, video, and audio effects. Follow the guidelines included throughout this guide for recommendations on using these elements in the presentation of information. In addition, the system provides some special support for Help topics.

Adding Menus and Toolbar Buttons

You can author additional menus and buttons to appear in the reference Help window. However, you cannot remove existing menus.

Because reference Help files typically include related topics, include Previous Topic and Next Topic browse buttons in your Help window toolbar. Another common button you may want to include is a See Also button that either displays a pop-up window or the Topics Found dialog box (as shown in Figure 12.14) with the related topics. Other common buttons include Up for moving to the parent or overview topic and History to display a list of the topics the user has viewed so they can return directly to a particular topic.

Make toolbar buttons contextual to the topic the user is viewing. For example, if the current topic is the last in the browse chain, disable the Next Topic button. When deciding whether to disable or remove a button, follow the guidelines defined in this guide for menus.

Topic Titles

Always provide a title for the current topic. The title identifies the topic and provides the user with a landmark within the Help system. The title should correspond to the entries you include in the Help Topics browser window. Use the title bar text of the window to identify the context and supplier of the topic. The Help filename should also match.

Nonscrolling Regions

If your topics are very long, you may want to include a nonscrollable region in your Help file. A nonscrolling region allows you to keep the topic title and other information visible when the user scrolls. A nonscrolling region appears with a line at its bottom edge to delineate it from the scrollable area. Display the scroll bar for the scrollable area of the topic so that its top appears below the nonscrolling region, not overlapped within that region.

Jumps

A jump is a button or interactive area that triggers an event when the user clicks on it. You can use a jump as a one-way navigation link from one topic to another, either within the same topic window, to another topic window, or a topic in another Help file.

You can also use jumps to display a pop-up window. As with pop-up windows for context-sensitive Help, use this form of interaction to support a definition or explanatory information about the word or object that the user clicks.

Jumps can also carry out particular commands. Shortcut buttons used in Help task topics are this form of a jump.

You need to provide visual indications to distinguish a jump from noninteractive areas of the window. You can do this by displaying a jump as a button, changing the pointer image to indicate an interactive element, formatting the item with some other visual distinction such as color or font, or a combination of these methods. The default system presentation for text jumps is green underlined text.

The Help Topics Browser

The Help Topics browser dialog box provides user access to Help information. To open this window, include a Help Topics menu item on the Help drop-down menu. Alternatively, you can include menu commands that open the window to a particular tabbed page — for example, Contents, Index, and Find Topic.

In addition, provide a Help Topics button in the toolbar of a task or reference Help topic window. When the user chooses this button, display the Help Topics browser window with the last page the user accessed. If you prefer, provide Contents, Index, and Find Topic buttons for direct access to a specific page. For example, by default, reference Help windows include Contents and Index button access to the Help Topics browser.

The Help Topics Tabs

Opening the Help Topics window displays a set of tabbed pages. The default pages include Contents, Index, and Find tabs. You can author additional tabs.

The Contents Page

The Contents page displays the list of topics organized by category, as shown in Figure 12.12. A book icon represents a category or group of related topics, and a page icon represents an individual topic. You can nest topic levels, but avoid more than three levels, as this can make access cumbersome.

Figure 12.12 The Contents page of the Help topics browser

The buttons at the bottom of the page allow the user to open or close a "book" of topics and display a particular topic. The Print button prints either a "book" of topics or a specific topic depending on which the user selects. The outline also supports direct interaction, such as double-clicking, for opening the outline or a topic.

Guidelines for Writing Help Contents Entries

The entries listed on the Contents page are based on what you author in your Help files. Define them to allow the user to see the organizational relationship between topics. Make the topic titles you include for your software brief, but descriptive, and correspond to the actual topic titles.

The Index Page

The Index page of the browser organizes the topics by keywords that you define for your topics, as shown in Figure 12.13.

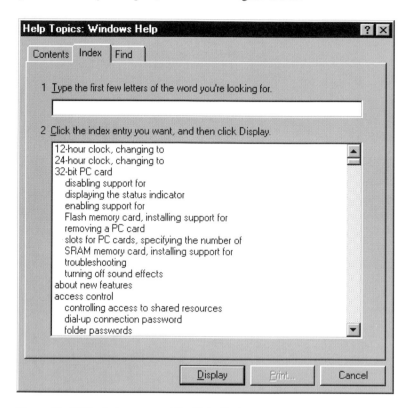

Figure 12.13 The Index page of the Help Topics browser

The user can enter a keyword or select one from the list. Choosing the Display button displays the topic associated with that keyword. If there are multiple topics that use the same keyword, then another secondary window is displayed that allows the user to choose from that set of topics, as shown in Figure 12.14. You can also use this dialog box to provide access to related topics by including a See Also button or Related Topics button in a topic window.

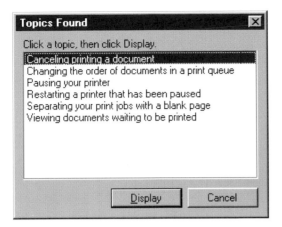

Figure 12.14 The Help topics window

Guidelines for Writing Help Index Keywords

Provide an effective keyword list to help users find the information
they are looking for. When deciding what keywords to provide for
your topics, consider the following categories:

- Words for a novice user.

- Words for an advanced user.

- Common synonyms of the words in the keyword list.

- Words that describe the topic generally.

- Words that describe the topic discretely.

The Find Page

The Find page, as shown in Figure 12.15, provides full-text search
functionality that allows the user to search for any word or phrase in
the Help file. This capability requires a full-text index file, which
you can create when building the Help file, or which the user can
create when using the Find page.

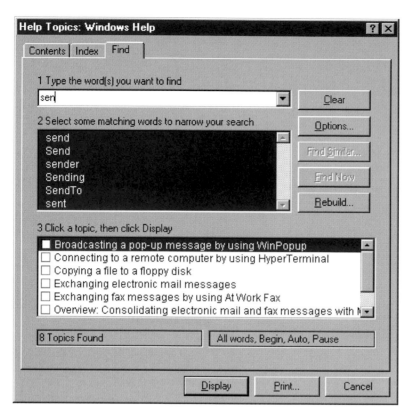

Figure 12.15 The Find page of the Help Topics browser

Wizards

A *wizard* is a special form of user assistance that automates a task through a dialog with the user. Wizards help the user accomplish tasks that can be complex and require experience. Wizards can automate almost any task, including creating new objects and formatting the presentation of a set of objects, such as a table or paragraph. They are especially useful for complex or infrequent tasks that the user may have difficulty learning or doing.

The system provides support for creating a wizard using the standard property sheet control. For more information about this control, see Chapter 7, "Menus, Controls, and Toolbars."

However, wizards are not well-suited to teach a user how to do something. Although wizards assist the user in accomplishing a task, they should be designed to hide many of the steps and much of the complexity of a given task. Similarly, wizards are not intended to be used for tutorials; wizards should operate on real data. For instructional user assistance, consider task Help or tutorial-style interfaces.

Do not rely on wizards as a solution for ineffective designs; if the user relies on a wizard too much it may be an indication of an overly complicated interface, not good wizard design. In addition, consider using a wizard to supplement, rather than replace, the user's direct ability to perform a specific task. Unless the task is fairly simple or done infrequently, experienced users may find a wizard to be inefficient or not provide them with sufficient access to all functionality.

Wizards may not always appear as an explicit part of the Help interface. You can provide access to them in a variety of ways, including toolbar buttons or even specific icons, such as templates.

For more information about templates, see Chapter 5, "General Interaction Techniques."

Guidelines for Designing Wizards

A wizard is a series of presentations or pages, displayed in a secondary window, that helps the user through a task. The pages include controls that you define to gather input from the user; that input is then used to complete the task for the user.

Optionally, you can define wizards as a series of secondary windows through which the user navigates. However, this can lead to increased modality and screen clutter, so using a single secondary window is recommended.

At the bottom of the window, include the following command buttons that allow the user to navigate through the wizard.

Command	Action
< Back	Returns to the previous page. (Remove or disable the button on the first page.)
Next >	Moves to the next page in the sequence, maintaining whatever settings the user provides in previous pages.
Finish	Applies user-supplied or default settings from all pages and completes the task.
Cancel	Discards any user-supplied settings, terminates the process, and closes the wizard window.

Use the title bar text of the wizard window to clearly identify the purpose of the wizard. But, because wizards are secondary windows, they should not appear in the taskbar. You may optionally include a context-sensitive What's This? Help title bar button as well.

On the first page of a wizard, include a graphic in the left side of the window, as shown in Figure 12.16. The purpose of this graphic is to establish a reference point, or theme — such as a conceptual rendering, a snapshot of the area of the display that will be affected, or a preview of the result. On the top right portion of the wizard window, provide a short paragraph that welcomes the user to the wizard and explains what it does. You may also include controls for entering or editing input to be used by the wizard, if there is sufficient space. However, avoid offering too many choices or choices that may be difficult to distinguish or understand without context.

Figure 12.16 An introductory page of a wizard

On subsequent pages you can continue to include a graphic for consistency or, if space is critical, use the entire width of the window for displaying instructional text and controls for user input. When using graphics, include pictures that help illustrate the process, as shown in Figure 12.17. Include default values or settings for all controls where possible.

Figure 12.17 Input page for a wizard

You can include the Finish button at any point that the wizard can complete the task. For example, if you can provide reasonable defaults, you can even include the Finish button on the first page. Place the Finish button to the right and adjacent to the Next button. This allows the user to step through the entire wizard or only the page on which they wish to provide input. Otherwise, if the user needs to step through each page of the wizard, replace the Next button with the Finish button on the last page of the wizard. Also on the last page of the wizard, indicate to the user that the wizard is prepared to complete the task and instruct the user to click the Finish button.

Design your wizard pages to be easy to understand. It is important that users immediately understand what a wizard is about so they don't feel like they have to read it very carefully to understand what they have to answer. It is better to have a greater number of simple pages with fewer choices than a smaller number of complex pages with too many options or text. In addition, follow the conventions outlined in this guide and consider the following guidelines when designing a wizard:

- Minimize the number of pages that require the display of a secondary window. Novice users are often confused by the additional complexity of secondary windows.

- Avoid a wizard design that requires the user to leave the wizard to complete a task. Less experienced users are often the primary users of a wizard. Asking them to leave the wizard to perform a function can make them lose their context. Instead, design your wizard so that the user can do everything from within the wizard.

- Make it visually clear that user-interface elements that are part of a graphic illustration on a wizard page are not interactive. You can do this by varying the graphic from their normal sizes or rendering them in a more abstract representation.

- Avoid advancing pages automatically. The user may not be able to read the information before a page advances. In addition, wizards are intended to allow the user to be in control of the process that the wizard automates.

- Display a wizard window so that the user can recognize it as the primary point of input. For example, if you display a wizard from a control the user chooses in a secondary window, you may need to place the wizard window so that it partially obscures that secondary window.

- Make certain that the design alternatives offered by your wizard provide the user with positive results. You can use the context, such as the selection, to determine what options may be reasonable to provide.

- Make certain that it is obvious how the user can proceed when the wizard has completed its process. This may be accomplished by the text you include on the last page of the wizard.

Guidelines for Writing Text for Wizard Pages

Use a conversational, rather than instructional, writing style for the text you provide on the screens. The following guidelines can be used to assist you in writing the textual information:

- Use words like "you" and "your."

- Start most questions with phrases like "Which option do you want..." or "Would you like...." Users respond better to questions that enable them to do a task than being told what to do. For example, "Which layout do you want?" works better in wizards than "Choose a layout."

- Use contractions and short, common words. In some cases, it may be acceptable to use slang, but you must consider localization when doing so.

  For more information about localization design, see Chapter 14, "Special Design Considerations."

- Avoid using technical terminology that may be confusing to a novice user.

- Try to use as few words as possible. For example, the question "Which style do you want for this newsletter?" could be written simply as "Which style do you want?"

- Keep the writing clear, concise, and simple, but remember not to be condescending.

Visual Design

What we see influences how we feel and what we understand. Visual information communicates nonverbally, but very powerfully. It can include cues that motivate, direct, or distract. This chapter covers the visual and graphic design principles and guidelines that you can apply to the interface design of your Microsoft Windows-based applications.

Visual Communication

Effective visual design serves a greater purpose than decoration; it is an important tool for communication. How you organize information on the screen can make the difference between a design that communicates a message and one that leaves a user feeling puzzled or overwhelmed.

Even the best product functionality can suffer if its visual presentation does not communicate effectively. If you are not trained in visual or information design, it is a good idea to work with a designer who has education and experience in this field and include that person as a member of the design team early in the development process. Good graphic designers provide a perspective on how to take the best advantage of the screen and how to use effectively the concepts of shape, color, contrast, focus, and composition. Moreover, graphic designers understand how to design and organize information, and the effects of fonts and color on perception.

Composition and Organization

We organize what we read and how we think about information by grouping it spatially. We read a screen in the same way we read other forms of information. The eye is always attracted to the colored elements before black and white, to isolated elements before elements in a group, and to graphics before text. We even read text by scanning the shapes of groups of letters. Consider the following principles when designing the organization and composition of visual elements of your interface: hierarchy of information, focus and emphasis, structure and balance, relationship of elements, readability and flow, and unity of integration.

Hierarchy of Information

The principle of hierarchy of information addresses the placement of information based on its relative importance to other visual elements. The outcome of this ordering affects all of the other composition and organization principles, and determines what information a user sees first and what a user is encouraged to do first. To further consider this principle, ask these questions:

- What information is most important to a user?

  In other words, what are the priorities of a user when encountering your application's interface. For example, the most important priority may be to create or find a document.

- What does a user want or need to do first, second, third, and so on?

  Will your ordering of information support or complicate a user's progression through the interface?

- What should a user see on the screen first, second, third, and so on?

  What a user sees first should match the user's priorities when possible, but can be affected by the elements you want to emphasize.

Focus and Emphasis

The related principle of focus and emphasis guides you in the placement of priority items. Determining focus involves identifying the central idea, or the focal point, for activity. Determine emphasis by choosing the element that must be prominent and isolating it from the other elements or making it stand out in other ways.

Where the user looks first for information is an important consideration in the implementation of this principle. Culture and interface design decisions can govern this principle. People in western cultures, for example, look at the upper left corner of the screen or window for the most important information. So, it makes sense to put a top-priority item there, giving it emphasis.

Structure and Balance

The principle of structure and balance is one of the most important visual design principles. Without an underlying structure and a balance of visual elements, there is a lack of order and meaning and this affects all other parts of the visual design. More importantly, a lack of structure and balance makes it more difficult for the user to clearly understand the interface.

Relationship of Elements

The principle of relationship of elements is important in reinforcing the previous principles. The placement of a visual element can help communicate a specific relationship of the elements of which it is a part. For example, if a button in a dialog box affects the content of a list box, there should be a spatial relationship between the two elements. This helps the user to clearly and quickly make the connection just by looking at the placement.

Readability and Flow

This principle calls for ideas to be communicated directly and simply, with minimal visual interference. Readability and flow can determine the usability of a dialog box or other interface component. When designing the layout of a window, consider the following:

- Could this idea or concept be presented in a simpler manner?

- Can the user easily step through the interface as designed?

- Do all the elements have a reason for being there?

Unity and Integration

The last principle, unity and integration, reflects how to evaluate a given design in relationship to its larger environment. When an application's interface is visually unified with the general interface of Windows, the user finds it easier to use because it offers a consistent and predictable work environment. To implement this principle, consider the following:

- How do all of the different parts of the screen work together visually?

- How does the visual design of the application relate to the system's interface or other applications with which it is used?

Color

Color is a very important property in the visual interface. Because color has attractive qualities, use it to identify elements in the interface to which you want to draw the user's attention — for example, the current selection. Color also has an associative aspect; we often assume there is a relationship between items of the same color. Color also carries with it emotional or psychological qualities. For example, colors are often categorized as cool or warm.

When used indiscriminately, color can have a negative or distracting effect. It can affect not only the user's reaction to your software but also productivity, by making it difficult to focus on a task.

In addition, there are a few more things to consider about using color:

- Although you can use color to show relatedness or grouping, associating a color with a particular meaning is not always obvious or easily learned.

- Color is a very subjective property. Everyone has different tastes in color. What is pleasing to you may be distasteful to someone else.

- Some percentage of your users may work with equipment that only supports monochrome presentation.

- Interpretation of color can vary by culture. Even within a single culture, individual associations with color can differ.

- Some percentage of the population may have color-identification problems. For example, about 9 percent of the adult male population have some form of color confusion.

The following sections summarize guidelines for using color: color as a secondary form of information, use of a limited set of colors, allowing the option to change colors.

Color as a Secondary Form of Information

Use color as an additive, redundant, or enhanced form of information. Avoid relying on color as the only means of expressing a particular value or function. Shape, pattern, location, and text labels are other ways to distinguish information. It is also a good practice to design visuals in black and white or monochrome first, then add color.

Use of a Limited Set of Colors

Although the human eye can distinguish millions of different colors, using too many usually results in visual clutter and can make it difficult for the user to discern the purpose of the color information. The colors you use should fit their purpose. Muted, subtle, complementary colors are usually better than bright, highly saturated ones, unless you are really looking for a carnival-like appearance where bright colors compete for the user's attention.

Color also affects color. Adjacent or background colors affect the perceived brightness or shade of a particular color. A neutral color (for example, light gray) is often the best background color. Opposite colors, such as red and green, can make it difficult for the eye to focus. Dark colors tend to recede in the visual space, light colors come forward.

Options to Change Colors

Because color is a subjective, personal preference, allow the user to change colors where possible. For interface elements, Windows provides standard system interfaces and color schemes. If you base your software on these system properties, you can avoid including additional controls, plus your visual elements are more likely to coordinate effectively when the user changes system colors. This is particularly important if you are designing your own controls or screen elements to match the style reflected in the system.

When providing your own interface for changing colors, consider the complexity of the task and skill of the user. It may be more helpful if you provide palettes, or limited sets of colors, that work well together rather than providing the entire spectrum. You can always supplement the palette with an interface that allows the user to add or change a color in the palette.

Fonts

Fonts have many functions in addition to providing letterforms for reading. Like other visual elements, fonts organize information or create a particular mood. By varying the size and weight of a font, we see text as more or less important and perceive the order in which it should be read.

At conventional resolutions of computer displays, fonts are generally less legible online than on a printed page. Avoid italic and serif fonts; these are often hard to read, especially at low resolutions. Figure 13.1 shows various font choices.

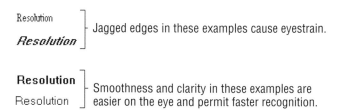

Figure 13.1 Effective and ineffective font choices

Limit the number of fonts and styles you use in your software's interface. Using too many fonts usually results in visual clutter.

Wherever possible, use the standard system font for common interface elements. This provides visual consistency between your interface and the system's interface and also makes your interface more easily scaleable. Because many interface elements can be customized by the user, check the system settings for the default system font and set the fonts in your interface accordingly. For more information about system font settings, see the section, "Layout," later in this chapter.

Dimensionality

Many elements in the Windows interface use perspective, highlighting, and shading to provide a three-dimensional appearance. This emphasizes function and provides real-world feedback to the user's actions. For example, command buttons have an appearance that provides the user with natural visual cues that help communicate their functionality and differentiate them from other types of information.

Windows bases its three-dimensional effects on a common theoretical light source, the conceptual direction that light would be coming from to produce the lighting and shadow effects used in the interface. The light source in Windows comes from the upper left.

When designing your own visual elements, be careful not to overdo the use of dimensionality. Avoid unnecessary nesting of visual elements and using three-dimensional effects for an element that is not interactive. Introduce only enough detail to provide useful visual cues and use designs that blend well with the system interface.

Design of Visual Elements

All visual elements influence one another. Effective visual design depends on context. In a graphical user interface, a graphic element and its function are completely interrelated. A graphical interface needs to function intuitively — it needs to look the way it works and work the way it looks.

Basic Border Styles

Windows provides a unified visual design for building visual components based on the border styles shown in Figure 13.2.

The basic border styles are based on standard system color settings.

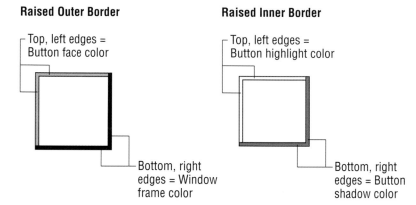

Raised Outer Border

Top, left edges = Button face color

Bottom, right edges = Window frame color

Raised Inner Border

Top, left edges = Button highlight color

Bottom, right edges = Button shadow color

Sunken Outer Button Border

Top, left edges = Button shadow color

Bottom, right edges = Button highlight color

Sunken Inner Button Border

Top, left edges = Window frame color

Bottom, right edges = Button face color

Figure 13.2 Basic border styles

Border style	Description
Raised outer border	Uses a single-pixel width line in the button face color for its top and left edges and the window frame color for its bottom and right edges.
Raised inner border	Uses a single-pixel width line in the button highlight color for its top and left edges and the button shadow color for its bottom and right edges.
Sunken outer border	Uses a single-pixel width line in the button shadow color for its top and left border and the button highlight color for its bottom and right edges.
Sunken inner border	Uses a single-pixel width line in the window frame color for its top and left edges and the button face color for its bottom and right edges.

If you use standard Windows controls and windows, these border styles are automatically supplied for your application. If you create your own controls, your application should map the colors of those controls to the appropriate system colors so that the controls fit in the overall design of the interface when the user changes the basic system colors.

The **DrawEdge** function automatically provides these border styles using the correct color settings. For more information about this function, see the documentation included in the Microsoft Win32 Software Development Kit (SDK).

Window Border Style

The borders of primary and secondary windows, except for pop-up windows, use the window border style. Menus, scroll arrow buttons, and other situations where the background color may vary also use this border style. The border style is composed of the raised outer and raised inner basic border styles, as shown in Figure 13.3.

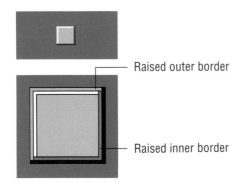

Raised outer border

Raised inner border

Figure 13.3 Window border style

Button Border Styles

Command buttons use the button border style. The button border style uses a variation of the basic border styles where the colors of the top and left outer and inner borders are swapped when combining the borders, as shown in Figure 13.4.

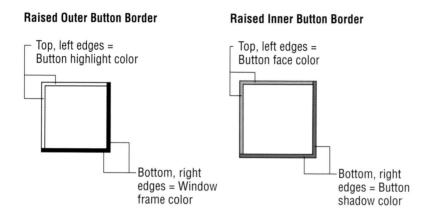

Raised Outer Button Border

┌ Top, left edges =
  Button highlight color

└ Bottom, right
  edges = Window
  frame color

Raised Inner Button Border

┌ Top, left edges =
  Button face color

└ Bottom, right
  edges = Button
  shadow color

Sunken Outer Button Border

┌ Top, left edges =
  Window frame color

└ Bottom, right
  edges = Button
  highlight color

Sunken Inner Button Border

┌ Top, left edges =
  Button shadow color

└ Bottom, right
  edges = Button
  face color

Figure 13.4 Button border styles

The normal button appearance combines the raised outer and raised inner button borders. When the user presses the button, the sunken outer and sunken inner button border styles are used, as shown in Figure 13.5.

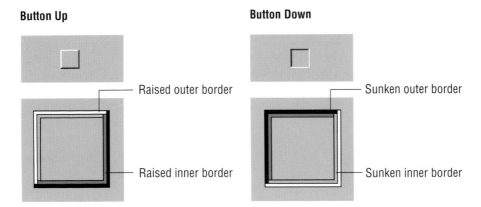

Button Up   **Button Down**

Raised outer border   Sunken outer border

Raised inner border   Sunken inner border

Figure 13.5 Button up and button down border styles

Field Border Style

Text boxes, check boxes, drop-down combo boxes, drop-down list boxes, spin boxes, list boxes, and wells use the field border style, as shown in Figure 13.6. You can also use the style to define the work area within a window. It uses the sunken outer and sunken inner basic border styles.

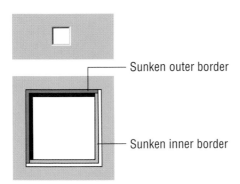

Sunken outer border

Sunken inner border

Figure 13.6 The field border style

For most controls, the interior of the field uses the button highlight color. However, in wells, the color may vary based on how the field is used or what is placed in the field, such as a pattern or color sample. For text fields, such as text boxes and combo boxes, the interior uses the button face color when the field is read-only or disabled.

Status Field Border Style

Status fields use the status field border style, as shown in Figure 13.7. This style uses only the sunken outer basic border style.

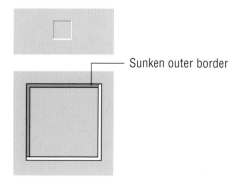

Sunken outer border

Figure 13.7 The status field border style

You use the status field style in status bars and any other read-only fields where the content of the file can dynamically change.

Grouping Border Style

Group boxes and menu separators use the grouping border style, as shown in Figure 13.8. The style uses the sunken outer and raised inner basic border styles.

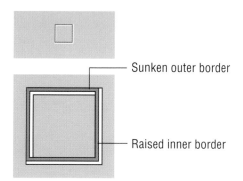

Sunken outer border

Raised inner border

Figure 13.8 The group border style

Visual States for Controls

The visual design of controls includes the various states supported by the control. If you use standard Windows controls, Windows automatically provides specific appearances for these states. If you design your own controls, use the information in the previous section for the appropriate border style and information in the following sections to make your controls consistent with standard Windows controls.

For more information about standard control behavior and appearance, see Chapter 7, "Menus, Controls, and Toolbars," and the documentation included in the Win32 SDK.

Pressed Appearance

When the user presses a control, it provides visual feedback on the down transition of the mouse button. (For the pen, the feedback provided is for when the pen touches the input surface and for the keyboard, upon the down transition of the key.)

For standard Windows check boxes and option buttons, the background of the button field is drawn using the button face color, as shown in Figure 13.9.

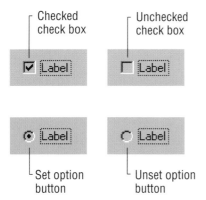

Figure 13.9 Pressed appearance for check boxes and option buttons

For command buttons, the button-down border style is used and the button label moves down and to the right by one pixel, as shown in Figure 13.10.

Figure 13.10 Pressed appearance for a command button

Option-Set Appearance

When using buttons to indicate when its associated value or state
applies or is currently set, the controls provide an *option-set appearance*. The option-set appearance is used upon the up transition of the
mouse button or pen tip, and the down transition of a key. It is visually distinct from the pressed appearance.

Standard check boxes and option buttons provide a special visual
indicator when the option corresponding to that control is set. A
check box uses a check mark, and an option button uses a dot that
appears inside the button, as shown in Figure 13.11.

Figure 13.11 Option-set appearance for check boxes and option buttons

When using command buttons to represent properties or other state
information, the button face reflects when the option is set. The
button continues to use the button-down border style, but a checkerboard pattern (dither) using the color of the button face and button
highlight is displayed on the interior background of the button, as
shown in Figure 13.12. For configurations that support 256 or more
colors, if the button highlight color setting is not white, the button
interior background is drawn in a halftone between button highlight
color and button face color. The glyph on the button does not otherwise change from the pressed appearance.

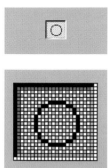

Figure 13.12 Option-set appearance for a command button

For well controls (shown in Figure 13.13), when a particular choice is set, place a border around the control, using the window text color and the button highlight color.

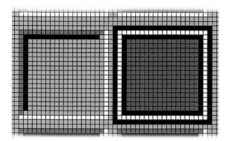

Figure 13.13 Option-set appearance for a well

Mixed-Value Appearance

When a control represents a property or other setting that reflects a set of objects where the values are different, the control is displayed with a *mixed-value* appearance (also referred to as indeterminate appearance), as shown in Figure 13.14.

For most standard controls, leave the field with no indication of a current set value if it represents a mixed value. For example, for a drop-down list, the field is blank.

Standard check boxes support a special appearance for this state that displays the check mark, in the button shadow color, against a checkerboard background that uses the button highlight color and button face color. For configurations that support 256 or more colors, if the button highlight color setting is not white, the interior of the control is drawn in a halftone between button highlight color and button face color.

The system defines the mixed-value states for check boxes as constants BS_3STATE and BS_AUTO3STATE when using the **CreateWindow** and **CreateWindowEx** functions. For more information about these functions, see the documentation included in the Win32 SDK.

Figure 13.14 Mixed-value appearance for a check box

For graphical command buttons, such as those used on toolbars, the checkerboard pattern, using the button highlight color and button face color, or the halftone color, is drawn on the background of the button face, as shown in Figure 13.15. The image is converted to a monochrome presentation and drawn in the button shadow color.

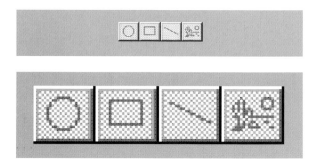

Figure 13.15 Mixed-value appearance for buttons

For check box and command button controls displaying mixed-value appearance, when the user clicks the button, the property value or state is set. Clicking a second time clears the value. As an option, you can support a third click to return the button to the mixed-value state.

Unavailable Appearance

When a control is unavailable (also referred to as disabled), its normal functionality is no longer available to the user (though it can still support access to contextual Help information) because the functionality represented does not apply or is inappropriate under the current circumstances. To reflect this state, the label of the control is rendered with a special *unavailable appearance*, as shown in Figure 13.16.

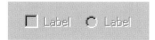

Figure 13.16 Unavailable appearance for check boxes and option buttons

For graphical or text buttons, create the engraved effect by converting the label to monochrome and drawing it in the button highlight color. Then overlay it, at a small offset, with the label drawn in the button shadow color, as shown in Figure 13.17.

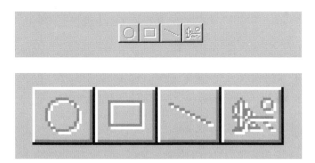

Figure 13.17 Unavailable appearance for buttons

If a check box or option button is set, but the control is unavailable, then the control's label is displayed with an unavailable appearance, and its mark appears in the button shadow color, as shown in Figure 13.18.

Figure 13.18 Unavailable appearance for check boxes and option buttons (when set)

If a graphical button needs to reflect both the set and unavailable appearance (as shown in Figure 13.19), omit the background checkerboard pattern and combine the option-set and the unavailable appearance for the button's label.

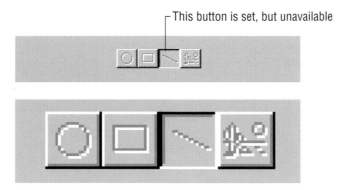

Figure 13.19 Unavailable and option-set appearance for buttons

Input Focus Appearance

You can provide a visual indication so the user knows where the input focus is. For text boxes, the system provides a blinking cursor, or insertion point. For other controls a dotted outline is drawn around the control or the control's label, as shown in Figure 13.20.

Figure 13.20 Example of input focus in a control

The system provides the input focus appearance for standard controls. To use it with your own custom controls, specify the rectangle to allow at least one pixel of space around the extent of the control. If the input focus indicator would be too intrusive, as an option, you can include it around the label for the control. Display the input focus when the mouse button (pen tip) is pressed while over a control; for the keyboard, display the input focus when a navigation or access key for the control is pressed.

The system provides support for drawing the dotted outline input focus indicator using the **DrawFocusRect** function. For more information about this function, see the documentation included in the Win32 SDK.

Flat Appearance

When you nest controls inside of a scrollable region or control, avoid using a three-dimensional appearance because it may not work effectively against the background. Instead, use the flat appearance style, as shown in Figure 13.21.

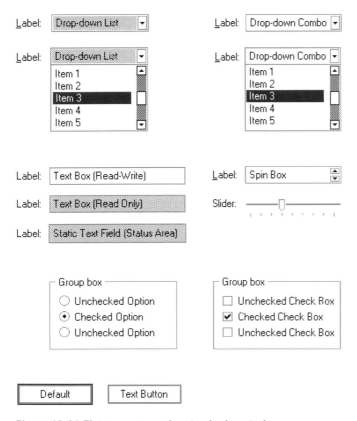

Figure 13.21 Flat appearance for standard controls

The system provides support for the flat appearance style for standard controls. It also includes support for drawing the edges of your own custom controls so you can match the appearance used by standard system controls.

The **DrawFrameControl** and **DrawEdge** functions support drawing the flat appearance. For more information about these functions, see the documentation included in the Win32 SDK.

Layout

Size, spacing, and placement of information are critical in creating a visually consistent and predictable environment. Visual structure is also important for communicating the purpose of the elements displayed in a window. In general, follow the layout conventions for how information is read. In western countries, this means left-to-right, top-to-bottom, with the most important information located in the upper left corner.

Font and Size

The default system font is a key metric in the presentation of visual information. The default font used for interface elements in Windows (U.S. release) is MS® Sans Serif for 8-point. Menu bar titles, menu items, control labels, and other interface text all use 8-point MS Sans Serif. Title bar text also uses the 8-point MS Sans Serif bold font, as shown in Figure 13.22. However, because the user can change the system font, make certain you check this setting and adjust the presentation of your interface appropriately rather than assuming a fixed size for fonts or other visual elements. Also adjust your presentation when the system notifies your application that these settings have changed.

The **GetSystemMetrics** (standard windows elements), **SystemParametersInfo** (primary windows fonts), and **GetStock-Object** (secondary windows fonts) functions provide the current system settings. The WM_SETTINGCHANGE message notifies applications when these settings change. For more information about these APIs, see the documentation included in the Win32 SDK.

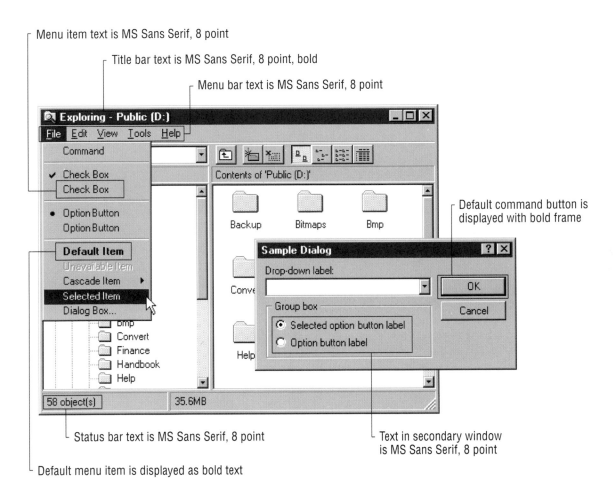

Menu item text is MS Sans Serif, 8 point

Title bar text is MS Sans Serif, 8 point, bold

Menu bar text is MS Sans Serif, 8 point

Default command button is displayed with bold frame

Default menu item is displayed as bold text

Status bar text is MS Sans Serif, 8 point

Text in secondary window is MS Sans Serif, 8 point

Figure 13.22 Default font usage in windows

The system also provides settings for the font and size of many system components including title bar height, menu bar height, border width, title bar button height, icon title text, and scroll bar height and width. When designing your window layouts, take these variables into consideration so that your interface will scale appropriately. In addition, use these standard system settings to determine the size of your custom interface elements.

The system defines the size and location of user-interface elements in a window based on dialog base units, not pixels. A *dialog base unit* is the device-independent measure to use for layout. One horizontal dialog base unit is equal to one-fourth of the average character width for the current system font. One vertical dialog base unit is equal to one-eighth of an average character height for the current system font. The default height for most single-line controls is 14 dialog base units. Be careful when using a pixel-based drawing program because this may not provide an accurate representation when you translate your design into dialog base units.

If a menu item represents a default command, the text is bold. Default command buttons use a bold outline around the button. In general, use nonbold text in your windows. Use bold text only when you want to call attention to an area or create a visual hierarchy.

Avoid displaying any secondary window larger than 263-dialog bases units x 263-dialog base units. The recommended sizes for property sheets are 252-dialog base units wide x 218-dialog base units high, 227-dialog bases units wide x 215-dialog base units high, and 212-dialog base units x 188-dialog base units high. These sizes keep the window from becoming too large to display at some resolutions, and still provide reasonable space to display supportive information, such as Help windows, that apply to the dialog box or property sheet.

For easy readability, make buttons a consistent length. However, if maintaining this consistency greatly expands the space required by a set of buttons, it may be reasonable to have one button larger than the rest.

Similarly, when using tabs, try to maintain a consistent width for all tabs in the same window (and same dimension). However, if a particular tab's label makes this unworkable, you can size it larger, and maintaining a smaller, consistent size for the other tabs. If a tab's label contains variable text, you may want to size the tab to fit the label, up to some reasonable maximum, after which you truncate and add an ellipsis.

Provide toolbar buttons in at least two different sizes: 24-pixels wide x 22-pixels high and 32-pixels wide x 30-pixels high. This includes the border. The image size you include as the button's label should be 16 x 16 pixels and 24 x 24 pixels, respectively. It is best to center

Your application can retrieve the number of pixels per base unit for the current display using the **GetDialogBaseUnits** function. For more information about this function, see the documentation included in the Win32 SDK.

For more information about common toolbar images, see Chapter 7 "Menus, Controls, and Toolbars."

the image on the button's face. Use the smaller size as your default presentation and provide an option for users to change the size. Be certain that you include button images to support all visual states for the buttons.

For larger buttons on very high resolution displays, you can proportionally size the button to be the same height as a text box control. This allows the button to maintain its proportion with respect to other controls in the toolbar. You can stretch the image when the button is an even multiple of the basic sizes. Alternatively, you can supply additional image sizes. This may be preferable, because it provides better visual results.

Toolbar buttons generally have only graphical labels and no accompanying textual label. You can use a tooltip to provide the name of the button.

Capitalization

When displaying text in menus, command buttons, and tabs, use conventional book title capitalization. For example, for U.S. versions, capitalize the first letter in each word unless it is an article or preposition not occurring at the beginning or end of the name, or unless the word's conventional usage is not capitalized. For example:

Insert Object
Paste Link
Save As
Go To
Always on Top
By Name

Use this same convention for default names you provide for filenames, title bar text, or icon labels. Of course, if the user supplies a name for an object, display the name as the user specifies it, regardless of case.

Field labels, such as those used for option buttons, check boxes, text boxes, group boxes, and page tabs, should use sentence-style capitalization. For U.S. versions, this means capitalize only the first letter of the initial word and any words that are normally capitalized. For example:

Extended (XMS) memory
Working directory
Print to
Find whole words only

Grouping and Spacing

Group related components together. You can use group box controls or spacing. Leave at least four dialog base units between controls. Although you can also use color to visually group objects, it is not a common convention and could result in undesirable effects when the user changes color schemes.

Maintain a consistent margin (seven dialog base units is recommended) from the edge of the window. Use spacing between groups within the window. Figure 13.23 shows the recommended spacing.

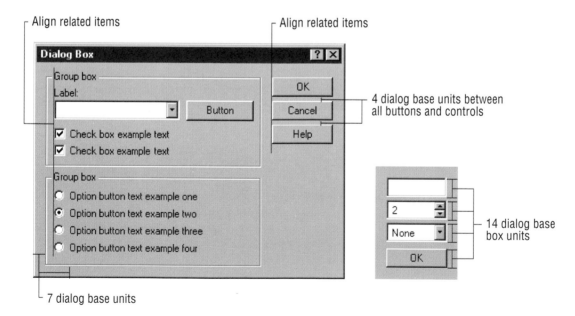

Figure 13.23 Recommended layout and spacing of controls and text

Position controls in a toolbar so that there is at least a window's border width from the edges of the toolbar. Use at least four dialog base units spacing between controls, unless you want to align a set of related toolbar buttons adjacently. Use adjacent alignment for toolbar buttons that are related. For example, when using toolbar buttons like a set of option buttons, align them without any spacing between them.

Alignment

When information is positioned vertically, align fields by their left edges (in western countries). This usually makes it easier for the user to scan the information. Text labels are usually left aligned and placed above or to the left of the areas to which they apply. When placing text labels to the left of text box controls, align the height of the text with text displayed in the text box.

Placement

Stack the main command buttons in a secondary window in the upper right corner or in a row along the bottom, as shown in Figure 13.24. If there is a default button, it is typically the first button in the set. Place OK and Cancel buttons next to each other. The last button is a Help button (if supported). If there is no OK button, but other command buttons, it is best to place the Cancel button at the end of a set of action buttons, but before a Help button. If a particular command button applies only to a particular field, group it with that field.

For more information about button placement in secondary windows, see Chapter 8, "Secondary Windows."

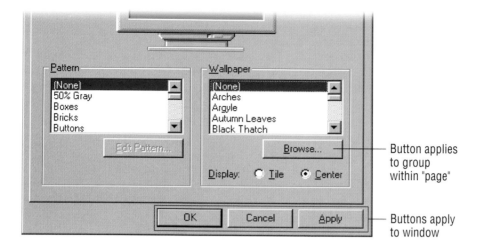

Button applies
to group
within "page"

Buttons apply
to window

Figure 13.24 Examples of layout of buttons

Placement of command buttons (or other controls) within a tabbed page implies the application of only the transactions on that page. If command buttons are placed within the window, but not on the tabbed page, they apply to the entire window.

Design of Graphic Images

When designing pictorial representations of objects, whether they are icons or graphical buttons, begin by defining the icon's purpose and its use. Brainstorm about possible ideas, considering real-world metaphors. It is often difficult to design icons that define operations or processes — activities that rely on verbs. Consider nouns instead. For example, scissors can represent the action of Cut.

Draw your ideas using an icon-editing utility or pixel (bitmapped) drawing package. Drawing them directly on the screen provides immediate feedback about their appearance. It is a good idea to begin the design in black and white. Consider color as an enhancing property. Also, test your images on different backgrounds. They may not always be seen against white or gray backgrounds.

Consistency is also important in the design of graphic images. As with other interface elements, design images assuming a light source from the upper left. In addition, make certain the scale (size) and orientation of your graphics are consistent with the other objects to which they are related and fit well within the working environment.

Avoid using a triangular arrow graphic similar to the one used in cascading menus, drop-down controls, and scroll arrows. When this image appears on a button, it implies that the control will display additional information. For example, you can use an arrow graphic to designate a menu button.

You may want to use a technique called anti-aliasing when designing graphic images. *Anti-aliasing* involves adding colored pixels to smooth the jagged edges of a graphic. However, avoid using anti-aliasing on the outside edge of an icon because the contrasting pixels may look jagged or fuzzy on varying backgrounds.

Finally, remember to consider the potential cultural impact of your graphics. What may have a certain meaning in one country or culture may have unforeseen meanings in another. It is best to avoid letters or words, if possible, as this may make the graphics difficult to apply for other cultures.

For more information about designing for international audiences, see Chapter 14, "Special Design Considerations."

Icon Design

Icons are used throughout the Windows interface to represent objects or tasks. Because the system uses icons to represent your software's objects, it is important to not only supply effective icons, but to design them to effectively communicate their purpose.

When designing icons, design them as a set, considering their relationship to each other and to the user's tasks. Do several sketches or designs and test them for usability.

Sizes and Types

Supply icons for your application in all standard sizes: 16 x 16 pixel (16 color), 32 x 32 pixel (16 color), and 48 x 48 pixel (256 color), as shown in Figure 13.25. Although you can also include greater color depth for the smaller sizes, it increases the storage requirements for the icons and may not be displayable on all computer configurations. Therefore, if you choose to provide 256 color icons in the smaller sizes, do so in addition to providing the standard (16 color) format.

To display icons at 48-x48-pixel resolution, the registry value Shell Icon Size, must be increased to 48. To display icons in color resolution depth higher than 16 colors, the registry value Shell Icon BPP must be set to 8 or more. These values are stored in **HKEY_ CURRENT_USER\Desktop\WindowMetrics**.

48 x 48   32 x 32   16 x 16

Figure 13.25 Three sizes of icons

The system automatically maps colors in your icon design for monochrome configurations. However, you should check your icon design in monochrome configuration. If the result is not satisfactory, author and supply monochrome icons as well.

Define icons not only for your application executable file, but also for all data file types supported by your application, as shown in Figure 13.26.

Application icons

Document icons

Figure 13.26 Application and supported document icons

Icons for documents and data files should be distinct from the application's icon. Include some common element of the application's icon, but focus on making the document icon recognizable and representative of the file's content.

Register the icons you supply in the system registry. If your software does not register any icons, the system automatically provides one based on your application's icon, as shown in Figure 13.27. However, it is unlikely to be as detailed or distinctive as one you can supply.

For more information about registering your icons, see Chapter 10, "Integrating with the System."

Figure 13.27 System-generated icon for file type without a registered icon

Icon Style

When designing your icons, use a common style across all icons. Repeat common characteristics, but avoid repeating unrelated elements.

An illustrative style tends to communicate metaphorical concepts more effectively than abstract symbols. However, in designing an image based on a real-world object, use only the amount of detail that is really necessary for user recognition and recall. Where possible and appropriate, use perspective and dimension (lighting and shadow) to better communicate the real-world representation, as shown in Figure 13.28.

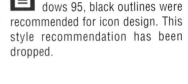 Previous to Microsoft Windows 95, black outlines were recommended for icon design. This style recommendation has been dropped.

Figure 13.28 Perspective and dimension improve graphics

User recognition and recollection are two important factors to consider in icon design. Recognition means that the icon is identifiable by the user and easily associated with a particular object. Support user recognition by using effective metaphors. Use real-world objects to represent abstract ideas so that the user can draw from previous learning and experiences. Exploit the user's knowledge of the world and allude to the familiar.

To facilitate recollection, design your icons to be simple and distinct. Applying the icon consistently also helps build recollection; therefore, design your small icons to be as similar as possible to their larger counterparts. It is generally best to try to preserve general shape and any distinctive detail. 48 x 48-pixel icons can be rendered in 256 colors. This allows very realistic-looking icons, but focus on simplicity and careful use of color. If your software is targeted at computers that can only display 256 colors, make certain you only use colors from the system's standard 256-color palette. If you aim at computers configured for 65,000 or more colors, you can use any combination of colors.

Pointer Design

You can use a pointer's design to help the user identify objects and provide feedback about certain conditions or states. However, use pointer changes conservatively so that the user is not distracted by excessive flashing of multiple pointer changes while traversing the screen. One way to handle this is to use a time-out before making noncritical pointer changes.

When you use a pointer to provide feedback, use it only over areas where that state applies. For example, when using the hourglass pointer to indicate that a window is temporarily noninteractive, if the pointer moves over a window that is interactive, change it to its appropriate interactive image. If a process makes the entire interface non-interactive, display the hourglass pointer wherever the user moves the pointer.

Pointer feedback may not always be sufficient. For example, for processes that last longer than a few seconds, it is better to use a progress indicator that indicates progressive status, elapsed time, estimated completion time, or some combination of these to provide more information about the state of the operation. In other situations, you can use command button states to reinforce feedback; for example, when the user chooses a drawing tool.

Use a pointer that best fits the context of the activity. The I-beam pointer is best used to select text. The normal arrow pointer works best for most drag and drop operations, modified when appropriate to indicate copy and link operations.

The location for the hot spot of a pointer (shown in Figure 13.29) is important for helping the user target an object. The pointer's design should make the location of the hot spot intuitive. For example, for a cross-hair pointer, the implied hot spot is the intersection of the lines.

For more information about some of the common pointers, see Chapter 4, "Input Basics." For information about displaying pointers for drag and drop operations, see Chapter 5, "General Interaction Techniques."

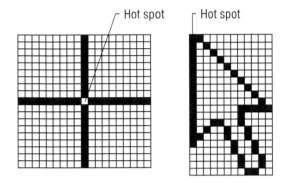

Figure 13.29 Pointer hot spots

Animating a pointer can be a very effective way of communicating information. However, remember that the goal is to provide feedback, not to distract the user. In addition, pointer animation should not restrict the user's ability to interact with the interface.

Selection Appearance

When the user selects an item, provide visual feedback to enable the user to distinguish it from items that are not selected. Selection appearance generally depends on the object and the context in which the selection appears.

Display an object with selection appearance as the user performs a selection operation. For example, display selection appearance when the user presses the mouse button to select an object.

For more information about selection techniques, see Chapter 5, "General Interaction Techniques."

It is best to display the selection appearance only for the scope, area, or level (window or pane) that is active. This helps the user recognize which selection currently applies and the extent of the scope of that selection. Therefore, avoid displaying selections in inactive windows or panes, or at nested levels.

However, in other contexts, it may still be appropriate to display
selection appearance simultaneously in multiple contexts. For example, when the user selects an object and then selects a menu item
to apply to that object, selection appearance is always displayed for
both the object and the menu item because it is clear where the user
is directing the input. In cases where you need to show simultaneous
selection, but with the secondary selection distinguished from the
active selection, you can draw an outline in the selection highlight
color around the secondary selection or use some similar variant of
the standard selection highlight technique.

Highlighting

For many types of objects, you can display the object or its background or some distinguishing part of the object using the system
highlight color. Figure 13.30 shows examples of selection
appearances.

The **GetSysColor** function
provides access to the current setting for the system selection
highlight color (COLOR_HIGH-
LIGHT). For more information about
this function, see the documentation included in the Win32 SDK.

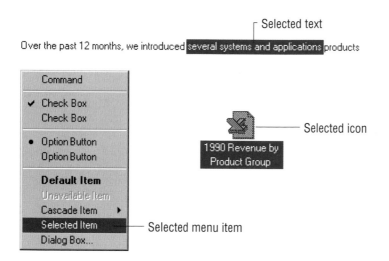

Figure 13.30 Examples of selection appearance

In a secondary window, it may be appropriate to display selection
highlighting when the highlight is also being used to reflect the
setting for a control. For example, in list boxes, highlighting often
indicates a current setting. In cases like this, provide an input focus
indication as well so the user can distinguish when input is being
directed to another control in the window; you can also use check
marks instead of highlighting to indicate the setting.

Handles

Handles provide access to operations for an object, but they can also indicate selection for some kinds of objects. The typical handle is a solid, filled square box that appears on the edge of the object, as shown in Figure 13.31.

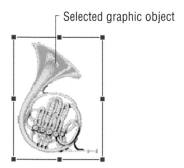

Selected graphic object

Figure 13.31 Selected graphic object with handles

The handle is "hollow" when the handle indicates selection, but is not a control point by which the object may be manipulated. Figure 13.32 shows a solid and a hollow handle.

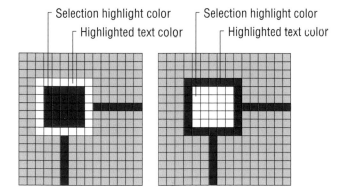

Selection highlight color
Highlighted text color
Selection highlight color
Highlighted text color

Figure 13.32 Solid and hollow handles

Base the default size of a handle on the current system settings for window border and edge metrics so that your handles are appropriately sized when the user explicitly changes window border widths or to accommodate higher resolutions. Similarly, base the colors you use to draw handles on system color metrics so that when the user changes the default system colors, handles change appropriately.

The system settings for window border and edge metrics can be accessed using the **GetSystemMetrics** function. For more information about this function, see the documentation included in the Win32 SDK.

When using handles to indicate selection, display the handle in the system highlight color. To help distinguish the handle from the variable background, draw a border and the edge of the handle using the system's setting for highlighted text. For hollow handles use the opposite: selection highlight color for the border and highlighted text color for the fill color. If you display handles for an object even when it is not selected, display handles in a different color, such as the window text color, so that the user will not confuse it as part of the active selection.

Transfer Appearance

When the user drags an object to perform an operation, for example, move, copy, print, and so on, display a representation of the object that moves with the pointer. In general, do not simply change the pointer to be the object, as this may obscure the insertion point at some destinations. Instead, use a translucent or outline representation of the object that moves with the pointer, as shown in Figure 13.33.

For more information about drag and drop transfer operations, see Chapter 5, "General Interaction Techniques."

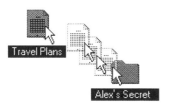

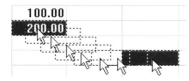

Figure 13.33 Translucent and outline representation (drag transfer)

You can create a translucent representation by using a checkerboard mask made up of 50 percent transparent pixels. When used together with the object's normal appearance, this provides a representation that allows part of the destination to show through. An outline representation should also use a translucent or transparent interior and a gray or dotted outline.

The presentation of an object being transferred displayed is always defined by the destination. Use a representation that best communicates how the transferred object will be incorporated when the user completes the drag transfer. For example, if the object being dragged will be displayed as an icon, then display an icon as its representation. If, on the other hand, it will be incorporated as native content, then display an appropriate representation. For example, you could display a graphics object as an outline or translucent image of its shape, a table cell as the outline of a rectangular box, and text selection as the first few characters of a selection with a transparent background.

Set the pointer image to be whatever pointer the target location uses for directly inserting information. For example, when dragging an object into normal text context, use the I-beam pointer. In addition, include the copy or link image at the bottom right of the pointer if that is the interpretation for the operation.

Open Appearance

Open appearance is most commonly used for an OLE embedded object, but it can also apply in other situations where the user opens an object into its own window. To indicate that an object is "open," display the object in its container's window overlaid with a set of hatched (45 degree) lines drawn every four pixels, as shown in Figure 13.34.

For more information about the use of open appearance for OLE embedded objects, see Chapter 11, "Working with OLE Embedded and OLE Linked Objects."

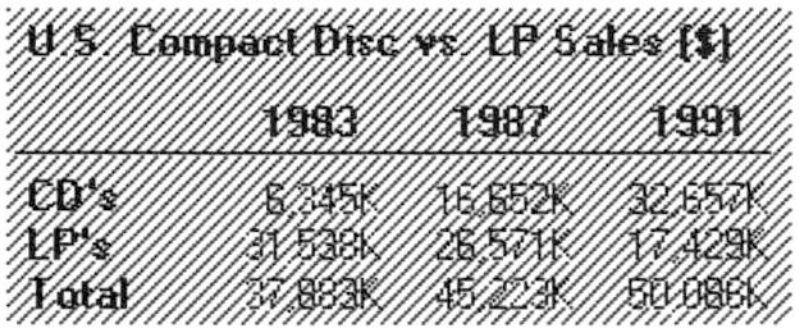

Figure 13.34 An object with opened appearance

If the opened object is selected, display the hatched lines using the system highlight color. When the opened object is not selected, display the lines using the system's setting for window text color.

Animation

Animation can be an effective way to communicate information. For example, it can illustrate the operation of a particular tool or reflect a particular state. It can also be used to include an element of fun in your interface. You can use animation effects for objects within a window and interface elements, such as icons, buttons, and pointers.

Effective animation involves many of the same design considerations as other graphics elements, particularly with respect to color and sound. Fluid animation requires presenting images at 16 (or more) frames per second.

When you add animation to your software, ensure that it does not affect the interactivity of the interface. Do not force the user to remain in a modal state to allow the completion of the animation. Unless animation is part of a process, make it interruptible by the user or independent of the user's primary interaction.

Avoid gratuitous use of animation. When animation is used for decorative effect it can distract or annoy the user. You may want to provide the user with the option of turning off the animation or otherwise customizing the animation effects.

Special Design Considerations

A well-designed application for Microsoft Windows must consider other factors to appeal to the widest possible audience. This chapter covers special user interface design considerations, such as support for sound, accessibility, internationalization, and network computing.

Sound

You can incorporate sound as a part of an application in several ways — for example, music, speech, or sound effects. Such auditory information can take the following forms:

- A primary form of information, such as the composition of a particular piece of music or a voice message.

- An enhancement of the presentation of information that is not required for the operation of the software.

- A notification or alerting of users to a particular condition.

Sound can be an effective form of information and interface enhancement when appropriately used. However, avoid using sound as the only means of conveying information. Some users may be hard-of-hearing or deaf. Others may work in a noisy environment or in a setting that requires that they disable sound or maintain it at a low volume. In addition, like color, sound is a very subjective part of the interface.

As a result, sound is best incorporated as a redundant or secondary form of information, or supplemented with alternative forms of communication. For example, if a user turns off the sound, consider flashing the window's title bar, taskbar button, presenting a message box, or other means of bringing the user's attention to a particular situation. Even when sound is the primary form of information, you can supplement the audio portion by providing visual representation of the information that might otherwise be presented as audio output, such as captioning or animation.

Always allow the user to customize sound support. Support the standard system interfaces for controlling volume and associating particular sounds with application-specific sound events. You can also register your own sound events for your application.

The system provides a global system setting, ShowSounds. The setting indicates that the user wants a visual representation of audio information. Your software should query the status of this setting and provide captioning for the output of any speech or sounds. Captioning should provide as much information visually as is provided in the audible format. It is not necessary to caption ornamental sounds that do not convey useful information.

Do not confuse ShowSounds with the system's SoundSentry option. When the user sets the SoundSentry option, the system automatically supplies a visual indication whenever a sound is produced. Avoid relying on SoundSentry alone if the ShowSounds option is set because SoundSentry only provides rudimentary visual indications, such as flashing of the display or screen border, and it cannot convey the meaning of the sound to the user. The system provides Sound-Sentry primarily for applications that do not provide support for ShowSounds. The user sets either of these options with the Microsoft Windows Accessibility Options.

The taskbar can also provide visual status or notification information. For more information about using the taskbar for this purpose, see Chapter 10, "Integrating with the System."

The **GetSystemMetrics** function provides access to the ShowSounds and SoundSentry settings. For more information about this function and the settings, see the documentation included in the Microsoft Win32 Software Development Kit (SDK).

In Microsoft Windows 95, SoundSentry only works for audio output directed through the internal PC speaker.

Accessibility

Accessibility means making your software usable and accessible to a wide range of users, including those with disabilities. Many users may require special accommodation because of temporary or permanent disabilities.

The issue of software accessibility in the home and workplace is becoming increasingly important. Nearly one in five Americans have some form of disability — and it is estimated that 30 million people in the U.S. alone have disabilities that may be affected by the design of your software. In addition, between seven and nine out of every ten major corporations employ people with disabilities who may need to use computer software as part of their jobs. As the population ages and more people become functionally limited, accessibility for users with disabilities will become increasingly important to the population as a whole. Legislation, such as the Americans with Disabilities Act, requires that most employers provide reasonable accommodation for workers with disabilities. Section 508 of the Rehabilitation Act is also bringing accessibility issues to the forefront in government businesses and organizations receiving government funding.

Designing software that is usable for people with disabilities does not have to be time consuming or expensive. However, it is much easier if you include this in the planning and design process rather than attempting to add it after the completion of the software. Following the principles and guidelines in this guide will help you design software for most users. Often recommendations, such as the conservative use of color or sound, often benefit all users, not just those with disabilities. In addition, keep the following basic objectives in mind:

- Provide a customizable interface to accommodate a wide variety of user needs and preferences.

- Provide compatibility with accessibility utilities that users install.

- Avoid creating unnecessary barriers that make your software difficult or inaccessible to certain types of users.

The following sections provide information on types of disabilities and additional recommendations about how to address the needs of customers with those disabilities.

Types of Disabilities

There are many types of disabilities, but they are often grouped into several broad categories. These include visual, hearing, physical movement, speech or language impairments, and cognitive and seizure disorders.

Visual Disabilities

Visual disabilities range from slightly reduced visual acuity to total blindness. Those with reduced visual acuity may only require that your software support larger text and graphics. For example, the system provides scalable fonts and controls to increase the size of text and graphics. To accommodate users who are blind or have severe impairments, make your software compatible with speech or Braille utilities, described later in this chapter.

Color blindness and other visual impairments may make it difficult for users to distinguish between certain color combinations. This is one reason why color is not recommended as the only means of conveying information. Always use color as an additive or enhancing property.

Hearing Disabilities

Users who are deaf or hard-of-hearing are generally unable to detect or interpret auditory output at normal or maximum volume levels. Avoiding the use of auditory output as the only means of communicating information is the best way to support users with this disability. Instead, use audio output only as a redundant, additive property or provide visual output as an option to supplement the audio information. For more information about supporting sound, see the section "Sound" earlier in this chapter.

Physical Movement Disabilities

Some users have difficulty or are unable to perform certain physical tasks — for example, moving a mouse or simultaneously pressing two keys on the keyboard. Other individuals have a tendency to inadvertently strike multiple keys when targeting a single key. Consideration of physical ability is important not only for users with disabilities, but also for beginning users who need time to master all the motor skills necessary to interact with the interface. The best way to support these users is by supporting all your basic operations using simple keyboard and mouse interfaces.

Speech or Language Disabilities

Users with language disabilities, such as dyslexia, find it difficult to read or write. Spell- or grammar-check utilities can help children, users with writing impairments, and users with a different first language. Supporting accessibility tools and utilities designed for users who are blind can also help those with reading impairments. Most design issues affecting users with oral communication difficulties apply only to utilities specifically designed for speech input.

Cognitive Disabilities

Cognitive disabilities can take many forms, including perceptual differences and memory impairments. You can accommodate users with these disabilities by allowing them to modify or simplify your software's interface, such as supporting menu or dialog box customization. Similarly, using icons and graphics to illustrate objects and choices can be helpful for users with some types of cognitive impairments.

Seizure Disorders

Some users are sensitive to visual information that alternates its appearance or flashes at particular rates — often the greater the frequency, the greater the problem. However, there is no perfect flash rate. Therefore, base all modulating interfaces on the system's cursor blink rate. Because users can customize this value, a particular frequency can be avoided. If that is not practical, provide your own interface for changing the flash rate.

The **GetCaretBlinkTime** function provides access to the current cursor blink rate setting. For more information about this function, see the documentation included in the Win32 SDK.

Types of Accessibility Aids

There are a number of accessibility aids to assist users with certain types of disabilities. To allow these users to effectively interact with your application, make certain it is compatible with these utilities. This section briefly describes the types of utilities and how they work.

One of the best ways to accommodate accessibility in your software's interface is to use standard Windows conventions wherever possible. Windows already provides a certain degree of customization for users and most accessibility aids work best with software that follows standard system conventions.

Screen Enlargement Utilities

Screen enlargers (also referred to as screen magnification utilities or large print programs) allow users to enlarge a portion of their screen. They effectively turn the computer monitor into a viewport showing only a portion of an enlarged virtual display. Users then use the mouse or keyboard to move this viewport to view different areas of the virtual display. Enlargers also attempt to track where users are working, following the input focus and the activation of windows, menus, and secondary windows, and can automatically move the viewport to the active area.

Screen Review Utilities

People who cannot use the visual information on the screen can interpret the information with the aid of a screen review utility (also referred to as a screen reader program or speech access utility). Screen review utilities take the displayed information on the screen and direct it through alternative media, such as synthesized speech or a refreshable Braille display. Because both of these media present only text information, the screen review utility must render other information on the screen as text; that is, determine the appropriate text labels or descriptions for graphical screen elements. They must also track users' activities to provide descriptive information about what the user is doing. These utilities often work by monitoring the system interfaces that support drawing on the screen. They build an off-screen database of the objects on the screen, their properties, and their spatial relationships. Some of this information is presented to users as the screen changes, and other information is maintained until users request it. Screen review utilities often include support for configuration files (also referred to as set files or profiles) for particular applications.

Voice Input Systems

Users who have difficulty typing can choose a voice input system (also referred to as a speech recognition program) to control software with their voice instead of a mouse and keyboard. Like screen reader utilities, voice input systems identify objects on the screen that users can manipulate. Users activate an object by speaking the label that identifies the object. Many of these utilities simulate keyboard interfaces, so if your software includes a keyboard interface, it can be adapted to take advantage of this form of input.

On-Screen Keyboards

Some individuals with physical disabilities cannot use a standard keyboard, but can use special devices designed to work with an on-screen keyboard. Switching devices display groups of commands displayed on the screen, and the user employs one or more switches to choose a selected group, then a command within the group. Another technique allows a user to use a special mouse or headpointer (a device that lets users manipulate the mouse pointer on the screen through head motion) to point to graphic images of keys displayed on the screen to generate keystroke input.

Keyboard Filters

Impaired physical abilities, such as erratic motion, tremors, or slow response, can sometimes be compensated by filtering out inappropriate keystrokes. The Windows Accessibility Options supports a wide range of keyboard filtering options. These are generally independent of the application with which users are interacting and therefore require no explicit support except for the standard system interfaces for keyboard input. However, users relying on these features may type slowly.

Compatibility with Screen Review Utilities

You can use the following techniques to ensure software compatibility with screen review utilities. The system allows your application to determine whether the system has been configured to provide support for a screen review utility, allowing your software to enable or disable certain capabilities.

You can check the SM_ SCREENREADER setting using the **GetSystemMetrics** function. For more information about this function and other information about supporting screen review utilities, see the documentation included in the Win32 SDK.

Controls

Use standard Windows controls wherever possible. Most of these have already been implemented to support screen review and voice input utilities. However, custom controls you create may not be usable by screen review utilities.

Always include a label for every control, even if you do not want the control's label to be visible. This applies regardless of whether you use standard controls or your own specialized controls, such as owner drawn controls or custom controls. If the control does not provide a label, you can create a label using a static text control.

Follow the normal layout conventions by placing the static text label before the control (above or to the left of the control). Also, set the keyboard TAB navigation order appropriately so that tabbing to a label navigates to the associated control it identifies instead of a label. To make certain that the label is recognized correctly, include a colon at the end of the label's text string, unless you are labeling a button, tab, or group box control. In cases where a label is not needed or would be visually distracting, provide the label but do not make it visible. Although the label is not visible, it is accessible to a screen review utility.

Text labels are also effective for choices within a control. For example, you can enhance menus or lists that display colors or line widths by including some form of text representation, as shown in Figure 14.1.

Text labels identify color choices

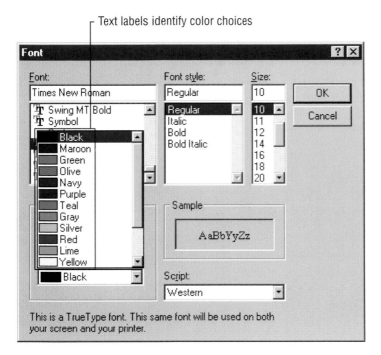

Figure 14.1 Using text to help identify choices

If providing a combined presentation is too difficult, offer users the choice between text and graphical representation, or choose one of them based on the system's screen review utility setting.

Text Output

Screen review utilities usually interpret text — including properties such as font, size, and face — that is displayed with standard system interfaces. However, text displayed as graphics (for example, bit-mapped text) is not accessible to a screen review utility. To make it accessible, your application can create an invisible text label and associate the graphical representation of text with it by drawing the text over the graphic with a null operator (NOP). Screen review utilities can read standard text representations in a metafile, so you can also use metafiles, instead of bitmap images, for graphics information that includes text.

Graphics Output

Users with normal sight may be able to easily distinguish different elements of a graphic or pictorial information, such as a map or chart, even if they are drawn as a single image; however, a screen review utility must distinguish between different components. There are a number of ways to do this. Any of these methods can be omitted when the system's screen review setting is not set.

When using bitmap images, consider separately drawing each component that requires identification. If performance is an issue, combine the component images in an off-screen bitmap using separate drawing operations and then display the bitmap on the screen with a single operation. You can also draw multiple bitmap images with a single metafile.

Alternatively, you can redraw each component separately, or draw a separate image to identify each region using a null operator. This will not have an effect on the visible image, but allows a screen review utility to identify the region. You can also use this method to associate a text label with a graphic element.

When drawing graphics, use standard Windows drawing functions wherever possible. If you change an image directly — for example, clearing a bitmap by writing directly into its memory — a screen review utility will not be able to recognize the content change and will inappropriately describe it to users.

Icons and Windows

Accompany icons that represent objects with a text label (title) of the object's name. Use the system font and color for icon labels, and follow the system conventions for placement of the text relative to the icon. This allows a screen review utility to identify the object without special support.

Similarly, make certain that all your windows have titles. Even if the title is not visible, it is still available to access utilities. The more unique your window titles, the easier users can differentiate between them, especially when using a screen review utility. Using unique window class names is another way to provide for distinct window identification, but providing appropriate window titles is preferred.

The User's Point of Focus

Many accessibility aids must follow where the user is working. For example, a screen review utility conveys to users where the input focus is; a screen enlarger pans its viewport to ensure that users' focus is always kept on the visible portion of the screen. Most utilities give users the ability to manually move the viewport, but this becomes a laborious process, especially if it has to be repeated each time the input focus moves.

When the system handles the move of the input focus, such as when the user selects a menu, navigates between controls in a dialog box, or activates a window, an accessibility utility can track the change. However, the utility may not detect when an application moves the input focus within its own window. Therefore, whenever possible, use standard system functions to place the input focus, such as the text insertion point. Even when you provide your own implementation of focus, you can use the system functions to indicate focus location without making the standard input focus indicator visible.

The **SetCaretPos** function is an example of a system function you can use to indicate focus location. For more information about this function, see the documentation included in the Win32 SDK.

Timing and Navigational Interfaces

Some users read text or press keys very slowly and do not respond to events as quickly as the average user. Avoid displaying critical feedback or messages briefly and then automatically removing them because many users cannot read or respond to them. Similarly, limit your use of time-out based interfaces. If you do include a time-based interface, always provide a way for users to configure the time-out.

Also, avoid displaying or hiding information based on the movement of the pointer, unless it is part of a standard system interface (for example, tooltips). Although such techniques can benefit some users, they may not be available for those using accessibility utilities. If you do provide such support, consider making these features optional so that users can turn them on or off when a screen review utility is installed.

Similarly, you should avoid using general navigation to trigger operations, because users of accessibility aids may need to navigate through all controls. For example, basic TAB keyboard navigation in a dialog box should not activate actions associated with a control, such as setting a check box or carrying out a command button. However, navigation can be used to facilitate further user interaction, such as validating user input or opening a drop-down control.

Color

Base the color properties of your interface elements on the system colors for window components, rather than defining specific colors. Remember to use appropriate foreground and background color combinations. If the foreground of an element is rendered with the button text color, use the button face color as its background rather than the window background color. If the system does not provide standard color settings that can be applied to some elements, you can include your own interface that allows users to customize colors. In addition, you can provide graphical patterns as an optional substitute for colors as a way to distinguish information.

For more information about the use of color and how it is used for interface elements, see Chapter 13, "Visual Design."

The system also provides a global setting called High Contrast Mode that users can set through the Windows Accessibility Options. The setting provides contrasting color settings for foreground and background visual elements. Your application should check for this setting's status when it starts, and whenever it receives notification of system setting changes. When set, adjust your interface colors based on those set for the high contrast color scheme. In addition, whenever High Contrast Mode is set, hide any images that are drawn behind text (for example, watermarks or logos) to maintain the legibility of the information on the screen. You can also display monochrome versions of bitmaps and icons using the appropriate foreground color.

The **GetSystemMetrics** function provides access to the SM_HIGHCONTRAST setting. For more information about this function, see the documentation included in the Win32 SDK.

Scalability

Another important way to provide for visual accessibility is to allow for the scalability of screen elements. Sometimes, this simply means allowing users to change the font for the display of information. The system allows users to change the size and font of standard Windows components. You should use these same metrics for appropriately adjusting the size of other visual information you provide. For your own custom elements, you can provide scaling by including a TrueType font or metafiles for your graphics images.

For more information about the system metrics for font and size, see Chapter 13, "Visual Design."

It may also useful to provide scaling features within your application. For example, many application provide a "Zoom" command that scales the presentation of the information displayed in a window, or other commands that make the presentation of information easier to read. You may need to add scroll bars if the scaled information exceeds the current size of the window.

Keyboard and Mouse Interface

Providing a good keyboard interface is an important step in accessibility because it affects users with a wide range of disabilities. For example, a keyboard interface may be the only option for users who are blind or use voice input utilities, and those who cannot use a mouse. The Windows Accessibility Options often compensate for users with disabilities related to keyboard interaction; however, it is more difficult to compensate for problems related to pointing device input.

You should follow the conventions for keyboard navigation techniques presented in this guide. For specialized interfaces within your software, model your keyboard interface on conventions that are familiar and appropriate for that context. Where they apply, use the standard control conventions as a guide for your defining interaction. For example, support TAB and SHIFT+TAB key and access keys to support navigation to controls.

Make certain the user can navigate to all objects. Avoid relying only on navigational design that requires the user to understand the spatial relationship between objects. Accessibility utilities may not be able to convey such relationships.

Providing a well-designed mouse interface is also important. Pointing devices may be more efficient than keyboards for some users. When designing the interface for pointing input, avoid making basic functions available only through multiple clicking, drag and drop manipulation, and keyboard-modified mouse actions. Such actions are best considered shortcut techniques for more advanced users. Make basic functions available through single click techniques.

The system also allows your application to determine when the user relies on the keyboard, rather than pointing device input. You can use this to present special keyboard interfaces that might otherwise be hidden.

Where possible, avoid making the implementation of basic functions dependent on a particular device. This is critical for supporting users with physical disabilities and users who may not wish to use or install a particular device.

Check the SM_KEYBOARD-PREF setting, using **GetSystemMetrics,** to determine whether a user relies on keyboard rather than pointing device input. For more information about this function, see the documentation included in the Win32 SDK.

Documentation, Packaging, and Support

Although this guide focuses primarily on the design of the user interface, a design that provides for accessibility needs to take into consideration other aspects of a product. For example, consider the documentation needs of your users. For users who have difficulty reading or handling printed material, provide online documentation for your product. If the documentation or installation instructions are not available online, you can provide documentation separately in alternative formats, such as ASCII text, large print, Braille, or audio tape format. Organizations that can help you produce and distribute such documentation are listed in the accessibility section of the Bibliography of this guide.

When possible, choose a format and binding for your documentation that makes it accessible for users with disabilities. As in the interface, information in color should be a redundant form of communication. Bindings that allow a book to lie flat are usually better for users with limited dexterity.

Packaging is also important because many users with limited dexterity can have difficulty opening packages. Consider including an easy-opening overlap or tab that helps users remove shrink-wrapping.

Finally, although support is important for all users, it is difficult for users with hearing impairments to use standard support lines. Consider making these services available to customers using text telephones (also referred to as "TT" or "TDD"). You can also provide support through public bulletin boards or other networking services.

Usability Testing

Just as it is important to test the general usability of your software, it is a good idea to test how well it provides for accessibility. There are a variety of ways of doing this. One way is to include users with disabilities in your prerelease or usability test activities. In addition, you can establish a working relationship with companies that provide accessibility aids. Information about accessibility vendors or potential test sites is included in the Bibliography.

You can also try running your software in a fashion similar to that used by a person with disabilities. Try some of the following ideas for testing:

- Use the Windows Accessibility Options and set your display to a high contrast scheme, such as white text on a black background. Are there any portions of your software that become invisible or hard to use or recognize?

- Try using your software for a week without using a mouse. Are there operations that you cannot perform? Was anything especially awkward?

- Increase the size of the default system fonts. Does your software still look good? Does your software fonts appropriately adjust to match the new system font?

Internationalization

To successfully compete in international markets, your software must easily accommodate differences in language, culture, and hardware. This section does not cover every aspect of preparing software for the international market, but it does summarize some of the key design issues.

For more information about the technical details for localizing your application, see the documentation included in the Win32 SDK.

The process of translating and adapting a software product for use in a different country is called *localization*. Like any part of the interface, include international considerations early in the design and development process. In addition to adapting screen information and documentation for international use, Help files, scenarios, templates, models, and sample files should all be a part of your localization planning.

Language is not the only relevant factor when localizing an interface. Several countries can share a common language but have different conventions for expressing information. In addition, some countries can share a language but use a different keyboard convention.

A more subtle factor to consider when preparing software for international markets is cultural differences. For example, users in the U.S. may recognize a rounded mail box with a flag on the side as an icon for a mail program, but this image may not be recognized by users in other countries. Sounds and their associated meanings may also vary from country to country.

It is helpful to create a supplemental document for your localization team that covers the terms and other translatable elements your software uses, and describes where they occur. Documenting changes between versions saves time in preparing new releases. Appendix E of this guide provides recommended translations of many words used in the Windows interface.

Text

A major aspect of localizing an interface involves translating the text used by the software in its title bars, menus and other controls, messages, and some registry entries. To make localization easier, store interface text as resources in your application's resource file rather than including it in the source code of the application. Remember to also translate menu commands your application stores for its file types in the system registry.

Translation is a challenging task. Each foreign language has its own syntax and grammar. Following are some general guidelines to keep in mind for translation:

- Do not assume that a word always appears at the same location in a sentence, that word order is always the same, that sentences or words always have the same length, or that nouns, adjectives, and verbs always keep the same form.

- Avoid using vague words that can have several meanings in different contexts.

- Avoid colloquialisms, jargon, acronyms, and abbreviations.

- Use good grammar. Translation is a difficult enough task without a translator having to deal with poor grammar.

- Avoid dynamic, or run-time, concatenation of different strings to form new strings — for example, composing messages by combining frequently used strings. An exception is the construction of filenames and names of paths.

- Avoid hard coding filenames in a binary file. Filenames may need to be translated.

- Avoid including text in images and icons. Doing so requires that these also be translated.

Translation of interface text from English to other languages often increases the length of text by 30 percent or more. In some extreme cases, the character count can increase by more than 100 percent; for example, the word "move" becomes "verschieben" in German. Accordingly, if the amount of the space for displaying text is strictly limited, as in a status bar, restrict the length of the English interface text to approximately one half of the available space. In contexts that allow more flexibility, such as dialog boxes and property sheets, allow 30 percent for text expansion in the interface design. Message text in message boxes, however, should allow for text expansion of about 100 percent. Avoid having your software rely on the position of text in a control or window because translation may require movement of the text.

Expansion due to translation affects other aspects of your product. A localized version is likely to affect file sizes, potentially changing the layout of your installation disks and setup software.

Translation is not always a one-to-one correspondence. A single word in English can have multiple translations in another language. Adjectives and articles sometimes change spelling according to the gender of the nouns they modify. Therefore, be careful when re-using a string in multiple places. Similarly, several English words may have only a single meaning in another language. This is particularly important when creating keywords for the Help index for your software.

Graphics

It is best to review the proposed graphics for international applicability early in your design cycle. Localizing graphics can be a time consuming process.

Although graphics communicate more universally than text, graphical aspects of your software — especially icons and toolbar button images — may also need to be revised to address an international audience. For example, a toolbar image that includes a magic wand to represent access to a wizard interface does not have meaning in many European countries and requires a different image.

When possible, choose generic images and glyphs. Even if you can create custom designs for each language, having different images for different languages can confuse users who work with more than one language version.

Many symbols with a strong meaning in one culture do not have any meaning in another. For example, many symbols for U.S. holidays and seasons are not shared around the world. Importantly, some symbols can be offensive in some cultures (for example, the open palm commonly used at U.S. crosswalk signals is offensive in some countries). Some metaphors also may not apply in all languages.

Keyboards

International keyboards also differ from those used in the U.S. Avoid using punctuation character keys as shortcut keys because they are not always found on international keyboards or easily produced by the user. Remember too, that what seems like an effective shortcut because of its mnemonic association (for example, CTRL+B for Bold) can warrant a change to fit a particular language. Similarly, macros or other utilities that invoke menus or commands based on access keys are not likely to work in an international version, because the command names on which the access keys are based differ.

Keys do not always occupy the same positions on all international keyboards. Even when they do, the interpretation of the unmodified keystroke can be different. For example, on U.S. keyboards, SHIFT+8 results in an asterisk character. However, on French keyboards, it generates the number 8. Similarly, avoid using CTRL+ALT combinations, because the system interprets this combination for some language versions as the ALTGR key, which generates some alphanumeric characters. Similarly, avoid using the ALT key as a modifier because it is the primary keyboard interface for accessing menus and controls. In addition, the system uses many specialized versions for special input. For example, ALT+~ invokes special input

editors in Far East versions of Windows. For text fields, pressing
ALT+*number* enters characters in the upper range of a character set.
Similarly, avoid using the following characters when assigning the
following shortcut keys.

@ £ $ { } [ ] \ ~ | ^ ' < >

Character Sets

Some international countries require support for different character
sets (sometimes referred to as *code pages*). The system provides a
standard interface for supporting multiple character sets and sort
tables. Use these interfaces wherever possible for sorting and case
conversion. In addition, consider the following guidelines:

The **SystemParametersInfo** function allows you to deter-mine the current keyboard configu-ration. For more information about this function, see the documenta-tion included in the Win32 SDK.

- Do not assume that the character set is U.S. ANSI. Many ANSI
  character sets are available. For example, the Russian version of
  Windows 95 uses the Cyrillic ANSI character set which is differ-ent
  than the U.S. ANSI set.

- Use the system functions for supporting font selection (such as the
  common font dialog box).

- Always save the character set with font names in documents.

Formats

Different countries often use substantially different formats for dates,
time, money, measurements, and telephone numbers. This collection
of language-related user preferences are referred to as a *locale*. De-signing
your software to accommodate international audiences re-quires
supporting these different formats.

Windows provides a standard means for inquiring what the default
format is and also allows the user to change those properties. Your
software can allow the user to change formats, but restrict these
changes to your application or document type, rather than affecting the
system defaults. Table 14.1 lists the most common format categories.

For more information about the functions that provide ac-cess to the current locale formats, see the documentation included in the Win32 SDK.

Table 14.1 Formats for International Software

Category	Format considerations
Date	Order, separator, long or short formats, and leading zero
Time	Separator and cycle (12-hour vs. 24-hour), leading zero
Physical quantity	Metric vs. English measurement system
Currency	Symbol and format (for example, trailing vs. preceding symbol)
Separators	List, decimal, and thousandths separator
Telephone numbers	Separators for area codes and exchanges
Calendar	Calendar used and starting day of the week
Addresses	Order and postal code format
Paper sizes	U.S. vs. European paper and envelope sizes

Layout

For layout of controls or other elements in a window, it is important to consider alignment in addition to expansion of text labels. In Hebrew and Arabic countries, information is written right to left. So when localizing for these countries, reverse your U.S. presentation.

Some languages include diacritical marks that distinguish particular characters. Fonts associated with these characters can require additional spacing.

In addition, do not place information or controls into the title bar area. This is where Windows places special user controls for configurations that support multiple languages.

References to Unsupported Features

Avoid confusing your international users by leaving in references to features that do not exist in their language version. Adapt the interface appropriately for features that do not apply. For example, some language versions may not include a grammar checker or support for bar codes on envelopes. Remove references to features such as menus, dialog boxes, and Help files from the installation program.

Network Computing

Windows provides an environment that allows the user to communicate and share information across the network. When designing your software, consider the special needs that working in such an environment requires.

Conceptually, the network is an expansion of the user's local space. The interface for accessing objects from the network should not differ significantly from or be more complex than the user's desktop.

Leverage System Support

When designing for network access, support standard conventions and interfaces, including the following:

- Use universal naming convention (UNC) paths to refer to objects stored in the file system. This convention provides transparent access to objects on the network.

- Use system-supported user identification that allows you to determine access without including your own password interface.

- Adjust window sizes and positions based on the local screen properties of the user.

- Avoid assuming the presence of a local hard disk. It is possible that some of your users work with diskless workstations.

Client-Server Applications

Users operating on a network may wish to run your application from a network server. For applications that store no state information, no special support is required. However, if your application stores state information, design your application with a server set of components and a client set of components. The server components include the main executable files, dynamic link libraries, and any other files that need to be shared across the network. The client components consist of the components of the application that are specific to the user, including local registry information and local files that provide the user with access to the server components.

For information about installing the client and server components of your application, see Chapter 10, "Integrating with the System."

Shared Data Files

When storing a file in the shared space of the network, it should be readily accessible to all users, so design the file to be opened multiple times. The granularity of concurrent access depends on the file type; that is, for some files you may only support concurrent access by word, paragraph, section, page, and so on. Provide clear visual cues as to what information can be changed and what cannot. Where multiple access is not easily supported, provide users with the option to open a copy of the file, if the original is already open.

Record Processing

Record processing or transaction-based applications may require somewhat different structuring than the typical productivity application. For example, rather than opening and saving discrete files, the interface for such applications focuses on accessing and presenting data as records through multiple views, forms, and reports. One of the distinguishing and most important design aspects of record-processing applications is the definition of how the data records are structured. This dictates what information can be stored and in what format.

However, you can apply much of the information in this guide to record-oriented applications. For example, the basic principles of design and methodology are just as applicable as they are for individual file-oriented applications. You can also apply the guide's conventions for input, navigation, and layout when designing forms and report designs. Similarly, your can apply other secondary window conventions for data-entry design, including the following:

- Provide reasonable default values for fields.

- Use the appropriate controls. For example, use drop-down list boxes instead of long lists of option buttons.

- Distinguish text entry fields from read-only text fields.

- Design for logical and smooth user navigation. Order fields as the user needs to move through them. Auto-exit text boxes are often good for input of predefined data formats, such as time or currency inputs.

- Provide data validation as close to the site of data entry as possible. You can use input masks to restrict data to specific types or list box controls to restrict the range of input choices.

Telephony

Windows provides support for creating applications with telephone communications, or *telephony*, services. Those services include the Assisted Telephony services for adding minimal, but useful telephonic functionality to applications, and the full Telephony API, for implementing full telephonic applications.

For more information about creating applications using the Microsoft Windows Telephony API (TAPI), see the documentation included in the Win32 SDK.

You should consider the following guidelines when developing telephony applications:

- Provide separate fields for users to enter country code, area code, and a local number. You may use auto-exit style navigation to facilitate the number entry. You can also use a drop-down list box to allow users to select a country code. The system provides support for listing available codes.

- Provide access to the TAPI Dialing Properties property sheet window wherever a user enters a phone number. This window provides a consistent and easy interface for users.

- Use the modem configuration interfaces provided by the system. If the user has not installed a modem, run the Windows TAPI modem installation wizard.

Microsoft Exchange

Microsoft Exchange is the standard Windows interface for email, voice mail, FAX, and other communication media. Applications interact with Microsoft Exchange by using the Messaging API (MAPI) and support services and components.

For more information about MAPI, see the documentation included in the Win32 SDK.

Microsoft Exchange allows you to create support for an information service. An information service is a utility that enables messaging applications to send and receive messages and files, store items in an information store, obtain user addressing information, or any combination of these functions.

Coexisting with Other Information Services

Microsoft Exchange is designed to simultaneously support different information services. Therefore when designing an information service, avoid:

- Initiating lengthy operations.

- Assuming exclusive use of key hardware resources, such as communications (COMM) ports and modems.

- Adding menu commands that are incompatible with other services.

Adding Menu Items and Toolbar Buttons

Microsoft Exchange allows you to add menu items and toolbar buttons to the main viewer window. Follow the recommendations in this guide for defining menu and toolbar entries. In addition, where possible, define your menu items and toolbar entries (or their tooltips) in a way that allows the user to clearly associate the functionality with a specific information service.

Supporting Connections

When the user selects an information service that you support, provide the user with a dialog box to confirm the choice and allow the user access to configuration properties. Because simultaneous services run at the same time, clearly identify the service. At the top of the window, display the icon and name of the service. You can include an option to not display the dialog box.

Installing Information Services

Microsoft Exchange includes a special wizard for installation of information services. You can support this wizard to allow the user to easily install your service.

The system also provides profiles and files that define which services are available to users when they log on. When the user installs your service, ask the user which profile they would like to include with your service, such as their default profile.

Appendixes

Mouse Interface Summary

The tables in this appendix summarize the basic mouse interface, including selection and direct manipulation (drag and drop).

Table A. 1 Interaction Guidelines for Common Unmodified Mouse Actions

Action	Target	Effect on current selection state	Effect on anchor point location	Resulting operation using button 1	Resulting operation using button 2
Press	Unselected object	Clears the active selection.	Resets the anchor point to the object.	Selects the object.	Selects the object.
	Selected object	None	None	None[1]	None
	White space (background)	Clears the active selection.	Resets the anchor point to the button down location.	Initiates a region (marquee) selection.	Initiates a region (marquee) selection.
Click	Unselected object	Clears the active selection.	Resets the anchor point to the object.	Selects the object.	Selects the object and displays its pop-up menu.
	Selected object	None[2]	None[2]	Selects the object.[1]	Selects the object[1] and displays the selection's pop-up menu.
	White space (background)	Clears the active selection.	None	None	Displays the pop-up menu for the white space.[3]

Table A. 1 Interaction Guidelines for Common Unmodified Mouse Actions *(continued)*

Action	Target	Effect on current selection state	Effect on anchor point location	Resulting operation using button 1	Resulting operation using button 2
Drag	Unselected object	Clears the active selection.	Resets the anchor point to the object.	Selects the object and carries out the default transfer operation[4] upon the button release at the destination.	Selects the object and displays the non-default transfer pop-up menu[4] upon the button release at the destination.
	Selected object	None	None	Carries out the default transfer operation[4] on the selection upon the button release at the destination.	Displays the nondefault transfer pop-up menu[4] upon the button release at the destination.
	White space (background)	Clears the active selection.	None	Selects everything logically included from anchor point to active end.	Selects everything logically included from anchor point to active end and displays pop-up menu for the resulting selection.
Double-click	Unselected object	Clears the active selection.	Resets the anchor point to the object.	Selects the object and carries out the default operation.	Selects the object.
	Selected object	None	None	Carries out the selection's default operation.	Selects the object.
	White space (background)	Clears the active selection.	None	Carries out the default operation for the white space.[3]	None.

[1]Alternatively, you can support subselection for this action. Subselection means to distinguish an object in a selection for some purpose. For example, in a selection of objects, subselecting an object may define that object as the reference point for alignment commands.

[2]Alternatively, you can support clearing the active selection and reset the anchor point to the object — if this better fits the context of the user's task.

[3] The white space (or background) is an access point for commands of the view, the container, or both. For example, white space can include commands related to selection (Select All), magnification (Zoom), type of view (Outline), arrangement (Arrange By Date), display of specific view elements (Show Grid), general operation of the view (Refresh), and containment commands that insert objects (Paste).

[4] The default transfer operation is determined by the destination of the drag and drop. Similarly, the destination determines the transfer commands displayed in the resulting pop-up menu when the mouse button is released. If the object cannot be dragged, then you can optionally use this action to create a range selection.

Table A. 2 Interaction Guidelines for Using the SHIFT Key to Modify Mouse Actions

Action	Target	Effect on current selection state	Effect on anchor point location	Resulting operation using button 1	Resulting operation using button 2
SHIFT+ Press	Unselected object	Clears the active selection.[1]	None	Extends the selection state from the anchor point to the object.[2]	Extends the selection state from the anchor point to the object.[3]
	Selected object	Clears the active selection.[1]	None	Extends the selection state from the anchor point to the object.[2]	Extends the selection state from the anchor point to the object.[3]
	White space (background)	Clears the active selection.[1]	None	Extends the selection state from the anchor point to the object logically included at the button down point.[2]	Extends the selection state from the anchor point to the object logically included at the button down point.[3]

Table A. 2 Interaction Guidelines for Using the SHIFT Key to Modify Mouse Actions *(continued)*

Action	Target	Effect on current selection state	Effect on anchor point location	Resulting operation using button 1	Resulting operation using button 2
SHIFT+ Click	Unselected object	Clears the active selection.[1]	None	Extends the selection state from the anchor point to the object.[2]	Extends the selection state from the anchor point to the object[2] and displays the pop-up menu for the resulting selection.[3]
	Selected object	Clears the active selection.[1]	None	Extends the selection state from the anchor point to the object.[2]	Extends the selection state from the anchor point to the object[2] and displays the pop-up menu for the resulting selection.[3]
	White space (background)	Clears the active selection.[1]	None	Extends the selection state from the anchor point to the object logically included at the button down point.[2]	Extends the selection state from the anchor point to the object[2] logically included at the button down point and displays the pop-up menu for the resulting selection.[3]

Table A. 2 Interaction Guidelines for Using the SHIFT Key to Modify Mouse Actions *(continued)*

Action	Target	Effect on current selection state	Effect on anchor point location	Resulting operation using button 1	Resulting operation using button 2
SHIFT+ Drag	Unselected object	Clears the active selection.[1]	None	Extends the selection state from the anchor point to the object.[2]	Extends the selection state from the anchor point to the object[2] and displays the pop-up menu for the resulting selection.[3]
	Selected object	Clears the active selection.[1]	None	Extends the selection state from the anchor point to the object.[2]	Extends the selection state from the anchor point to the object[2] and displays the pop-up menu for the resulting selection.[3]
	White space (background)	Clears the active selection.[1]	None	Extends the selection state from the anchor point to the object logically included at the button down point.[2]	Extends the selection state from the anchor point to the object logically included at the button down point[2] and displays the pop-up menu for the resulting selection.[3]

Table A. 2 Interaction Guidelines for Using the SHIFT Key to Modify Mouse Actions *(continued)*

Action	Target	Effect on current selection state	Effect on anchor point location	Resulting operation using button 1	Resulting operation using button 2
SHIFT+ Double-click	Unselected object	Clears the active selection.[1]	Resets the anchor point to the object.	Extends the selection state from the anchor point to the object[2] and carries out the default command on the resulting selection.[3]	Extends the selection state from the anchor point to the object.[2]
	Selected object	None	None	Extends the selection state from the anchor point to the object[2] and carries out the default command on the resulting selection.[3]	Extends the selection state from the anchor point to the object.[2]
	White space (background)	Clears the active selection.[1]	None	Extends the selection state from the anchor point to the object logically included at the button down point[2] and carries out the default command on the resulting selection.[3]	Extends the selection state from the anchor point to the object logically included at the button down point.[2]

[1] Only the active selection is cleared. The active selection is the selection made from the current anchor point. Other selections made by disjoint selection techniques are not affected, unless the new selection includes those selected elements.

[2] The resulting selection state is based on the selection state of the object at the anchor point. If that object becomes selected, all the objects included in the range are selected. If the object is not selected, all the objects included in the range are also not selected.

[3] If the effect of extending the selection unselects the object or a range of objects, the operation applies to the remaining selected objects.

Table A. 3 Interaction Guidelines for Using the CTRL Key to Modify Mouse Actions

Action	Target	Effect on selection state	Effect on anchor point location	Resulting operation using button 1	Resulting operation using button 2
CTRL+ Press	Unselected object	None	Resets the anchor point to the object.	Selects the object.[1]	Selects the object.[1]
	Selected object	None	Resets the anchor point to the object.	None	None
	White space (background)	None	Resets the anchor point to the button down location.	Initiates a disjoint region selection.	Initiates a disjoint region selection.
CTRL+ Click	Unselected object	None	Resets the anchor point to the object.	Selects the object.[1]	Selects the object[1] and displays the pop-up menu for the entire selection.
	Selected object	None	Resets the anchor point to the object.	Unselects the object.[1]	Unselects the object[1] and displays the pop-up menu for the remaining selection.
	White space (background)	None	None	None	Displays the pop-up menu for the existing selection.
CTRL+ Drag	Unselected object	None	Resets the anchor point to the object.	Selects the object[1] and copies the entire selection.[2]	Selects the object[1] and displays the transfer pop-up menu upon button release at the destination.
	Selected object	None	Resets the anchor point to the object.	Copies the entire selection to the destination defined at the button up location.[2]	Selects the object[1] and displays the transfer pop-up menu upon button release at the destination.

Table A. 3 Interaction Guidelines for Using the CTRL Key to Modify Mouse Actions *(continued)*

Action	Target	Effect on selection state	Effect on anchor point location	Resulting operation using button 1	Resulting operation using button 2
CTRL+ Drag *(cont.)*	White space (background)	None	None	Toggles the selection state of objects logically included by region selection.[3]	Toggles the selection state of objects logically included by region selection[3] and displays the pop-up menu for the resulting selection.[4]
CTRL+ Double-click	Unselected object	None	Resets the anchor point to the object.	Selects the object[1] and carries out the default command on the selection set.	Selects the object.[1]
	Selected object	None	Resets the anchor point to the object.	Unselects the object and carries out the default command on the selection set.[4]	Unselects the object.
	White space (background)	None	None	Carries out the default command on the existing selection.[5]	None

[1] The CTRL key toggles the selection state of an object; this table entry shows the result.

[2] If the user releases the CTRL key before releasing the mouse button, the operation reverts to the default transfer operation (as determined by the destination). If the destination does not support a copy operation, it may reinterpret operation. If the object cannot be dragged, you can optionally use this operation to create a disjoint range selection.

[3] The range of objects included are all toggled to the same selection state, which is based on the first object included by the bounding region (marquee).

[4] If the effect of toggling cancels the selection of the object, the operation applies to the remaining selected objects.

[5] The white space (background) is an access point to the commands of the view, the container, or both.

Keyboard Interface Summary

This appendix summarizes the common keyboard operations, short-cut keys, and access key assignments.

Table B.1 displays a summary of the keys used for navigation.

Table B.1 Common Navigation Keys

Key	Cursor movement	CTRL+cursor movement
LEFT ARROW	Left one unit.	Left one proportionally larger unit.
RIGHT ARROW	Right one unit.	Right one proportionally larger unit.
UP ARROW	Up one unit or line.	Up one proportionally larger unit.
DOWN ARROW	Down one unit or line.	Down one proportionally larger unit.
HOME	To the beginning of the line.	To the beginning of the data (topmost position).
END	To the end of the line.	To the end of the data (bottommost position).
PAGE UP	Up one screen (previous screen, same position).[1]	Left one screen (or previous unit, if left is not meaningful).
PAGE DOWN	Down one screen (next screen, same position).[1]	Right one screen (or next unit, if right is not meaningful).
TAB[2]	Next field.	To next tab position (in property sheets, next page).

[1] "Screen" is defined as the height of the visible area being viewed. When scrolling, leave a nominal portion of the previous screen to provide context. For example in text, PAGE DOWN includes the last line of the previous screen as its first line.

[2] Using the SHIFT key with the TAB key navigates in the reverse direction.

Table B.2 lists the common shortcut keys. Avoid assigning these keys to functions other than those listed.

Table B.2 Common Shortcut Keys

Key	Meaning
CTRL+C[1]	Copy
CTRL+O	Open
CTRL+P	Print
CTRL+S	Save
CTRL+V[1]	Paste
CTRL+X[1]	Cut
CTRL+Z[1]	Undo
F1	Display contextual Help window.
SHIFT+F1	Activate context-sensitive Help mode (What's This?).
SHIFT+F10	Display pop-up menu.
SPACEBAR[2]	Select (same as mouse button 1 click).
ESC	Cancel
ALT	Activate or inactivate menu bar mode.
ALT+TAB[3]	Display next primary window (or application).
ALT+ESC[3]	Display next window.
ALT+SPACEBAR	Display pop-up menu for the window.
ALT+HYPHEN	Display pop-up menu for the active child window (MDI).
ALT+ENTER	Display property sheet for current selection.
ALT+F4	Close active window.
ALT+F6[3]	Switch to next window within application (between modeless secondary windows and their primary window).
ALT+PRINT SCREEN	Capture active window image to the Clipboard.
PRINT SCREEN	Capture desktop image to the Clipboard.
CTRL+ESC	Access Start button in taskbar.

Table B.2 **Common Shortcut Keys** *(continued)*

Key	Meaning
CTRL+F6	Display next child window (MDI).
CTRL+TAB	Display next tabbed page or child window (MDI).
CTRL+ALT+DEL	Reserved for system use.

[1] The system still supports shortcut assignments available in earlier versions of Microsoft Windows (ALT+BACKSPACE, SHIFT+INSERT, CTRL+INSERT, SHIFT+DELETE). You should consider supporting them (though not documenting them) to support the transition of users.

[2] If the context (for example, a text box) uses the SPACEBAR for entering a space character, you can use CTRL+SPACEBAR. If that is also defined by the context, define your own key.

[3] Using the SHIFT key with this key combination navigates in the reverse direction.

Table B.3 lists shortcut key assignments for keyboards supporting the new Windows keys. The Left Windows key and Right Windows key are handled the same. All Windows key combinations, whether currently assigned or not, are strictly reserved for definition by the system only. Do not use this key for your own application-defined functions.

Table B.3 **Windows Keys**

Windows key and Application key

Key	Meaning
APPLICATION key	Display pop-up menu for the selected object.
WINDOWS key	Display Start button menu.
WINDOWS+F1	Display Help Topics browser dialog box for the main Windows Help file.
WINDOWS+TAB	Activate next application window.
WINDOWS+E	Explore My Computer.
WINDOWS+F	Find a file.
WINDOWS+CTRL+F	Find a computer.
WINDOWS+M	Minimize All.
SHIFT+WINDOWS+M	Undo Minimize All.
WINDOWS+R	Display Run dialog box.
WINDOWS+BREAK	Reserved system function.
WINDOWS+*number*	Reserved for computer manufacturer use.

Table B.4 lists the key combinations and sequences the system uses to support accessibility. Support for these options is set by users with the Windows Accessibility Options.

Table B.4 Accessibility Keys

Key	Meaning
LEFT ALT+LEFT SHIFT+PRINT SCREEN	Toggle High Contrast mode
LEFT ALT+LEFT SHIFT+NUM LOCK	Toggle MouseKeys
SHIFT (pressed five consecutive times)	Toggle StickyKeys
RIGHT SHIFT (held eight or more seconds)	Toggle FilterKeys (SlowKeys, RepeatKeys, and BounceKeys)
NUM LOCK (held five or more seconds)	Toggle ToggleKeys

Table B.5 lists the recommended access key assignments for common commands. While the context of a command may affect specific assignments, you should use these access keys when you including these commands in your menus and command buttons.

Table B.5 Access Key Assignments

About	Insert Object	Quick View
Always on Top	Link Here	Redo
Apply	Maximize	Repeat
Back	Minimize	Restore
Browse	Move	Resume
Close	Move Here	Retry
Copy	New	Run
Copy Here	Next	Save
Create Shortcut	No	Save As
Create Shortcut Here	Open	Select All
Cut	Open With	Send To
Delete	Paste	Show
Edit	Paste Link	Size
Exit	Paste Shortcut	Split
Explore	Page Setup	Stop
File	Paste Special	Undo
Find	Pause	View
Help	Play	What's This?
Help Topics	Print	Window
Hide	Print Here	Yes
Insert	Properties	

Avoid assigning access keys to OK and Cancel when the ENTER key and ESC key, respectively, are assigned to them by default.

Guidelines Summary

The following checklist summarizes the guidelines covered in this guide. You can use this guideline summary to assist you in your planning, design, and development process.

Remember, the objective of the recommendations and suggestions in this guide is to benefit your users, not to enforce a rigid set of rules. Consistency in design makes it easier for a user to transfer skills from one task to another. When you need to diverge from or extend these guidelines, follow the principles and spirit of this guide.

General Design

☐ Supports user initiation of actions

☐ Supports user customization of the interface

☐ Supports an interactive and modeless environment

☐ Supports direct manipulation interfaces

☐ Uses familiar, appropriate metaphors

☐ Is internally consistent; similar actions have a similar interface

☐ Makes actions reversible where possible; where not possible, requests confirmation

☐ Makes error recovery easy

☐ Eliminates possibilities for user errors, where possible

☐ Uses visual cues to indicate user interaction

☐ Provides prompt feedback

☐ Provides feedback that is appropriate to the task

☐ Makes appropriate use of progressive disclosure

Design Process

☐ Employs a balanced team

☐ Uses an iterative design cycle

☐ Incorporates usability assessment as a part of the process

☐ Designs for user limitations

Input and Interaction

☐ Follows basic mouse interaction guidelines

☐ Uses appropriate modifier keys for adjusting or adding elements to a selection

☐ Uses appropriate visual feedback, such as highlighting or handles, to indicate selected objects

☐ Supports default and nondefault drag and drop

☐ Supports standard transfer commands, where appropriate

☐ Provides keyboard interface for all basic operations

☐ Follows keyboard guidelines for navigation, shortcut keys, and access keys

☐ Keeps foreground activity as modeless as possible

☐ Indicates use of modes visually

☐ Provides access to common, basic operations through single click interaction

☐ Provides shortcut methods (such as double-clicking) to common or frequently used operations for experienced users

Windows

☐ Provides title text for all windows and follows guidelines for defining correct title bar text and icon

☐ Supports single window instance model: brings the existing window to the top of the Z order when the user attempts to reopen a view or window that is already open

☐ Uses common dialog boxes, where applicable

☐ Follows common dialog box conventions when substituting these dialog boxes

☐ Saves and restores the window state

☐ Adjusts window size and position to the appropriate screen size

☐ Uses modeless secondary windows, wherever possible

☐ Avoids system modal secondary windows, except in the case of possible loss of data

☐ Automatically supplies a proposed name upon the creation of a new object

☐ Uses the appropriate message symbol in message boxes

☐ Provides a brief but clear statement of problem and possible remedies in message boxes

☐ Organizes properties into property sheets, using property pages for peer properties and list controls for hierarchical navigation

☐ Places command buttons that apply to the page inside a tabbed page (for example, a property sheet), and outside of a page when the user applies by window (as a set)

☐ Follows single document window interface (SDI) or multiple document interface (MDI or MDI alternatives) conventions

Control Usage

☐ Uses system-supplied controls, wherever possible

☐ Provides an object pop-up menu for the title bar icon

☐ Provides a pop-up menu for the window

☐ Avoids multiple level hierarchical interfaces (menus, secondary windows) for frequently used access operations

☐ Uses an ellipsis only for commands that require additional input or parameters

☐ Uses the menu (triangular) arrow image to indicate when a control can display more information (cascading menus, drop-down control arrows, scroll bar arrows)

☐ Provides pop-up menus for selections and other user identifiable objects

☐ Supports the display of pop-up menus using mouse button 2, the keyboard shortcut keys, and action handles

☐ Displays pop-up menus upon the release of the mouse button

☐ Follows guidelines for ordering the commands on pop-up menus

☐ Limits commands on pop-up menus to those that apply to the selection and its immediate context

☐ Makes toolbars user configurable (display, position, content)

☐ Uses defined toolbar label images when supporting common actions

☐ Defines custom controls to be visually and operationally consistent with standard system controls

Integration

☐ Makes full and correct use of the registry, including registration
   of file extensions, file types, and icons

☐ Avoids use of Autoexec.bat, Config.sys, or initialization
   (.INI) files

☐ Supports and registers entries for Print and Print To interfaces
   for file types that are printable

☐ Provides and registers icons in 32-x 32-, 16-x 16-, and 48-x 48-
   pixel sizes for application, and all document and data file types
   (in both color and monochrome versions)

☐ Registers file types supported under the system's New
   command

☐ Uses system interfaces when adding property pages for types

☐ Supports long filenames and universal naming convention
   (UNC) paths, where files are used

☐ Displays filenames correctly

☐ Follows appropriate conventions when using the taskbar to
   support notification and status information

☐ Supports appropriate behavior for creating and integrating
   scrap objects

☐ Follows guidelines for installation

☐ Provides an uninstall program

☐ Provides appropriate support for network installation

☐ Supports all OLE user interface guidelines, including transfer interfaces (drag and drop and nondefault drag and drop), pop-up menus, and property sheets for OLE embedded and linked objects

User Assistance

☐ Provides context-sensitive Help information for elements (including controls)

☐ Provides task Help topics for basic procedures

☐ Provides tooltips for all unlabeled controls, such as in toolbars

☐ Follows guidelines for messages, status bar information, contextual Help, task Help, online Reference Help, and wizards

Visual Design

☐ Uses color only as an enhancing, secondary form of information

☐ Uses a limited set of colors

☐ Uses system metrics for all display elements (such as color settings and fonts)

☐ Uses standard border styles

☐ Uses appropriate appearance for visual states of controls

☐ Supports dimensionality using light source from the upper left

☐ Supports guidelines for design and appearance of controls and icons

☐ Supports guidelines for layout and font use

☐ Uses correct capitalization for control labels

Sound

☐ Uses audio only for secondary cues (applicable only where audio is not the primary form of information, for example, music)

☐ Supports system interface for sound volume

☐ Supports and provides appropriate visual output for system ShowSounds setting

Accessibility

☐ Clearly labels all controls, icons, windows, and other screen elements (even if not visible) so they can be identified by screen review and voice input utilities

☐ Indicates keyboard focus

☐ Uses standard functions for displaying text

☐ Makes components of graphic images that must be separately discernible by using metafiles, drawing each component separately, or by redrawing components with null operation (NOP) when the user has installed a screen review utility

☐ Avoids time-out interaction or makes timing interaction user configurable

☐ Avoids triggering actions on user navigation in the interface

- ☐ Supports scaling or magnification views where possible and applicable

- ☐ Supports system accessibility settings (such as High Contrast Mode) and appropriately adjusts the user interface elements

- ☐ Tests for compatibility with common accessibility aids

- ☐ Includes people with disabilities in testing process

- ☐ Provides documentation in nonprinted formats, such as online

- ☐ Provides telephone support to users using text telephones (TT/TDD)

International Users

- ☐ Provides sufficient space for character expansion for localization

- ☐ Avoids jargon and culturally dependent words or ideas

- ☐ Avoids using punctuation keys in shortcut key combinations

- ☐ Supports displaying information based on local formats

- ☐ Uses layout conventions appropriate to reading conventions

- ☐ Adjusts references to unsupported features

Network Users

- ☐ Supports system naming and identification conventions

- ☐ Supports shared access for application and data files

Supporting Specific Versions of Windows

This guide is primarily intended for applications designed for Microsoft Windows 95 and later releases. However, you can apply many of the conventions to other releases of Windows. This appendix covers the differences you may need to consider.

Microsoft Windows 3.1

The Windows Interface: An Application Design Guide provided guidelines for applications designed for Microsoft Windows 3.1. It was included in the Microsoft Windows 3.1 Software Development Kit (SDK) and published by Microsoft Press®.

Many of the recommendations in *The Windows Interface: An Application Design Guide* were carried forward and extended into this guide to reflect the new conventions in Microsoft OLE and Microsoft Windows 95. These extended, revised, or new conventions include:

• Recommendations for applying command and direct manipulation transfer methods between applications and the system's shell components.

• Recommendations for mouse button 2, specifically, displaying pop-up menus upon a button 2 click and supporting nondefault drag and drop.

- The replacement of the Control (System) menu with the pop-up menu for the window.

- New conventions for minimizing and re-opening windows.

- Recommendations for using the title bar Close button, the What's This? button, and title bar icons and their accompanying pop-up menus.

- New guidelines for ordering the title bars of document or data file windows.

- New common dialog box interfaces and new controls — list views, tree views, column headings, progress indicators, toolbars, tooltips, property sheets, tabs, status bars, rich-text boxes, sliders, spin boxes, proportional scroll bars, and pen controls.

- Recommendations for displaying and editing properties; including guidelines for using the Properties command, property sheets, and property inspectors.

- New conventions for context-sensitive (What's This?) Help and task Help and recommendations for wizard design.

- New registry entries and shell integration conventions — support for storing application state and path information, file type association, file creation, adding commands for files, file installation, providing access to your application, extending the shell, file viewing using the Quick View command, adding sound events, icon support, and AutoPlay.

- Support for long filenames and access to network resources using universal naming conventions (UNC) pathnames.

- New OLE recommendations — container supplied pop-up menus, Properties command, and property sheets.

- Revised design conventions for window components and icons.

- Recommended conventions for supporting Microsoft telephony application programming interfaces (TAPI), messaging application programming interfaces (MAPI), Plug and Play, pen application programming interfaces, and accessibility utilities.

Microsoft Windows NT 3.51

Windows NT 3.51 (and Windows NT Server 3.51) includes a special dynamic-link library (COMCTL32.DLL) that supports the new controls in Windows 95. As a result, you can develop applications for Windows 95 and Windows NT that have general functional and operational compatibility. However, when applying the conventions in this guide to applications designed for Windows NT, be aware of the following differences in release 3.51:

- Window visuals and shell components follow the Windows 3.1 appearance and operation.

- Close buttons and title bar icons are not supported.

- Open and Save As common dialog boxes follow Windows 3.1 appearance and conventions.

- Message box symbols follow Windows 3.1 conventions.

- Pen API interfaces are not supported.

- Registry formats and entries — support for application state and path information, shell creation, the Quick View command, adding commands for files, shell extensions, and sound event registration.

- Program Manager is still the primary interface for providing user access to applications. File Manager, rather than Windows Explorer, supports file browsing and file management.

- There is no support for the Add/Remove Programs installation object (included in Control Panel). Instead, provide an object in your application's Program Manager group.

- AutoPlay is not supported.

- Taskbar and desktop toolbars are not supported.

- The Recycle Bin is not supported.

- The Passwords object (in Control Panel) is not supported. Use the Windows NT User Manager instead.

- Microsoft MAPI 1.0, TAPI, and Plug and Play are not supported. (Simple MAPI support is included.)

- Some system shortcut key assignments, such as CTRL+ESC and CTRL+ALT+DEL, operate differently.

For more information about these interfaces, see the documentation included in the Microsoft Win32 Software Development Kit (SDK).

International Word Lists

This appendix contains translations of the English word list that appears on the following two pages. The intent of this list is to provide, for each of the following languages, a comprehensive set of words and phrases that either appear in the Microsoft Windows user interface or are used in describing key concepts of the operating system. Note that bold indicates command names that appear on buttons and menus. Translations are not available for some pen-based terms.

Arabic	French	Polish
Basque	German	Portuguese
Catalan	Greek	Portuguese (Brazil)
Chinese (Simplified)	Hebrew	Russian
Chinese (Traditional)	Hungarian	Slovenian
Czech	Italian	Spanish
Danish	Japanese	Swedish
Dutch	Korean	Turkish
Finnish	Norwegian	

English

1	**About**	54	document	107	link (v.)
2	access key	55	double-click	108	**Link Here**
3	accessibility	56	double-tap	109	list box
4	action handle	57	drag	110	list view (control)
5	active	58	drag-and-drop	111	manual link
6	active end	59	drop-down combo box	112	**Maximize**
7	active object	60	drop-down list box	113	maximize button
8	active window	61	drop-down menu	114	menu
9	adornment	62	**Edit**	115	menu bar
10	**Always on Top**	63	**Edit menu**	116	menu button
11	anchor point	64	ellipsis	117	menu item
12	**Apply**	65	embedded object	118	menu title
13	auto-exit	66	**Exit**	119	message box
14	auto-repeat	67	expand (an outline)	120	**Minimize**
15	automatic link	68	**Explore**	121	minimize button
16	automatic scrolling (autoscroll)	69	extended selection	122	mixed-value
17	**Back**	70	extended selection list box	123	modal
18	barrel button (pen)	71	file	124	mode
19	barrel-tap	72	File menu	125	modeless
20	boxed edit (control)	73	**Find**	126	modifier key
21	**Browse**	74	**Find Next**	127	mouse
22	**Cancel**	75	**Find What**	128	**Move**
23	cascading menu	76	folder	129	**Move Here**
24	check box	77	font	130	Multiple Document Interface (MDI)
25	check mark	78	font size	131	multiple selection list box
26	child window	79	font style	132	My Computer (icon)
27	choose	80	function key	133	Network Neighborhood (icon)
28	click	81	gesture	134	**New**
29	Clipboard	82	glyph	135	**Next**
30	**Close**	83	group box	136	object
31	Close button	84	handle	137	**OK**
32	collapse (outline)	85	**Help**	138	OLE
33	column heading (control)	86	Help menu	139	OLE drag and drop
34	combo box	87	**Hide**	140	OLE embedded object
35	command button	88	hierarchical selection	141	OLE linked object
36	container	89	hold	142	OLE nondefault drag and drop
37	context-sensitive Help	90	hot spot	143	**Open**
38	contextual	91	hot zone	144	**Open With**
39	control	92	icon	145	option button
40	**Copy**	93	inactive	146	option-set
41	**Copy Here**	94	inactive window	147	package
42	**Create Shortcut**	95	ink	148	**Page Setup**
43	**Create Shortcut Here**	96	ink edit	149	palette window
44	**Cut**	97	input focus	150	pane
45	default	98	**Insert**	151	parent window
46	default button	99	**Insert Object**	152	password
47	**Delete**	100	insertion point	153	**Paste**
48	desktop	101	italic	154	**Paste Link**
49	destination	102	label	155	**Paste Shortcut**
50	dialog box	103	landscape	156	**Paste Special**
51	disability	104	lasso-tap	157	path
52	disjoint selection	105	lens (control)	158	**Pause**
53	dock	106	link (n.)	159	pen

English

160	**Play**	193	rich-text box	226	StartUp folder
161	Plug and Play	194	**Run**	227	status bar
162	point	195	**Save**	228	**Stop**
163	pointer	196	**Save As**	229	tab control
164	pop-up menu	197	scroll	230	tap
165	pop-up window	198	scroll arrow	231	task bar
166	portrait	199	scroll bar	232	task-oriented Help
167	press (a key)	200	scroll box	233	template
168	press (and hold a mouse button)	201	secondary window	234	text box
169	primary container	202	select	235	title bar
170	primary window	203	**Select All**	236	title text
171	**Print**	204	selection	237	toggle key
172	printer	205	selection handle	238	toolbar
173	progress indicator (control)	206	**Send To**	239	tooltip
174	project	207	separator	240	tree view control
175	**Properties**	208	**Settings**	241	type (n.)
176	property inspector	209	**Setup**	242	type (v.)
177	property page	210	shortcut	243	unavailable
178	property sheet	211	shortcut button	244	**Undo**
179	property sheet control	212	shortcut icon	245	**Uninstall**
180	**Quick View**	213	shortcut key	246	**View**
181	read-only	214	shortcut key control	247	visual editing
182	recognition	215	**Show**	248	well control
183	Recycle Bin (icon)	216	**Shutdown**	249	**What's This?**
184	**Redo**	217	single selection list box	250	window
185	region selection	218	**Size**	251	**Window**
186	registry	219	size grip	252	Windows Explorer
187	**Repeat**	220	slider	253	wizard
188	**Replace**	221	spin box	254	workbook
189	**Restore**	222	**Split**	255	workgroup
190	Restore button	223	split bar	256	workspace
191	**Resume**	224	split box	257	**Yes**
192	**Retry**	225	Start button		

Arabic

#		#		#	
1	حول	45	افتراضي	90	نقطة فعالة
2	مفتاح التشغيل	46	زر افتراضي	91	منطقة فعالة
2	مفتاح الوصول	47	حذف	92	رمز
3	إمكانية التشغيل	48	سطح المكتب	93	غير نشط
3	إمكانية الوصول	49	الوجهة	94	إطار غير نشط
4	مقبض الأداء	50	مربع حوار	95	كتابة غير مقروءة
5	نشط	51	إعاقة	96	تحرير كتابة غير مقروءة
6	نقطة النهاية النشطة	52	تحديد غير متصل	97	مركز النشاط
7	كائن نشط	53	رصف	98	إدراج
8	إطار نشط	54	مستند	99	إدراج كائن
9	عنصر إضافي	55	انقر نقراً مزدوجاً	100	نقطة الإدراج
10	دوماً في المقدمة	55	النقر نقراً مزدوجاً	101	مائل
11	نقطة الارتساء	56	اضغط بالقلم مرتين	102	عنونة
12	تطبيق	56	الضغط بالقلم مرتين	102	اسم
13	إنهاء تلقائي	57	سحب	103	طباعة عرضية
14	تكرار تلقائي	58	السحب والإفلات	103	اتجاه عرضي
15	ارتباط تلقائي	59	مربع تحرير وسرد منسدل	104	تحديد حر
16	تحرير تلقائي	60	مربع قائمة منسدلة	105	عدسة
17	السابق	61	قائمة منسدلة	106	ارتباط
18	زر غلاف القلم	62	تحرير	107	ربط
19	الضغط بزر غلاف القلم	63	تحرير	108	الربط هنا
20	عنصر تحرير مربع	64	علامة القطع	109	مربع قائمة
21	استعراض	65	كائن مضمّن	110	العرض كقائمة
22	إلغاء الأمر	66	إنهاء	111	ارتباط يدوي
23	قائمة متعاقبة	67	توسيع	112	الحد الأقصى
24	خانة اختيار	68	استكشاف	113	زر التكبير
25	علامة الاختيار	69	تحديد ممتد	114	قائمة
26	إطار فرعي	70	مربع قائمة تحديد ممتد	115	شريط القوائم
27	احجز	71	ملف	116	زر قائمة
28	انقر	72	ملف	117	عنصر قائمة
28	النقر	73	بحث	118	عنوان القائمة
29	الحافظة	74	بحث عن التالي	119	مربع رسائل
30	إغلاق	75	البحث عن	120	الحد الأدنى
31	زر الإغلاق	76	مجلد	121	زر التصغير
32	طي	77	حط	122	قيمة مختلطة
33	عنوان العمود	78	حجم الخط	123	مشروط
34	مربع تحرير وسرد	79	نمط الخط	124	وضع
35	زر الأمر	80	مفتاح وظيفي	125	غير مشروط
36	كائن ضام	81	إشارة	126	زر معدّل
37	تعليمات تتبع السياق	82	صورة رمزية	127	الماوس
38	سياقي	83	مربع مجموعة	128	تحريك
39	عنصر تحكم	84	مقبض	128	نقل
40	نسخ	85	تعليمات	129	التحريك هنا
41	النسخ هنا	86	تعليمات	129	النقل إلى هنا
42	إنشاء اختصار	87	إخفاء	130	واجهة تعدد المستندات
43	إنشاء اختصار هنا	88	تحديد هيكلي	131	مربع قائمة تحديدات متعددة
44	قص	89	الاستمرار في الضغط	132	الكمبيوتر الخاص

Arabic

133	حوار شبكة الاتصال	174	خطة	217	مربع قائمة أحادية التحديد
134	**جديد**	175	**خصائص**	218	**حجم**
135	**التالي**	176	كاشف الخصائص	219	مقبض تغيير الحجم
136	كائن	177	صفحة الخصائص	220	مربع التمرير
137	**موافق**	178	كشف بالخصائص	221	مربع زيادة ونقصان
138	ربط الكائنات وتضمينها	179	عنصر تحكم الكشف بالخصائص	222	**انقسام**
139	السحب والإفلات في ربط الكائنات وتضمينها	180	**عرض سريع**	223	شريط الانقسام
140	كائن مضمّن في نظام ربط الكائنات وتضمينها	181	للقراءة فقط	224	مربع الانقسام
141	كائن مرتبط في نظام ربط الكائنات وتضمينها	182	التعرف على	225	زر البدء
142	السحب والإفلات غير الافتراضي في ربط الكائنات وتضمينها	183	سلة المحذوفات	226	مجلد بدء التشغيل
143	**فتح**	184	**إعادة**	227	شريط الوضع
144	**فتح بواسطة**	185	تحديد منطقة	227	شريط المعلومات
145	زر الخيار	186	سجل النظام	228	**توقف**
146	مجموعة خيارات	187	**تكرار**	229	تبويب
147	حزمة	188	**استبدال**	230	ضغط
148	**إعداد الصفحة**	189	**استرجاع**	231	شريط المهام
149	إطار لوح خيارات	190	زر الاسترجاع	232	تعليمات تتبع المهام
150	جزء	191	**استئناف**	233	قالب
151	إطار أصلي	192	**إعادة المحاولة**	234	مربع نص
152	كلمة مرور	193	مربع نص منسق	235	شريط العنوان
153	**لصق**	194	**تشغيل**	236	نص العنوان
154	**لصق الارتباط**	194	**تنفيذ**	237	مفتاح مقلب
155	**لصق الاختصار**	195	**حفظ**	238	شريط الأدوات
155	**اختصار اللصق**	196	**حفظ باسم**	239	تعريف الأدوات
156	**لصق خاص**	197	تمرير	240	عنصر عرض هيكلي
157	مسار	198	سهم التمرير	241	نوع
158	**إيقاف مؤقت**	199	شريط التمرير	242	اكتب
159	قلم	200	حانة التمرير	243	غير متوفر
160	**قراءة**	201	إطار ثانوي	243	غير متاح
161	التوصيل والتشغيل	202	تحديد	244	**تراجع**
162	نقطة	203	**تحديد كلي**	245	**إلغاء التثبيت**
163	مؤشر	204	تحديد	246	**عرض**
164	قائمة منبثقة	205	مقبض التحديد	247	تحرير مرئي
165	إطار منبثق	206	**إرسال إلى**	248	
166	طباعة طولية	207	فاصل	249	**ما هذا**
166	اتجاه طولي	208	**إعدادات**	250	إطار
167	اضغط	209	**برنامج الإعداد**	251	**إطار**
168	اضغط	210	اختصار	252	المستكنف
169	كائن ضام أساسي	211	زر اختصار	253	معالج
170	إطار أساسي	212	رمز اختصار	254	مصنف
171	**طباعة**	213	مفتاح اختصار	255	مجموعة عمل
172	طابعة	214	عنصر تحكم لمفتاح اختصار	256	مساحة العمل
173	مشير التقدم	215	**إظهار**	257	**نعم**
		216	**إيقاف التشغيل**		

Basque

1	**...i buruz**	54	dokumentua	104	lazo-kolpea
2	atzipen-tekla	55	klik bikoitza egin (v.) klik bikoitza	105	lentea
3	erabilerraztasuna		(n.)	106	esteka
4	ekintza-heldulekua	56	kolpe bikoitza eman (v.) kolpe	107	estekatu
5	aktiboa		bikoitza (n.)	108	**Estekatu hemen**
6	amaiera aktiboa	57	arrastatu	109	zerrenda-koadroa
7	objektu aktiboa	58	arrastatu eta jaregin	110	zerrenda-ikuspegia
8	leiho aktiboa	59	goitibeherako konbinazio-koadroa	111	eskuzko esteka
9	apaingarria	60	goitibeherako zerrenda-koadroa	112	**Maximizatu**
10	**Beti gainean**	61	goitibeherako menua	113	"Maximizatu" botoia
11	aingura-puntua	62	**Editatu**	114	menua
12	**Aplikatu**	63	**Edizioa menua**	115	menu-barra
13	auto-irteera	64	eten-puntuak	116	menu-botoia
14	auto-errepikapena	65	objektu kapsulatua	117	menu-elementua
15	esteka automatikoa	66	**Irten**	118	menu-titulua
16	korritze automatikoa	67	destolestu	119	mezu-koadroa
17	**Atzera**	68	**Esploratu**	120	**Ikonotu**
18	arkatz-botoia	69	hautapen hedatua	121	"Ikonotu" botoia
19	arkatzaren botoi-kolpea	70	hautapen hedatuko zerrenda-	122	balio nahasia
20	koadrodun edizioa		koadroa	123	modala
21	**Arakatu**	71	fitxategia	124	modua
22	**Utzi**	72	Fitxategia menua	125	modugabea
23	kaskada-menua	73	**Aurkitu**	126	tekla aldatzailea
24	kontrol-laukia	74	**Aurkitu hurrengoa**	127	sagua
25	hautamarka	75	**Zer aurkitu**	128	**Mugitu**
26	leiho umea	76	karpeta	129	**Mugitu hona**
27	aukeratu	77	letra-tipoa	130	dokumentu anitzeko interfazea
28	klik egin (v.) klik (n.)	78	letra-tamaina		(MDI)
29	Arbela	79	letra-estiloa	131	hautapen anitzeko zerrenda-koadroa
30	**Itxi**	80	funtzio-tekla	132	Ordenadorea
31	"Itxi" botoia	81	keinua	133	Sarearen auzoa
32	tolestu	82	glifoa	134	**Berria**
33	zutabe-izenburua	83	talde-koadroa	135	**Hurrengoa**
34	konbinazio-koadroa	84	heldulekua	136	objektua
35	komando-botoia	85	**Laguntza**	137	**Ados**
36	edukigailua	86	Laguntza menua	138	OLE
37	testuinguruaren araberako leguntza	87	**Ezkutatu**	139	OLE arrastatu eta jaregin
38	testuingurukoa	88	hautapen hierarkikoa	140	OLE objektu kapsulatua
39	kontrola	89	mantendu	141	OLE objektu estekatua
40	**Kopiatu**	90	eragin-puntua	142	OLE arrastatu eta jaregin
41	**Kopiatu hemen**	91	eragin-zona		lehenetsigabea
42	**Sortu lasterbidea**	92	ikonoa	143	**Ireki**
43	**Sortu lasterbidea hemen**	93	inaktiboa	144	**Ireki honekin**
44	**Ebaki**	94	leiho inaktiboa	145	aukera-botoia
45	lehenetsia	95	trazua	146	aukera-multzoa
46	botoi lehenetsia	96	trazu-edizioa	147	paketea
47	**Ezabatu**	97	sarrera-fokua	148	**Prestatu orrialdea**
48	mahaia	98	**Txertatu menua**	149	paleta-leihoa
49	helburua	99	**Txertatu objektua**	150	panela
50	elkarrizketa-koadroa	100	txertapuntua	151	leiho gurasoa
51	ezgaitsuna	101	etzana	152	pasahitza
52	hautapen desjarraia	102	etiketa	153	**Itsatsi**
53	ertzeratu	103	horizontala	154	**Itsatsi estekatuz**

Basque

155	**Itsatsi lasterbidea**	190	"Leheneratu" botoia	224	zatitze-koadroa
156	**Itsatsi berezia**	191	**Berrekin**	225	"Hasi" botoia
157	bide-izena	192	**Saiatu berriro**	226	"Abioa" karpeta
158	**Pausa**	193	testu aberastua-koadroa	227	egoera-barra
159	Arkatza	194	**Exekutatu**	228	**Gelditu**
160	**Erreproduzitu**	195	**Gorde**	229	fitxa-kontrola
161	Plug and Play	196	**Gorde honela**	230	kolpea eman
162	seinalatu (v.) puntua (n.)	197	korritu	231	ataza-barra
163	erakuslea	198	korritze-gezia	232	atazei orientatutako Laguntza
164	pop-up menua	199	korritze-barra	233	txantiloia
165	pop-up leihoa	200	korritze-koadroa	234	testu-koadroa
166	bertikala	201	bigarren mailako leihoa	235	titulu-barra
167	sakatu (tekla bat)	202	hautatu	236	titulu-testua
168	sakatu (eta mantendu sagu-botoia)	203	**Hautatu dena**	237	txanda-tekla
169	lehen mailako edukigailua	204	hautapena	238	tresna-barra
170	lehen mailako leihoa	205	hautapen-heldulekua	239	argibidea
171	**Inprimatu**	206	**Bidali hona**	240	zuhaitza ikusteko kontrola
172	inprimagailua	207	bereizlea	241	mota
173	progresio-adierazlea	208	**Ezarpenak**	242	idatzi
174	proiektua	209	**Instala**	243	ez-erabilgarria
175	**Propietateak**	210	lasterbidea	244	**Desegin**
176	propietate-begiralea	211	laster-botoia	245	**Desinstalatu**
177	propietate-orrialdea	212	laster-ikonoa	246	**Ikusi menua**
178	propietate-orria	213	laster-tekla	247	edizio bisuala
179	propietate-orriaren kontrola	214	laster-teklaren kontrola	248	kaxa-kontrola
180	**Ikustaldi bizkorra**	215	**Erakutsi**	249	**Zer da hau?**
181	irakurtzeko soilik	216	**Itzali**	250	leihoa
182	ezagutzea	217	hautapen bakarreko zerrenda-koadroa	251	**Leihoa menua**
183	Zakarrontzia			252	Windows esploradorea
184	**Berregin**	218	**Tamaina**	253	morroia
185	eskualde-hautapena	219	tamaina-heldulekua	254	laneko liburua
186	erregistroa	220	irristaria	255	lantaldea
187	**Errepikatu**	221	koadro birakaria	256	laneko espazioa
188	**Ordeztu**	222	**Zatitu**	257	**Bai**
189	**Leheneratu**	223	zatitze-barra		

Catalan

1	**Quant a**	53	estiba	106	enllaç (n.)
2	tecla d'accés	54	document	107	enllaça (v.)
3	accessibilitat	55	doble clic	108	**Enllaça aquí**
4	manipulador d'acció	56		109	quadre de llista
5	actiu (masc.) / activa (fem.)	57	arrossega	110	visualització de llista (control)
6	extrem actiu	58	arrossega i deixa anar	111	enllaç manual
7	objecte actiu	59	quadre combinat desplegable	112	**Amplia a la grandària màxima**
8	finestra activa	60	quadre de llista desplegable	113	botó de grandària màxima
9	orla	61	menú desplegable	114	menú
10	**Sempre visible**	62	**Edita**	115	barra de menús
11	punt d'ancoratge	63	**menú Edició**	116	botó de menú
12	**Aplica**	64	punts suspensius	117	opció de menú
13	sortida automàtica	65	objecte inserit	118	nom de menú
14	repetició automàtica	66	**Surt**	119	quadre de missatge
15	enllaç automàtic	67	expandeix (un esquema)	120	**Redueix a la grandària mínima**
16	desfilada automàtica	68	**Explora**	121	botó de grandària mínima
17	**Enrera**	69	selecció millorada	122	barreja de valors
18		70	llista de selecció millorada	123	modal
19		71	fitxer	124	mode
20		72	menú Fitxer	125	amodal
21	**Navegació**	73	**Busca**	126	tecla modificadora
22	**Anul·la**	74	**Següent**	127	ratolí
23	menú en cascada	75	**Cerca de**	128	**Desplaça**
24	quadre de verificació	76	carpeta	129	**Desplaça aquí**
25	marca de verificació	77	tipus de lletra	130	interfície de múltiples documents (IMD)
26	finestra fill	78	cos (del tipus de lletra)		
27	fes un clic damunt de/selecciona/tria	79	estil (del tipus de lletra)	131	quadre de llista de selecció múltiple
28	fes un clic damunt de	80	tecla de funció	132	El meu ordinador (icona)
29	Carpeta	81		133	Veïnatge de xarxa (icona)
30	**Tanca**	82		134	**Crea**
31	botó de tancament	83	quadre de grup	135	**Següent**
32	contrau (un esquema)	84	manipulador	136	objecte
33	capçalera de columna (control)	85	**Ajuda**	137	**D'acord**
34	quadre combinat	86	menú Ajuda	138	arrossega i deixa anar amb l'OLE
35	botó d'opció	87	**Amaga**	139	arrossegar i deixar anar amb l'OLE
36	contenidor	88	selecció jerarquitzada	140	objecte inserit amb l'OLE
37	ajuda segons el context	89	sense deixar anar	141	objecte enllaçat amb l'OLE
38	contextual	90	cap de punter	142	arrossega i deixa anar amb l'OLE personalitzat
39	control	91	extrem actiu/zona activa		
40	**Copia**	92	icona	143	**Obre**
41	**Copia aquí**	93	inactiu (masc.) / inactiva (fem.)	144	Obre amb
42	**Crea un element d'accés ràpid**	94	finestra inactiva	145	botó d'opció
43	**Crea aquí un element d'accés ràpid**	95		146	Presentació d'opció
		96		147	envàs
44	**Retalla**	97	focus d'introducció	148	**Format de pàgina**
45	per defecte	98	**menú Inserció**	149	finestra paleta
46	botó per defecte	99	**Insereix un objecte**	150	subfinestra
47	**Esborra**	100	punt d'inserció	151	finestra pare
48	escriptori	101	cursiva	152	contrasenya
49	destinació	102	etiqueta	153	**Enganxa**
50	quadre de diàleg	103	horitzontal	154	**Enganxa enllaçant**
51	incapacitat	104		155	**Enganxa amb accés ràpid**
52	selecció disjunta	105		156	**Enganxa amb format**

Catalan

157	camí	190	botó de restauració	224	quadre de divisió
158	**Pausa**	191	**Reprèn**	225	botó d'inici
159		192	**Reintenta**	226	carpeta d'inici
160	**Toca**	193	quadre de text ric	227	barra d'estat
161	Connexió universal (n.)/universal (adj.)	194	**Executa**	228	**Para**
		195	**Desa**	229	control tabulador
162	punt	196	**Anomena i desa**	230	
163	punter	197	desplaçament	231	barra de tasques
164	menú desplegable	198	fletxa de desplaçament	232	ajuda orientada a tasques
165	finestra desplegable	199	barra de desplaçament	233	plantilla
166	vertical	200	quadre de desplaçament	234	quadre de text
167	prem (una tecla)	201	finestra secundària	235	barra de títol
168	prem (sense deixar anar un botó del ratolí)	202	selecciona	236	títol
		203	Selecciona-ho tot	237	tecla commutadora
169	contenidor principal	204	element(s)/bloc seleccionat(s)	238	barra d'eines
170	finestra principal	205	manipulador de l'element seleccionat	239	descripció d'eina
171	**Imprimeix**			240	control de visualització d'arbre
172	impressora	206	Envia a	241	tipus (n.)
173	indicador de progrés (control)	207	separador	242	tecleja (v. intr.)
174	projecte	208	**Paràmetres**	243	no disponible
175	**Característiques**	209	Instal·lació / Configuració	244	**Desfés**
176	inspector de propietats	210	accés ràpid	245	**Desinstal·la**
177	pàgina de propietats	211	botó d'accés ràpid	246	**menú Visualització**
178	full de propietats	212	icona d'accés ràpid	247	edició visual
179	control del full de propietats	213	combinació de tecles (d'accés ràpid)	248	control d'aspecte
180	**Visualització ràpida**	214	control de combinació de tecles	249	**Què és?**
181	informació només amb accés de lectura	215	**Visualitza**	250	finestra
		216	**Tanca**	251	**menú Finestra**
182		217	quadre de llista de selecció única	252	Explorador del Windows
183	Paperera de reciclatge (icona)	218	**Grandària**	253	auxiliar
184	**Refés**	219	manipulador de grandària	254	llibre de treball
185	àrea seleccionada	220	corredor	255	grup de treball
186	registre	221	**Divideix**	256	àrea de treball
187	**Repeteix**	222	**Divisió**	257	**Sí**
188	**Substitueix**	223	mainell		
189	**Restaura**				

Chinese (Simplified)

1	关于	47	删除	93	非活动
2	热键	48	桌面	94	非活动窗口
3	无障碍	49	目标	95	线条
4	动作句柄	50	对话框	96	线条编辑
5	活动的	51	不可用	97	输入焦点
6	活动终点	52	分离选定	98	**插入菜单**
7	活动目标	53	沿边	99	**插入对象**
8	活动窗口	54	文档	100	插入指针
9	控制栏	55	双击	101	斜体
10	前端显示	56	双点	102	标识
11	起始点	57	拖动	103	横向
12	应用	58	拖放	104	圈住并敲击
13	自动跳转	59	下拉式组合框	105	视镜
14	自动重复	60	下拉式列表	106	链接
15	自动链接	61	下拉式菜单	107	链接
16	自动滚动	62	**编辑**	108	**在此处链接**
17	**后退**	63	**编辑菜单**	109	列表框
18	柱状按钮	64	省略号	110	视图列表
19	按	65	内嵌对象	111	手工链接
20	框编辑区	66	**退出**	112	**最大化**
21	**浏览**	67	扩充	113	**最大化按钮**
22	取消	68	**资源总管**	114	菜单
23	层叠菜单	69	扩展选定	115	菜单栏
24	复选框	70	扩展选定列表框	116	菜单按钮
25	复选标记	71	文件	117	菜单项
26	子窗口	72	**文件菜单**	118	菜单标题
27	选择	73	**查找**	119	消息框
28	单击	74	**查找下一个**	120	**最小化**
29	剪帖板	75	**查找目标**	121	**最小化按钮**
30	关闭	76	文件夹	122	复合值
31	关闭按钮	77	字体	123	模式的
32	折叠	78	字体大小	124	模式
33	栏标题	79	字体样式	125	无模式
34	组合框	80	功能键	126	修改键
35	命令按钮	81	条行码	127	鼠标
36	容器	82	图形符号	128	**移动**
37	上下文关联帮助	83	组合框	129	**移动到此处**
38	上下文关联的	84	控点	130	多文档界面
39	控制	85	**帮助**	131	多重选定列表框
40	**复制**	86	**帮助菜单**	132	
41	**复制到此处**	87	**隐藏**	133	网上邻居
42	**创建快捷键**	88	阶层式选定	134	**新建**
43	**在此处创建快捷键**	89	保持	135	**下一个**
44	剪切	90	热点	136	对象
45	默认	91	热区	137	**确定**
46	默认按钮	92	图标	138	OLE

Chinese (Simplified)

139 OLE 拖放	179 属性夹控制	219 尺寸控制
140 OLE 内嵌对象	180 **快速浏览**	220 滑杆
141 OLE 链接对象	181 只读	221 选值框
142 OLE 非默认拖放	182 识别	222 **分割**
143 **打开**	183 回收站	223 分隔条
144 **用... 打开**	184 **重做**	224 分隔块
145 选项按钮	185 区域选定	225 启动按钮
146 选项设置	186 注册表	226 启动文件夹
147 包	187 **重复**	227 状态栏
148 **页面设置**	188 **替换**	228 **停止**
149 调色板窗口	189 **还原**	229 制表符控制
150 窗格	190 还原按钮	230 按
151 父窗口	191 **继续**	231 任务栏
152 口令	192 **重试**	232 任务关联帮助
153 **粘贴**	193 多信息文本框	233 模板
154 **粘贴链接**	194 **运行**	234 文本框
155 **粘贴快捷键**	195 **保存**	235 标题栏
156 **选择性粘贴**	196 **另存为**	236 标题文本
157 路径	197 滚动	237 切换键
158 **暂停**	198 滚动箭头	238 工具栏
159 笔	199 滚动栏	239 工具提示
160 **播放**	200 滚动块	240 树形显示控制
161 即插即用	201 二级窗口	241 键入
162 指向	202 选定	242 键入
163 指针	203 **全选**	243 不可用
164 弹出式菜单	204 选定	244 **撤消**
165 弹出式窗口	205 选定句柄	245 **卸装**
166 纵向	206 **发送**	246 **"查看"菜单**
167 按	207 分隔符	247 可视化编辑
168 按下	208 **设置**	248 图形属性控制
169 主容器	209 **安装**	249 **这是什么?**
170 主窗口	210 捷径	250 窗口
171 **打印**	211 快捷按钮	251 **窗口菜单**
172 打印机	212 快捷图标	252 Windows 资源总管
173 进展指示窗	213 快捷键	253 向导
174 项目	214 快捷键控制	254 工作簿
175 **属性**	215 **显示**	255 工作组
176 属性查看	216 **关闭系统**	256 工作区
177 属性页	217 单选列表框	257 **是**
178 属性夹	218 **大小**	

Chinese (Traditional)

1	關於	45	預設值	89	按住
2	便捷鍵	46	預設按鈕	90	觸敏點
3	存取的便利性	47	刪除	91	敏感區
4	動作控點	48	桌面	92	圖示
5	作用中	49	目的地	93	候用中
6	作用範圍邊緣	50	對話方塊	94	候用視窗
7	作用中物件	51	低階	95	未辨認筆勢
8	作用中視窗	52	不連續選擇	96	未辨認筆勢編輯
9	浮貼物件	53	定址工具列	97	待命點
10	頂端顯示設定	54	文件	98	插入功能表
11	錨點	55	輕按兩下(n.)	99	插入物件
12	應用	55	按兩下滑鼠按鈕(v.)	100	插入點
13	自動結束	56	輕點兩下(n.)	101	斜體
14	自動重複	56	輕點兩下光筆(v.)	102	標籤
15	自動連結	57	拖曳	103	橫印
16	自動捲動	58	拖放	103	橫向
17	倒退	59	下拉式組合方塊	104	勾勒光筆範圍
17	上一步	60	下拉式清單方塊	105	字框 (光筆控制項)
18	按鍵 (光筆)	61	下拉式功能表	106	連結 (n.)
19	輕按按鍵(光筆專用)	62	編輯	107	連結 (v.)
20	編輯方塊 (控制項)	63	編輯功能表	108	連結至此
21	瀏覽	64	更多選項記號	109	清單方塊
22	取消	65	內嵌物件	110	列示清單 (控制項)
23	階層式功能表	66	結束	111	手動連結
24	核取方塊	67	展開 (大綱)	112	最大化
25	核取符號	68	檔案總管	113	最大化按鈕
26	子視窗	69	擴展選定	114	功能表
27	選取	70	擴展選定清單方塊	115	功能表列
28	輕按一下(n.)	71	檔案	116	功能表按鈕
28	按一下滑鼠按鈕(v.)	72	檔案功能表	117	功能表項目
29	剪貼簿	73	尋找	118	功能表標題
30	關閉	74	找下一個	119	訊息方塊
31	關閉按鈕	75	尋找目標	120	最小化
32	隱藏細節 (大綱)	76	檔案夾	121	最小化按鈕
33	欄位標題 (控制項)	77	字型	122	混合值
34	組合方塊	78	字型大小	123	限制模式的
35	指令按鈕	79	字型樣式	124	模式
36	容器	80	功能鍵	125	非限制模式的
37	文意感應說明	81	可辨認筆勢	126	修正鍵
38	文意的	82	圖像	127	滑鼠
39	控制項	83	群組方塊	128	移動
40	複製	84	控點	129	移動至此
41	複製至此	85	說明	130	複式文件介面(MDI)
42	建立捷徑	86	說明功能表	131	複選定清單方塊
43	在此建立捷徑	87	隱藏	132	我的電腦 (圖示)
44	剪下	88	階層式選定	133	網路上的芳鄰 (圖示)

Chinese (Traditional)

134	開新檔案	174	計劃	217	單選清單方塊
135	下一步	175	屬性	218	大小
135	下一個	175	內容	219	大小控點
136	物件	176	檢視屬性工具	220	連續調節控制
137	確定	177	屬性畫面	221	調節方塊
138	object linking and embedding (OLE)	178	內容表	222	分割
		179	內容表控制項	223	分割軸
139	OLE 拖放	180	快速檢視	224	分割方塊
140	OLE 內嵌物件	181	唯讀	225	開始按鈕
141	OLE 連結物件	182	辨識	226	啓動資料夾
142	OLE 非預設拖放	183	資源回收桶 (圖示)	227	狀態列
143	開啓舊檔	184	重做	228	停止
144	開啓	185	區域選定	229	標籤控制項
145	選項按鈕	186	登錄	230	輕按
146	選項設定	187	重複	231	工作列
147	分封	188	取代	232	作業流程說明
147	包裝	189	還原	233	範本
148	設定列印格式	190	還原按鈕	234	文字方塊
149	色盤視窗	191	重新開始	235	標題列
150	窗格	192	重試	236	標題文字
151	母視窗	193	繁複樣式文字方塊	237	切換鍵
152	密碼	194	執行	238	工具列
153	貼上	195	儲存檔案	239	工具提示
154	貼上連結	196	另存新檔	240	樹狀結構檢視控制項
155	貼上捷徑	197	捲動	241	類型 (n.)
156	選擇性貼上	198	捲動箭頭	242	鍵入 (v.)
157	路徑	199	捲軸	243	無法使用
158	暫停	200	捲動方塊	244	復原
159	光筆	201	次要視窗	245	解除安裝
160	播放	202	選定	246	檢視功能表
161	Plug and Play	203	選定全部	247	就地編輯
162	指到(v.)	204	選定範圍	248	圖形屬性控制項
162	點(n.)	205	選定控點	249	這是什麼?
163	游標	206	傳送至	250	視窗
164	快顯功能表	207	分隔字元	251	視窗功能表
165	快顯視窗	208	設定	252	Windows 檔案總管
166	直印	209	安裝程式	253	精靈
166	縱向	209	設定	254	活頁簿
167	按 (按鍵)	210	捷徑	255	工作群組
168	按住 (滑鼠按鈕)	211	捷徑按鈕	256	工作環境
169	主容器	212	捷徑圖示	257	是
170	主要視窗	213	快速鍵		
171	列印	214	快速鍵控制項		
172	印表機	215	顯示		
173	進展指標 (控制項)	216	關機		

Czech

1	**Co je**	53	ukotvit; dok (mobile)	105	
2	přístupová klávesa	54	dokument	106	propojení
3	přístupnost; usnadnění přístupu	55	poklepat	107	propojit
4	výkonný úchyt	56		108	**Propojit sem**
5	aktivní	57	přetáhnout; táhnout	109	seznam
6	aktivní konec	58	umístit tažením	110	seznam
7	aktivní objekt	59	pole s rozevíracím seznamem	111	ruční propojení
8	aktivní okno	60	rozevírací seznam	112	**Maximalizovat**
9	lem	61	rozevírací nabídka; nabídka	113	maximalizační tlačítko
10	**Vždy navrchu**	62	**Úpravy**	114	nabídka
11	kotevní bod	63	**nabídka Úpravy**	115	řádek nabídek
12	**Použít, Provést**	64	výpustek	116	vstup nabídky; tlačítko nabídky
13	automatický výstup	65	vložený objekt	117	položka nabídky
14	automatické opakování	66	**Konec**	118	název nabídky
15	automatické propojení	67	rozbalit (přehled)	119	zpráva
16	automatický posuv	68	**Prozkoumat**	120	**Minimalizovat**
17	**Zpět**	69	rozšířený výběr	121	minimalizační tlačítko
18		70	seznam s rozšířeným výběrem	122	neurčitý
19		71	soubor	123	modální
20		72	nabídka Soubor	124	režim
21	**Procházet**	73	**Najít**	125	nemodální
22	**Storno**	74	**Najít další**	126	modifikační klávesa
23	vedlejší nabídka	75	**Co hledat**	127	myš
24	zaškrtávací políčko	76	složka	128	**Přesunout**
25	zaškrtnutí	77	písmo	129	**Přesunout sem**
26	dceřiné okno	78	velikost písma	130	prostředí více dokumentů (MDI)
27	zvolit	79	řez písma	
28	klepnout	80	funkční klávesa	131	seznam s násobným výběrem
29	schránka	81		132	Tento počítač
30	**Zavřít**	82		133	Okolní počítače
31	Závěr	83	rámeček skupiny	134	**Nový**
32	sbalit (přehled)	84	úchyt	135	**Další**
33	hlavička sloupce	85	**Nápověda**	136	objekt
34	pole se seznamem	86	nabídka Nápověda	137	**OK**
35	příkazové tlačítko; tlačítko	87	**Skrýt**	138	OLE (propojování a vkládání objektů)
36	kontejner	88	víceúrovňový výběr	
37	kontextová nápověda	89	držet (hold down - přidržet)	139	přetažení OLE
38	kontextový	90	aktivní bod	140	vložený objekt OLE
39	ovládací prvek	91	citlivá oblast	141	propojený objekt OLE
40	**Kopírovat**	92	ikona	142	přetažení OLE s nabídkou
41	**Kopírovat sem**	93	neaktivní	143	**Otevřít**
42	**Vytvořit zástupce**	94	neaktivní okno	144	**Otevřít čím**
43	**Vytvořit zástupce zde**	95		145	přepínač
44	**Vyjmout**	96		146	skupina přepínačů; nastavená možnost
45	výchozí	97	místo vstupu; zvýraznění	
46	výchozí tlačítko	98	**nabídka Vložit**	147	balíček
47	**Odstranit**	99	**nabídka Objekt**	148	**Vzhled stránky**
48	pracovní plocha	100	kurzor	149	paleta
49	cíl	101	kurzíva	150	část okna
50	dialogové okno; dialog	102	popis	151	mateřské okno
51	postižení	103	na šířku	152	heslo
52	nespojitý výběr	104		153	**Vložit**

Czech

154	**Vložit propojení**	189	**Obnovit**	225	tlačítko Start
155	**Vložit zástupce**	190	tlačítko Obnovit	226	složka Po spuštění
156	**Vložit jinak**	191	**Pokračovat**	227	stavový řádek
157	cesta	192	**Znovu**	228	**Stop**
158	**Pozastavit**	193	formátované textové pole	229	karta
159		194	**Spustit**	230	
160	**Zahrát**	195	**Uložit**	231	hlavní panel
161	kokamžitému použití	196	**Uložit jako**	232	nápověda postupu
162	(v.) ukázat,(n.) bod	197	posunout	233	šablona
163	ukazatel	198	šipka posuvníku	234	textové pole
164	místní nabídka	199	posuvník	235	záhlaví okna
165	překryvné okno	200	táhlo posuvníku	236	text záhlaví
166	na výšku	201	druhotné okno; vedlejší okno	237	zámek
167	stisknout	202	vybrat	238	panel nástrojů
168	stisknout (a přidržet tlačítko)	203	**Vybrat vše**	239	název
169	prvotní kontejner	204	výběr	240	strom
170	prvotní okno; hlavní okno	205	úchyt výběru	241	druh
171	**Tisk**	206	**Odeslat**	242	napsat
172	tiskárna	207	oddělovač	243	nedostupný
173	ukazatel průběhu	208	**Nastavení**	244	**Zpět**
174	projekt	209	**Instalátor**	245	**Odstranit instalaci**
175	**Vlastnosti**	210	zástupce	246	**nabídka Zobrazit**
176	inspektor vlastností	211	tlačítko zástupce	247	místní úpravy
177	karta vlastností	212	ikona zástupce	248	paleta
178	okno vlastností	213	klávesová zkratka	249	**Co je to?**
179	ovládací prvek okna vlastností	214	pole klávesové zkratky	250	okno
180	**Zběžné zobrazení**	215	**Zobrazit**	251	**nabídka Okno**
181	jen číst	216	**Vypnout**	252	Průzkumník
182		217	seznam s jediným výběrem	253	průvodce
183	Koš	218	**Velikost**	254	sešit
184	**Znovu**	219	volný roh	255	pracovní skupina
185	obtah; obtažení; obtahová křivka	220	táhlo	256	pracovní prostor
186	registr	221	číselník	257	**Ano**
187	**Opakovat**	222	**Rozdělit**		
188	**Zaměnit**	223	příčka		
		224	dělící táhlo; táhlo příčky		

Danish

1	**Om**	54	dokument	107	sammenkæde (v.)
2	hurtigtast	55	dobbeltklikke	108	**Indsæt kæde her**
3	brugervenlighed	56		109	liste
4	genvejshåndtag	57	trække	110	listevisningsboks (kontrolelement)
5	aktiv	58	trække og slippe	111	manuel kæde
6	markeringsafslutning	59	kombinationsboks med rullepil	112	**Maksimer**
7	aktivt objekt	60	rulleliste	113	maksimeringsknap
8	aktivt vindue	61	rullemenu	114	menu
9	værktøjselement	62	**Rediger**	115	menulinje
10	**Altid øverst**	63	**Menuen Rediger**	116	menuknap
11	forankringspunkt	64	ellipse	117	menupunkt
12	**Anvend**	65	integreret objekt	118	menutitel
13	tekstboks med automatisk udgang	66	**Afslut**	119	meddelelsesboks
14	automatisk gentagelse	67	udvide (en disposition)	120	**Minimer**
15	automatisk kæde	68	**Stifinder**	121	minimeringsknap
16	automatisk rulning	69	udvidet markering	122	blandet værdi
17	**Tilbage**	70	liste, der tillader udvidet markering	123	modal
18		71	fil	124	tilstand
19		72	Menuen Filer	125	ikke-modal
20		73	**Søg**	126	ændringstast
21	**Gennemse**	74	**Find næste**	127	mus
22	**Annuller**	75	**Søg efter**	128	**Flyt**
23	undermenu	76	mappe	129	**Flyt hertil**
24	afkrydsningsfelt	77	skrifttype	130	multiple document interface (MDI)
25	afkrydsning	78	skriftstørrelse	131	liste, der tillader flere markeringer
26	underordnet vindue	79	typografi	132	Denne computer (ikon)
27	vælge	80	funktionstast	133	Andre computere (ikon)
28	klikke	81		134	**Ny**
29	Udklipsholder	82		135	**Næste**
30	**Luk**	83	gruppeboks	136	objekt
31	lukknap	84	håndtag	137	**OK**
32	skjule (disposition)	85	**Hjælp**	138	OLE
33	kolonneoverskrift (kontrolelement)	86	Menuen Hjælp	139	OLE-træk og slip
34	kombinationsboks	87	**Skjul**	140	integreret OLE-objekt
35	kommandoknap	88	hierarkisk markering	141	sammenkædet OLE-objekt
36	objektbeholder	89	holde nede	142	interaktiv OLE-træk og slip
37	kontekstafhængig hjælp	90	aktivt punkt	143	**Åbn**
38	kontekstafhængig	91	aktiv zone	144	**Åbn med**
39	kontrolelement	92	ikon	145	alternativknap
40	**Kopier**	93	ikke-aktiv	146	aktiveret indstilling
41	**Kopier hertil**	94	ikke-aktivt vindue	147	objektpakke
42	**Opret genvej**	95		148	**Sideopsætning**
43	**Opret genvej her**	96		149	paletvindue
44	**Klip**	97	inputfokus	150	rude
45	standard	98	**Menuen Indsæt**	151	overordnet vindue
46	standardknap	99	**Indsæt objekt**	152	adgangskode
47	**Slet**	100	indsætningspunkt	153	**Sæt ind**
48	skrivebord	101	kursiv	154	**Indsæt kæde**
49	destination	102	etiket	155	**Indsæt genvej**
50	dialogboks	103	liggende	156	**Indsæt speciel**
51	handicap	104		157	sti
52	usammenhængende markering	105		158	**Pause**
53	forankre	106	kæde (n.)	159	

Danish

Dutch

1	**Info**		persoon met een handicap (beter dan	103	liggend
2	toegangstoets		gehandicapte))	104	
3	toegankelijkheid	52	niet-aaneengesloten selectie	105	
4	bewerkingsgreep	53	in werkbalkdok plaatsen	106	koppeling
5	actief	54	document	107	koppelen
6	selecie-einde	55	dubbelklikken	108	**Hier koppeling maken**
7	actief object	56		109	keuzelijst
8	actief venster	57	slepen	110	weergaveknoppen
9	grafisch hulpmiddel	58	slepen en neerzetten	111	handmatige koppeling
10	**Altijd op voorgrond**	59	vervolgkeuzelijst met invoervak	112	**Maximaliseren**
11	fixeerpunt	60	vervolgkeuzelijst	113	knop Maximaliseren
12	**Toepassen**	61	menu	114	menu
13	automatisch verlaten	62	**Bewerken**	115	menubalk
14	(zich) automatisch herhalen	63	**menu Bewerken**	116	menuknop
15	automatische koppeling	64	puntjes (...)	117	opdracht
16	automatisch schuiven	65	ingesloten object	118	menunaam
17	**Vorige** (wanneer het een logisch	66	**Afsluiten**	119	berichtvak
	paar vormt met **Volgende**)	67	uitvouwen	120	**Minimaliseren**
18		68	**Verkennen**	121	knop Minimaliseren
19		69	uitgebreide selectie	122	met gemengde waarden
20		70	keuzelijst met uitgebreide selectie	123	modusgebonden
21	**Bladeren**	71	bestand	124	modus (pl. = modi)
22	**Annuleren**	72	menu Bestand	125	niet-modusgebonden
23	vervolgmenu	73	**Zoeken**	126	modificatietoets
24	selectievakje	74	**Volgende zoeken**	127	muis
25	vinkje	75	**Zoeken naar**	128	**Verplaatsen**
26	subvenster	76	map	129	**Hierheen verplaatsen**
27	kiezen	77	lettertype	130	interface voor meerdere documenten
28	klikken	78	tekengrootte		(MDI)
29	Klembord	79	tekenstijl	131	keuzelijst met meervoudige selectie
30	**Sluiten**	80	functietoets	132	Deze computer (pictogram)
31	knop Sluiten	81		133	Netwerkomgeving (pictogram)
32	samenvouwen	82		134	**Nieuw**
33	kolomnaam	83	groepsvak	135	**Volgende**
34	keuzelijst met invoervak	84	greep	136	object
35	opdrachtknop	85	**Help**	137	**OK**
36	hoofdobject	86	menu Help	138	OLE (OLE (objecten koppelen en
37	contextafhankelijke Help	87	**Verbergen**		insluiten): voluit alleen in doc en
38	contextafhankelijk	88	hiërarchische selectie		Help)
39	besturingselement	89	ingedrukt houden	139	slepen en neerzetten (via OLE)
40	**Kopiëren**	90	selectiepunt	140	ingesloten OLE-object
41	**Hierheen kopiëren**	91	selectiegebied	141	gekoppeld OLE-object
42	**Snelkoppeling maken**	92	pictogram	142	Aangepast slepen en neerzetten (via
43	**Hier snelkoppeling maken**	93	niet-actief		OLE)
44	**Knippen**	94	niet-actief venster	143	**Openen**
45	standaard	95		144	**Openen met**
46	standaardknop	96		145	keuzerondje
47	**Verwijderen**	97	invoerfocus	146	opties
48	bureaublad	98	**menu Invoegen**	147	OLE-pakket
49	doel	99	**Object invoegen**	148	**Pagina-instelling**
50	dialoogvenster	100	invoegpositie	149	paletvenster
51	handicap (voorzichtig in context,	101	cursief	150	deelvenster
	maar handicap niet verbloemen:VB:	102	label (gender, Masc.: de)	151	hoofdvenster

Dutch

152	wachtwoord	187	**Herhalen**	224	splitsblokje
153	**Plakken**	188	**Vervangen**	225	knop Start
154	**Koppeling plakken**	189	**Vorig formaat**	226	map Opstarten
155	**Snelkoppeling plakken**	190	knop Vorig formaat	227	statusbalk
156	**Plakken speciaal**	191	**Doorgaan**	228	**Stoppen**
157	pad	192	**Nogmaals**	229	tab
158	**Pauze**	193	RTF-vak	230	
159		194	**Uitvoeren (Maar: macro starten)**	231	taakbalk
160	**Afspelen**	195	**Opslaan**	232	taakgeoriënteerde Help
161	Plug en Play	196	**Opslaan als**	233	sjabloon (de)
162	aanwijzen	197	schuiven door	234	tekstvak
163	aanwijzer	198	schuifpijl	235	titelbalk
164	pop-up-menu	199	schuifbalk	236	venstertitel
165	pop-up-venster	200	schuifblok	237	wisseltoets
166	staand	201	secundair venster	238	werkbalk
167	drukken op (een toets)	202	selecteren	239	knopinfo
168	(een muisknop) ingedrukt houden (press a mouse button = een muisknop indrukken)	203	**Alles selecteren**	240	(besturingselement voor) structuurweergave
		204	selectie	241	type
		205	selectiegreep	242	typen
169	primair hoofdobject	206	**Kopiëren naar**	243	niet beschikbaar
170	primair venster	207	scheidingsteken	244	**Ongedaan maken**
171	**Afdrukken**	208	**Instellingen**	245	**Installatie ongedaan maken**
172	printer	209	**Instellen (Setup** als het programma Setup wordt bedoeld)	246	**menu Beeld**
173	voortgangsindicator			247	direct bewerken
174	project	210	snelkoppeling	248	keuzelijst met grafische opties
175	**Eigenschappen**	211	snelkoppelingsknop	249	**Wat is dit?**
176	eigenschappenweergave	212	snelkoppelingspictogram	250	venster
177	eigenschappenpagina	213	sneltoets	251	**menu Venster**
178	eigenschappenblad	214	sneltoetsvak	252	Windows Verkenner
179	besturingselement op een eigenschappenblad	215	**Weergeven**	253	wizard (geen hoofdletter meer in lopende tekst)
		216	**Afsluiten**		
180	**Snel weergeven**	217	keuzelijst met enkelvoudige selectie	254	werkmap
181	alleen-lezen	218	**Formaat wijzigen**	255	werkgroep
182		219	formaatgreep	256	werkruimte
183	Prullenbak (pictogram)	220	schuifregelaar	257	**Ja**
184	**Opnieuw**	221	kringveld		
185	gebiedsselectie	222	**Splitsen**		
186	het Register	223	splitsbalk		

Finnish

1	**Tietoja**	53	telakoida	106	linkki
2	valintanäppäin	54	asiakirja; tiedosto	107	linkittää
3	helppokäyttötoiminto	55	kaksoisnapsauttaa	108	**Linkitä tähän**
4	toimintokahva	56		109	luetteloruutu
5	aktiivinen	57	vetää	110	luettelonäyttö (ohjausobjekti)
6	valinnan aktiivinen päätöskohta	58	vetää ja pudottaa	111	manuaalinen linkki
7	aktiivinen objekti	59	avattava yhdistelmäruutu	112	**Suurenna**
8	aktiivinen ikkuna	60	avattava luetteloruutu	113	suurennuspainike
9	graafinen lisäke	61	avattava valikko	114	valikko
10	**Aina päällimmäisenä**	62	**Muokkaa**	115	valikkorivi
11	ankkurikohta	63	**Muokkaa-valikko**	116	valikkopainike
12	**Käytä**	64	kolme pistettä	117	valikon vaihtoehto
13	automaattinen siirtyminen	65	upotettu objekti	118	valikon otsikko
14	automaattinen toisto	66	**Lopeta**	119	sanomaruutu
15	automaattinen linkki	67	laajentaa (jäsennys)	120	**Pienennä**
16	automaattinen vieritys	68	**Selaa**	121	pienennyspainike
17	**Takaisin**	69	laajennettu valinta	122	monitila
18		70	laajennettu valinta-luetteloruutu	123	modaalinen
19		71	tiedosto	124	tila
20		72	Tiedosto-valikko	125	ei-modaalinen
21	**Selaa**	73	**Etsi**	126	yhdistelmänäppäin
22	**Peruuta**	74	**Etsi seuraava**	127	hiiri
23	alivalikko	75	**Etsittävä**	128	**Siirrä**
24	valintaruutu	76	kansio	129	**Siirrä tähän**
25	valintamerkki	77	fontti	130	MDI-liittymä
26	ali-ikkuna	78	fonttikoko	131	monivalintainen luetteloruutu
27	valita	79	fonttityyli	132	Oma tietokone (kuvake)
28	napsauttaa	80	funktionäppäin	133	Verkkoympäristö (kuvake)
29	Leikepöytä	81		134	**Uusi**
30	**Sulje**	82		135	**Seuraava**
31	sulkemispainike	83	ryhmän kehys	136	objekti
32	kutistaa; tiivistää (jäsennys)	84	kahva	137	**OK**
33	sarakeotsikko; saraketunnus	85	**Ohje**	138	OLE
	(ohjausobjekti)	86	Ohje-valikko	139	vedä ja pudota-OLE-toiminto
34	yhdistelmäruutu	87	**Piilota**	140	upotettu OLE-objekti
35	(komento) painike	88	hierarkkinen valinta	141	linkitetty OLE-objekti
36	säilö	89	pitää painettuna	142	käyttäjän määrittämä vedä ja
37	tilannekohtainen ohje	90	kohdepiste		pudota-OLE-toiminto
38	tilannekohtainen	91	kohdealue	143	**Avaa**
39	ohjausobjekti	92	kuvake	144	**Avaa sovelluksessa**
40	**Kopioi**	93	passiivinen	145	valintanappi
41	**Kopioi tähän**	94	passiivinen ikkuna	146	valitsimen tila
42	**Luo pikakuvake**	95		147	pakkaus
43	**Luo pikakuvake tähän**	96		148	**Sivun asetukset**
44	**Leikkaa**	97	syöttöalue	149	valikoimaikkuna
45	oletus	98	**Lisää-valikko**	150	ruutu
46	oletuspainike	99	**Lisää objekti**	151	ylemmän tason ikkuna
47	**Poista**	100	lisäyskohta	152	salasana
48	työpöytä	101	kursivoitu	153	**Liitä**
49	kohde	102	nimi; otsikko	154	**Liitä linkki**
50	valintaikkuna	103	vaaka	155	**Liitä pikakuvake**
51	invaliditeetti	104		156	**Liitä määräten**
52	hajavalinta	105		157	polku

Finnish

158	**Tauko**	191	**Jatka**	225	Käynnistä-painike
159		192	**Yritä uudelleen**	226	Käynnistys-kansio
160	**Soita**	193	monimuotoruutu	227	tilarivi
161	Plug and Play	194	**Suorita**	228	**Pysäytä**
162	osoittaa	195	**Tallenna**	229	välilehti (ohjausobjekti)
162	piste	196	**Tallenna nimellä**	230	
163	osoitin	197	vierittää	231	tehtäväpalkki
164	pikavalikko	198	vieritysnuoli	232	tehtäväohje
165	ponnahdusikkuna	199	vierityspalkki	233	malli
166	pysty	200	vieritysruutu	234	muokkausruutu
167	painaa (näppäintä)	201	toissijainen ikkuna	235	otsikkorivi
168	painaa (ja pitää painettuna	202	valita	236	otsikkoteksti
	hiiripainiketta)	203	**Valitse kaikki**	237	tilanvaihtonäppäin
169	ensisijainen säilö	204	valinta	238	työkalurivi
170	ensisijainen ikkuna	205	valintakahva	239	työkaluvihje
171	**Tulosta**	206	**Lähetä tiedosto**	240	puunäyttö (ohjausobjekti)
172	kirjoitin	207	erotin	241	tyyppi; laji
173	tilanneilmaisin (ohjausobjekti)	208	**Asetukset**	242	kirjoittaa
174	projekti	209	**Asennus**	243	ei käytettävissä
175	**Ominaisuudet**	210	pika-	244	**Kumoa**
176	ominaisuuksien tarkastelu	211	pikapainike	245	**Pura asennus**
177	ominaisuusryhmä	212	pikakuvake	246	**Näytä-valikko**
178	ominaisuusikkuna	213	pikanäppäin	247	visuaalinen muokkaus
179	ominaisuusikkuna-ohjausobjekti	214	pikanäppäin-ohjausobjekti	248	graafisen valinnan ohjausobjekti
180	**Pikanäyttö**	215	**Näytä**	249	**Lisätietoja**
181	vain luku	216	**Sammuta**	250	ikkuna
182		217	yksivalintainen luetteloruutu	251	**Ikkuna-valikko**
183	Roskakori (kuvake)	218	**Muuta kokoa**	252	Resurssienhallinta
184	**Tee uudelleen**	219	koonmuuttokahva	253	ohjattu toiminto
185	aluevalinta	220	liukusäädin	254	työkirja
186	rekisteri	221	askellusruutu	255	työryhmä
187	**Toista**	222	**Jaa**	256	työtila
188	**Korvaa**	223	jakopalkki	257	**Kyllä**
189	**Palauta**	224	jakoruutu		
190	palautuspainike				

French

1	**A propos**	53	aligner	106	liaison
2	touche d'accès rapide	54	document	107	lier
3	accessibilité	55	cliquer deux fois	108	**Lier ici**
4	handle d'action	56	toucher deux fois	109	zone de liste
5	actif/active	57	faire glisser	110	Liste icônes
6	point de fin de sélection	58	glisser-déplacer	111	liaison manuelle
7	objet actif	59	zone de liste déroulante modifiable	112	**Agrandissement**
8	fenêtre active	60	zone de liste déroulante fixe	113	agrandir
9	barre	61	menu déroulant	114	menu
10	**Toujours visible**	62	**Edition**	115	barre de menus
11	point de début de sélection	63	**modifier**	116	bouton de menu
12	**Appliquer**	64	points de suspension	117	élément de menu
13	sortie automatique	65	objet incorporé	118	titre de menu
14	répétition automatique	66	**Quitter**	119	boîte de message
15	Liaison automatique	67	développer	120	**Réduction**
16	défilement automatique	68	**Explorer**	121	réduire
17	**Précédent**	69	sélection étendue	122	valeurs multiples
18	Bouton du stylet	70	zone de liste à sélection étendue	123	modal
19	toucher-maintenir enfoncé	71	fichier	124	mode
20	édition contrôlée	72	Fichier	125	non modal
21	**Parcourir**	73	**Rechercher**	126	touche de modification
22	**Annuler**	74	**Suivant**	127	souris
23	menu en cascade	75	**Rechercher**	128	**Déplacement**
24	case à cocher	76	dossier	129	**Transférer ici**
25	coche	77	police	130	Interface documents multiples
26	fenêtre enfant	78	taille de police	131	zone de liste à sélection multiple
27	choisir	79	style de police	132	Poste de travail
28	(v.) cliquer sur (à l'écran) / cliquer le (bouton souris) - (n.) clic	80	touche de fonction	133	Voisinage réseau
		81	signe	134	**Nouveau**
29	Presse-papiers	82	glyphe	135	**Suivant**
30	**Fermer/Fermeture**	83	zone de groupe	136	objet
31	Fermer	84	handle	137	**OK**
32	réduire	85	**Aide**	138	OLE
33	en-tête de colonne	86	?	139	glisser-déplacer OLE
34	zone de liste modifiable	87	**Masquer**	140	Objet OLE incorporé
35	bouton de commande	88	sélection hiérarchique	141	Objet OLE lié
36	conteneur (d'objets)	89	maintenir	142	glisser-déplacer OLE non standard
37	aide contextuelle	90	point d'impact	143	**Ouvrir**
38	contextuel/contextuelle	91	zone critique	144	**Ouvrir avec**
39	contrôle	92	icône	145	case d'option
40	**Copier**	93	inactif/inactive	146	état des caractéristiques
41	**Copier ici**	94	fenêtre inactive	147	ensemble
42	**Créer un raccourci**	95	dessin à main levée	148	**Mise en page**
43	**Créer un raccourci ici**	96	éditeur de dessin à main levée	149	palette
44	**Couper**	97	zone d'interaction	150	volet
45	par défaut	98	**Insertion**	151	fenêtre parent
46	bouton par défaut	99	**Insérer un objet**	152	mot de passe
47	**Supprimer**	100	point d'insertion	153	**Coller**
48	bureau	101	italique	154	**Coller avec liaison**
49	destination	102	nom de volume / étiquette	155	**Coller le raccourci**
50	boîte de dialogue	103	paysage	156	**Collage spécial**
51	incapacité	104	toucher lasso	157	chemin
52	sélection d'objets disjoints	105	loupe	158	**Pause**

French

159	stylet	193	zone de texte RTF (Rich Text Format)	226	dossier de démarrage
160	**Exécuter**	194	**Exécuter**	227	barre d'état
161	Plug and Play	195	**Enregistrer**	228	**Arrêter**
162	(v.) amener le pointeur sur (n.) point	196	**Enregistrer sous**	229	onglet
163	pointeur	197	faire défiler	230	toucher
164	menu autonome	198	flèche de défilement	231	barre des tâches
165	fenêtre autonome	199	barrre de défilement	232	aide spécifique aux tâches
166	portrait	200	curseur de défilement	233	modèle
167	appuyer (sur une touche)	201	fenêtre secondaire	234	zone de texte
168	appuyer (et maintenir enfoncé)	202	sélectionner	235	barre de titre
169	conteneur principal	203	**Tout sélectionner**	236	texte de la barre de titre
170	fenêtre principale	204	sélection	237	touche bascule
171	**Imprimer**	205	handle de sélection	238	barre d'outils
172	imprimante	206	**Envoyer vers**	239	info-bulle
173	indicateur d'état	207	séparateur	240	arborescence
174	projet	208	**Paramètres**	241	type
175	**Propriétés**	209	**Installation / INSTALL**	242	taper
176	inspecteur de propriétés	210	raccourci	243	pas disponible
177	page de propriétés	211	raccourci	244	**Annuler**
178	feuille de propriétés	212	raccourci	245	**Désinstaller**
179	feuille de propriétés	213	touche de raccourci	246	**Affichage**
180	**Aperçu**	214	touche de raccourci	247	activation sur place
181	en lecture seule	215	**Afficher**	248	sélection graphique
182	reconnaissance	216	**Arrêter l'ordinateur**	249	**Qu'est-ce que c'est ?**
183	Corbeille	217	zone de liste à sélection unique	250	fenêtre
184	**Annuler Annuler**	218	**Dimension**	251	**Fenêtre**
185	sélection par zone	219	poignée de redimensionnement	252	Explorateur Windows
186	base des registres	220	défileur	253	assistant
187	**Répéter**	221	compteur	254	classeur
188	**Remplacer**	222	**Fractionner**	255	groupe de travail
189	**Restauration**	223	barre de fractionnement	256	espace de travail
190	Restaurer	224	curseur de fractionnement	257	**Oui**
191	**Reprendre**	225	**Démarrer**		
192	**Essayer de nouveau**				

German

1	**Info**	54	Dokument	107	Verknüpfen	
2	Zugriffstaste	55	Doppelklicken	108	**Hiermit verknüpfen**	
3	Eingabehilfe	56	Doppeltippen	109	Listenfeld	
4	Aktionspunkt	57	Ziehen	110	Listenansicht	
5	Aktiv	58	Drag & Drop	111	Manuelle OLE-Verknüpfung	
6	Aktives Ende	59	Dropdown-Kombinationsfeld	112	**Maximieren**	
7	Aktives Objekt	60	Dropdown-Listenfeld	113	Maximieren (Schaltfläche)	
8	Aktives Fenster	61	Dropdown-Menü	114	Menü	
9	Zubehör	62	**Bearbeiten**	115	Menüleiste	
10	**Immer im Vordergrund**	63	**Bearbeiten (Menü)**	116	Menü (Schaltfläche)	
11	Ankerpunkt	64	Auslassungspunkte	117	Menüelement	
12	**Zuweisen**	65	Eingebettetes Objekt	118	Menütitel	
13	Textfeld mit automatischer Freigabe	66	**Beenden**	119	Meldungsfeld	
14	Automatische Wiederholung	67	Einblenden (einer Struktur)	120	**Minimieren**	
15	Automatische OLE-Verknüpfung	68	**Explorer (Befehl)**	121	Minimieren (Schaltfläche)	
16	Automatischer Bildlauf	69	Erweiterte Auswahl	122	Gemischt	
17	**Zurück**	70	Listenfeld für erweiterte Auswahl	123	Modal	
18	Pen-Knopf	71	Datei	124	Modus	
19	Tippen mit Pen-Knopf	72	Datei (Menü)	125	Interaktiv	
20	Texteditor (Steuerelement)	73	**Suchen**	126	Zusatztaste	
21	**Durchsuchen**	74	**Weitersuchen**	127	Maus	
22	**Abbrechen**	75	**Suchen nach**	128	**Verschieben**	
23	Überlappendes Menü	76	Ordner	129	**Hierher verschieben**	
24	Kontrollkästchen	77	Schriftart	130	MDI (Multiple Document Interface)	
25	Markierung (Kontrollkästchen)	78	Schriftgrad	131	Listenfeld für Mehrfachauswahl	
26	Untergeordnetes Fenster	79	Schriftschnitt	132	Arbeitsplatz (Symbol)	
27	Wählen	80	Funktionstaste	133	Netzwerk (Symbol)	
28	Klicken	81	Schriftzug	134	**Neu**	
29	Zwischenablage	82	Zeichen	135	**Weiter**	
30	**Schließen**	83	Gruppenfeld	136	Objekt	
31	Schließen (Schaltfläche)	84	Ziehpunkt	137	**OK**	
32	Ausblenden (Gliederung)	85	**Hilfe**	138	OLE	
33	Spaltenüberschrift (Steuerelement)	86	? (Menü)	139	OLE-Drag & Drop	
34	Kombinationsfeld	87	**Ausblenden**	140	Eingebettetes OLE-Objekt	
35	Schaltfläche	88	Hierarchische Auswahl	141	Verknüpftes OLE-Objekt	
36	Container	89	Halten	142	Vom Standard abweichendes OLE-Drag & Drop	
37	Kontextbezogene Hilfe	90	Hot Spot			
38	Kontextbezogen	91	Hot Zone	143	**Öffnen**	
39	Steuerelement	92	Symbol	144	**Öffnen mit**	
40	**Kopieren**	93	Inaktiv	145	Optionsfeld	
41	**Hierher kopieren**	94	Inaktives Fenster	146	Aktivierte Option	
42	**Verknüpfung erstellen**	95	Ink	147	Paket	
43	**Hiermit verknüpfen**	96	Inkeditor	148	**Seite einrichten**	
44	**Ausschneiden**	97	Eingabefokus	149	Palettenfenster	
45	Standard	98	**Einfügen (Menü)**	150	Fensterbereich	
46	Standardschaltfläche	99	**Objekt einfügen**	151	Übergeordnetes Fenster	
47	**Löschen**	100	Einfügemarke	152	Kennwort	
48	Desktop	101	Kursiv	153	**Einfügen**	
49	Ziel	102	Bezeichnung	154	**Verknüpfung einfügen**	
50	Dialogfeld	103	Querformat	155	**Verknüpfung einfügen**	
51	Behinderung	104	Lasso-Tippen	156	**Inhalte einfügen**	
52	Nichtzusammenhängende Auswahl	105	Lupe	157	Pfad	
53	Verankern	106	Verknüpfung	158	**Anhalten**	

German

159	Pen	192	**Wiederholen**	226	Autostart (Ordner)	
160	**Wiedergeben**	193	RTF-Textfeld	227	Statusleiste	
161	Plug & Play	194	**Ausführen**	228	**Beenden**	
162	Zeigen	195	**Speichern**	229	Register	
163	Zeiger	196	**Speichern unter**	230	Tippen	
164	Kontextmenü	197	Bildlauf durchführen	231	Task-Leiste	
165	Popup-Fenster	198	Bildlaufpfeil	232	Vorgangsbezogene Hilfe	
166	Hochformat	199	Bildlaufleiste	233	Vorlage	
167	Drücken (einer Taste)	200	Bildlauffeld	234	Textfeld	
168	Drücken (und Halten einer Maustaste)	201	Sekundärfenster	235	Titelleiste	
169	Primär-Container	202	Auswählen	236	Titeltext	
170	Primärfenster	203	**Alle markieren**	237	Ein-/Aus-Taste	
171	**Drucken**	204	Auswahl	238	Symbolleiste	
172	Drucker	205	Auswahlpunkt	239	QuickInfo	
173	Statusanzeige	206	**Senden an**	240	Strukturansicht	
174	Projekt	207	Trennelement	241	Typ	
175	**Eigenschaften**	208	**Einstellungen**	242	Eingeben	
176	Eigenschaftenanzeige	209	**Einrichten**	243	Nicht verfügbar	
177	Eigenschaftengruppe	210	Verknüpfung	244	**Rückgängig**	
178	Eigenschaftenfenster	211	Verknüpfte Schaltfläche	245	**Deinstallieren**	
179	Eigenschaftenfenster-Steuerelement	212	Verknüpfungssymbol	246	**Ansicht (Menü)**	
180	**Schnellansicht**	213	Tastenkombination	247	Direkte Bearbeitung	
181	Schreibgeschützt	214	Steuerelement für Tastenbelegung	248	Steuerelement zur Grafikanzeige	
182	Schrifterkennung	215	**Anzeigen**	249	**Direkthilfe**	
183	Papierkorb (Symbol)	216	**Beenden**	250	Fenster	
184	**Wiederherstellen**	217	Listenfeld für Einfachauswahl	251	**Fenster (Menü)**	
185	Bereichsauswahl	218	**Größe ändern**	252	Explorer	
186	Registrierung	219	Element für Größenänderung	253	Assistent	
187	**Wiederholen**	220	Schieber	254	Arbeitsmappe	
188	**Ersetzen**	221	Drehfeld	255	Arbeitsgruppe	
189	**Wiederherstellen**	222	**Teilen**	256	Arbeitsbereich	
190	Wiederherstellen (Schaltfläche)	223	Fensterteiler	257	**Ja**	
191	**Fortsetzen**	224	Teilungsfeld			
		225	Start (Schaltfläche)			

Greek

1	Περίτου (της)	49	προορισμός	101	πλάγια (γραφή)
2	πλήκτρο πρόσβασης	50	παράθυρο διαλόγου	102	ετικέτα
3	προσβασιμότητα	51	ειδικές ανάγκες	103	οριζόντια (σελίδα)
4	λαβή ενεργειών	52	ασυνεχής επιλογή	104	
5	ενεργός (-ή, ό)	53	αποθέτω (v.)	105	
6	ενεργό τέλος (επιλογών)	54	έγγραφο	106	δεσμός
7	ενεργό αντικείμενο	55	διπλό κλικ	107	συνδέω
8	ενεργό παράθυρο	56	διπλό χτύπημα	108	**Σύνδεσηεδώ**
9	διάκοσμος	57	σύρω	109	πλαίσιο λίστας
10	**Πάντα σε πρώτο πλάνο**	58	μεταφορά και απόθεση	110	προβολή λίστας
11	σημείο αγκύρωσης	59	αναπτυσσόμενο σύνθετο	111	μη αυτόματος δεσμός
12	**Εφαρμογή**		πλαίσιο	112	**Μεγιστοποίηση**
13	αυτόματης εξόδου (πλαίσιο)	60	αναπτυσσόμενο πλαίσιο λίστας	113	κουμπί μεγιστοποίησης
14	αυτόματης επανάληψης	61	αναπτυσσόμενο μενού	114	μενού
	(πλαίσιο)	62	**Επεξεργασία**	115	γραμμή μενού
15	αυτόματος δεσμός	63	**ΜενούΕπεξεργασία**	116	κουμπί μενού
16	αυτόματη κύλιση	64	αποσιωπητικά	117	στοιχείο μενού
17	**Προηγούμενος(-η, ο)**	65	ενσωματωμένο αντικείμενο	118	τίτλος μενού
18		66	**Έξοδος**	119	παράθυρο μηνύματος
19		67	ανάπτυξη (διάρθρωσης)	120	**Ελαχιστοποίηση**
20		68	**Εξερεύνηση Διερεύνηση**	121	πλήκτρο ελαχιστοποίησης
21	**Αναζήτηση**	69	διευρυμένη επιλογή	122	μεικτής τιμής
22	**Άκυρο**	70	πλαίσιο λίστας για διευρυμένη	123	περιοριστικός (-ή, -ό) σε
23	επικαλυπτόμενα μενού,		επιλογή		συγκεκριμένες καταστάσεις
	δευτερεύον μενού, διαδοχικά	71	αρχείο		λειτουργίας
	μενού	72	Μενού Αρχείο	124	κατάσταση (λειτουργίας),
24	πλαίσιο ελέγχου	73	**Εύρεση**		τρόπος (λειτουργίας)
25	μαρκάρισμα, σημάδι	74	**Εύρεση επομένου**	125	μη περιοριστικός (-ή, ό)
26	θυγατρικό παράθυρο	75	**Εύρεσητου**	126	πλήκτρο τροποποίησης
27	επιλογή (n.), επιλέγω, διαλέγω	76	φάκελος	127	ποντίκι
	(v.)	77	γραμματοσειρά	128	**Μετακίνηση**
28	κλικ, κάντε κλικ	78	μέγεθος γραμματοσειράς	129	**Μετακίνησηεδώ**
29	Πρόχειρο	79	στυλ γραμματοσειράς	130	περιβάλλον πολλών εγγράφων
30	**Κλείσιμο**	80	πλήκτρο ειδικής λειτουργίας		(MDI)
31	Κουμπί "Κλείσιμο"	81		131	πλαίσιο λίστας για πολλαπλές
32	σύμπτυξη (διάρθρωσης)	82			επιλογές
33	επικεφαλίδα στήλης	83	πλαίσιο ομάδας	132	Ο υπολογιστής μου
34	σύνθετο πλαίσιο	84	λαβή	133	Περιοχή του δικτύου
35	κουμπί εντολής	85	**Βοήθεια**	134	**Δημιουργία**
36	κοντέινερ	86	Μενού Βοήθεια	135	**Επόμενος(-η, ο)**
37	βοήθεια συναφής με το	87	**Απόκρυψη**	136	αντικείμενο
	περιβάλλον	88	ιεραρχική επιλογή	137	OK
38	συναφής, στο πλαίσιο, στο	89	κρατώ πατημένο	138	OLE
	περιβάλλον	90	σημείο αιχμής	139	μεταφορά και απόθεση OLE
39	στοιχείο ελέγχου	91	ζώνη αιχμής	140	ενσωματωμένο αντικείμενο
40	**Αντιγραφή**	92	εικονίδιο		OLE
41	**Αντιγραφήεδώ**	93	ανενεργός (-ή, ό)	141	συνδεδεμένο αντικείμενο OLE
42	**Δημιουργίασυντόμευσης**	94	ανενεργό παράθυρο	142	Μη προεπιλεγμένη μεταφορά
43	**Δημιουργίασυντόμευσηςεδώ**	95			και απόθεση OLE
44	**Αποκοπή**	96		143	**Άνοιγμα**
45	προεπιλεγμένος (-η, ο), εξ	97	χώρος εισαγωγής στοιχείων	144	**Άνοιγμαμε**
	ορισμού		(από το χρήστη)	145	κουμπί επιλογής
46	προεπιλεγμένο κουμπί	98	**ΜενούΕισαγωγή**	146	ορισμός επιλογής
47	**Διαγραφή**	99	**Εισαγωγήαντικειμένου**	147	πακέτο
48	επιφάνεια εργασίας	100	σημείο παρεμβολής	148	**Διαμόρφωσησελίδας**

Greek

149	παράθυρο παλέτας	186	μητρώο	221	Πλαίσιο τιμών
150	τμήμα (παραθύρου)	187	**Επανάληψη**	222	**Διαίρεση**
151	γονικό παράθυρο	188	**Αντικατάσταση**	223	γραμμή διαίρεσης
152	κωδικός πρόσβασης	189	**Επαναφορά**	224	πλαίσιο διαίρεσης
153	**Επικόλληση**	190	Κουμπί επαναφοράς	225	Κουμπί έναρξης
154	**Επικόλλησημε δεσμό**	191	**Επιστροφή Επανεκκίνηση**	226	Φάκελος εκκίνησης
155	**Επικόλλησησυντόμευσης**	192	**Επανάληψη(n.)**, επαναλαμβάνω	227	γραμμή κατάστασης
156	**Ειδικήεπικόλληση**		(v.), ξαναπροσπαθώ (v.)	228	**Διακοπή**
157	Διαδρομές (στο δίσκο)	193	πλαίσιο εμπλουτισμένου	229	στοιχείο καρτέλας
158	**Παύση**		κειμένου	230	
159		194	**Εκτέλεση**	231	Γραμμή εργασιών
160	**Αναπαραγωγή Εκτέλεση**	195	**Αποθήκευση**	232	βοήθεια σχετική με την εργασία
161	Τοποθέτηση και άμεση	196	**Αποθήκευσηως**	233	Πρότυπο
	λειτουργία	197	κύλιση	234	πλαίσιο κειμένου
162	σημαδέψτε με το δείκτη	198	βέλος κύλισης	235	γραμμή τίτλου
163	δείκτης	199	γραμμή κύλισης	236	κείμενο τίτλου
164	αναδυόμενο μενού	200	πλαίσιο κύλισης	237	πλήκτρο-διακόπτης
165	αναδυόμενο παράθυρο	201	δευτερεύον παράθυρο	238	γραμμή εργαλείων
166	κατακόρυφη σελίδα	202	επιλέγω	239	επεξήγηση εργαλείου
167	πάτημα (πλήκτρου)	203	**Επιλογήόλων**	240	στοιχείο (ελέγχου) προβολής
168	πάτημα (και κράτημα ενός	204	επιλογή		δέντρου
	πλήκτρου ποντικιού)	205	λαβή επιλογής	241	τύπος
169	πρωτεύον κοντέινερ	206	**Αποστολήσε**	242	πληκτρολόγηση
170	πρωτεύον παράθυρο	207	**Διαχωριστικό**	243	μη διαθέσιμος (-η, -ο)
171	**Εκτύπωση**	208	**Παράμετροι**	244	**Αναίρεση**
172	εκτυπωτής	209	**Εγκατάσταση Ορισμός**	245	**Κατάργησηεγκατάστασης**
173	δείκτης προόδου		παραμέτρων	246	**Μενού Προβολή**
174	έργο	210	συντόμευση	247	επιτόπια επεξεργασία
175	**Ιδιότητες**	211	κουμπί συντόμευσης	248	στοιχείο (ελέγχου) πηγής
176	επιθεώρηση ιδιοτήτων	212	εικονίδιο συντόμευσης	249	**Τι είναι...**
177	σελίδα ιδιοτήτων	213	πλήκτρο συντόμευσης	250	παράθυρο
178	φύλλο ιδιοτήτων	214	στοιχείο (ελέγχου) πλήκτρου	251	**Μενού Παράθυρο**
179	στοιχείο (ελέγχου) φύλλου		συντόμευσης	252	Εξερεύνηση των Windows
	ιδιοτήτων	215	**Επίδειξη Εμφάνιση**	253	οδηγός
180	**Γρήγορηπροβολή**	216	**Τερματισμόςλειτουργίας**	254	βιβλίο εργασίας
181	μόνο για ανάγνωση	217	πλαίσιο λίστας για μεμονωμένες	255	ομάδα εργασίας
182			επιλογές	256	χώρος εργασίας
183	Κάδος ανακύκλωσης	218	**Μέγεθος**	257	**Ναι**
184	**Ακύρωσηαναίρεσης**	219	λαβή μεταβολής μεγέθους		
185	επιλογή περιοχής	220	Αυξομειωτής		

Hebrew

#		#		#	
1	אודות	53	עגן	101	הטיה
2	מקש גישה	54	מסמך	102	תווית
3	נגישות	55	לחץ פעמיים	103	לרוחב
4	נקודת אחיזה לביצוע פעולה	55	לחיצה כפולה	104	הקפה ונקישה
5	פעיל	56	הקש פעמיים	105	
6	קצה אזור פעיל	56	נקישה כפולה	106	קישור
7	אובייקט פעיל	57	גרור	107	קשר
8	חלון פעיל	58	גרור ושחרר	108	**קשר כאן**
9		59	תיבה משולבת נפתחת	109	תיבת רשימה
10	**תמיד עליון**	60	תיבת רשימה נפתחת	110	תצוגת רשימה (פקד)
11	נקודת עוגן	61	תפריט נפתח	111	קישור ידני
12	**החל**	62	**עריכה**	112	**הגדל**
13	יציאה אוטומטית	63	תפריט עריכה	113	לחצן הגדל
14	חזרה אוטומטית	64	שלוש נקודות	114	תפריט
15	קישור אוטומטי	65	אובייקט מוטבע	115	שורת תפריט
16	גלילה אוטומטית	66	**יציאה**	116	לחצן תפריט
17	**הקודם**	67	הרחב (חלוקה לרמות)	117	פריט תפריט
18	לחצן העט	68	**סייר**	118	כותרת תפריט
19	נקישת עט	69	בחירה מורחבת	119	תיבת הודעה
20	תיבת עריכה	70	תיבת רשימה עם אפשרות בחירה מורחבת	120	**מזער**
21	**עיון**			121	לחצן מזער
22	**ביטול**	71	קובץ	122	ערכים מעורבים
23	תפריט מדורג	72	תפריט קובץ	123	מודאלי
24	תיבת סימון	73	**חפש**	124	מצב
25	סימן ביקורת	74	**חפש את הבא**	125	לא מודאלי
26	חלון צאצא	75	**חפש את**	126	מקש משנה מצב
27	בחר	76	תיקיה	127	עכבר
28	לחץ	77	גופן	128	**הזז**
29	לוח	78	גודל גופן	129	**העבר**
30	**סגור**	79	סגנון גופן	128	הזז
31	לחצן סגור	80	מקש ייעודי	129	העבר כאן
32	כווץ (חלוקה לרמות)	81	תנועת יד	130	ממשק ריבוי מסמכים (MDI)
33	כותרת עמודה	82	תמונה	131	תיבת רשימה עם אפשרות בחירה מרובה
34	תיבה משולבת	83	תיבת קבוצה		
35	לחצן פקודה	84	נקודת אחיזה	132	המחשב שלי (סמל)
36	כלי קיבול	85	**עזרה**	133	שכנים ברשת (סמל)
37	עזרה תלויית הקשר	86	תפריט עזרה	134	**חדש**
38	תלוי הקשר	87	**הסתר**	135	**הבא**
39	פקד	88	בחירה בשלבים/הדרגתית	136	אובייקט
40	**העתק**	89	החזק (לחוץ)	137	**אישור**
41	**העתק כאן**	90	נקודת מגע	138	OLE
42	**צור קיצור דרך**	91	אזור מגע	139	
43	**צור קיצור דרך כאן**	92	סמל	140	
44	**גזור**	93	לא פעיל	141	
45	ברירת מחדל	94	חלון לא פעיל	142	
46	לחצן ברירת מחדל	95	שרבוט	143	פתיחה
47	**מחק**	96	עריכת שרבוט	144	פתחבאמצעות
48	שולחן עבודה	97	מוקד קלט	145	לחצן אפשרויות
49	יעד	98	**תפריט הוספה**	146	אפשרות מוגדרת
50	תיבת דו-שיח	99	**הוספתאובייקט**	147	מנה
51	מגבלה	100	נקודת כניסה	148	**הגדרת עמוד**
52	בחירה לא רציפה	101	נטוי	149	חלון ערכת כלים

Hebrew

Hungarian

1	**Névjegy**	52	szakaszos kijelölés, nem összefüggő	104	
2	hívóbetű	53	kiköt	105	
3	kisegítő lehetőségek	54	dokumentum	106	csatolás
4	kezelő	55	duplán kattint	107	csatol
5	aktív	56		108	**Csatolás (ide)**
6	végpont	57	húz	109	listapanel
7	aktív objektum	58	"Fogd és vidd"	110	listatárló (vezérlés)
8	aktív ablak	59	legördülő kombinált lista	111	kézi csatolás
9	kényelmi eszközök	60	legördülő lista	112	**Teljes méret**
10	**Mindig látható**	61	legördülő menü	113	Teljes méret gomb
11	kezdőpont	62	**Szerkesztés**	114	menü
12	**Alkalmaz, Legyen, Érvényesít**	63	**Szerkesztés menü**	115	menüsor
13	automatikus kilépés	64	három pont	116	menügomb
14	automatikus ismétlés	65	beágyazott objektum	117	menüelem
15	automatikus csatolás	66	**Kilépés**	118	menücím
16	automatikus görgetés	67	kibont	119	üzenetpanel
17	**Vissza**	68	**Intéz, Szervez**	120	**Kis méret**
18		69	univerzális kijelölés	121	Kis méret gomb
19		70	lista univerzális kijelöléssel	122	kevert érték
20		71	fájl	123	modális
21	**Tallózás**	72	Fájl menü	124	mód
22	**Mégse**	73	**Keresés**	125	nem modális, független
23	almenü	74	**Továbbkeresés**	126	módosítóbillentyű
24	jelölőnégyzet	75	**Mit**	127	egér
25	pipa, iksz	76	mappa	128	**Áthelyezés**
26	származtatott ablak	77	betűtípus	129	**Áthelyezés ide**
27	választ	78	betűméret	130	többdokumentumos felület
28	kattint	79	betűstílus	131	többválasztós lista
29	Vágólap	80	funkcióbillentyű, F-billentyű,	132	Sajátgép (ikon)
30	**Bezárás**	81		133	Hálózatok (ikon)
31	Bezárás gomb	82		134	**Új**
32	összecsuk	83	(vezérlőelem-) csoport	135	**Következő**
33	hasábfej (vezérlés)	84	kezelő	136	objektum
34	kombinált lista	85	**Súgó**	137	**OK**
35	parancsgomb	86	Súgó menü	138	OLE
36	tároló,tartály	87	**Elrejtés**	139	irányított áthúzás
37	környezetfüggő súgó	88	hierachikus kiválasztás	140	OLE beágyazott objektum
38	környezetfüggő	89	nyomva tartás	141	OLE csatolt objektum
39	vezérlőelem	90	hatáspont	142	OLE választó áthúzás/irányított
40	**Másolás**	91	érzékeny mező/terület/rész		fogd és vidd eljárás
41	**Másolás ide**	92	ikon	143	**Megnyitás**
42	**Parancsikon létrehozása**	93	inaktív	144	**Társítás**
43	**Parancsikon létrehozása**	94	inaktív ablak	145	választógomb
44	**Kivágás**	95		146	beállítás
45	alap, alapértelmezett,	96		147	csomag
	alapértelmezés	97	beviteli terület	148	**Oldalbeállítás**
46	alapgomb	98	**Beszúrás menü**	149	paletta ablak
47	**Törlés**	99	**Objektum beszúrása**	150	ablaktábla
48	asztal	100	beszúrási pont	151	szülőablak
49	cél	101	dőlt	152	jelszó
50	párbeszédpanel	102	címke, felirat	153	**Beillesztés**
51	kezdő	103	fekvő	154	**Csatolva beillesztés**

Hungarian

Italian

Italian

149	casella degli strumenti/tavolozza di colori
150	riquadro
151	finestra principale
152	password
153	**Incolla**
154	**Incolla collegamento**
155	**Incolla collegamento**
156	**Incolla speciale**
157	percorso
158	**Interrompi**
159	penna
160	**Riproduci**
161	Plug and Play
162	punto
163	puntatore
164	menu di scelta rapida
165	finestra popup
166	verticale
167	premere (un tasto)
168	premere (e tenere premuto un pulsante del mouse)
169	contenitore principale
170	finestra principale
171	**Stampa**
172	stampante
173	indicatore di avanzamento del processo
174	progetto
175	**Proprietà**
176	visualizzatore proprietà
177	scheda proprietà
178	finestra proprietà
179	controllo finestra proprietà
180	**Anteprima**
181	sola lettura
182	riconoscimento
183	Cestino
184	**Ripeti**
185	selezione dell'area

186	registro di configurazione
187	**Ripeti**
188	**Sostituisci**
189	**Ripristina**
190	pulsante di ripristino
191	**Riprendi**
192	**Riprova**
193	casella di testo RTF
194	**Esegui**
195	**Salva**
196	**Salva con nome**
197	scorrere (v.)
198	freccia di scorrimento
199	barra di scorrimento
200	casella di scorrimento
201	finestra secondaria
202	selezionare (v.)
203	**Seleziona tutto**
204	selezione
205	quadratino di selezione
206	**Invia a**
207	separatore
208	**Impostazioni**
209	**Imposta**
210	collegamento
211	pulsante di collegamento
212	icona di collegamento
213	tasto di scelta rapida
214	controllo tasto di scelta rapida
215	**Mostra**
216	**Arresta il sistema** (pulsanti e opzioni)
216	**Chiudi sessione** (comando del menu Avvio)
217	casella di riepilogo a selezione singola
218	**Dimensione**
219	punto di ridimensionamento
220	dispositivo di scorrimento
221	casella di selezione

222	**Dividi**
223	barra di divisione
224	casella di divisione
225	pulsante Avvio
226	cartella Esecuzione automatica
227	barra di stato
228	**Ferma**
229	controllo a schede
230	toccare (v.)
230	tocco (n.)
231	barra delle applicazioni
232	guida orientata alle attività
233	modello
234	casella di testo
235	barra del titolo
236	testo della barra del titolo
237	tasto interruttore
238	barra degli strumenti
239	descrizione comando
240	controllo per la visualizzazione ad albero
241	tipo
242	digitare/inserire
243	non disponibile
244	**Annulla**
245	**Rimozione**
246	**menu Visualizza**
247	modifica diretta
248	controllo di selezione grafica
249	**Guida rapida**
250	finestra
251	**menu Finestra**
252	Gestione risorse
253	installazione guidata
254	cartella di lavoro
255	gruppo di lavoro
256	area di lavoro
257	**Sì**

Japanese

1	バージョン情報	46	デフォルト ボタン	90	ホット スポット
2	アクセス キー	47	削除	91	ホット ゾーン
3	ユーザー補助	48	デスクトップ	92	アイコン
4	アクション ハンドル	49	OLE 先	93	非アクティブ
5	アクティブ	50	ダイアログ ボックス	94	非アクティブ ウィンドウ
6	アクティブ エンド	51	ディザビリティ	95	インク
7	アクティブなオブジェクト	52	非連続の複数選択	96	インク編集
8	アクティブ ウィンドウ	53	ドッキング	97	入力フォーカス
9	ウィンドウの付属要素	54	ドキュメント	98	［挿入］ メニュー
10	つねに手前に表示	55	ダブルクリック	99	オブジェクトの挿入
11	アンカー ポイント	56	ダブルタップ	100	挿入ポイント
12	更新	57	ドラッグ	101	斜体
13	自動フォーカス	58	ドラッグ アンド ドロップ	102	ラベル
14	オート リピート	59	ドロップダウン コンボ ボックス	103	横
15	自動リンク			103	横置き
16	自動スクロール	60	ドロップダウン リスト ボックス	104	囲んで選択
17	戻る			105	レンズ
18	サイド ボタン	61	ドロップダウン メニュー	106	リンク
19	サイド ボタンを押しながらタップ	62	編集	107	リンクする
		63	［編集］ メニュー	108	ここにリンク
20	ボックス編集	64	省略記号	109	リスト ボックス
21	参照	65	埋め込みオブジェクト	110	一覧表示
22	キャンセル	66	～の終了	111	手動リンク
23	カスケード メニュー	67	下位階層の表示	112	最大化
24	チェック ボックス	67	開く	113	最大化ボタン
25	チェック マーク	68	エクスプローラ	114	メニュー
26	子ウィンドウ	69	拡張選択	115	メニューバー
27	選ぶ	70	拡張選択リスト ボックス	116	メニュー ボタン
28	クリック	71	ファイル	117	メニュー項目
29	クリップボード	72	［ファイル］ メニュー	118	メニュー タイトル
30	閉じる	73	検索	119	メッセージ ボックス
31	閉じるボタン	74	次を検索	120	最小化
32	下位階層の非表示	75	検索する文字列	121	最小化ボタン
32	閉じる	75	検索する値	122	混在設定
33	列見出し	76	フォルダ	123	モーダル
34	コンボ ボックス	77	フォント	124	モード
35	コマンド ボタン	78	フォント サイズ	125	モードレス
36	コンテナ	79	フォント スタイル	126	修飾キー
37	状況依存のヘルプ	80	ファンクション キー	127	マウス
38	状況依存の	81	ジェスチャ	128	移動
39	コントロール	82	グリフ	129	ここに移動
40	コピー	83	グループ ボックス	130	複数ドキュメント インターフェイス
41	ここにコピー	84	ハンドル		
42	ショートカットの作成	85	ヘルプ	131	複数選択リスト ボックス
43	ショートカットをここに作成	86	［ヘルプ］ メニュー	132	マイ コンピュータ
44	切り取り	87	隠す	133	ネットワーク コンピュータ
45	標準	88	階層的な選択	134	新規作成
45	デフォルト	89	押したまま	135	次へ

Japanese

136	オブジェクト
137	OK
138	OLE
139	OLE ドラッグ アンド ドロップ
140	OLE オブジェクトの埋め込み
141	OLE でリンクされたオブジェクト
142	選択型 OLE ドラッグ アンド ドロップ
143	開く
144	アプリケーションから開く
145	オプション ボタン
146	オプション設定
147	パッケージ
148	ページレイアウトの設定
149	パレット ウィンドウ
150	ペイン
151	親ウィンドウ
152	パスワード
153	貼り付け
154	リンク貼り付け
155	ショートカットの貼り付け
156	形式を選択して貼り付け
157	パス
158	一時停止
159	ペン
160	再生
161	プラグ アンド プレイ
162	ポイント
163	ポインタ
164	ポップアップ メニュー
165	ポップアップ ウィンドウ
166	縦
166	縦置き
167	押す
168	押したまま
169	メイン コンテナ
170	メイン ウィンドウ
171	印刷
172	プリンタ
173	進行状況インジケータ
174	プロジェクト
175	プロパティ
176	プロパティ インスペクタ

177	プロパティ ページ
178	プロパティ シート
179	プロパティ シート コントロール
180	クイック表示
181	読み取り専用
182	認識
183	ごみ箱
184	やり直し
185	領域選択
186	レジストリ
187	リピート
188	置換
189	復元
190	元のサイズに戻すボタン
191	再開
192	再試行
193	リッチテキスト ボックス
194	ファイル名を指定して実行
195	保存
196	名前を付けて保存
197	スクロール
198	スクロールバーの矢印ボタン
199	スクロールバー
200	スクロールバーのつまみ
201	2 次ウィンドウ
202	選択する
203	すべて選択
204	選択範囲
205	選択ハンドル
206	送る
207	区分線
208	設定
209	セットアップ
210	ショートカット
211	ショートカット ボタン
212	ショートカット アイコン
213	ショートカット キー
214	ショートカット キー コントロール
215	表示
216	シャットダウン
216	Windows の終了
217	単一選択リストボックス
218	サイズ

219	サイズ変更ハンドル
220	つまみ
221	スピン ボックス
222	境界の変更
223	分割バー
224	分割ボックス
225	［スタート］ボタン
226	スタートアップ フォルダ
227	ステータスバー
228	中止
228	停止
228	終了
228	解除
229	タブ コントロール
230	タップ
231	タスクバー
232	タスク対応ヘルプ
233	テンプレート
234	テキスト ボックス
235	タイトルバー
236	タイトルバーの文字
237	トグル キー
238	ツールバー
239	ツールのヒント
240	ツリー表示コントロール
241	種類
241	タイプ
242	入力
243	利用不可
244	元に戻す
245	アンインストール
245	削除
246	［表示］メニュー
247	埋め込み先編集
248	ビジュアル コントロール
249	ヘルプ
250	ウィンドウ
251	［ウィンドウ］メニュー
252	エクスプローラ
253	ウィザード
254	ワークブック
255	ワークグループ
256	ワークスペース
257	はい

Korean

1	정보	47	삭제	94	비활성 창
2	선택키	48	바탕 화면	95	잉크
3	장애인용	49	대상	96	잉크 편집
4	작업 핸들	50	대화 상자	97	입력 가능 영역
5	활성	51	장애	98	삽입 메뉴
6	선택 끝점	52	다중 선택	99	개체 삽입
7	활성 개체	53	고정	100	삽입 포인터
8	활성 창	54	문서	101	기울임꼴
9	사용하기 편리하도록 화면에	55	두 번 누르기	102	레이블
	표시	56	두 번 누르기	102	이름표
10	항상 위	57	끌기	103	가로 방향
11	선택 시작점	58	끌어서 놓기	104	원형으로 영역 선택
11	기준 위치점	59	나열형 콤보 상자	105	렌즈(제어)
12	적용	60	나열형 목록 상자	106	연결
13	자동 종료	61	나열형 메뉴	107	연결하다
14	자동 반복	62	편집	108	연결 대상
15	자동 연결	63	편집 메뉴	109	목록 상자
16	자동 이동	64	생략 기호	110	목록 표시(제어)
17	뒤로	65	포함된 개체	111	수동 연결
18	펜 단추	66	종료	112	전체 화면 표시
19	펜 두들기기	67	하위 수준 표시(개요)	113	전체 화면 표시 단추
20	상자형 편집 영역(제어)	68	파일 탐색	114	메뉴
21	찾아보기	69	선택 영역 확장	115	메뉴 표시줄
22	취소	70	선택 영역을 확장할 수 있는	116	메뉴 단추
23	계단식 메뉴		목록 상자	117	메뉴 항목
24	확인란	71	파일	118	메뉴 이름
25	확인 표시	72	파일 메뉴	119	메시지 상자
26	하위 문서 창	73	찾기	120	아이콘 표시
27	선택	74	다음 찾기	121	아이콘 표시 단추
28	누르기	75	찾을 문자열	122	혼합값
29	클립보드	76	폴더	123	모달
30	닫기	77	글꼴	124	모드
31	닫기 단추	78	글꼴 크기	125	모드리스
32	하위 수준 숨기기(개요)	79	글꼴 유형	126	수정키
33	열 머리글(제어)	80	기능키	127	마우스
34	콤보 상자	81	제스처	128	이동
35	명령 단추	82	모양	129	여기에 이동
36	다른 개체를 포함하는 개체	83	그룹 창	130	다중 문서 인터페이스
37	현재 상황에 맞는 도움말	84	핸들	131	다중 선택 목록 상자
38	상황에 맞는	84	조종	132	내 컴퓨터(아이콘)
39	제어	85	도움말	133	네트워크 환경(아이콘)
39	조절	86	도움말 메뉴	134	새 파일
40	복사	87	숨기기	135	다음
41	여기에 복사	88	계층적 선택	136	개체
42	단축 아이콘 만들기	89	쥐기	137	확인
43	여기에 단축 아이콘 만들기	90	핫 스폿	138	개체 연결 및 포함
44	잘라내기	91	핫 존	139	OLE 끌어서 놓기
45	기본값	92	아이콘	140	OLE 포함 개체
46	기본 단추	93	비활성	141	OLE 연결 개체

Korean

142	OLE 조건적 끌어서 놓기	180	잠깐 보기	220	슬라이더
143	열기	181	읽기 전용	221	스핀 상자
144	파일을 열 프로그램	182	인식	222	나눔
145	옵션 단추	183	휴지통(아이콘)	223	나눔줄
146	옵션 설정	184	재 실행	224	나눔 상자
147	꾸러미	185	영역 선택	225	시작 단추
148	쪽 설정	186	시스템 등록	226	시작 폴더
149	모음 창	187	반복	227	상태 표시줄
149	색상표 창	188	바꾸기	228	정지
150	틀	189	화면 복귀	229	탭 제어
151	상위 창	190	화면 복귀 단추	230	두들기기
152	암호	191	재시작	231	작업 표시줄
153	붙여넣기	192	재시도	232	작업 순서 도움말
154	연결하여 붙여넣기	193	서식 유지 입력란	233	서식 파일
155	단축 붙여넣기	194	실행	234	입력란
156	선택하여 붙여넣기	195	저장	235	제목 표시줄
157	경로	196	다른 이름으로 저장	236	제목 문자열
158	일시 중지	197	이동	237	전환키
159	펜	198	이동 화살표	238	도구 모음
160	재생	199	이동줄	239	도구 설명
161	플러그 앤 플레이(주변기기 자동 설치)	200	이동 위치표	240	트리 표시 제어
162	포인트	201	부속 창	241	유형
163	포인터	202	선택하다	241	종류
164	돌출 메뉴	203	전체 선택	242	입력한다
165	돌출 창	204	선택	243	사용 불가능
166	세로 방향	205	선택 핸들	244	실행 취소
167	(키) 두들기기	206	보내기	245	설치 삭제
168	(마우스 단추) 누르기	207	구분자	246	보기 메뉴
169	다른 개체를 포함하는 기본 개체	208	설정	247	포함된 위치를 현재 위치에서 편집
170	기본 창	209	설치	248	그래픽 정보 표시
171	인쇄	210	단축	249	설명
172	프린터	211	단축 단추	250	창
173	작업 진행 표시등(제어)	212	단축 아이콘	251	창 메뉴
174	프로젝트	213	단축키	252	파일 탐색기
175	등록 정보	214	단축키 제어	253	마법사
175	속성	215	표시	254	통합 문서
176	등록 정보 보기	215	보기	255	작업 그룹
177	등록 정보 쪽	216	시스템 종료	256	작업 영역
178	등록 정보 시트	217	단일 선택 목록 상자	257	예
179	등록 정보 제어	218	크기		
		219	창 크기 조절 핸들		

Norwegian

1	**Om**	54	dokument	107	koble	
2	tilgangstast	55	dobbeltklikke	108	**Lag kobling her**	
3	tilgjengelighet	56		109	listeboks	
4	handlingshåndtak	57	dra	110	listevisning (kontroll)	
5	aktiv	58	dra og slippe	111	manuell kobling	
6	markeringsavslutning	59	kombinasjonsboks	112	**Maksimer**	
7	aktivt objekt	60	rullegardinliste	113	maksimeringsknapp	
8	aktivt vindu	61	rullegardinmeny	114	meny	
9	verktøyselement	62	**Rediger**	115	menylinje	
10	**Alltid øverst**	63	**Rediger-menyen**	116	menyknapp	
11	forankringspunkt	64	ellipse	117	menyelement	
12	**Bruk**	65	innebygd objekt	118	menytittel	
13	automatisk avslutning	66	**Avslutt**	119	meldingsboks	
14	automatisk gjentagelse	67	utvide (en disposisjon)	120	**Minimer**	
15	automatisk kobling	68	**Utforsk**	121	minimeringsknapp	
16	automatisk rulling (autorulling)	69	utvidet merking	122	blandet verdi	
17	**Tilbake**	70	liste med utvidet merking	123	modal	
18		71	fil	124	modus	
19		72	Fil-menyen	125	ikke-modal	
20		73	**Søk etter**	126	modifiseringstast	
21	**Bla gjennom**	74	**Søk etter neste**	127	mus	
22	**Avbryt**	75	**Søk etter**	128	**Flytt**	
23	undermeny	76	mappe	129	**Flytt hit**	
24	avmerkingsboks	77	skrift	130	flerdokumentgrensesnitt (MDI)	
25	merke	78	skriftstørrelse	131	flervalgsliste	
26	undervindu	79	skriftstil	132	Min datamaskin (ikon)	
27	velge	80	funksjonstast	133	Andre maskiner (ikon)	
28	klikke	81		134	**Ny**	
29	utklippstavle	82		135	**Neste**	
30	**Lukk**	83	gruppeboks	136	objekt	
31	lukkeknapp	84	håndtak	137	**OK**	
32	skjule (disposisjon)	85	**Hjelp**	138	OLE	
33	kolonneoverskrift (kontroll)	86	Hjelp-menyen	139	OLE dra og slipp	
34	kombinasjonsboks	87	**Skjul**	140	innebygd OLE-objekt	
35	kommandoknapp	88	hierarkisk merking	141	koblet OLE-objekt	
36	beholder	89	holde	142	utvidet OLE dra og slipp	
37	kontekstavhengig hjelp	90	fokus	143	**Åpne**	
38	kontekstavhengig	91	fokuseringssone	144	**Åpne i**	
39	kontroll	92	ikon	145	alternativknapp	
40	**Kopier**	93	inaktiv	146	valgt alternativ	
41	**Kopier hit**	94	inaktivt vindu	147	pakke	
42	**Lag snarvei**	95		148	**Utskriftsformat**	
43	**Lag snarvei her**	96		149	palettvindu	
44	**Klipp ut**	97	inndatafokus	150	rute	
45	standard	98	**Sett inn-menyen**	151	hovedvindu	
46	standardknapp	99	**Sett inn objekt**	152	passord	
47	**Slett**	100	innsettingspunkt	153	**Lim inn**	
48	skrivebord	101	kursiv	154	**Lim inn kobling**	
49	mål	102	etikett	155	**Lim inn snarvei**	
50	dialogboks	103	liggende	156	**Lim inn utvalg**	
51	funksjonshemning	104		157	bane	
52	ikke sammenhengende utvalg	105		158	**Pause**	
53	forankre	106	kobling	159		

Norwegian

Polish

1	**Informacje**	52	wybór nieciągły	104		
2	klawisz dostępu	53	dokowanie	105		
3	dostępność	54	dokument	106	łącze	
4	obsługa	55	dwukrotne kliknięcie	107	łącz	
5	aktywny	56		108	**Łącz tutaj**	
6	aktywne zakończenie	57	przeciągnij	109	pole listy	
7	aktywny obiekt	58	przeciągnij i upuść	110	widok listy	
8	aktywne okno	59	rozwijalne pole kombi	111	łączenie ręczne	
9	zwieńczenie	60	pole listy rozwijalnej	112	**Maksymalizuj**	
10	**Zawsze na wierzchu**	61	menu rozwijalne	113	przycisk maksymalizacji	
11	punkt zakotwiczenia	62	**Edycja**	114	menu	
12	**Zastosuj**	63	**menu Edycja**	115	pasek menu	
13	autozakończenie	64	wielokropek	116	przycisk menu	
14	autopowtarzanie	65	obiekt osadzony	117	element menu	
15	łączenie automatyczne	66	**Zakończ**	118	tytuł menu	
16	automatyczne przewijanie	67	rozwiń	119	pole komunikatu	
	(autoprzewijanie)	68	**Eksploruj**	120	**Minimalizuj**	
17	**Wstecz**	69	wybór rozszerzony	121	przycisk minimalizacji	
18		70	pole listy z rozszerzonym wyborem	122	wartość mieszana	
19		71	plik	123	modalny	
20		72	menu Plik	124	tryb	
21	**Przeglądaj**	73	**Znajdź**	125	niemodalny	
22	**Anuluj**	74	**Znajdź następne**	126	klawisz modyfikujący	
23	menu kaskadowe	75	**Znajdź**	127	mysz	
24	pole wyboru	76	folder	128	**Przenieś**	
25	znacznik wyboru	77	czcionka	129	**Przenieś tutaj**	
26	okno podrzędne	78	rozmiar czcionki	130	interfejs wielodokumentowy	
27	wybierz	79	styl czcionki		(MDI)	
28	kliknij	80	klawisz funkcyjny	131	pole listy z wielokrotnym wyborem	
29	Schowek	81		132	Mój komputer (ikona)	
30	**Zamknij**	82		133	Otoczenie sieciowe (ikona)	
31	przycisk Zamknij	83	pole grupy	134	**Nowy**	
32	zwiń	84	uchwyt	135	**Następny**	
33	nagłówek kolumny (formant)	85	**Pomoc**	136	obiekt	
34	pole kombi	86	menu Pomoc	137	**OK**	
35	przycisk polecenia	87	**Ukryj**	138	OLE	
36	kontener	88	wybór hierarchiczny	139	OLE-przeciągnij i upuść	
37	pomoc kontekstowa	89	trzymaj	140	osadzony obiekt OLE	
38	kontekstowy	90	punkt aktywny	141	łączony obiekt OLE	
39	formant	91	strefa aktywna	142	OLE-niestandadowe przeciągnij i	
40	**Kopiuj**	92	ikona		upuść	
41	**Kopiuj tutaj**	93	nieaktywny	143	**Otwórz**	
42	**Utwórz skrót**	94	okno nieaktywne	144	**Otwórz z**	
43	**Utwórz skrót tutaj**	95		145	przycisk opcji	
44	**Wytnij**	96		146	zestaw opcji	
45	domyślny	97	fokus wejściowy	147	pakiet	
46	przycisk domyślny	98	**menu Wstaw**	148	**Ustawienia strony**	
47	**Usuń**	99	**Wstaw obiekt**	149	okno palety	
48	pulpit	100	punkt wstawiania	150	okienko	
49	przeznaczenie	101	kursywa	151	okno nadrzędne	
50	okno dialogowe	102	etykieta	152	hasło	
51	niepełnosprawność	103	pozioma	153	**Wklej**	

Polish

154	**Wklej łączenia**	189	**Przywróć**	224	pole podziału
155	**Wklej skrót**	190	przycisk Przywróć	225	przycisk Start
156	**Wklej specjalnie**	191	**Wznów**	226	folder startowy
157	ścieżka	192	**Ponów próbę**	227	pasek stanu
158	**Pauza**	193	pole tekstu RTF	228	**Zatrzymaj**
159		194	**Uruchom**	229	formant karty
160	**Odtwarzaj**	195	**Zapisz**	230	
161	Plug and Play	196	**Zapisz jako**	231	pasek zadań
162	punkt	197	przewiń	232	Pomoc zorientowana zadaniowo
163	wskaźnik	198	strzałka przewijania	233	szablon
164	menu podręczne	199	pasek przewijania	234	pole tekstowe
165	okno podręczne	200	pole przewijania	235	pasek tytułu
166	pionowa	201	okno podrzędne	236	tekst tytułu
167	naciśnij (klawisz)	202	zaznacz	237	klawisz przełącznikowy
168	naciśnij (i przytrzymaj przycisk)	203	**Zaznacz wszystko**	238	pasek narzędzi
169	główny kontener	204	zaznaczenie	239	etykietka narzędziowa
170	główne okno	205	uchwyt zaznaczenia	240	formant widoku drzewa
171	**Drukuj**	206	**Wyślij do**	241	typ
172	drukarka	207	separator	242	wpisz
173	wskaźnik postępu	208	**Ustawienia**	243	niedostępny
174	projekt	209	**Instalator**	244	**Cofnij**
175	**Właściwości**	210	skrót	245	**Odinstaluj**
176	inspektor właściwości	211	przycisk skrótu	246	**menu Widok**
177	strona właściwości	212	ikona skrótu	247	edycja wizualna
178	arkusz właściwości	213	klawisz skrótu	248	formant graficzny
179	formant arkusza właściwości	214	formant klawisza skrótu	249	**Co to jest?**
180	**Krótki przegląd**	215	**Pokaż**	250	okno
181	tylko-odczyt	216	**Zamknięcie systemu**	251	**menu Okno**
182		217	pole listy z pojedynczym wyborem	252	Eksplorator Windows
183	Kosz (ikona)	218	**Rozmiar**	253	kreator
184	**Ponów**	219	uchwyt rozmiaru	254	skoroszyt
185	wybór obszaru	220	suwak	255	grupa robocza
186	rejestracja	221	pokrętło	256	obszar roboczy
187	**Powtórz**	222	**Podział**	257	**Tak**
188	**Zamień**	223	pasek podziału		

Portuguese

1	**Acerca de**		seleccionar	109	caixa de listagem
2	tecla de acesso	53	ancorar	110	vista da lista (controlo)
3	acessibilidade	54	documento	111	ligação manual
4	ponto de controlo de acção	55	duplo clique, fazer duplo clique	112	**Maximizar**
5	activo(s)/a(s)		(sobre)	113	botão Maximizar
6	extremidade activa	57	arrastar	114	menu
7	objecto activo	58	arrastar e largar	115	barra de menus
8	janela activa	59	caixa de combinação pendente	116	botão de menu
9	ornamento	60	caixa de listagem pendente	117	item de menu
10	**Sempre Visível**	61	menu pendente	118	título do menu
11	ponto de fixação	62	**Editar**	119	caixa da mensagem
12	**Aplicar**	63	**menu Editar**	120	**Minimizar**
13	saída automática	64	elipse (if graphic object), reticências	121	botão Minimizar
14	repetição automática		(if punctuation)	122	valor misto
15	ligação automática	65	objecto incorporado	123	modal
16	rolamento automático	66	**Sair**	124	modo
17	**Retroceder**	67	expandir (um destaque)	125	sem modo
18		68	**Explorar**	126	tecla modificadora
19		69	selecção alargada	127	rato
20		70	caixa de listagem de selecção	128	**Mover**
21	**Procurar**		alargada	129	**Mover Aqui**
22	**Cancelar**	71	ficheiro	130	interface de múltiplos documentos
23	menu em cascata	72	menu Ficheiro		(MDI, multiple document interface)
24	caixa de verificação	73	**Localizar**	131	caixa de listagem de selecção
25	marca de verificação	74	**Localizar Seguinte**		múltipla
26	janela filha	75	**Localizar**	132	O Meu Computador (ícone)
27	seleccionar	76	pasta	133	Redondezas na Rede (ícone)
28	clique, fazer clique (sobre)	77	tipo de letra	134	**Novo**
29	Área de Transferência	78	tamanho do tipo de letra	135	**Seguinte**
30	**Fechar**	79	estilo do tipo de letra	136	objecto
31	botão Fechar	80	tecla de função	137	**OK**
32	fechar (destaque)	83	caixa de grupo	138	OLE (ligação e incorporação de
33	título de coluna (controlo)	84	ponto de controlo		objectos)
34	caixa de combinação	85	**Ajuda**	139	arrastar e largar OLE
35	botão de comando	86	menu Ajuda	140	objecto incorporado por OLE
36	recipiente, depósito	87	**Ocultar**	141	objecto ligado por OLE
37	ajuda contextual	88	selecção hierárquica	142	arrastar e largar OLE não
38	contextual	89	manter premido(s)/a(s)		predefinido
39	controlo	90	ponto interactivo	143	**Abrir**
40	**Copiar**	91	área interactiva	144	**Abrir Com**
41	**Copiar Aqui**	92	ícone	145	botão de opção
42	**Criar Atalho**	93	inactivo(s)/a(s)	146	conjunto de opções
43	**Criar Atalho Aqui**	94	janela inactiva	147	conjunto de programas
44	**Cortar**	97	foco de introdução	148	**Configurar Página**
45	predefinir; predefinido;	98	**menu Inserir**	149	janela da paleta
	predefinição; predefinições	99	**Inserir Objecto**	150	painel
46	botão predefinido	100	ponto de inserção	151	janela mãe
47	**Eliminar**	101	itálico	152	palavra-passe
48	ambiente de trabalho	102	etiqueta/nome	153	**Colar**
49	destino	103	horizontal	154	**Colar Ligação**
50	caixa de diálogo	106	ligação	155	**Colar Atalho**
51	incapacidade	107	ligar	156	**Colar Especial**
52	selecção descontínua (n.),	108	**Ligar Aqui**	157	caminho

Portuguese

158	**Pausa/Interromper**	191	**Continuar**	225	botão Iniciar
159		192	**Repetir/Tentar de Novo**	226	pasta de Arranque
160	**Reproduzir**	193	caixa de texto melhorado	227	barra de estado
161	Plug and Play	194	**Executar**	228	**Parar**
162	ponto	195	**Guardar**	229	controlo de tabulação
163	ponteiro	196	**Guardar Como**	230	
164	menu de sobreposição	197	rolar	231	barra de tarefas
165	janela de sobreposição	198	seta de deslocamento	232	Ajuda relacionada com a tarefa
166	vertical	199	barra de deslocamento	233	modelo
167	premir (uma tecla)	200	caixa de deslocamento	234	caixa de texto
168	premir (e manter premido um botão do rato)	201	janela secundária	235	barra de título
		202	seleccionar	236	texto do título
169	recipiente principal	203	**Seleccionar Tudo**	237	tecla de comutação
170	janela principal	204	selecção	238	barra de ferramentas
171	**Imprimir**	205	ponto de controlo de selecção	239	descrição
172	impressora	206	**Enviar Para**	240	controlo da vista da árvore
173	indicador de progresso (controlo)	207	separador	241	tipo (n.)
174	projecto	208	**Definições**	242	escrever (v.)
175	**Propriedades**	209	**Configurar**	243	indisponível
176	inspector de propriedades	210	atalho	244	**Anular**
177	página de propriedades	211	botão de atalho	245	**Desinstalar**
178	folha de propriedades	212	ícone de atalho	246	**menu Ver**
179	controlo de folha de propriedades	213	tecla de atalho	247	edição visual
180	**Apresentação**	214	controlo de teclas de atalho	248	controlo de propriedades gráficas
181	Só de Leitura	215	**Mostrar**	249	**O Que É Isto?**
182		216	**Encerrar**	250	janela
183	Reciclagem (ícone)	217	caixa de listagem de selecção única	251	**menu Janela**
184	**Repetir**	218	**Dimensionar (v.), Tamanho (n.)**	252	Explorador do Windows
185	selecção de grupo	219	controlo de dimensionamento	253	assistente
186	registo	220	controlo de escala	254	(o) livro
187	**Repetir**	221	caixa de controlo rotativo	255	grupo de trabalho
188	**Substituir**	222	**Dividir**	256	área de trabalho
189	**Restaurar**	223	barra de divisão	257	**Sim**
190	botão Restaurar	224	caixa de divisão		

Portuguese – Brazil

1	**Sobre**	52	seleção descontínua (n.),		rótulo
2	tecla de acesso		descontinuar seleção (v.)	103	paisagem
3	acessibilidade	53	encaixar	104	
4	alças de manipulação	54	documento	105	
5	ativo(a)	55	clicar duas vezes	106	vínculo (n.)
6	fim ativo	56		107	vincular (v.)
7	objeto ativo	57	arrastar	108	**Vincular Aqui**
8	janela ativa	58	arrastar-e-soltar	109	caixa de listagem
9	controle de opções gráficas	59	caixa de combinação suspensa	110	modo de lista (controle)
10	**Sempre Visível**	60	caixa de listagem suspensa	111	vínculo manual
11	ponto de âncora	61	menu suspenso	112	**Maximizar**
12	**Aplicar**	62	**Editar**	113	botão Maximizar
13	saída automática (n.), sair	63	**Menu Editar**	114	menu
	automaticamente (v.)	64	reticências	115	barra de menu
14	repetição automática (n.), repetir	65	objeto incorporado	116	botão de menu
	automaticamente (v.)	66	**Sair**	117	item de menu
15	vínculo automático	67	expandir (tópicos)	118	título de menu
16	rolagem automática	68	**Explorar**	119	caixa de mensagem
17	**Voltar**	69	seleção estendida	120	**Minimizar**
18		70	caixa de listagem de seleção	121	botão Minimizar
19			estendida	122	valor misto
20		71	arquivo	123	modal
21	**Procurar**	72	Menu Arquivo	124	modo
22	**Cancelar**	73	**Localizar**	125	sem modo
23	menu em cascata	74	**Localizar Próxima**	126	tecla de modificação
24	caixa de verificação	75	**Localizar**	127	mouse
25	marca de verificação	76	pasta	128	**Mover**
26	janela filho	77	fonte	129	**Mover Aqui**
27	escolher	78	tamanho da fonte	130	interface de múltiplos documentos
28	clicar	79	estilo da fonte		(MDI)
29	Área de Transferência	80	tecla de função	131	caixa de listagem de seleção
30	**Fechar**	81			múltipla
31	botão Fechar	82		132	Meu Computador (ícone)
32	ocultar (tópicos)	83	caixa de grupo	133	Ambiente de Rede (ícone)
33	cabeçalho da coluna (controle)	84	alças	134	**Novo**
34	caixa de combinação	85	**Ajuda**	135	**Avançar**
35	botão de comando	86	Menu Ajuda	136	objeto
36	recipiente	87	**Ocultar**	137	**OK**
37	Ajuda relacionada ao contexto	88	seleção hierárquica	138	OLE
38	relacionado(a) ao contexto	89	manter pressionado(a)	139	arrastar-e-soltar OLE
39	controle	90	ponto interativo	140	objeto incorporado OLE
40	**Copiar**	91	área interativa	141	objeto vinculado OLE
41	**Copiar Aqui**	92	ícone	142	arrastar-e-soltar OLE não padrão
42	**Criar Atalho**	93	inativo(a)	143	**Abrir**
43	**Criar Atalho Aqui**	94	janela inativa	144	**Abrir Com**
44	**Recortar**	95		145	botão de opção
45	padrão	96		146	conjunto de opções
46	botão padrão	97	foco de entrada	147	pacote
47	**Excluir**	98	**Menu Inserir**	148	**Configurar Página**
48	área de trabalho	99	**Inserir Objeto**	149	janela de paleta
49	destino	100	ponto de inserção	150	painel
50	caixa de diálogo	101	itálico	151	janela pai
51	incapacidade	102	according to context: nome, etiqueta,	152	senha

Portuguese – Brazil

153	**Colar**	188	**Substituir**	224	caixa de divisão
154	**Colar Vínculo**	189	**Restaurar**	225	botão Iniciar
155	**Colar Atalho**	190	botão Restaurar	226	pasta Iniciar
156	**Colar Especial**	191	**Continuar**	227	barra de status
157	caminho	192	**Repetir**	228	**Parar**
158	**Pausa**	193	caixa de rich-text	229	controle de tabulação (if it refers to tabul.), controle de guias (if it refers to 'tabs' in a dial. box)
159		194	**Executar**		
160	**Reproduzir; Jogar**	195	**Salvar**		
161	Plug and Play	196	**Salvar Como**	230	
162	ponto	197	rolar	231	barra de tarefas
163	ponteiro	198	seta de rolagem	232	Ajuda relacionada à tarefa
164	menu pop-up	199	barra de rolagem	233	modelo
165	janela pop-up	200	caixa de rolagem	234	caixa de texto
166	retrato	201	janela secundária	235	barra de título
167	pressione (uma tecla)	202	selecionar	236	texto do título
168	pressione (e mantenha pressionado o botão do mouse)	203	**Selecionar Tudo**	237	tecla de alternância
		204	seleção	238	barra de ferramentas
169	recipiente primário	205	alças de seleção	239	descrição de ferramenta
170	janela primária	206	**Enviar Para**	240	modo de árvore (controle)
171	**Imprimir**	207	separador	241	tipo
172	impressora	208	**Configurações**	242	digitar
173	indicador de progresso (controle)	209	**Programa de Instalação**	243	não disponível
174	projeto	210	atalho	244	**Desfazer**
175	**Propriedades**	211	botão de atalho	245	**Desinstalar**
176	inspetor de propriedades	212	ícone de atalho	246	**Menu Exibir**
177	página de propriedades	213	tecla de atalho	247	edição visual
178	folha de propriedades	214	controle de tecla de atalho	248	controle de entalhe
179	controle da folha de propriedades	215	**Mostrar**	249	**O Que É Isto?**
180	**Visualização Rápida**	216	**Desligar**	250	janela
181	somente leitura	217	caixa de listagem de seleção única	251	**Menu Janela**
182		218	**Tamanho**	252	Windows Explorer
183	Lixeira (ícone)	219	alças de dimensionamento	253	assistente
184	**Refazer**	220	controle deslizante	254	pasta de trabalho
185	seleção de região	221	caixa de rotação	255	grupo de trabalho
186	registro	222	**Divisão (n.), Dividir (v.)**	256	área de trabalho
187	**Repetir**	223	barra de divisão	257	**Sim**

Russian

1	О программе	46	основная кнопка	87	Скрыть
2	клавиша доступа	47	Удалить	88	Иерархическое выделение
3	доступность; легкость использования	48	рабочий стол	89	удерживать
		49	место назначения, получатель	90	острие
4	ручка	50	диалоговое окно	91	область взаимодействия
5	активный	51	физический недостаток	92	значок
6	активный край	52	несвязное выделение	93	неактивный
7	активный объект	53	закрепить; пристыковать	94	неактивное окно
8	активное окно	54	документ	95	
9	элемент обрамления	55	(v.) дважды щелкнуть; дважды нажать кнопку мыши; (n.) двойной щелчок;двойное нажатие кнопки мыши	96	
10	Поверх остальных[окон]			97	фокус ввода
11	начало выделения			98	Вставка
12	Применить			99	Вставить объект
13	автопереход; поле с автоматическим переходом	56		100	курсор
		57	1) перетащить (объект); 2) протащить (указатель по списку, тексту и т.п.; линию); 3) выделить (фрагмент текста, элементы списка, объекты и т.п.); 4) переместить указатель при нажатой кнопке мыши (если ни одно из предыдущих выражений не подходит)	101	наклонное (начертание); курсивное
14	самоповторяющийся (событие и т.п.)			102	наклейка; подпись
15	автоматически обновляемая связь			103	альбомная
				104	
16	автопрокрутка			105	
17	Назад			106	связь
18				107	связать
19				108	Связать здесь
20		58	перетащить [с помощью мыши]	109	список
21	Обзор (кнопка); обзор, просмотр	59	поле с раскрывающимся списком	110	список
		60	раскрывающийся список	111	связь, обновляемая вручную
22	Отмена (кнопка)	61	меню; раскрывающееся меню	112	Развернуть
	Отменить (команда)	62	править, изменять	113	кнопка развертывания окна
23	подменю	63	Правка	114	меню
24	флажок	64	многоточие	115	строка меню
25	отметка; галочка	65	встроенный объект	116	кнопка раскрытия меню
26	дочернее окно	66	Выход	117	пункт меню
27	выбрать	67	развернуть (иерархию, структуру)	118	заглавие меню
28	(v.) щелкнуть; нажать кнопку мыши; выбрать с помощью мыши; (n.) щелчок; нажатие кнопки мыши	68	Просмотр	119	окно сообщения
		69	расширенное выделение	120	Свернуть
		70	список с расширенным выделением	121	Кнопка свертывания [окна]
29	Буфер обмена			122	смешанное (состояние элемента интерфейса)
30	Закрыть	71	файл		
31	Кнопка закрытия окна	72	Документ; Файл	123	модальный
32	свернуть (структуру)	73	Найти	124	режим
33	заголовок столбца	74	Поиск далее	125	немодальный
34	поле со списком	75	Образец	126	преобразующая клавиша
35	кнопка	76	папка	127	мышь
36	[объект-]контейнер	77	шрифт	128	Переместить
37	контекстная справка	78	размер шрифта	129	Переместить сюда
38	контекстный	79	начертание	130	многодокументная среда (MDI)
39	элемент управления	80	функциональная клавиша		
40	Копировать	81		131	список с множественным выбором
41	Копировать сюда	82			
42	Создать ярлык	83	рамка группы, группа	132	Мой компьютер
43	Создать ярлык здесь	84	ручка	133	Сетевая окрестность
44	Вырезать	85	Справка	134	Создать
45	используемый по умолчанию; предустановленный	86	?	135	Далее (Next/Back);Следующий (Next/Previous)
				136	объект

Russian

137 ОК (русскиебуквы)
138 OLE
139 OLE-перетаскивание
140 внедренный OLE-объект
141 связанный OLE-объект
142 условное OLE-перетаскивание
143 Открыть
144 Открытьс помощью
145 переключатель
146 параметр установлен
147 сверток
148 Макетстраницы
149 окно палитры
150 область (окна)
151 родительское окно
152 пароль
153 Вставить
154 Вставитьсвязь
155 Вставитьярлык
156 Специальнаявставка
157 путь
158 Пауза
159
160 Воспроизведение
161 [самонастраиваемое]
устройство   (Plug and Play)
162 указать на; подвести указатель
к; установить указатель на
163 указатель
164 всплывающее меню
165 всплывающее окно
166 книжная (ориентация)
167 нажать (клавишу)
168 нажать и удержать кнопку
мыши
169 главный контейнер
170 главное окно
171 Печать
172 принтер
173 индикатор выполнения,
показатель выполнения
174 проект
175 Свойства
176 инспектор свойств объекта
177 карточка свойств

178 окно свойств
179 элемент управления из
таблицы свойств
180 Быстрыйпросмотр
181 только для чтения, только
чтение (флажок)
182
183 Корзина
184 Вернуть
185 охват
186 [системный] реестр
187 Повторить
188 Заменить
189 Восстановить
190 Кнопка восстановления
размеров окна
191 Продолжить
192 Повтор(кнопка); повторить
193 форматируемое поле
194 Выполнить
195 Сохранить
196 Сохранитькак
197 прокручивать
198 кнопка прокрутки
199 полоса прокрутки
200 бегунок
201 вспомогательное окно
202 выбрать; выделить
203 Выделитьвсе
204 выделение; выделенные
объекты
205 ручка выделения
206 Отправить
207 разделитель
208 Настройка
209 Установка
210 ярлык
211 кнопка действия
212 значок ярлыка, ярлык
213 быстрая клавиша; сочетание
клавиш; клавиши быстрого
вызова
214 поле определения сочетания
клавиш
215 Вывести, Отобразить

Показать
216 Завершениеработы
217 простой список
218 Размер
219 ручка размера
220 ползунок
221 счетчик
222 Разбить
223 линия разбивки
224 вешка разбивки
225 кнопка Пуск
226 Загружаемые при запуске;
Автозапуск
227 строка состояния
228 Останов, Остановить, Стоп
229 ярлычок
230
231 панель задач
232 справка по задачам
233 шаблон
234 поле
235 заголовок окна
236 текст заголовка
237 переключатель; клавиша-
переключатель
238 панель инструментов
239 всплывающая подсказка
240 средство просмотра дерева
241 тип
242 вводить
243 недоступный
244 Отменить
245 Удалить
246 Вид
247 правка на месте
248 клетка
249 Что это такое?
250 окно
251 Окно
252 Проводник
253 мастер
254 рабочая книга
255 рабочая группа
256 рабочее пространство
257 Да

Slovenian

1	**Vizitka**	53	združitev	105		
2	tipka za dostop	54	dokument	106	povezava	
3	Pripomočki za invalide	55	dvoklik	107	povezati	
4	oprimek dejanja	56		108	**Poveži sem**	
5	aktivno	57	povleči	109	okence seznama	
6	aktivni konec	58	povleči in spustiti	110	seznamski pogled (krmilo)	
7	aktivni predmet	59	spustni kombinirani seznam	111	ročna povezava	
8	aktivno okno	60	okence za spustni seznam	112	**Maksimiraj**	
9	prirobnik	61	spustni meni	113	gumb Maksimiraj	
10	**Vedno na vrhu**	62	**Uredi**	114	meni	
11	sidrišče	63	**meni Uredi**	115	menijska vrstica	
12	**Uporabi**	64	tri pike	116	menijski gumb	
13	samodejni izhod	65	vdelani predmet	117	menijski element	
14	samodejna ponovitev	66	**Izhod**	118	naslov menija	
15	samodejna povezava	67	razširiti (oris)	119	sporočilno okno	
16	samodejno drsenje (samodrsenje)	68	**Raziskuj**	120	**Minimiraj**	
17	**Nazaj**	69	razširjeni izbor	121	gumb Minimiraj	
18		70	okence seznama za razširjeni izbor	122	neenotno	
19		71	datoteka	123	načinovno	
20		72	meni Datoteka	124	način	
21	**Prebrskaj**	73	**Najdi**	125	breznačinovno	
22	**Prekliči**	74	**Nadaljuj iskanje**	126	modifikacijska tipka	
23	stopničasti meni	75	**Najdi (Kaj)**	127	miška	
24	potrditveno polje	76	mapa	128	**Premakni**	
25	potrditveni znak	77	pisava	129	**Premakni sem**	
26	podrejeno okno	78	velikost pisave	130	večdokumentni vmesnik (MDI)	
27	izbrati	79	slog pisave	131	okence seznama za večkratni izbor	
28	klikniti	80	funkcijska tipka	132	Moj računalnik (ikona)	
29	odložišče	81		133	Omrežna soseščina (ikona)	
30	**Zapri**	82		134	**Novi**	
31	gumb Zapri	83	okvirček skupine	135	**Naslednji / Naprej**	
32	strniti (oris)	84	oprimek	136	predmet	
33	naslov stolpca (krmilo)	85	**Pomoč**	137	**V redu**	
34	kombinirani seznam	86	meni Pomoč	138	OLE	
35	ukazni gumb	87	**Skrij**	139	OLE povleci in spusti	
36	vsebnik	88	hierarhični izbor	140	OLE vdelan predmet	
37	pomensko občutljiva pomoč	89	zadržati	141	OLE povezan predmet	
38	pomensko skladno	90	občutljiva točka	142	OLE neprivzeto povleci in spusti	
39	krmilo	91	občutljivo področje	143	**Odpri**	
40	**Kopiraj**	92	ikona	144	**Odpri z**	
41	**Kopiraj sem**	93	neaktivno	145	izbirni gumb	
42	**Ustvari bližnjico**	94	neaktivno okno	146	možnost je izbrana	
43	**Ustvari bližnjico tu**	95		147	paket	
44	**Izreži**	96		148	**Priprava strani**	
45	privzeto	97	vnosno žarišče	149	paletno okno	
46	privzeti gumb	98	**meni Vstavi**	150	podokno	
47	**Izbriši**	99	**Vstavi predmet**	151	nadrejeno okno	
48	namizje	100	mesto vstavljanja	152	geslo	
49	cilj	101	ležeče (pisava)	153	**Prilepi**	
50	pogovorno okno	102	oznaka	154	**Prilepi s povezavo**	
51	telesna okvara	103	ležeče (format)	155	**Prilepi bližnjico**	
52	nepovezani izbor	104		156	**Posebno lepljenje**	

Slovenian

157	pot	191	**Nadaljuj**	225	gumb Start
158	**Premor / Začasna prekinitev**	192	**Poskusi znova**	226	Mapa - Zagon
159		193	vnosno polje za obogateno besedilo	227	statusna vrstica
160	**Predvajaj**	194	**Poženi**	228	**Ustavi**
161	Plug and Play	195	**Shrani**	229	jeziček
162	pokazati	196	**Shrani kot**	230	
163	kazalec	197	drseti	231	opravilna vrstica
164	pojavni meni	198	drsna puščica	232	opravilno usmerjena pomoč
165	pojavno okno	199	drsni trak	233	predloga
166	pokončno	200	drsnik	234	vnosno polje
167	pritisniti (tipko)	201	dodatno okno	235	naslovna vrstica
168	pritisniti (in zadržati miškino tipko)	202	izbrati	236	besedilo naslova
169	osnovni vsebnik	203	**Izberi vse**	237	preklopna tipka
170	osnovno okno	204	izbor	238	orodna vrstica
171	**Tiskaj**	205	izbirni oprimek	239	opis orodja
172	tiskalnik	206	**Pošlji**	240	krmilo za drevesni pogled
173	kazalnik poteka (krmilo)	207	ločilo	241	vrsta
174	projicirati	208	**Nastavitve**	242	natipkati
175	**Lastnosti**	209	**Priprava**	243	ni na voljo
176	prikaz lastnosti	210	bližnjica	244	**Razveljavi**
177	stran z lastnostmi	211	gumb bližnjice	245	**Odstrani**
178	okno z lastnostmi	212	ikona bližnjice	246	**meni Pogled**
179	krmilo v oknu z lastnostmi	213	tipka bližnjice	247	neposredno urejanje
180	**Hitri vpogled**	214	krmilo za tipko bližnjice	248	krmilo za grafično izbiro
181	samo za branje	215	**Pokaži**	249	**Kaj je to?**
182		216	**Zaustavitev sistema**	250	okno
183	Koš (ikona)	217	okence seznama za enojno izbiro	251	**meni Okno**
184	**Uveljavi**	218	**Velikost**	252	Raziskovalec
185	izbira področja	219	velikostni oprimek	253	čarovnik
186	register	220	drsna letev	254	delovni zvezek
187	**Ponovi**	221	vrtilno polje	255	delovna skupina
188	**Zamenjaj**	222	**Razdeli**	256	delovni prostor
189	**Obnovi**	223	delilna črta	257	**Da**
190	gumb Obnovi	224	okenski delilnik		

Spanish

1	**Acerca de**	54	documento	106	vínculo (n.)	
2	tecla de acceso	55	hacer doble clic	107	vincular (v.)	
3	accesibilidad	56	puntear dos veces	108	**Vincular aquí**	
4	controlador de acciones	57	arrastrar	109	cuadro de lista	
5	activo	58	arrastrar y colocar	110	presentación de iconos or "ver lista"	
6	fin de la selección activa	59	cuadro combinado desplegable		depending on context.	
7	objeto activo	60	cuadro de lista desplegable	111	vínculo manual	
8	ventana activa	61	menú desplegable	112	**Maximizar**	
9	opción gráfica	62	**Edición**	113	botón de maximizar	
10	**Siempre visible**	63	**menú Edición**	114	menú	
11	inicio de la selección activa	64	puntos suspensivos	115	barra de menús	
12	**Aplicar**	65	objeto incrustado	116	botón de menú	
13	salida automática	66	**Salir**	117	elemento de menú	
14	repetición automática	67	expandir (un esquema)	118	título de menú	
15	vínculo automático	68	**Explorar**	119	cuadro de mensaje	
16	desplazamiento automático	69	selección extendida	120	**Minimizar**	
17	**Atrás**	70	cuadro de lista de selección	121	botón de minimizar	
18	botón del lápiz		extendida	122	valores mezclados	
19	puntear con el botón presionado	71	archivo	123	modal	
20	edición en casilla (control)	72	menú Archivo	124	modo	
21	**Examinar**	73	**Buscar**	125	sin modo	
22	**Cancelar**	74	**Buscar siguiente**	126	tecla modificadora	
23	menú en cascada	75	**Buscar**	127	mouse	
24	casilla de verificación	76	carpeta	128	**Mover**	
25	marca de verificación	77	fuente	129	**Mover aquí**	
26	ventana secundaria	78	tamaño de fuente	130	interfaz de documentos múltiples	
27	elegir	79	estilo de fuente		(MDI)	
28	hacer clic	80	tecla de función	131	cuadro de lista de selección múltiple	
29	Portapapeles	81	signo	132	Mi PC (icono)	
30	Cerrar	82	símbolo gráfico	133	Entorno de red (icono)	
31	botón "Cerrar"	83	cuadro de grupo	134	**Nuevo**	
32	contraer (esquema)	84	controlar (v.) controlador (n.)	135	**Siguiente**	
33	encabezado de columna (control)	85	**Ayuda**	136	objeto	
34	cuadro combinado	86	menú Ayuda	137	**Aceptar**	
35	botón de comando	87	**Ocultar**	138	OLE	
36	contenedor	88	selección jerárquica	139	Arrastrar y colocar de OLE	
37	ayuda interactiva	89	mantener presionado	140	Objeto incrustado de OLE	
38	contextual	90	punto interactivo	141	Objeto vinculado de OLE	
39	control	91	zona interactiva	142	Arrastrar y colocar no	
40	**Copiar**	92	icono		predeterminado de OLE	
41	**Copiar aquí**	93	inactivo	143	**Abrir**	
42	**Crear acceso directo**	94	ventana inactiva	144	**Abrir con**	
43	**Crear acceso directo aquí**	95	trazo	145	botón de opción	
44	**Cortar**	96	editor de trazos	146	opción establecida	
45	predeterminado	97	zona de entrada [de datos]	147	paquete	
46	botón predeterminado	98	**menú Insertar**	148	**Preparar página**	
47	**Eliminar**	99	**Insertar objeto**	149	ventana de paleta	
48	escritorio	100	punto de inserción	150	panel	
49	destino	101	cursiva	151	ventana principal	
50	cuadro de diálogo	102	etiqueta	152	contraseña	
51	Discapacidades	103	horizontal	153	**Pegar**	
52	selección disjunta	104	punteo en la selección	154	**Pegar vínculo**	
53	acoplar	105	lente (control)	155	**Pegar acceso directo**	

Spanish

Swedish

1	**Om**	53	docka	106	länk
2	snabbtangent	54	dokument	107	länka
3	Hjälpmedel (ikonen	55	dubbelklicka på	108	**Länka hit**
	Accessibility)/tillgänglighet	56		109	listruta
4	funktionshandtag	57	dra	110	listvy
5	aktiv	58	dra och släpp	111	manuell länk
6	aktiv slutpunkt	59	nedrullningsbar kombinationsruta	112	**Maximera**
7	aktivt objekt	60	nedrullningsbar listruta	113	maximeringsknapp
8	aktivt fönster	61	nedrullningsbar meny	114	meny
9	fönsterfält	62	**Redigera**	115	menyrad
10	**Alltid överst**	63	**Redigera-meny**	116	menyknapp
11	startpunkt	64	punkter	117	menyobjekt
12	**Verkställ**	65	inbäddat objekt	118	menytitel
13	flytta automatiskt	66	**Avsluta**	119	meddelanderuta
14	upprepa automatiskt	67	expandera	120	**Minimera**
15	automatisk länk	68	**Utforska**	121	minimeringsknapp
16	automatisk rullning	69	utökad markering	122	blandvärde
17	**Föregående**	70	listruta för utökad markering	123	modal
18		71	fil	124	läge
19		72	Arkiv-meny	125	icke-modal
20		73	**Sök**	126	ändringstangent
21	**Bläddra**	74	**Sök nästa**	127	mus
22	**Avbryt**	75	**Sök efter**	128	**Flytta**
23	undermeny	76	mapp	129	**Flytta hit**
24	kryssruta	77	teckensnitt	130	multiple document interface (MDI)
25	markering	78	teckenstorlek	131	listruta för multipel markering
26	underfönster	79	teckenstil	132	Den här datorn
27	välj	80	funktionstangent	133	Nätverket
28	klicka	81		134	**Ny/nytt**
29	Urklipp	82		135	**Nästa**
30	**Stäng**	83	gruppruta	136	objekt
31	stängningsknapp	84	handtag	137	**OK**
32	komprimera	85	**Hjälp**	138	OLE
33	kolumnrubrik	86	Hjälp-meny	139	dra och släpp (OLE)
34	kombinationsruta	87	**Dölj**	140	inbäddat objekt (OLE)
35	kommandoknapp	88	hierarkisk markering	141	länkat objekt (OLE)
36	behållare	89	hålla ned	142	utökat dra och släpp (OLE)
37	sammanhangsberoende hjälp	90	aktiv punkt	143	**Öppna**
38	sammanhangsberoende	91	aktiveringszon	144	**Öppna med**
39	kontroll	92	ikon	145	alternativknapp
40	**Kopiera**	93	inaktiv	146	valt alternativ
41	**Kopiera hit**	94	inaktivt fönster	147	paket
42	**Skapa genväg**	95		148	**Utskriftsformat**
43	**Skapa genväg här**	96		149	palettfönster
44	**Klipp ut**	97	inmatningsfokus	150	fönsterruta
45	standard	98	**Infoga-meny**	151	moderfönster
46	standardknapp	99	**Infoga objekt**	152	lösenord
47	**Ta bort**	100	insättningspunkt	153	**Klistra in**
48	skrivbord	101	kursiv	154	**Klistra in länk**
49	mål	102	titel	155	**Klistra in genväg**
50	dialogruta	103	liggande	156	**Klistra in special**
51	oförmåga	104		157	sökväg
52	osammanhängande markering	105		158	**Paus**

Swedish

Turkish

1	**Hakkında**	54	belge	107	bağla
2	erişim tuşu	55	çift tıklama	108	**Buraya Bağla**
3	erişilebilirlik	56		109	liste kutusu
4	eylem tutacağı	57	sürüklemek	110	liste görünümü (denetim)
5	etkin	58	sürükle ve bırak	111	el ile bağlantı
6	bitiş ucu	59	açılan bileşim kutusu	112	**Ekranı Kapla**
7	etkin nesne	60	açılan liste kutusu	113	ekranı kaplama düğmesi
8	etkin pencere	61	açılan menü	114	menü
9	takı	62	**Düzenle**	115	menü çubuğu
10	**Devamlı Üstte**	63	**Düzen menüsü**	116	menü düğmesi
11	başlangıç ucu	64	üç nokta	117	menü öğesi
12	**Uygula**	65	katılmış nesne	118	menü başlığı
13	otomatik çıkış	66	**Çıkış**	119	ileti kutusu
14	otomatik yineleme	67	(seviye) genişlet	120	**Simge Durumuna Küçült**
15	otomatik bağlantı	68	**Araştır**	121	simge dürumuna küçültme düğmesi
16	otomatik kaydırma	69	genişletilmiş seçim	122	karışık değer
17	**Geri**	70	genişletilmiş seçim listesi kutusu	123	kipsel
18		71	dosya	124	kip
19		72	Dosya menüsü	125	kipsiz
20		73	**Bul**	126	değiştirici tuş
21	**Gözat**	74	**Sonrakini Bul**	127	fare
22	**İptal Et**	75	**Ne Bulunsun**	128	**Taşı**
23	basamaklı menü	76	klasör	129	**Buraya Taşı**
24	onay kutusu	77	yazıtipi	130	Çoklu Belge Arabirimi
25	onay imi	78	yazıtipi boyutu	131	çoklu seçim listesi kutusu
26	alt pencere	79	yazıtipi biçemi	132	Bilgisayarım (simge)
27	seçmek	80	işlev tuşu	133	Ağ Komşuları (simge)
28	tıklamak	81		134	**Yeni**
29	Pano	82		135	**Sonraki**
30	**Kapat**	83	grup kutusu	136	nesne
31	Kapat düğmesi	84	tutaç	137	**Tamam**
32	(seviye) daralt	85	**Yardım**	138	OLE
33	sütun başlığı	86	Yardım menüsü	139	OLE sürükle ve bırak
34	bileşim kutusu	87	**Gizle**	140	OLE katılmış nesne
35	komut düğmesi	88	sırasal seçim	141	OLE bağlanmış nesne
36	kap	89	basılı tutmak	142	OLE varsayılan dışı sürükleme ve bırakma
37	içeriğe duyarlı yardım	90	sıcak nokta	143	**Aç**
38	içeriksel	91	sıcak bölge	144	**Birlikte Aç**
39	denetim	92	simge	145	seçenek düğmesi
40	**Kopyala**	93	etkin değil	146	seçim ayarı
41	**Buraya Kopyala**	94	etkin olmayan pencere	147	paket
42	**Kısayol Yarat**	95		148	**Sayfa Yapısı**
43	**Burada Kısayol Yarat**	96		149	palet penceresi
44	**Kes**	97	giriş odağı	150	yarı pencere
45	ön değer	98	**Ekle menüsü**	151	ana pencere
46	saptanan düğme	99	**Nesne Ekle**	152	parola
47	**Sil**	100	ekleme noktası	153	**Yapıştır**
48	masaüstü	101	italik	154	**Bağlantı Yapıştır**
49	hedef	102	etiket	155	**Kısayol Yapıştır**
50	iletişim kutusu	103	yatay	156	**Özel Yapıştır**
51	engellilik	104		157	yol
52	düzensiz seçim	105			
53	yapışık	106	bağlantı		

Turkish

158	**Durakla**	191	**Devam Et**	225	Başlat düğmesi
159		192	**Yeniden Dene**	226	Başlangıç klasörü
160	**Çal**	193	zengin metin kutusu	227	durum çubuğu
161	Tak ve Kullan	194	**Çalıştır**	228	**Dur**
162	yazıtipi boyutu birimi (n.) /	195	**Kaydet**	229	sekme denetimi
	işaretleme (v.)	196	**Farklı Kaydet**	230	
163	işaretçi	197	kaydırmak	231	görev çubuğu
164	açılır menü	198	kaydırma oku	232	göreve duyarlı Yardım
165	açılır pencere	199	kaydırma çubuğu	233	şablon
166	düşey	200	kaydırma kutusu	234	metin kutusu
167	basmak	201	ikincil pencere	235	başlık çubuğu
168	basın (ve basılı tutun)	202	seçmek (n.) / Seç (v.)	236	başlık metni
169	birincil kap	203	**Tümünü Seç**	237	değiştirme tuşu
170	ön pencere	204	seçim	238	araç çubuğu
171	**Yazdır**	205	seçim tutacağı	239	araç bilgisi
172	yazıcı	206	**Gönder**	240	araç görünümlü denetim
173	durum göstergesi (denetim)	207	ayırıcı	241	tür
174	proje	208	**Ayarlar**	242	yaz
175	**Özellikler**	209	**Kur**	243	kullanılamaz
176	özellik denetleyicisi	210	kısayol	244	**Geri Al**
177	özellik sayfası	211	kısayol düğmesi	245	**Kaldır**
178	özellik tablosu	212	kısayol simgesi	246	**Görünüm menüsü**
179	özellik tablosu denetimi	213	kısayol tuşu	247	yerinde düzenleme
180	**Hızlı Bakış**	214	kısayol tuşu denetimi	248	görüntüsel denetim
181	salt okunur	215	**Göster**	249	**Bu Nedir?**
182		216	**Oturumu Kapat**	250	pencere
183	Geri Dönüşüm Kutusu (simge)	217	tek seçim listesi kutusu	251	**Pencere menüsü**
184	**Yinele**	218	**Boyut**	252	Windows Gezgini
185	bölge seçimi	219	boyutlandırma tutacağı	253	sihirbaz
186	kayıt	220	kaydırıcı	254	çalışma kitabı
187	**Yinele**	221	fırıldak kutusu	255	çalışma grubu
188	**Değiştir**	222	**Böl**	256	çalışma alanı
189	**Eski Durumuna Getir**	223	bölme çubuğu	257	**Evet**
190	Eski Durumuna Getir düğmesi	224	bölme kutusu		

Glossary

A

accelerator key *See* shortcut key**.**

access bar *See* desktop toolbar.

access key The key that corresponds to an underlined letter on a menu or control (also referred to as a mnemonic or mnemonic access key).

accessibility Designing software to be usable and accessible to the widest range of users, including users with disabilities.

action handle A special handle, primarily designed for pen-based interaction, that provides access to a selected object's operations, through a pop-up menu, drag and drop, or both.

active The state when an object is the focus of user input and its operations are available.

active end The ending point for a selected range of objects. It is usually established at the object logically nearest the hot spot of the pointer when a user releases a mouse button or lifts the tip of a pen from the input surface. *Compare* anchor point.

active window The window in which a user is currently working or directing input. An active window is typically at the top of the Z order and is distinguished by the color of its title bar. *Compare* inactive window.

adornment A control or status area that is attached to the edge of a pane or window, such as a toolbar or ruler.

anchor point The starting point for a selected range of objects. An anchor point is usually established at the object logically nearest the hot spot of the pointer when a user presses a mouse button or touches the tip of a pen to the input surface. *Compare* active end.

anti-aliasing A graphic design technique that involves adding colored pixels to smooth the jagged edges of a graphic.

apply To commit a set of changes or pending transactions made in a secondary window, typically without closing that window.

auto-exit A text box in which the input focus automatically moves to the next control as soon as a user types the last character.

auto-joining The movement of text to fill a remaining gap after a user deletes other text.

automatic scrolling A technique where a display area automatically scrolls without direct interaction with a scroll bar.

auto-repeat An event or interaction that is automatically repeated. Auto-repeat events usually occur when a user holds down a keyboard key or presses and holds a special control (for example, scroll bar buttons).

B

barrel-tap A pen action that involves holding down the barrel button of a pen while tapping. It is the equivalent of clicking mouse button 2.

box edit A standard Microsoft Windows pen interface control that provides a discrete area for entering each character. A user can also edit text within the control.

C

cancel To halt an operation or process and return to the state before it was invoked. *Compare* stop.

caret *See* insertion point.

cascading menu A menu that is a submenu of a menu item (also referred to as a hierarchical menu, child menu, or submenu).

check box A standard Windows control that displays a setting, either checked (set) or unchecked (not set). *Compare* option button.

child menu *See* cascading menu.

child window A document window used within an MDI window. *See also* multiple document interface.

chord To press more than one mouse button at the same time.

click (v.) To position the pointer over an object and then press and release a mouse button. (n.) The act of clicking. *See also* press.

Clipboard The area of storage for objects, data, or their references after a user carries out a Cut or Copy command.

close To remove a window.

code page A collection of characters that make up a character set.

collection A set of objects that share some common aspect.

column heading A standard Windows control that can be used to provide interactive column titles for a list.

combo box A standard Windows control that combines a text box and interdependent list box. *Compare* drop-down combo box.

command button A standard Windows control that initiates a command or sets an option (also referred to as a push button).

composite A set or group of objects whose aggregation is recognized as an object itself (for example, characters in a paragraph, a named range of cells in a spreadsheet, or a grouped set of drawing objects).

constraint A relationship between a set of objects, such that making a change to one object affects another object in the set.

container An object that holds other objects.

context menu *See* pop-up menu.

context-sensitive Help Information about an object and its current condition. It answers the questions "What is this" and "Why would I want to use it?" *Compare* reference Help and task-oriented Help.

contextual Specific to the conditions in which something exists or occurs.

contiguous selection A selection that consists of a set of objects that are logically sequential or adjacent to each other (also referred to as range selection). *Compare* disjoint selection.

control An object that enables user interaction or input, often to initiate an action, display information, or set values.

Control menu The menu, also referred to as the System menu, displayed on the left end of a title bar in Windows 3.1. A pop-up menu of a window replaces the Control menu.

cursor A generic term for the visible indication of where a user's interaction will occur. *See also* input focus, insertion point, and pointer.

D

data-centered design A design in which users interact with their data directly without having to first start an appropriate editor or application.

data link A link that propagates a value between two objects or locations.

default An operation or value that the system or application assumes, unless a user makes an explicit choice.

default button The command button that is invoked when a user presses the ENTER key. A default button typically appears in a secondary window.

delete To remove an object or value.

desktop The visual work area that fills the display. The desktop is also a container and can be used as a convenient location to place objects stored in the file system.

desktop toolbar A toolbar that docks to the desktop, similar to the taskbar. *See also* taskbar.

dialog base unit A device-independent measure to use for layout. One horizontal unit is equal to one-fourth of the average character width for the current system font. One vertical unit is equal to one-eighth of an average character height for the current system font.

dialog box A secondary window that gathers additional information from a user. *Compare* message box, palette window, and property sheet.

dimmed *See* unavailable.

disabled *See* unavailable.

disjoint selection A selection that consists of a set of objects that are not logically sequential or physically adjacent to each other. *Compare* contiguous selection. *See also* extended selection.

dock To manipulate an interface element, such as a toolbar, such that it aligns itself with the edge of another interface element, typically a window or pane.

document A common unit of data (typically a file) used in user tasks and exchanged between users.

document window A window that provides a primary view of a document (typically its content).

double-click (v.) To press and release a mouse button twice in rapid succession. (n.) The act of double-clicking.

double-tap (v.) To press and lift the pen tip twice in rapid succession. It is typically interpreted as the double-click of the mouse. (n.) The act of double-tapping.

drag To press and hold a mouse button (or press the pen tip) while moving the mouse (or pen).

drag and drop A technique for moving, copying, or linking an object by dragging. The destination determines the interpretation of the operation. *Compare* nondefault drag and drop.

drop-down combo box A standard Windows control that combines the characteristics of a text box with a drop-down list box. *Compare* combo box.

drop-down list box A standard Windows control that displays a current setting, but can be opened to display a list of choices.

drop-down menu A menu that is displayed from a menu bar. *See also* menu and pop-up menu.

edit field *See* text box.

Edit menu A common drop-down menu that includes general purpose commands for editing objects displayed within a window, such as Cut, Copy, and Paste.

ellipsis The "..." suffix added to a menu item or button label to indicate that the command requires additional information to be completed. When a user chooses the command, a dialog box is usually displayed for user input of this additional information.

embedded object *See* OLE embedded object.

event An action or occurrence to which an application can respond. Examples of events are clicks, key presses, and mouse movements.

explicit selection A selection that a user intentionally performs with an input device. *Compare* implicit selection.

extended selection A selection technique that is optimized for the selection of a single object or single range using contiguous selection techniques (that is, canceling any existing selection when a new selection is made). However, it also supports modifying an existing selection using disjoint selection techniques. *See also* disjoint selection.

extended selection list box A list box that supports multiple selection, but is optimized for a selection of a single object or single range. *See also* extended selection and list box. *Compare* multiple selection list box.

File menu A common drop-down menu that includes commands for file operations, such as Open, Save, and Print.

flat appearance The recommended visual display of a control when it is nested inside another control or scrollable region.

folder A type of container for objects — typically files.

font A set of attributes for text characters.

font size The size of a font, typically represented in points.

font style The stylistic attributes of a font — such as bold, italic, and underline.

G

gesture A set of lines or strokes (inking) drawn on the screen that is recognized and interpreted as a command or character. *See also* recognition and ink.

glyph A generic term used to refer to any graphic or pictorial image that can be used on a button or in a message box. *Compare* icon.

grayed *See* unavailable.

group box A standard Windows control that groups a set of controls.

H

handle An interface element added to an object that provides a control point for moving, sizing, reshaping, or other operations pertaining to that object.

Help menu A common drop-down menu that includes commands that provide access to Help information or other forms of user assistance. *See* also context-sensitive Help and task-oriented Help.

heterogeneous selection A selection that includes objects with different properties or type. *Compare* homogeneous selection.

hierarchical menu *See* cascading menu.

hold To continue pressing a keyboard key, mouse button, or pen tip.

homogeneous selection A selection that includes objects with the same properties or type. *Compare* heterogeneous selection.

hot spot The specific portion of the pointer (or pointing device) that defines the exact location, or object, to which a user is pointing.

hot zone The interaction area of a particular object or location with which a pointer or pointing device's hot spot must come in contact.

icon A pictorial representation of an object. *Compare* glyph.

implicit selection A selection that is the result of inference or the context of some other operation. *See also* explicit selection.

inactive The state of an object when it is not the focus of a user's input.

inactive window A window in which a user's input is not currently being directed. An inactive window is typically distinguished by the color of its title bar. *Compare* active window.

indeterminate *See* mixed-value appearance.

ink The unrecognized, freehand drawing of lines on the screen with a pen. *See also* gesture and ink edit.

ink edit A standard Windows control for input and editing of "ink." *See also* ink.

input focus The location where the user is currently directing input.

input focus appearance The visual display of a control or other object that indicates when it has the input focus.

insertion point The location where text or graphics will be inserted (also referred to as the caret). Also used for text box controls to indicate input focus.

inside-out activation A technique that allows a user to directly interact with the content of an OLE embedded object without executing an explicit activation command. *Compare* outside-in activation.

J

jump A special form of a link that navigates to another location (also referred to as a hyperlink).

L

label The text (or graphic) that identifies a control (also referred to as a caption).

landscape An orientation where the long dimension of a rectangular area (for example, screen or paper) is horizontal.

lasso-tap A pen gesture that results in a region selection by drawing a circle around the object to be selected and tapping within that circle.

lens *See* writing tool.

link (v.) To form a connection between two objects. (n.) A reference to an object that is linked to another object. *See also* OLE linked object.

link path The descriptive form of referring to the location of a link source (also referred to as a moniker).

list box A standard Windows control that displays a list of choices. *See also* extended selection list box.

list view A standard Windows list box control that displays a set of objects. The control also supports different views and drag and drop.

locale A collection of language-related user preferences for formatting information, such as time, currency, or dates.

localization The process of adapting software for different countries, languages, or cultures.

M

marquee *See* region selection.

maximize To make a window its largest size. *See also* minimize.

MDI *See* multiple document interface.

menu A list of textual or graphical choices from which a user can choose. *See also* drop-down menu and pop-up menu.

menu bar A horizontal bar at the top of a window, below the title bar, that contains menus. *See also* drop-down menu.

menu button A command button that displays a menu.

menu item A choice on a menu.

menu title A text or graphic label that designates a particular menu. For drop-down menus, the title is the entry in the menu bar; for cascading menus the menu title is the name of its parent menu item.

message box A secondary window that is displayed to inform a user about a particular condition. *Compare* dialog box, palette window, and property sheet.

minimize To minimize the size of a window; in some cases this means to hide the window. *See also* maximize.

mixed-value appearance The visual display for a control when it reflects a mixed set of values.

mnemonic *See* access key.

modal A restrictive or limiting interaction because of operating in a mode. Modal often describes a secondary window that restricts a user's interaction with other windows. A secondary window can be modal with respect to its primary window or to the entire system. *Compare* modeless.

mode A particular state of interaction, often exclusive in some way to other forms of interaction.

modeless Not restrictive or limiting interaction. Modeless often describes a secondary window that does not restrict a user's interaction with other windows. *Compare* modal.

modifier key A keyboard key that, when pressed (and held), changes the actions of ordinary input.

moniker *See* link path.

mouse A commonly used input device that has one or more buttons used to interact with a computer. It is also used as a generic term to include other pointing devices that operate similarly (for example, trackballs and headpointers).

multiple document interface (MDI) A technique for managing a set of windows whereby documents are opened into windows (sometimes called child windows) that are constrained to a single primary (parent) window. *See also* child window and parent window.

multiple selection list box A list box that is optimized for making multiple, independent selections. *Compare* extended selection list box and single selection list box.

My Computer A standard Windows icon that represents a user's private, usually local, storage.

N

Network Neighborhood A standard Windows icon that represents access to objects that are stored on the network file system.

nondefault drag and drop A drag (transfer) operation whose interpretation is determined by a user's choice of command. These commands are included in a pop-up menu displayed at the destination when the object is dropped. *Compare* drag and drop.

O

object An entity or component identifiable by a user that can be distinguished by its properties, operations, and relationships.

object-action paradigm The basic interaction model for the user interface in which the object to be acted upon is specified first, followed by the command to be executed.

OLE (Microsoft OLE) The name that describes the technology and interface for implementing support for object interaction.

OLE embedded object A data object that retains the original editing and operating functionality of the application that created it, while physically residing in another document.

OLE linked object An object that represents or provides an access point to another object that resides at another location in the same container or a different, separate container. *See also* link.

OLE visual editing The ability to edit an OLE embedded object in place, without opening it into its own window.

open appearance The visual display of an object when the user opens the object into its own window.

operation A generic term that refers to the actions that can be done to or with an object.

option button A standard Windows control that allows a user to select from a fixed set of mutually exclusive choices (also referred to as a radio button). *Compare* check box.

option-set appearance The visual display for a control when its value is set.

outside-in activation A technique that requires a user to perform an explicit activation command to interact with the content of an OLE embedded object. *Compare* inside-out activation.

P

package An OLE encapsulation of a file so that it can be embedded in an OLE container.

palette window A modeless secondary window that displays a toolbar or other choices, such as colors or patterns. *Compare* dialog box and message box. *See also* property sheet.

pane One of the separate areas in a split window.

parent window A primary window that provides window management for a set of child windows. *See also* child window and multiple document interface.

pen An input device that consists of a pen-shaped stylus that a user employs to interact with a computer.

persistence The principle that the state of an object is automatically preserved.

point (v.) To position the pointer over a particular object and location. (n.) A unit of measurement for type (1 point equals approximately 1/72 inch).

pointer A graphic image displayed on the screen that indicates the location of a pointing device (also referred to as a cursor).

pop-up menu A menu that is displayed at the location of a selected object (also referred to as a context menu or shortcut menu). The menu contains commands that are contextually relevant to the selection.

pop-up window A secondary window with no title bar that is displayed next to an object; it provides contextual information about that object.

portrait An orientation where the long dimension of a rectangular area (for example, screen or paper) is vertical.

press To press and release a keyboard key or to touch the tip of a pen to the screen. *See also* click.

pressed appearance The visual display for an object, such as a control, when it is being pressed.

primary window The window in which the main interaction takes place. *See also* secondary window and window.

progress indicator Any form of feedback that provides the user with information about the state of a process.

progress indicator control A standard Windows control that displays the percentage of completion of a particular process as a graphical bar.

project A window or task management technique that consists of a container holding a set of objects, such that when the container is opened, the windows of the contained objects are restored to their former positions.

properties Attributes or characteristics of an object that define its state, appearance, or value.

property inspector A dynamic properties viewer that displays the properties of the current selection, usually of a particular type of object. *Compare* property sheet.

property page A grouping of properties on a tabbed page of a property sheet. *See also* property sheet.

property sheet A secondary window that displays the properties of an object when a user chooses its Properties command. *Compare* dialog box and property inspector. *See also* property page.

property sheet control A standard Windows control used to create property sheet interfaces.

proximity The ability of some pen devices to detect the presence of the pen without touching the pen to the input surface.

push button *See* command button.

R

radio button *See* option button.

range selection *See* contiguous selection.

recognition The interpretation of strokes or gestures as characters or operations. *See also* gesture.

reference Help A form of online Help information that can contain conceptual and explanatory information. *Compare* task-oriented Help and context-sensitive Help.

region selection A selection technique that involves dragging out a bounding outline (also referred to as a marquee) to define the selected objects.

Recycle Bin The standard Windows icon that represents the repository for deleted files.

relationship The context or way an object relates to its environment.

rich-text box A standard Windows control that is similar to a standard text box, except that it also supports individual character and paragraph properties.

S

scope The definition of the extent that a selection is logically independent from other selections. For example, selections made in separate windows are typically considered to be independent of each other.

scrap An icon created when the user transfers a data selection from within a file to a shell container.

scroll To move the view of an object or information to make a different portion visible.

scroll arrow button A component of a scroll bar that allows the information to be scrolled by defined increments when the user clicks it. The direction of the arrow indicates the direction in which the information scrolls.

scroll bar A standard Windows control that supports scrolling.

scroll box A component of a scroll bar that indicates the relative position (and optionally the proportion) of the visible information relative to the entire amount of information. The user can drag the scroll box to view areas of information not currently visible. *See also* scroll bar shaft.

scroll bar shaft The component of a scroll bar that provides the visual context for the scroll box. Clicking (or tapping) in the scroll bar shaft scrolls the information by a screenful. *See also* scroll box.

secondary window A window that provides information or supplemental interaction related to objects in a primary window.

select To identify one or more objects upon which an operation can be performed.

selection An object or set of objects that have been selected.

selection appearance The visual display of an object when it has been selected.

selection handle A graphical control point of an object that provides direct manipulation support for operations of that object, such as moving, sizing, or scaling.

separator An entry in a menu used to group menu items together.

shell A generic term that refers to the interface that allows the user control over the system.

shortcut A generic term that refers to an action or technique that invokes a particular command or performs an operation with less interaction than its usual method.

shortcut icon A link presented as an icon that provides a user with access to another object.

shortcut key A keyboard key or key combination that invokes a particular command (also referred to as an accelerator key).

shortcut menu *See* pop-up menu.

single selection list box A list box that only supports selection of a single item in the list.

size grip A special control that appears at the junction of a horizontal and vertical scroll bar or the right end of a status bar and provides an area that a user can drag to size the lower right corner of a window.

slider A standard Windows control that displays and sets a value from a continuous range of possible values, such as brightness or volume.

spin box A control composed of a text box and increment and decrement buttons that allows a user to adjust a value from a limited range of possible values.

split bar A division between panes that appears where a window has been split; the split bar visually separates window panes.

split box A special control added to a window, typically adjacent to the scroll bar, that allows a user to split a window or adjust a window split.

status bar An area that allows the display of state information of the information being viewed in the window, typically placed at the bottom of a window.

status bar control A standard Windows control that provides the functionality of a status bar.

stop To halt a process or action, typically without restoring the state before the process began. *Compare* cancel.

submenu *See* cascading menu.

System menu *See* Control menu.

tab control A standard Windows control that looks similar to a notebook or file divider and provides navigation between different pages or sections of information.

tap To press and lift the pen tip from the screen, usually interpreted as a mouse click.

targeting To determine where pen input is directed.

taskbar A special toolbar that docks on an edge of the desktop supplied by the system. The taskbar includes the Start button, buttons for each open primary window, and a status area.

task-oriented Help Information about the steps involved in carrying out a particular task. *Compare* context-sensitive Help and reference Help.

template An object that automates the creation of new objects of a particular type.

text box A standard Windows control in which a user can enter and edit text (also referred to as the edit field).

thread A process that is part of a larger process or program.

title bar The horizontal area at the top of a window that identifies the window. The title bar also acts as a handle for dragging the window.

toggle key A keyboard key that alternates between turning a particular operation, function, or mode on or off.

toolbar A frame or special area that contains a set of other controls.

toolbar button A command button used in a toolbar (or status bar).

toolbar control A standard Windows control designed with the same characteristics as the toolbar.

tooltip A standard Windows control that provides a small pop-up window that provides descriptive text, such as a label, for a control or graphic object.

transfer appearance The visual feedback displayed during a transfer operation.

transaction A unit of change to an object.

tree control A standard Windows control that allows a set of hierarchically related objects to be displayed as an expandable outline.

type (v.) To enter a character from the keyboard. (n.) A classification of an object based on its characteristics, behavior, and attributes.

unavailable The state of a control whose normal functionality is not presently available to a user (also referred to as grayed, dimmed, and disabled).

unavailable appearance The visual display for a control when it is unavailable.

undo To reverse a transaction.

unfold button A command button used to expand a secondary window to a larger size to reveal additional controls or information.

visual editing *See* OLE visual editing.

W

well control A control that is used to display color or pattern choices, typically used like an option button.

white space The background area of a window. (The color need not literally be white.)

window A standard Windows object that displays information. A window is a separately controllable area of the screen that typically has a rectangular border. *See also* primary window and secondary window.

wizard A form of user assistance that automates a task through a dialog with the user.

wordwrap The convention where, as a user enters text, existing text is automatically moved from the end of a line to the next line.

workbook A window or task management technique that consists of a set of views that are organized like a tabbed notebook.

workspace A window or task management technique that consists of a container holding a set of objects, where the windows of the contained objects are constrained to a parent window. Similar to the multiple document interface, except that the windows displayed within the parent window are of objects that are also contained in the workspace.

writing tool A standard Windows pen interface control that supports text editing.

Z

Z order The layered relationship of a set of objects, such as windows, on the display screen.

Bibliography

General Design

Baecker, Ronald M., and Buxton, William A. S. *Readings in Human-Computer Interaction: A Multidisciplinary Approach.* Los Altos, Calif.: M. Kaufmann, 1987.

Brooks, Frederick P. *The Mythical Man-Month: Essays on Software Engineering.* Reading, Mass.: Addison-Wesley Pub. Co., 1975.

Heckel, Paul. *The Elements of Friendly Software Design.* New Ed., San Francisco: SYBEX, 1991.

Lakoff, George, and Johnson, Mark. *Metaphors We Live By.* Chicago: University of Chicago Press, 1980.

Laurel, Brenda, Ed. *The Art of Human-Computer Interface Design.* Reading, Mass.: Addison-Wesley Pub. Co., 1990.

Norman, Donald A. *The Design of Everyday Things.* New York: Basic Books, 1990.

Norman, Donald A., and Draper, Stephen, W., Eds. *User Centered System Design*: *New Perspectives on Human-Computer Interaction.* Hillsdale, N.J.: L. Erlbaum Associates, 1986.

Shneiderman, Ben. *Designing the User Interface: Strategies for Effective Human-Computer Interaction.* Reading, Mass.: Addison-Wesley, 1992.

Tognazzini, Bruce. *Tog on Interface.* Reading, Mass.: Addison-Wesley, 1992.

Graphic Information Design

Blair, Preston. *Cartoon Animation.* How to Draw and Paint Series. Tustin, Calif.: Walter Foster Pub., 1989.

Dreyfuss, Henry. *Symbol Sourcebook: An Authoritative Guide to International Graphic Symbols.* New York: Van Nostrand Reinhold Co., 1984.

Thomas, Frank., and Johnston, Ollie. *Disney Animation: The Illusion of Life.* New York: Abbeville Press, 1984.

Tufte, Edward R. *Envisioning Information.* Cheshire, Conn.: Graphics Press, 1990.

Tufte, Edward R. *The Visual Display of Quantitative Information.* Cheshire, Conn.: Graphics Press, 1983.

Usability

Dumas, Joseph S., and Redish, Janice C. *A Practical Guide to Usability Testing.* Norwood, N.J.: Ablex Pub. Corp., 1993.

Nielsen, Jakob. *Usability Engineering.* Boston: Academic Press, 1993.

Rubin, Jeffrey. *Handbook of Usability Testing: How to Plan, Design, and Conduct Effective Tests.* New York: Wiley, 1994.

Whiteside, John, Bennett, John, and Holtzblatt, Karen. "Usability Engineering: Our Experience and Evolution." In *Handbook of Human-Computer Interaction*, Martin Helander (Ed.), Elsevier Science Pub. Co., Amsterdam, 1988.

Wiklund, Michael E., Ed. *Usability in Practice: How Companies Develop User-Friendly Products.* Boston: AP Professional, 1994.

Object-Oriented Design

Booch, Grady. *Object-Oriented Analysis and Design with Applications.* Redwood City, Calif.: Benjamin/ Cummings Pub. Co., 1994.

Peterson, Gerald E., Ed. *Tutorial: Object-Oriented Computing: Volume 2: Implementations.* Washington, D.C.: Computer Society Press of the IEEE, 1987.

Rumbaugh, James, et al. *Object-Oriented Modeling and Design.* Englewood Cliffs, N.J.: Prentice Hall, 1991.

Organizations

The following organizations publish journals and sponsor conferences on topics related to user interface design.

SIGCHI (Special Interest Group in Computer Human Interaction)
Association for Computing Machinery
1515 Broadway
New York, NY 10036-5701
212-869-7440

SIGGRAPH (Special Interest Group on Graphics)
Association for Computing Machinery
1515 Broadway
New York, NY 10036-5701
212-869-7440

Human Factors and Ergonomics Society
P.O. Box 1369
Santa Monica, CA 90406-1369
310-394-1811

Accessibility

For a list of accessibility aids available for Microsoft Windows, accessibility software vendors, potential test sites, or facilities for producing accessible documentation, contact:

Microsoft Sales Information Center
One Microsoft Way
Redmond, WA 98052-6399
(800) 426-9400 (voice)
(800) 892-5234 (text telephone)
(206) 936-7329 (FAX)

An assistive technology program in your area can provide referrals to programs and services available to you. To locate the assistive technology program nearest to your location, contact:

National Information System
Center for Development Disabilities
University of South Carolina
Benson Building
Columbia, SC 29208
(803) 777-4435 (voice or text telephone)
(803) 777-6058 (FAX)

The Trace Research and Development Center publishes references and materials on accessibility, including:

Vanderheiden, Gregg C., and Vanderheiden, Katherine R. *Accessible Design of Consumer Products: Guidelines for the Design of Consumer Products to Increase Their Accessibility to People with Disabilities or Who Are Aging.* Madison, Wis.: Trace Research and Development Center, 1991.

Vanderheiden, Gregg C. *Application Software Design Guidelines: Increasing the Accessibility of Applications Software to People with Disabilities and Older Users (Version 1.1).* Madison, Wis.: Trace Research and Development Center, 1994.

Borden, Fatherly, Ford, and Vanderheiden, Eds. *Trace Resource Book: Assistive Technologies for Communication, Control and Computer Access.* Madison, Wis.: Trace Research and Development Center, 1993.

For information on these books and other resources available from the Trace Research and Development Center, contact them at:

Trace Research and Development Center
University of Wisconsin - Madison
S-151 Waisman Center
1500 Highland Avenue
Madison, WI 5705-2280
(608) 263-2309 (voice)
(608) 263-5408 (text telephone)
(608) 262-8848 (FAX)

Index

Index

Advanced users, designing for 15

Aesthetics 7

Alignment of interface elements 389

ALT key

  See also Keyboard interface

  accessing drop-down menus 123

  activating menu bars 123

  avoiding in shortcut key assignments 36

  canceling a drop-down menu 123

  international considerations 418

  using in modifier key combinations 35

  using with access keys 33

ALT+~ key combination 418

ALT+arrow key combination 123, 130

ALT+double-click 61

ALT+ENTER key combination 61

ALT+ESC key combination 36, 103

ALT+F4 key combination 61

ALT+F6 key combination 181

ALT+HYPHEN key combination 130

ALT+*number* key combinations 36

ALT+SPACEBAR key combination 36, 130

ALT+TAB key combination 35, 36, 103, 109

Always on Top property

  for application desktop toolbars 271

  for palette windows 208

  providing for secondary windows 181

Anchor point

  See also Mouse interface summary

  keyboard selection 56

  mouse selection 48

Animating pointers 395

Animation, designing 400

ANSI character sets 419

Anti-aliasing 391

Appbars *See* Desktop toolbars

Application desktop toolbars *See* Desktop toolbars

Application icons 392

Application key 36, 129

Application path information, registering 241

Application shortcuts, placing in the Programs menu 260

Application state information, registering 238 – 240

Apply command 65, 190

Arrow keys

  accessing drop-down lists 153

  accessing drop-down menus 123

  accessing window pop-up menus 130

  basic function of 45

  navigating between controls 185

  selecting items in list boxes 150

  switching between tabs 165

  using for contiguous selections 56

  using for scrolling 115

  using with the ALT key 123, 130

  using with the SHIFT key 56

Arrow pointers 30

Assessment *See* Usability testing

Attributes of objects *See* Properties

Audio feedback

  accessibility considerations 404

  importance of 7

  summary of guidelines 449

  using sound as notification 401 – 402

Auto-exit text boxes 158

Auto-joining 63

Auto-repeat 111

Autoexec.bat file 259

Automatic scrolling 82 – 83, 114 – 115

AutoPlay feature, supporting 264 – 266

Autorun.inf file 264

B

BACKSPACE key 63

Barrel button

  barrel-dragging 38, 77

  barrel-tapping 38

Basic elements of the Windows environment

  desktop 23

  icons 26

  Start button 25

  status area 26

  taskbar 24

  window buttons 26

  windows 28

Beginning users, designing for 15

C

Index

Index

D

Index

Index

Index

Register Today!

Return this
The Windows® Interface Guidelines for Software Design registration card for:

✔ a Microsoft Press® catalog

✔ exclusive offers on specially priced books

U.S. and Canada addresses only. Fill in information below and mail postage-free. Please mail only the bottom half of this page.

1-55615-679-0A   *The Windows Interface Guidelines for Software Design*   *Owner Registration Card*

_____
NAME

_____
INSTITUTION OR COMPANY NAME

_____
ADDRESS

_____
CITY   STATE   ZIP

Microsoft®*Press*

Quality Computer Books

For a free catalog of
Microsoft Press® products, call
1-800-MSPRESS